Providing
Psychological
and Related Services
to Children
and Adolescents

Providing Psychological and Related Services to Children and Adolescents

A Comprehensive Guidebook

by

Sebastian Striefel, Ph.D.
Professor of Psychology
Director of Clinical and Education
  Services
Developmental Center for
  Handicapped Persons
Utah State University
Logan

and

Phyllis Cole, Ph.D.
Coordinator of Clinical Services
Exceptional Child Center
Utah State University
Logan

·P A U L·H·
BROOKES
PUBLISHING CO.

Baltimore • London

Paul H. Brookes Publishing Co.
Post Office Box 10624
Baltimore, Maryland 21285-0624

Typeset by The Composing Room, Grand Rapids, Michigan.
Manufactured in the United States of America by
The Maple Press Company, York, Pennsylvania.

Library of Congress Cataloging-in-Publication Data
Striefel, Sebastian, 1941–
  Providing psychological and related services to children and
adolescents.

  Includes bibliographies and index.
  1. Child mental health services. 2. Child psychiatry. I. Cole,
Phyllis. II. Title. [DNLM: 1. Community Mental Health
Services—in adolescence—handbooks. 2. Community Mental
Health Services—in infancy & childhood—handbooks. 3.
Handicapped—handbooks. 4. Mental Retardation—rehabilitation—
handbooks. WM 34 S917p]
RJ499.S814   1987   618.92′89′0068   86-29925
ISBN 0-933716-68-0 (pbk.)

Contents

Preface vii
Acknowledgments ix

Chapter 1   Establishing and Operating a
Clinic: An Overview 1

Chapter 2   Marketing the Program and
Equipping the Facility 19

Chapter 3   Personnel Policies, Practices,
and Procedures 43

Chapter 4   Client-Related Policies,
Practices, and Procedures 65

Chapter 5   Family Involvement in
Assessment/Evaluation,
Treatment, and Training 91

Chapter 6   Assessment/Evaluation
Practices and Procedures 105

Chapter 7   Developing, Implementing,
and Evaluating Treatment 149

Chapter 8   Additional Assessment and
Treatment Information and
Issues 179

Chapter 9   Functional Clinical Reports 201

Chapter 10   Consultation 223

Chapter 11   Legal and Ethical Aspects 243

Chapter 12   Current Status and Future
Directions 267

Appendix A   Ethical Principles of
Psychologists 273

Appendix B   Self-Evaluation Checklists for
Administrators and Clinicians 283

Index 295

Preface

The intent of this guidebook is to provide a single comprehensive source of procedures and practices on how to provide psychological and related services to children and adolescents. The methods described here are in use today. Some have been developed or refined by us over a 9-year period in the child and adolescent clinic at the Developmental Center for Handicapped Persons at Utah State University; the rest are borrowed from other sources. In the process of writing this book we have reviewed and assimilated information from many sources and have improved our own knowledge base and skills. The insights we have gained are also being used to improve the operation of the clinic at the Developmental Center for Handicapped Persons.

Specifically, this book delineates information, procedures, and considerations relevant to setting up, operating, and working in a clinic that provides psychological and related services to children and adolescents, while simultaneously identifying the general goals, philosophy, and operating procedures for such a clinic. Details are also provided on approaches that have specific applicability with children and adolescents. Sample forms, record sheets, recommended assessment and treatment materials, and suggested clinic operating procedures are included. Working with families and family issues are also dealt with as they relate to the problems of children and adolescents. Whereas the major focus is on psychological and related services, much of the material in this guidebook is equally applicable to establishing and operating clinics with other primary areas of focus (e.g., speech clinics, physical therapy clinics, and occupational therapy clinics, to name but a few).

As a scholarly, yet practical compendium covering a range of administrative, programmatic, and treatment concerns, this guidebook hopes to serve a broad audience, including the direct service provider, clinic administrators, supervisors, and staff. Administrators are given numerous ideas for fulfilling responsibilities in overall operations and in specific areas of policy, including legal and ethical concerns. Psychologists who provide psychological services, as well as staff such as psychiatrists, social workers, medical doctors, occupational therapists, recreation therapists, nutritionists, nurses, and others who provide related services for a child and adolescent clinic will find a wealth of helpful suggestions for day to day intervention activities. Parents and clients will find the information useful in understanding the service process and in learning how they can contribute to that process. The book could also serve as a text for college students enrolled in courses concerned with providing psychological and related services. Clearly, entire books have been and could be written on many of the topics covered by the individual chapters. Our aim has been to integrate information into a format for clinical use and include references to allow you to delve deeper into specific topics. Combined, we have a total of 34 years of experience working in clinics, hospitals, schools, and communities as psychological service providers and administrators. We hope this guidebook reflects the depth of our experience, while also endeavoring to point to future directions in answering the psychological needs of children and adolescents.

A note on semantics: The terms *clinician, service provider,* and *therapist* can each have similar or different meanings depending on their use and context. For the purposes of this book, the terms are used interchangeably, with the possibility that one or another term may be used more frequently in a given chapter because of its relationship to a specific area of psychology. For example, although the terms *clinician* and *service provider* are perfectly acceptable in connection with Chapter 7's discussion of therapy interventions, the term *therapist* is used more frequently because therapy is what therapists do.

Acknowledgments

Appreciation is expressed to Richard Baer, Ph.D., Glen Latham, Ed.D., Damian McShane, Ph.D., William Dobson, Ph.D., Grayson Osborne, Ph.D., Maria Quintero, Gina Green, Kim Marvel, and the staff of the Paul H. Brookes Publishing Company for their review of and comments on various parts of the book. Without these reviews, the book content would have suffered. We also appreciate the efforts of Patti Baird, Ruth Cartee, Jane Meadows, Christy Woffinden, and other secretaries who typed the many revisions. To all of these people, we say thank you.

Providing Psychological and Related Services to Children and Adolescents

1

Establishing and Operating a Clinic
An Overview

After reading this chapter, you should understand:
1. The definition of the terms *clinic, psychological and related services,* and *psychological service unit,* as well as be familiar with alternative clinic models
2. The advantages and disadvantages of specialty versus comprehensive clinics
3. The importance of each clinic establishing a clearcut philosophy, mission, and goals
4. Other factors to consider in setting up a clinic
5. The scope and limitations of this guidebook

This chapter provides the necessary foundation for developing and operating a clinic offering psychological and related services to children and adolescents. In addition to giving background information for the remainder of the book, this chapter seeks to stimulate you to evaluate your own ideas for providing psychological and related services in light of the material provided here.

DEFINING A CLINIC, PSYCHOLOGICAL AND RELATED SERVICES, AND PSYCHOLOGICAL SERVICE UNIT

One need only look in the Yellow Pages of a telephone directory to get a quick impression of the diversity of activities and areas covered under the label "Clinic." The gamut runs from chiropractic, to mental health, to weight control, to nutrition, to pregnancy counseling, to medicine, and so on. Of the numerous meanings of the term *clinic,* Guralnik's definition (1982) is especially suited to our purposes. Guralnik defines a clinic as "an organization or institution that offers some kind of advice, treatment, or instruction" (p. 267). This definition is appropriate for this guidebook, since we are focusing on the operations of a facility that provides outpatient or outclient services. However, defining the psychological clinic's organization alone is not sufficient; one must also define its functions, the primary one being the provision of psychological services.

Psychological services have been defined in the *Standards for Providers of Psychological Services* (American Psychological Association [APA], 1977) to include one or more of the following:

1

A. Evaluation, diagnosis, and assessment of the functioning of individuals and groups in a variety of settings and activities.
B. Interventions to facilitate the functioning of individuals and groups. Such intervention may include psychological counseling, psychotherapy, and process consultation.
C. Consultation relating to A and B above.
D. Program development services in the areas of A, B, and C above.
E. Supervision of psychological services. (p. 4)

Thus, *a clinic is a facility, or part of a facility, that houses a psychological service unit and provides psychological services.* A *clinic* and a *service unit* can be similar or different entities, depending on their purpose and function. When a clinic provides mainly psychological services, as defined in the next paragraph, then a clinic (facility) and a psychological service unit (function) are related and similar; the clinic is the facility within which the psychological service unit functions. A clinic could, however, house several different service units (e.g., psychological service unit, physical therapy service unit, recreation therapy service unit). In such cases, the clinic offers a broader range of services than a psychological service clinic per se. Thus, a large agency, such as a hospital, could have one or more clinics and a clinic could have several service units.

A psychological service unit:

A. Provides mainly psychological services (as previously defined) and consists of one or more professional psychologists and support staff.
B. Operates as an independent psychological service or as part of a larger organization or agency (e.g., educational).
C. Includes any psychologist who provides professional services in a multioccupational setting.
D. Consists of an individual or a group providing psychological services in a private practice or consulting firm. (APA, 1977, p. 5)

Psychological issues confronting clients are the major focus of a psychological clinic. Such services are most often provided by professional psychologists, that is, doctoral-level psychologists[1] with training and experience in the area of services offered. Representatives from other disciplines such as psychiatrists, social workers, psychiatric nurses, nutritionists, occupational therapists, and recreation therapists often become involved in providing *related services* (i.e., services that are directly connected with an individual's mental and behavioral adjustment to his or her environment). For example, a medical doctor and nutritionist, along with a psychologist, might be members of a team dealing with a client who is overweight, or bulemic, or anorexic. Each professional would provide the services germane to his or her area of expertise. Inclusion of *related services* may be critical in providing a coordinated intervention program.

---

[1]Note that the American Psychological Association's *Standards for Providers of Psychological Services* (1977) do not recognize master's-level psychologists as professional psychologists.

ALTERNATIVE CLINIC MODELS

Clinics for serving children and adolescents vary considerably, depending upon factors such as: space and funding available; whether the clinic is publicly or privately owned; philosophy, background, experience, and professional discipline of the director; whether the clinic is specialized or general; and location and size of the population served. For example, a specialized clinic would be a private clinic operated by a person working in a single discipline who provides one specialized service for children (e.g., a psychologist who works only with child and adolescent phobias). On a more general level would be a large community mental health clinic with staff members from all of the professional disciplines dealing with the many psychological and related problems of children and adolescents, and possibly of adults as well. Between these two extremes are many other options. In all likelihood, it is within these options that most clinics operate. A general description of different clinic models will help set the stage for the rest of the book.

Specialty Clinics

Staff in clinics operated by one or more persons and specializing in treating one kind of problem provide a useful service in that the staff can offer the state of the art "treatment of choice" for the specific problem area selected to be served. The clinic can be quite successful if the provider is well trained and competent. The disadvantages of this type of clinic, however, are many. First, a problem seldom occurs in total isolation (for example, a child experiencing personal stress in school may likely also lack social and assertiveness skills). Second, in order for clients to be referred to such a clinic, they must have been seen and evaluated by someone else. If staff of one service agency have already assessed a client, the probability of referral to the specialized clinic is low, unless the presenting problem is extremely resistant to treatment. In addition, referrals from other sources on an ongoing basis require that a fair amount of time and effort be devoted to public relations activities such as presentations to local community groups. The expense of such activities can be high. If clinic staff try to evaluate and screen their own clients for treatment, they may well spend most of their time evaluating clients that need to be referred elsewhere.

For specialty clinics with only one staff member, the problems just mentioned are compounded when that individual has: to do all the tasks; has no one readily available with whom to consult: has little or no peer review or ongoing feedback from others; has no internal options for inservice training; and has no one to cover his or her clients when he or she is sick, needs a day off, or wishes to go on vacation. Most of these difficulties can be overcome, but at a high cost in time and money. One less-expensive resolution is for the administrators to arrange for consultations, peer review, inservice training, and client coverage with another agency on the basis of a fee or direct exchange of similar services.

Comprehensive Clinics

By contrast, the advantages of comprehensive clinics for serving children and adolescents include:

1. All staff need not possess all possible skills, so long as the staff collectively possess the skills.
2. Team members can be assigned roles that take advantage of their individual strengths (e.g., intake, assessment, treatment, or staff supervision).
3. Funding is usually more stable, since it typically comes from public sources.
4. A wider variety of disciplines is generally represented by the staff. Services become more cost efficient because the need justifies hiring a full-time director, an administrator, and a secretary.
5. The clinic can serve low-income as well as high-income clients.
6. The clinic is more visible in the community.
7. Third-party collections are easier to obtain.

Although the advantages are numerous, disadvantages exist, including:

1. Communication problems increase in proportion to the number of disciplines and staff employed.
2. Staff personality conflicts are more likely.
3. Administrative and supervisory problems are more frequent.
4. Operating procedures are generally less flexible.
5. Staff turnover can be an ongoing problem.
6. Making staff feel part of the clinic may be more problematic.
7. Maintaining quality services can be more difficult to monitor.

Model Child and Adolescent Clinics

A multiplicity of clinics operate along the spectrum between specialty and comprehensive clinics, maximizing the advantages of the two extremes, while minimizing their disadvantages. From a team-building vantage point, a suitable clinic would have a staff of 10–15 professionals, representing different disciplines and expertise, including: one or more child or clinical psychologists, psychiatrists, clinical social workers, psychiatric nurses, and possibly a speech therapist, an occupational or physical therapist, and representatives of other disciplines depending upon clinic goals. Such a staffing pattern would allow staff to address the referral problems of most children and adolescents, while simultaneously providing a balance between operating costs and income. In addition, the clinic would need a business manager, a receptionist-secretary, and possibly other ancillary staff. A model child and adolescent clinic would operate on an *outpatient,* or *outclient,*[2] basis, but could be located in a hospital building as readily as

[2]The term *outpatient* is really not accurate in defining the clientele served by a psychological services unit; however, it is the term most commonly used in existing literature, and clients often need to be classified as patients in order for third-party payments to be collected. Therefore, the terms *outpatient* and *outclient* are used interchangeably throughout this book.

within a private or other community building. The way a clinic is operated is affected by a broad range of factors, as previously mentioned, in addition to personnel factors such as the staff hierarchy. A clinic with 10 to 15 professionals should be of sufficient size to be financially self-sufficient.

PHILOSOPHY, MISSION, AND GOALS

Every service program should have a clearly specified philosophy, mission, and goals, in written form, to guide the development of all other aspects of its development, operation, and progress (Striefel & Cadez, 1983).

Philosophy

A philosophy is basically a set of principles and assumptions to guide the behavior of the clinic staff in conducting its programs. We believe that every clinic's philosophy should, first of all, stress the provision of *quality services* (defined later in this chapter). In addition, clinic management should specify the other components of their philosophy. A nonexhaustive list of important philosophic components of a clinic for children and adolescents is presented in Table 1.1.

Various disciplines' principles of ethics often contain items worth including in a clinic's philosophy in the document's preamble. The "Ethical Principles of Psychologists" published by the APA (1981) are a good example (see Appendix A at the end of this guidebook).

Mission

A mission statement should reflect the major purpose and focus of a clinic. It is usually a statement that answers the question; "Why do we exist?" (Seattle Mental Health Institute, 1984, p. 1). It should make clear whether a clinic's primary focus is service, training, research, or some combination thereof. A hypothetical mission statement is as follows:

> The mission of this clinic is to optimize the psychological well-being of children and adolescents by providing quality services to children and adolescents primarily in need of psychological services, by providing related services when necessary, and by serving other family members as necessary to achieve this end. In so doing, clinic staff will cooperate with other agencies and professionals in providing services to the same individuals, will cooperate in training new professionals, and will engage in applied research related to the goals and mission of the clinic.

This mission statement emphasizes that children and adolescents are the primary targets for service of a psychological nature. Related services, services to family members, and cooperation with other agencies and professionals occur only if an individual in need primarily of psychological services is a client. Research and training are included to further the clinic's mission and other goals such as improving or maintaining "exemplary services." This mission statement sets the boundaries of the clinic's sphere of operation and provides a direction for developing specific goal statements. Mission statements can be broad, such as the aforementioned statement, or narrow (e.g., "to provide relaxation training

Table 1.1. Nonexhaustive list of philosophy statements

1. The human rights and the dignity and worth of all children, adolescents, and their families should be respected, preserved, and protected, regardless of race, religion, sex, or presenting problems.

2. No child or adolescent should be refused services because of age, intellectual functioning, inability to pay, or other factors over which he or she has no control (e.g., a child with AIDS).

3. Children and adolescents have a right to treatment directed toward the achievement of some specific goal or end result, regardless of whether they enter the service system voluntarily or involuntarily. They also have the right to know the type of treatment they will receive and the rationale for that specific treatment. Procedures should be established whereby parents, legal guardians, and others who have a need to know can obtain the information.

4. Children and adolescents, in conjunction with their parent or legal guardian, or in some cases in opposition to them, should have the right to refuse treatment unless judged by appropriate authorities to have severe disabilities or to be dangerous to self or others.

5. Every child and adolescent can learn new methods for coping with his or her environment. If progress does not occur, it may be because of an inadequate treatment plan or its implementation, and not the child or adolescent per se.

6. Longstanding and severe problems are resolved at a slower rate than new or less severe problems. Thus, long-term and severe problems will require more intensive and more structured interventions and probably more interdisciplinary and interagency cooperation.

7. A service system effectively addresses the long-term needs of children and adolescents when based on a model, or models, that emphasize both prevention and treatment.

8. Services should be provided in the least restrictive environment, using the least restrictive methods.

9. Persons with severe or chronic problems may need inpatient treatment for short or long periods of time because of control problems. Thus, the therapist must be willing to maintain contact with the client in the hospital or in transition placements; to turn over treatment of the client to staff from other facilities; and to resume treatment of the client when he or she is returned to the natural environment.

10. There is no way to predetermine the extent to which an individual child or adolescent will progress, other than by intervention and ongoing evaluation of that intervention. A therapist must be prepared to take a child or adolescent through treatment as fast and as far as possible, remaining flexible and changing the intervention as necessary.

11. Public and private agencies should work cooperatively to ensure maximum utilization of limited resources. The roles and responsibilities of the public and private sectors in meeting the psychological and related needs of children and adolescents should be clearly articulated.

12. The quality of life, both for individuals and a society, is directly related to the level of psychological health of everyone, including its children and youth. It is important that psychological and related services maximize clients' psychological health and lead to an improved quality of life.

13. Incentives should be built into psychological service clinics to provide the best and most cost efficient services possible.

14. Staff of psychological and related service clinics should be accountable to the public they serve, seeking public input whenever possible.

15. Public policy concerning the provision of psychological and related services should be clear and specific, and should drive the clinic's service delivery system.

16. The clinic's mission, goals, assumptions, policies, and standards should be reviewed annually and updated as necessary.

Source: Items 9–17 are revisions of the *Mental Health Assumptions for Utah* (Striefel et al., 1984).

and systematic desensitization therapy for children and adolescents diagnosed as phobic'').

Goals

Goals help administrators decide what should be included or excluded from the work scope, how to allocate resources, what resources (funds) to pursue, what kinds of standard operating procedures are needed, staff competencies needed, and so on. Setting goals for a clinic is not a one-time task but a continuing exercise requiring review and revision as the status, circumstances, and operations of a clinic change. Long-term goals can be established that are appropriate for several years, with subgoals outlined for a specific year or part of a year. Since goals are accomplishments that clinic staff will strive to achieve, long-term goals should address the main purposes for which the clinic was established (e.g., "to provide diagnostic and prescriptive services to all children and adolescents referred to the clinic"), whereas subgoals address purposes whose activities will help achieve long-term goals (e.g., "to hire a psychologist able to administer and interpret projective tests for use with children and adolescents"). Again, the more clearly these two types of goals are specified, the more direction staff and administrators have in deciding where and how to utilize the available resources. The special education and psychology literature includes a variety of resources concerned with formulating goals. The process is the same regardless of the goals. Two resources include Lee (1978) and Striefel and Cadez (1983). Following are some general suggestions on goal setting.

Goals should focus on answering questions such as "What do we want to accomplish?" and "Where do we want to go?" (Seattle Mental Health Institute, 1984, p. 1). Goals should also be stated in measurable terms, should be outcome oriented, and should have specified timelines in order to allow both clients and therapists to measure client progress. Goals should, moreover, be achievable, practical, and understandable (Christian & Hannah, 1983). Otherwise, a client may become dissatisfied when his or her problems do not lessen over time. Finally, goals need to focus clearly on whom will be served (e.g., children ages 2 to 10 only or all children and adolescents who need service). Some sample long-term goals for a clinic operating within a university setting and based on a broad mission statement such as that presented in the preceding section are provided in Table 1.2.

The goals in Table 1.2 cover a wide spectrum of activities and include a method for evaluating whether each is achieved. Evaluation procedures could also be specified in more detail, along with timelines, person(s) responsible, and specific activities to be conducted to achieve each goal. Evaluation will again help to delineate the focus and limits of a clinic's operation. The goals mentioned would not be appropriate for all clinics and may even change for a specific clinic over time. Goals should be reviewed at least annually. Setting goals also provides an excellent basis for evaluating achievement of a clinic per se and the performance of individual staff members.

Table 1.2. Sample long-term goals

1. Within the next 12 months, the clinic staff will provide *quality* (see definition in this chapter) psychological and related services to 500 children and adolescents to improve their lives. Each child or adolescent accepted for treatment will have been referred primarily because of a need for psychological services. Goal achievement will be determined on the basis of the referral question, case outcome, and consumer satisfaction.

2. Within the next 12 months, the clinic staff will provide quality services to family members of children and adolescents served by the clinic to help the family function better. Goal achievement will be determined by case outcome and consumer satisfaction.

3. Within the next 12 months, the clinic staff will cooperate with other agencies and professionals who are providing services to the same consumers in order to best meet the needs of those consumers. Goal achievement will be determined on the basis of ongoing written cooperative agreements, outcomes achieved for clients jointly served, and consumer and agency satisfaction.

4. During the next 12 months, the clinic staff will maintain and improve the professional skills of the service staff via ongoing and timely supervision and feedback, inservice training, attendance at workshops and conferences, enrollment in university courses, and other self-development activities. Goal achievement will be determined on the basis of a log of these activities, on the basis of how the activities relate to the skills of each staff member, and on the basis of staff input.

5. During the next 12 months, the clinic staff will strive to maintain good public relations with agencies, professionals, parents, and the public. Goal achievement will be determined on the basis of a log of staff-community involvement activities, an annual request to selected community members for feedback, and comments received spontaneously during the course of the year from various sources.

6. During the next 12 months, the clinic staff will provide a quality training internship to five individuals on how to serve children and adolescents. The internship will be in cooperation with university training programs or other agencies. Goal achievement will be determined on the basis of a log of training activities provided, the number of interns, the evaluation of the interns' skills, and intern-completed satisfaction questionnaires.

7. During the next 12 months, the clinic staff will cooperate in or engage in one or more applied research activities related to improving services to children, adolescents, and their families. Goal achievement will be determined on the basis of the number of research activities in progress or completed, the quality of the research in terms of practicality and/or publishability, the researchers involved, and their affiliations.

8. During the next 12 months, clinic staff will conduct systematic research and data collection within the clinic in order to improve the services provided to clients and to monitor staff and administrative activities. Goal achievement will be determined on the basis of research data available in the files and on changes made in program administrative procedures.

Other Considerations

A clinic might have as its mission the provision of direct services, but in clarifying its mission and setting its goals (or in reviewing an existing mission and goals), a variety of factors need to be considered, including items such as (Christian & Hannah, 1983):

1. Will assessment services be provided? What type? Psychological? Educational? Related areas?
2. Will treatment services be provided? What type?
3. Will prevention services be provided? What type and at what level?

4. Whom will the clinic serve? Children? Adolescents? Families? Is ability to pay a factor?

5. Will services be provided for all types of problems, or will services be limited in scope to include or exclude specific areas such as substance abuse or social skills? What are the most common problems for the population selected for service?

6. What will the staff consist of? One person? One discipline? Multi-disciplines? What skills will be needed to accomplish the clinic's goals?

7. Will the clinic be public or private, and profit or nonprofit? Nonprofit clinics often offer services without charge, below cost, or at cost.

8. How will the clinic be funded? Fee for service only, including third-party payments? Tax dollars? Contracts and grants? What funds are available at the outset?

9. How much space is needed for the clinic? What type of space is needed? Where should it be located?

10. Where will referrals come from? What must be done to establish and maintain referrals?

11. Are interagency agreements needed? Should they be oral or in written form? What are the advantages and disadvantages of oral versus written agreements? What should be the context of these agreements?

SERVICES

Psychological and *related services* were defined earlier in this chapter. Several issues pertaining to services remain to be discussed, including quality, comprehensiveness, standards and guidelines, and referrals.

Quality Services

Definition

The importance of quality services cannot be overemphasized. Quality services can be defined as: services that represent the "state of the art"; are worthy of replication; are research based and validated by peer review; conform to relevant codes of ethics, standards of operation, and laws; protect the rights of those served; are outcome oriented; and, most importantly, are effective. Services that fit this definition can be expected to establish trust in consumer groups; increase client flow; attract highly competent staff; establish good public relations; contribute to a well-organized delivery system; maximize third-party payments; minimize funding problems; and minimize the probability of litigation. An active approach should be taken whereby monitoring is used to improve quality to the point where it surpasses minimum standards and prevents potential problems before they develop (Bradley, Ashbaugh, Harder, Stoddard, & Shea, 1984).

State of the Art

To be "state of the art" means that service providers must be competent in using the best currently available techniques for dealing with the specific presenting problems of children and adolescents. In addition, providers need to receive ongoing education in order to keep abreast of the many new service options. The earlier-mentioned APA standards (1977) have assumed that consumers will benefit if providers are well trained, organized, keep good records, engage in peer review, keep informed on new information in their field, and have adequate staff and supporting resources (Jacobs, 1983). In addition, ideally, service providers will receive ongoing feedback on their effectiveness in the form of client progress and satisfaction, peer case staffings, and supervisor evaluations to assure that their knowledge and skills are "state of the art."

Ongoing Education

Typically, many providers function in isolated settings where the only feedback they receive is that of their own subjective impression of client progress and satisfaction. Work load and location often preclude arranging for ongoing education in the form of inservice training or keeping abreast of literature in the field. Such providers must make difficult decisions concerning whether to try to serve all clients in need of service or to allocate time for developing or updating skills. Our bias is that unless service providers allocate time for their own professional development on a regular basis, they may quickly lose touch with those treatment approaches proven most effective. In addition, they may become high risk for burnout, a syndrome typified by emotional exhaustion and cynicism (Greenberg & Valletutti, 1980). When professional development ceases, service providers often end up implementing treatment programs that are more complex and time consuming than necessary or that fail because they are not the "treatment of choice" for a particular problem.

In order to be worthy of replication or of use by others, services must respond to the needs of residents in the geographic area served by the clinic. Programs must include a range of exemplary diagnostic, assessment, intervention, consultation, program development, program evaluation, and supervisory services. Each of these elements is discussed more fully in other chapters of this book.

Peer Review

For a service to be validated by peer review, it is essential that standards exist outlining what is necessary to maintain a satisfactory pattern of service. For example, the APA standards and guidelines for providing professional services (1977) can serve as a yardstick for verifying the acceptability of services provided by a specific discipline, if peer evaluation is conducted. Such standards, however, need to be applied carefully and within the context of the circumstances that exist in the specific clinic setting at the time of review. Peer reviews in the form of accreditation by the Joint Commission on Accreditation of Hospitals (JCAH), case record reviews by the Office of the Civilian Health and Medical Program of the Uniformed Services (CHAMPUS), or third-party payer reviews are becoming more common, and have a high probability of also serving an educational function by identifying existing deficiencies in clinic activities. As such, peer reviews should be sought rather than feared. In addition, seeking accreditation or peer review voluntarily rather than when mandated by the courts or a third-party payer enables a clinic to be prepared in advance for any mandated review that might occur. Such prior review could, in fact, preclude the need for a mandated review, because all possible questions that could arise may have been dealt with by appropriate, in-place written operating procedures.

Document Review

Conforming to relevant codes of ethics, standards of operation, and laws necessitates that staff be trained and have available copies of all relevant documents. Each staff member and the clinic administrator need to regularly monitor any changes that occur in ethics, standards, and laws. For example, the APA has revised its code of ethics and standards three times in the last 10 years. It is easy for a practitioner to be unaware of these changes. At a minimum, clinic staff should review yearly the changes in ethics, standards, and laws that are relevant to their disciplines and to the clinic's operation, and act to *update the education* of staff.

To provide services that violate the rights of those served cannot legally, and should not ethically, occur; thus, providing quality services requires both that a clinic have available in written form an acceptable listing of the rights of clients and that those rights be enforced. A full discussion and listing of such rights is found in Chapter 11.

Outcome

Last, but not least, quality services must be outcome oriented; that is, they must be directed toward overcoming the presenting problems of the clients served. Jacobs (1983) has stated it is obvious that quality services must be defined in terms of the results obtained. Competence in the future may well mean that the client leaves services *satisfied with the outcome achieved,* and that anything less may be defined as a lack of quality services. Such an orientation has serious implications for service providers and raises many questions, not the least of which is, "Can and should service providers be evaluated for competence on the basis of outcomes achieved?" If a provider is not 100% successful, is he or she incompetent? If so, then probably all providers are incompetent, since few, if any, are 100% successful. More realistically, outcome is only one of several factors that contribute to a professional's level of competence (extensive coverage of staff competence is included in Chapter 3). Realistically, providers need to be aware of what can and cannot be accomplished within a specific client content, and they must explain that to the client/family. They should then strive to achieve the identified goal.

Issues such as defining competence are a "trend of the times" and must be considered by all service providers, both alone and within the context of their own disciplines. Failure to do so may result in other groups legislating requirements that are totally unacceptable to service providers. For example, the state of Utah is trying to require licensed psychologists to be supervised by a physician in order for an agency to collect Title XIX funds (Utah Psychological Association, 1984). Much national legislation has focused on whether particular services are efficacious, safe, and appropriate (DeLeon, VandenBos, & Cummings, 1983).

Comprehensiveness of Services Offered

Cummings (1978) and Fox (1982) stress the importance of psychologists establishing their own comprehensive psychological service centers. The issue of comprehensiveness of services is complex. Following are several considerations to take into account.

Questions to Address

After determining the psychological and related services needed by children and adolescents in a specific geographic area, existing clinic directors (and possibly staff) or those considering opening a psychological clinic face a number of interrelated issues, including: a) how comprehensive should the offered services be? b) Should the comprehensiveness of services offered now be the same in future years? c) Should only psychological services be offered, or should related services also be provided? d) If only psychological services are to be provided, will they be restricted to evaluation and assessment only or will treatment services also be offered? e) Will treatment be restricted to only one problem area (e.g., phobias), or will it be available for all psychological problems? f) Should psychological staff represent only one theoretical orientation (e.g., behavioral), or should several orientations be included? g) Should the clinic provide consultation services to other agencies? After these and other questions have been answered, the issue of staff and other resources needed can be addressed.

Staffing

Comprehensiveness can be considered from several vantage points. One perspective assumes that a clinic must be staffed by psychologists representing all of the major theoretical schools of psychology in order to be considered a comprehensive clinic. A second perspective assumes that a clinic is comprehensive when staffed not only by psychologists from all the various theoretical orientations for service to children but also by staff from other disciplines that provide related services such as psychiatry, physical therapy, nutrition, psychiatric nursing, social work, and speech therapy. On a practical level, a clinic might be considered comprehensive if the staff are able to provide the most common services needed by children and adolescents experiencing psychological difficulties. These services might include assessment and evaluation; intervention and family support services; consultation to agencies; program development; evaluation; and supervision (APA, 1981), with a cooperative arrangement for medical support services. It is important that each of these components have fully qualified staff; for example, if an assessment service is offered, staff should be able to assess intellectual and cognitive factors, educational skills and deficits, personality variables, vocational interests and aptitudes, and psychological pathology. Morganstern (1976) pointed out that assessment should expose "everything that is relevant to the development of effective, efficient, and durable treatment intervention" (p. 52).

Clearly, one person is unable to provide the comprehensive psychological services that may be needed by all different types of children, adolescents, and their families. This is not to say that one individual cannot or should not operate a private practice, but, rather, that he or she should clearly delineate which services can be provided in accordance with his or her areas of competence, and which services would need to be provided through interagency agreement or referral of the client elsewhere. A clinician working independently may arrange for supervision prior to accepting clients in areas in which expertise is lacking. Indeed, ethical principles for the human service professions require that he or she do so. For example, it seems unlikely that an individual trained in traditional behavior modification but without training in norm referenced testing would be qualified to provide comprehensive psychological and related services to all children and adolescents referred. Few if any practitioners have had experience with all of the various types of problems that might be referred to a clinic. In addition, experience does not necessarily imply competence in treating various problems, or even interest in treating them. Trying to provide service to individuals with drug-related problems, alcoholism, sexual acting-out tendencies, delinquency patterns, criminal behavior, behavioral problems, family problems, abuse, and so forth, could be overwhelming to any provider and, moreover, would be unethical.

It is important for professional staff members to know their limitations and strengths when confronted with specific problems, and know when to seek assistance either from a peer within the clinic or by referring a client elsewhere. A self-assessment may be helpful. We believe that, at a minimum, it takes a staff team with different areas of expertise to provide appropriate services in a well-functioning child and adolescent clinic. The more staff members there are with diversified training and experience, the more comprehensive the services. In addition, Klein (1983) points out that clients are often attracted to group practices because they think the clinicians are more competent.

Crisis Coverage

Crisis intervention and staff coverage during vacations and days off are two specific services that may need to be arranged through external sources. Any professional in psychological or related services must arrange for adequate coverage of clients who might go into crisis during hours when the clinic is closed or when the professional must be absent for whatever reason. Without arranging for coverage, a sole clinician would be on call 24 hours a day, 7 days a week. Professionals working alone in a clinic also have difficulty arranging for time off because other professionals do not want to take responsibility for someone else's clients. In addition, directors of crisis centers within a community mental health agency may often react negatively to professionals who do not provide their own crisis coverage for their clients. When there is more than one staff member, individuals can take a day off during the week, take off the weekend, or take an annual vacation while knowing that their clients are adequately covered.

Referral Services

Each clinic should determine the available and appropriate community and state options to which referrals can be made when: a) the clinic does not have the appropriate services available; b) the client needs services provided by a different type of agency (e.g., subsistence payments); c) the clinic staff are unsuccessful in dealing with a client's problem. Before referrals are made, a clinic's administrative staff should be familiar with all possible options, public and private. The options for each type of service can be typed on a separate sheet and distributed as handouts. We recommend that clients not be referred to one specific provider or agency; instead, they should be given lists with as many options as possible. Such a practice may avoid litigation that can result if a referral is made to an incompetent or inappropriate provider or agency. (Given a list with several options, it is the client's decision as to which to choose, and not that of the service clinic making the referral.) In reality, however, many clinics make direct referrals to a specific provider because they know of the provider's reputation and the quality of services provided. Although legally a bit more risky, they find it practical because a good working relationship between agencies can thus be established, resulting in reciprocal referrals when appropriate to the needs of a specific client.

Continuum of Services

As previously stated, a clinic operated by one discipline or for one kind of problem would be considered a "specialty" clinic, whereas a "comprehensive" clinic would involve more than one discipline and more than one service. A comprehensive child and adolescent clinic would provide directly, or arrange for via interagency agreements, the majority of the continuum of services mandated in different state statutes such as the State of Utah's *State Standards for Community Mental Health Centers* (1980) and *Board of Mental Health Policies* (1981, 1985). See Table 1.3 for Utah's continuum of services.

Whether all components of a comprehensive clinic are provided directly or through arrangements with other agencies depends largely on whether the clinic is operated by public tax dollars or by private fees. A child or adolescent clinic that provides all 10 services listed in Table 1.3 would certainly be considered a comprehensive clinic. Other clinics could be considered comprehensive if they provided the first 5 services and had written cooperative arrangements with other

Table 1.3. The Utah continuum of mental health services

1. Emergency services to meet the needs of children and adolescents.
2. Outclient services to meet the needs of children and adolescents.
3. Consultation and education services to increase public awareness of mental health problems and services available to children and adolescents. This activity might be considered optional by some, but it is one of the best means of generating an ongoing flow of clients.
4. Screening and evaluation services to help determine for courts and other agencies the need for inpatient care for children and adolescents.
5. A range of modalities acceptable for treating the problems of children and adolescents, such as behavioral and humanistic approaches, and individual, group, family, crisis, and day treatment.
6. Case-finding services adequate to meet the needs of the catchment area.
7. Providing and arranging for inpatient services for those children and adolescents who need 24-hour intensive treatment because they cannot cope successfully or are dangerous to self or others. This includes hospitalization and other residential care and services.
8. Transitional and residential services to provide appropriate community-based living services to a) prevent inappropriate admissions to inpatient care and b) assist children and adolescents in transition from one level of care to a less restrictive one.
9. Pharmacy services adequate to meet the needs of children and adolescents served by the clinic.
10. Partial care, therapeutic services, and rehabilitative services aimed at maximizing independent living in the community for children and adolescents. These related services should serve as an intermediary between inpatient services and the natural environment.

Source: State of Utah (1981, 1985).

agencies for the other 5 services. In terms of treatment areas, a comprehensive clinic must also be prepared to provide services for all of the psychological and related problems faced by children and adolescents, including but not limited to: aggression and social skills problems, developmental problems, school problems, substance abuse problems, sexual or other acting-out problems, hyperactivity, custody problems, and abuse and neglect.

Standards and Guidelines

The more fully a clinic's services are described, including what services will be provided directly and indirectly, the easier it is to establish standards and guidelines for service delivery. Some of these standards and guidelines, along with codes of ethics and law, are often mandated from outside a clinic; but operating procedures are usually an internal matter. At least 10 features must be dealt with and resolved by clinic staff in distinguishing standards and guidelines for service delivery (Jacobs, 1983). These include:

1. Defining the training and education necessary to be a service provider
2. Defining the level of supervision required over paraprofessionals
3. Describing the service options available and outlining the organizational elements of the service delivery system

4. Defining the functions and standard operating procedures that are to be maintained
5. Defining staff responsibilities and authority, staff privileges, voting status on key committees, and other factors related to governance of the committee
6. Defining interdisciplinary relationships within the clinic and with agencies with whom cooperative arrangements exist
7. Defining procedures for protecting the human and civil rights of consumers
8. Defining the methods for evaluating services at a local level (peer review) or elsewhere
9. Specifying clearly when the standards and guidelines will be reviewed and revised, and by whom
10. Specifying how the standards will be applied and enforced

An example of a set of standards for service delivery is provided in Table 1.4.

If each of these features is dealt with and the resolution is put into the form of a written document, the clinic has a beginning set of standards by which staff

Table 1.4. Example of a mental health center standard for service delivery

A COMPREHENSIVE PLAN OF SERVICES

Standard

There shall be a Comprehensive Plan of Services that shall be reviewed and updated at least annually to reflect changing needs. The plan shall include the following:

Criteria

1. A description of the community to be served in terms of demographic and economic data, using already-existing data whenever possible
2. A description of the human services system serving the target population, including social services, public health services, rehabilitation services, employment services, sheltered living arrangements, and services of private agencies
3. Estimates based on available data of the types and extent of significant social, health, and mental health problems in the community, including estimates of the types and extent of emotional and substance abuse disabilities in children, adolescents, adults, and elderly
4. A description of existing services dealing with the above problems, including an evaluation of the degree to which the services match the estimated needs
5. A description of the purposes, goals, and objectives of the center
6. A description of how, when and where proposed programs will be implemented, including the methods to be used, the projected costs, and the means of financing
7. Where proposed programs are to be provided through affiliation with community agencies, the authorities and responsibilities of the center vis-à-vis the affiliating agencies must be clearly spelled out in writing
8. A description of the hours of operation of the various services
9. A description of efforts to assure accessibility and availability of services, including arrangements for making services available to those in public and private facilities
10. A description of working relationships with health, health planning, and other human service agencies serving the catchment area
11. A description of the means for assuring citizen and client input to program planning

Source: State of Utah (1980, p. 2).

can operate and a way to determine needed changes. The more planning that occurs before a clinic opens its doors, the greater the likelihood of success. Like any other business, psychological and related services can fail unless proper attention is paid to planning (Drucker, 1954).

SCOPE AND LIMITATIONS OF THIS GUIDEBOOK

Clearly, the factors to be considered in establishing and operating a clinic are many and complex and include type of clinic; clinic philosophy, mission, and goals; quality and comprehensiveness of services; and standards and guidelines. This book provides guidelines for *setting up clinics primarily concerned with psychological services for children and adolescents.* Issues similar to those connected with psychological services would also need to be considered by clinics interested in providing other types of services, such as speech therapy, physical therapy, or medical services. The factors considered would need to be adjusted for the specific discipline and its strengths. Clinics already in operation, which have not undergone a planning stage in which a philosophy, mission, and goals were prepared, might find it useful to participate in the process described in this chapter as a form of self-evaluation and self-improvement.

The remainder of this guidebook describes other clinic and service-related aspects and how to implement services. It would be impossible to cover all of the possible clinic and treatment approaches. Rather, this book concentrates on factors common to the establishment and operation of most clinics for children and adolescents.

To help you incorporate major ideas, to plan, and to review content, reader activities are provided at the end of each chapter. In addition, Appendix B contains separate self-evaluation checklists for administrators and clinicians which reiterate some of the major points of each chapter.

READER ACTIVITIES

Are you familiar with the philosophy, mission, and goals of the clinic you administer, are employed by, or are establishing? Have the philosophy, mission, and goals been developed and/or reviewed to ensure that they are appropriate and functional? If not, we suggest you take time *now* to review and/or establish a philosophy, mission, and goals according to this chapter's guidelines. Do so now and write them down for later use. Have you clearly specified what the continuum of services to be offered is and how comprehensive the clinic is or will be in terms of services offered? If not, do so now.

REFERENCES

American Psychological Association. (1977). *Standards for providers of psychological services.* Washington, DC: American Psychological Association.

American Psychological Association. (1981). Ethical principles of psychologists. *American Psychologist, 36*(6), 633–638.

Bradley, V. J., Ashbaugh, J. W., Harder, W. P., Stoddard, S., & Shea, S. (1984). *Assessing and enhancing the quality of services.* Boston: Human Services Research Institute.

Christian, W. P., & Hannah, G. T. (1983). *Effective management in human services.* Englewood Cliffs, NJ: Prentice-Hall.

Cummings, N. A. (1978). Testimony before Senate Finance Committee. In *Proposals to expand coverage of mental health under Medicare-Medicaid.* Washington, DC: U.S. Government Printing Office.

DeLeon, P. H., VandenBos, G. R., & Cummings, N. A. (1983). Psychotherapy—Is it safe, effective, and appropriate? *American Psychologist, 38*(8), 907–911.

Drucker, P. F. (1954). *The practice of management.* New York: Harper & Row.

Fox, R. E. (1982). The need for a reorientation of clinical psychology. *American Psychologist, 37*(9), 1051–1057.

Greenberg, S. F., & Valletutti, P. J. (1980). *Stress and the helping professions.* Baltimore: Paul H. Brookes Publishing Co.

Guralnik, D. B. (1982). *Webster's new world dictionary of the American language.* New York: Simon & Schuster.

Jacobs, D. F. (1983). The development and application of standards of practice for professional psychologists. In B. D. Sales (Ed.), *The professional psychologist's handbook* (pp. 19–75). New York: Plenum.

Klein, H. E. (1983). How to improve the marketing of therapy services. In P. E. Keller & L. G. Ritt (Eds.), *Innovations in clinical practice: A source book* (Vol. 2, pp. 233–241). Sarasota, FL: Professional Resources Exchange.

Lee, W. (1978). *Formulating and reaching goals.* Champaign, IL: Research Press.

Morganstern, K. P. (1976). Behavioral interviewing: The initial stages of assessment. In M. Hersen & A. S. Bellack (Eds.), *Behavioral assessment: A practical handbook* (pp. 51–76). New York: Pergamon.

Seattle Mental Health Institute. (1984). *What's in your future? The steps in the development of a mental health long range plan.* Seattle: Author.

State of Utah. (1980). *State standards for community mental health centers.* Salt Lake City: Department of Social Services.

State of Utah. (1981). *Board of Mental Health policies.* Salt Lake City: Department of Social Services.

State of Utah. (1985). *Board of Mental Health policies.* Salt Lake City: Department of Social Services.

Striefel, S., Burnside, J., Callister, S., Cardon, B., Stroud, K., Patterson, C., & Forbush, B., (1984). *Mental health assumptions for Utah.* Salt Lake City: Department of Social Services.

Striefel, S., & Cadez, M. J. (1983). *Serving children and adolescents with developmental disabilities in the special education classroom: Proven methods.* Baltimore: Paul H. Brookes Publishing Co.

Utah Psychological Association.(1984).*UPA Summer Newsletter, (3).*

2

Marketing the Program and Equipping the Facility

After reading this chapter, you will be acquainted with issues related to the:
1. Development of a new clinic, including funding and marketing issues
2. Clinic facilities needed for staff
3. Clinic facilities needed for clients and client families
4. Specialized portable and nonportable equipment useful in a clinic setting
5. Specialized materials, consumable and nonconsumable, used in a clinic
6. The role of the computer in the clinic
7. Insurance needs

THE NEW CLINIC

Starting Slowly

Based on available or anticipated resources, administrators must decide what services to offer within your clinic. You may decide to start with a small operation and expand as funds begin to flow into the system, or funds could be borrowed to begin a larger operation. Financial prudence dictates starting small and expanding as funds become available. It is not essential that a clinic open with all available services, or that it even be a full-time clinic. Rather, it could begin as a part-time activity and as the referral sources grow and funding permits, it could expand to a full-time clinic. Subsequently, components and staff could be added to become a comprehensive clinic.

Relationship of Services and Clinic Goals

Within the context of determining what services to provide, it is essential that the mission and goals of the clinic be articulated, if that has not already been done (see Chapter 1). Preparing mission and goal statements will help alleviate the problems of "jumping into something" without a well-conceptualized plan. As emphasized in Chapter 1, planning is essential if the clinic is to be successful. One marketing firm indicates that during "start-up" the administrator will probably spend 90% of his or her time on planning, 5% on implementation, and 5% on staff control issues (Serco, 1984).

Funding Issues

Decisions concerning what clinic facilities, equipment, and materials will be available as resources now and in the future will depend upon funding. A clinic may obtain funds prior to opening via: a) personal funds of the owners; b) obtaining a loan; c) backing by individuals who would fund the clinic as a business venture; and d) obtaining service contracts or grants from local, state, or national government or private sources (e.g., the State Mental Health Division, the National Institute of Mental Health, or private corporations).

After the clinic is operating, services will be financed by, a) payments received from clients; b) payments received through federal, state, and local government agencies; c) payments received from insurance companies; and d) payments received from private contributors, including individuals and corporations (Christian & Hannah, 1983). (Client billing and payment issues are discussed in Chapter 4). Appropriate sources of financial information include bankers, accountants, lawyers, government agencies, foundations within corporations, and other professionals who provide human services.

Along with determining available funding for facilities, equipment, and materials, you will need to know what actual resources (e.g., staff, facilities, equipment) are needed to begin the desired programs. Existing clinics will need to ascertain what resources are already available, what resources might become available (Seattle Mental Health Institute, 1984), and what resources need to be sought. The mission and goals of a clinic cannot be accomplished without adequate resources.

Naming the Psychological Service Clinic

An often overlooked aspect of planning concerns the selection of an appropriate name for the service clinic. Klein (1983) has recommended that the word *clinic* not be included in the name because clinics are often regulated in special ways by state law. Names such as, "Center for Child and Adolescent Services" or "The Children and Youth Therapy Institute," have an immediate appeal because they designate the population to be served and how they will be served. In selecting a name, a marketing firm can be hired to do a market survey to determine the potential impact of different names; however, that can be expensive. Alternatively, the administrator and staff (if available) can select a name themselves. Start by generating a list of tentative names. A survey can then be conducted by contacting a variety of community members and asking them to rate several names for their desirability. It is suggested that a clinic not be named after the owner(s) because if the business should not succeed, negative associations will accompany that name in the future (Mancuso, 1985). Mancuso also suggests that the business not be named after the street it is on, or the community where it is located, to avoid possible confusion for consumers. Since the name of the service clinic will appear on all advertising, letterhead, envelopes, and on the facility itself, it is important that the name convey the appropriate image and activity of the service unit. The name should also be easy to remember, dignified, and not readily confused with that of other agencies.

MARKETING ACTIVITIES

General Factors

Beginning a new service unit or deciding to expand referrals for existing units requires attention to marketing considerations. Kurtz and Boone (1984) characterize service as a product designed to produce "consumer want satisfaction"; thus, a psychological service clinic is in a sense selling services.

As stated in Chapter 1, a clinic providing psychological and related services is a business. Every business must ultimately attract customers in order to survive (Drucker, 1954). Marketing, the process of creating customers, is achieved through an organized group of activities adopted by management with the intent of matching organizational activities and consumer need, for mutual satisfaction (Serco, 1984). The activities include planning and implementation.

Planning and Implementation

Creating a customer (client) means identifying existing or future needs, deciding which needs the clinic can serve, and converting potential into actual clients (Guiltenan & Paul, 1982). In a service clinic (defined in Chapter 1), the administrator is responsible for planning and implementation. An overview of planning and implementation activities is contained in Table 2.1.

Planning is the process of projecting what the future will be like and deciding what activities to engage in to achieve organizational goals (Kurtz & Boone, 1984). Planning can help you achieve several clinic goals as specified in Table 2.2.

Identifying Needs

Marketing is based on an exchange process in which two or more parties give something of value to each other to satisfy needs (Kurtz & Boone, 1984). A service clinic's need is to have clients who pay for services, whereas the client's need is for the services. Identifying needs requires that the specific public to be served, often called the market (e.g., children and adolescents), be specified first. The general process for identifying the market to be served was discussed in Chapter 1 in the sections addressing the establishment of clinic goals. The subsections that follow in the present chapter provide more specific pointers for selecting the market segment to be served.

The administrator makes decisions on whom to serve by considering factors such as willingness to buy, purchasing power, and authority to buy (Kurtz & Boone, 1984). Each of these factors poses unique problems for a clinic serving or

Table 2.1. Planning and implementation activities

1. Identifying the needs of potential clients (in this case the needs of children, adolescents, and their families).
2. Developing services that meet those needs.
3. Making the services available at times that meet client needs (e.g., making office hours convenient for clients and keeping waiting lists short).
4. Making the services available at a convenient, safe, and attractive location. It is also important to consider accessibility that protects the client's need for privacy, since many individuals (especially teenagers) do not want others to know they are receiving psychological services.
5. Providing services at fees that reflect competition, cost, and the ability of clients to pay. (This is discussed in the section, "Fees for Client Services," in Chapter 4.)
6. Providing quality services and follow-up to ensure client satisfaction with the services received.

Source: Adapted from Guiltinan & Paul (1982).

planning to serve children and adolescents, because these groups do not often willingly seek services, nor do they have the authority or dollars to purchase services. Thus, you must consider the needs of this population, while simultaneously determining which of those needs parents or agencies are willing to address by seeking out and paying for services. For example, if targeting a nonaffluent group, you might direct the marketing effort to personnel from agencies who are likely to work with that population and who typically seek and/or fund services of the type provided by the clinic.

Market Segmentation

Attempting to satisfy everyone may readily result in failure, since there are so many diverse groups with different needs. Market segmentation is the process of dividing the total market into several relatively homogeneous groups in order to target a particular segment for services (e.g., middle class children within the city limits of Salt Lake City). A market segment can be distinguished from other market segments on the basis of factors such as age, sex, geographic location, income, expenditure patterns, population size, and mobility. Based on such factors, administrators can decide what segments of the market they plan to serve.

Table 2.2. A sample of planning outcomes

1. Achieve a more favorable position in the market
2. The clinic progress in the direction favored by management
3. Each administrator to think, decide, and act more effectively in achieving desired outcomes
4. Keep the clinic flexible
5. Stimulate a cooperative, integrated, and enthusiastic approach to organizational problems
6. Administrators to evaluate progress toward the planned goals
7. Achieve economically and socially useful results

Source: Adapted from Jain (1981).

Needs

The more precisely the market segment to be served is defined, the easier it is to identify the needs of that market. Precision can be achieved by developing profiles of the typical client from different market segments. Included in the profile could be items such as attitudes toward psychological services in general and specific services per se, life-style patterns, service use patterns (by parents rather than the children), geographic location, and demographic characteristics (Kurtz & Boone, 1984). To identify specific needs you can collect new data (primary data) by interviewing members of the market segment or staff from agencies who serve that segment. You can also collect data already available (secondary data) in published form from within the clinic (e.g., who has been served, for what problems, how well they were served with existing resources, their ability to pay, and what problems arose), or you can collect data from external sources such as local, state, and federal government agencies (e.g., census data). Common methods of data collection include observation and surveys (telephone, mail, and face-to-face interviews). Conducting surveys necessitates attending to all of the following: questionnaire design; selecting, training, and controlling interviews; editing, coding, tabulating and interpreting data; presenting results; and determining the validity and reliability of the data (Kurtz & Boone, 1984).

The more you can utilize existing data, the more economical in time and dollars it will be to identify market segment needs. Keep in mind, though, that existing sources may not include all of the information you need for decision making.

The final concern in selecting a target segment is to ensure that the needs of the segment match the services to be offered. For a new clinic, services can be designed, resources allocated, and staff hired to meet the specific needs of the target clients. For existing clinics the task can be more difficult. The choice is either to find the specific market segments that need the services currently offered or to redesign the services for the target groups chosen. In all probability a little of each will be necessary.

Matching Client Needs and Services

In order to match market segment needs with services, both needs and services must be identified. The previous section specified procedures for identifying needs. Identifying the services to be offered is discussed in detail in Chapter 3, and thus is not covered here. Suffice it to say that the better the match between needs and services, the more progress clients will make and the more satisfied they will be with the services.

Christian and Hannah (1983, p. 4) stated that the correlation between consumer needs and services received is affected by several factors, including:

> (1) the accuracy and appropriateness of diagnostic (need) assessment and service planning (goals, objectives, and criteria for success); (2) the advantages and limitations of the program's physical environment and available resources; (3) the quality

and quantity of program personnel (for example, expertise of staff, staff-to-client ratio); (4) the extent of the consumer's understanding and participation (for example, informed consent); (5) the training, supervision, and evaluation provided for program personnel; (6) the effectiveness of program evaluation and accountability systems (for example, client progress reviews, client tracking systems); and (7) the effectiveness of regulatory agencies.

Promotion

The next task is to make the potential consumer (client and client family) aware of their needs and of the services offered by your clinic. This is accomplished via promotional activities. Once the administrator has decided whom is to be served, he or she must also decide how to attract clients and how to publicize the clinic as a qualified provider of psychological and related services. Several marketing-related activities are associated with a clinic's relative success (Kurtz & Boone, 1984):

1. The relative strength of the new service and how it is publicized
2. The nature and quality of information available as the service is developed
3. The relative proficiency of the new service development efforts
4. The characteristics of the marketplace at which the service is aimed
5. The compatibility of the new service with the unit's resource base
6. The specific characteristics of the new service effort

Care must be taken in dealing with each of these categories as part of the planning and promotion process.

Advertising

As already stated, the clinic's name represents a vital initial and ongoing advertisement for the facility. In addition, Klein (1983) suggests that a number of promotional steps be taken after an appropriate name has been selected, including: a) tell your friends and ask them to advise their colleagues that the clinic is interested in referrals; b) announce the existence of the service program through tasteful and ethical announcements in the local newspapers, cross listings in the Yellow Pages of the telephone directory (it is estimated that for every $1,000 spent here, $6,000–$7,000 in new income is generated), and tasteful brochures that specify the services offered (one for the public and one for professionals); c) contact local groups and offer free lectures and workshops; d) contact large organizations and let them know what services are available; e) use the local newspapers, radio, and television to gain exposure via talk shows, interviews, or articles; f) have professional clinic staff affiliate with known organizations such as the Mental Health Association to build local contacts and visibility: g) distribute inexpensive business tokens that will remind people of the clinic's existence (e.g., pens imprinted with the name of the organization); h) provide special services that set the service unit apart from others (e.g., provide therapy on pediatric wards at hospitals or services not offered by other providers): and i) arrange to meet with professionals outside the clinic to find out what services they offer so that referrals can be made to them; often, they in turn will ask about services provided and may make referrals to the clinic.

Administrators can influence the public and improve the clinic's marketing position by using what is called identification advertising, which refers to conveying a message with which a consumer can identify (Serco, 1984). Brochures, radio and television spots, and face-to-face contacts can be used to present such messages. For example, a television spot could present a message such as the following, "My teenage son and I were constantly fighting over his school performance until I sought counseling for him. Things are better now," followed by a printed message, "This announcement has been sponsored by the Center for Adolescent Services," followed by the center's telephone number. Messages must be presented at a level understandable to the consumer group.

In developing messages, administrators should consider (Serco, 1984):

1. What the ad is expected to accomplish
2. The degree of existing interest or lack of interest
3. The physical way the message will be communicated
4. The nature of the audience in terms of ability to buy, customs, prejudices, knowledge, and intelligence
5. What is being advertised in terms of the specific qualities or attributes of the services and the clinic
6. How the services or clinic compares with others in generating revenue and in advertising volume

All advertisements for psychologists must adhere to the *Ethical Principles of Psychologists* (APA, 1981).

PUBLIC RELATIONS

The establishment or continuation of a clinic is heavily dependent upon how the clinic is viewed by the community. Indicators of public approval of the clinic operation are reflected by the number of clients referred to the clinic; consistency of client referrals; requests for professional interactions and consultation from other community agencies and professionals; and funding support.

Clinic management should be aware, however, that the delivery of exemplary services to clients, although a significant factor in maintaining public relations, is not the sole effort needed to ensure that the clinic has community acceptance and is viewed as a vital community service. Public relations efforts should be ongoing throughout a clinic's operation. Christian and Hannah (1983) have proposed that a positive image of a progressive human service program is created through coordinated efforts both within the clinic and with professionals and agencies outside the clinic. They suggest the following public relations activities:

1. Development of a clinic brochure and other promotional literature that can be mailed or provided to members of local community organizations and

other individuals at state and national levels who could support the clinic operation. An identifying clinic logo on all printed materials distributed by a clinic helps to create recognition.

2. Development of a standard package of materials that can be mailed to those inquiring about available services.

3. An audiovisual program describing the clinic and clinic services that could be shown at no cost at conferences, workshops, or other public presentations. This program could also be shown to groups invited to tour the clinic, or to clients when they come to the clinic for services.

4. Professional participation by staff in community activities and organizations; presentations at local and national conferences; articles in journals, newsletters, and local newspapers; press releases and other media reports or interviews on clinic functions and activities.

5. Appointment of a community advisory board responsible for specific public relations activities.

FACILITIES FOR STAFF AND CLIENT USE

A clinic's image is aided by the availability of facilities that are comfortable, esthetically pleasing, and appropriate for the specific activities to be conducted there.

Office Space

Each staff member will need office space, either private or shared with other staff. Space allocation should be made on the basis of: a) staff roles and assignments; b) clinic functions carried out in office areas; c) client use of staff office areas; and d) clinic space available. If clinicians are assigned private offices, some client services may also be provided within these areas, thus increasing their use. Whenever office space is shared by clinicians, the need for separate client service areas is increased because of the need for client privacy and confidentiality.

Lounge and Restrooms

If at all possible, the clinic should contain a lounge area for staff (which may be equipped with food preparation areas and vending machines) and restroom facilities separate from those available to clients. The size of the clinic facility and number of staff employed will be major factors in determining the extent of clinic facilities available for staff.

Each clinic serving preschool/kindergarten age children should ideally contain one restroom that is fitted with child-sized plumbing equipment in addition to the regular restroom facilities available. Parents or legal guardians should be expected to accompany young children to the restroom or monitor use by older children for the child/adolescent's safety, particularly in buildings where restrooms are available to the public (e.g., hospital settings), or are not observable from waiting or treatment areas.

Multipurpose Rooms

Each clinic should contain at least one multipurpose room large enough to be used for staff meetings, case staffings, staff inservices and training, and other group activities (e.g., parent workshops). Room schedules for each multipurpose room within the clinic should be maintained so that staff can reserve the space in advance. Whenever only one multipurpose room is available within a clinic, it should be large enough to accommodate the maximum number of occupants that could conceivably use the room at any one time. The room should: a) be furnished with chairs and tables easily movable to allow for flexibility in room arrangement: b) contain a chalkboard (portable or wall mounted); and c) have space for a film projector or other audiovisual equipment (e.g., overhead projectors) and a projection screen (portable or wall-mounted). In larger clinics, especially those located within hospital facilities, small auditoriums or conference rooms in the same building may be available for clinic use, particularly when large groups are to be accommodated. The needs of children and adolescents who will use the facilities should also be considered (e.g., chairs should be of appropriate size).

Waiting Areas

Most clinics have a central waiting area for those who have appointments to see service providers, or are accompanying such clients (i.e., parents) or who are waiting to see other clinic staff (e.g., business office staff). Depending on the number of clients served and the number of staff available, it is generally not possible to avoid having more than one client and client family in the waiting area at the same time, although this would be most desirable for maintaining privacy rights.

Whenever children or adolescents are to be kept waiting for appointments with clinicians, they should be supplied with age-appropriate toys, and reading or other materials, to occupy them during the waiting period. It is also desirable that parents of clients be provided with current periodicals or articles, including those related to parenting and other family issues. If it is clinic policy to allow client families to bring siblings or other children or adolescents to the clinic at the time of the client's appointment, it will also be necessary to have toys and/or materials to occupy them. We recommend that client families be discouraged from bringing children other than the client to the clinic because it can be disruptive for both parents and clinicians. Parents should be encouraged to make arrangements for child care outside of the clinic so that their attention can be devoted fully to the task at hand. Some parents may find it impossible to either obtain child care or leave children in the care of others (e.g., nursing infants). If so, clinic staff will have to accept these special circumstances and make whatever arrangements they can (i.e., arrange for child care within the clinic).

If space is available, a play area or playground may be set up, either within the building or outdoors, for the use of children and adolescents. If such an area is to be available, it is essential that specific rules for the use of the playground be posted within that area and that parents be informed of these rules and their responsibilities for monitoring any minor-age children using the play facilities. For example, in a large hospital clinic setting where a playground area is available, it could be a rule that children up to age 12 are not allowed access to the playground area unless a parent or guardian is present. Clinics cannot afford to assign a staff member to playground duty.

Clients/client families should have access to drinking fountains or bottled water and paper cups conveniently located in, or close to, the waiting areas. If young children are served, a low water fountain or stool will be needed to make the drinking fountain accessible. Some clinic waiting areas also contain vending machines with hot and cold drinks and snacks. These are particularly useful if waiting times are long (i.e., when the child or adolescent client is in a session with a clinician and the parents are waiting). Installation and maintenance of vending machines, however, are usually practical only in clinics serving a large number of clients.

It may be easier to plan and equip waiting areas in new clinics than in older clinics, particularly if clinics are being built to specification. Rearrangement of rooms or remodeling may sometimes be accomplished in older clinics, without extensive cost, and should be considered when existing client facilities are inappropriate and inadequate.

Assessment and Treatment Rooms

If client services are not to be provided in clinicians' offices, rooms will need to be designated for client services. In general, client service rooms should be furnished in accordance with their intended use. For example, rooms used for assessment services should not only contain appropriate-sized furniture to accommodate clients of different ages (discussed more fully later in this chapter) but should contain minimal distractors (e.g., pictures, bric-a-brac, toys). Rooms designated for individual, group, or family counseling, however, if not also used for assessment purposes, do not need to be as simply furnished and may be set up as casual living rooms. Depending upon the clinic orientation and size, one or more rooms may also be designated for play therapy. If so, such rooms should be furnished in accordance with the type of therapy to be conducted.

Lighting, Wall, and Floor Coverings

It is essential that rooms used for client services have adequate lighting for conducting assessment and treatment. Permanent overhead lighting fixtures are desirable in assessment/treatment rooms. Portable floor or table lamps are less desirable for safety reasons. If preschool-age children are to be served, all electric wall plugs should be fitted with inexpensive close-off adaptors when not in use. Wall and floor coverings should be of materials that can be easily cleaned and maintained. This is crucial in rooms designated for play therapy, where messy materials are likely to be used (e.g., clay and sand).

Soundproofing

Insofar as possible, walls between clinical treatment rooms, offices, and hallways should be soundproofed so that conversations are not overheard in adjacent areas. If clinic rooms are not soundproof, then other methods may be employed to mask out verbal interchanges, such as use of a white noise generator, FM radio, or other masking devices. These are low-cost options and are easy to install in an existing facility not originally built as a clinic.

Location of Client Service Areas within the Clinic

In planning a new facility or in remodeling an existing one, rooms used for client services should be located so that opportunities for face-to-face encounters between different clients and their families are minimized. Again, as already stated, whenever children or adolescents are to interact with clinicians apart from their parents or legal guardians (e.g., for assessment or treatment), waiting areas or rooms will be needed for the adults.

Observation Rooms

Ideally, some clinic offices or treatment rooms will be located adjacent to rooms designated for observation. Connecting walls between observation and clinic rooms should contain a one-way observation window (mirrored on the side facing the clinic room). Observation rooms can be used by: a) clinicians, to observe parent/child interactions (e.g., during child management training); b) trainees, to observe more experienced staff working with clients; and c) supervisors, to monitor various staff or trainees during their performance of clinical activities. Parents or legal guardians may also be invited at times and in accordance with clinic policy to observe their child/adolescent during interactions, assessment, or treatment.

Each observation room should be equipped with some type of audio receiver with volume and off/on controls connected to an audio output system in the clinic room (e.g., a wall microphone). Two-way communication systems could also be useful for training and instructional purposes (e.g., a therapist in the observation room could cue a parent with a child in the clinic room). In addition, permanent wall-mounted video cameras installed in the clinic rooms adjacent to observation rooms and operated from the observation room could be quite useful for many clinical purposes (e.g., to obtain video records of performance that can be used in later training sessions). As another option, a telephone system could be installed between the clinic and observation rooms, thus allowing intercommunication between the two areas.

Observation room regulations should be posted on doors both outside of the room and on the inside. A suggested list of observation room regulations is provided in Table 2.3. When no observations are to be allowed, a sign to this effect should be placed on the outside door of the observation room. Observations may not be appropriate for some clinic activities (e.g., during private child or adolescent interviews dealing with sensitive issues such as abuse). It may be

Table 2.3. Observation room regulations

1. Keep door to observation room closed when room is in use.
2. Lights in the observation room must remain out while observing.
3. Adjust volume on intercoms just loud enough to hear, and turn off the intercoms when leaving.
4. Any conversation in the observation room should be quiet, and avoid making noises that could be audible in adjacent rooms.
5. What is seen and heard while in the observation room is confidential information, and should only be discussed with staff, practicum interns, and supervisors involved with the case.
6. Be discrete in comments made to other staff or trainees while in the observation room, as frequently parents and others involved in the case may be present.
7. If observations are not to be allowed, uncover the sign to that effect that is on the outside of the observation room door.

desirable to have the doors to the observation rooms fitted with locks so that unauthorized observation can be prevented.

Exits

Some clinics have two separate exits/entrances. One is used solely for arriving clients and the other for exiting clients. This arrangement allows clients and parents/legal guardians to leave the clinic without contact with others, thus providing greater privacy. The availability of such exits, unless routed through a business office, precludes the collection of payment for the services at that time. Options to circumvent this are to have payments for services made upon arrival, or to have the clinician collect for services rendered. This latter option is not desirable, however, because of the time involved, the need for receipt books, and because it forces the clinician to be both a helper and a bill collector. In one-person clinics, however, this may be the way fee payments are handled because there are no other alternatives.

SPECIALIZED FURNITURE, EQUIPMENT, AND MATERIALS

The clinic must be equipped with items necessary for staff to provide quality client services and to conduct assigned responsibilities. Included are: a) office furnishings such as desks, chairs, bookcases, lockable filing cabinets, typewriters, copy machines, and computers; b) other supplies and miscellaneous items such as paper, pencils and pens, pencil sharpeners, staplers, rulers, files, and forms; and c) reference materials such as dictionaries, professional books and journals. The clinic should also be furnished with items to accommodate and serve child and adolescent clients. In newly organized clinics, budget allocations for such specialized items must be a major priority. In established clinics, annual budget allocations should be made for replacement of used, worn out, or outdated items, and for updating or increasing clinic inventories.

Clinic managers should maintain updated lists of specialized furniture, equipment, and materials that are desired or needed. As monies become available, items may be procured in order of their priority. However, certain items (i.e., expendable materials such as test protocols) are essential to clinic functioning, and budget allocations must be made for replacement of such materials.

Specialized Furniture for Client Use

The clinic should be equipped with age-appropriate (as well as disability-appropriate, for clients with physical handicaps) chairs and tables. Specialized furniture items should be placed in clinic waiting areas as well as in interview and assessment rooms. Numerous types of child-sized furniture are available, and items may be purchased readymade through commercial outlets (e.g., school equipment distributors). If suppliers are not locally available, items may be purchased by catalog. If ordering by catalog, arrange, whenever possible, for an inspection period with return privileges, so that you or other staff can determine whether items are satisfactory before actual expenditures are made. In some areas, local craftsmen may be located who will make specialized furniture items to order at nominal prices.

Although your staff will identify furniture items that are most appropriate for your clients, the following factors should be considered in selecting specialized child furniture items:

Factors to Consider in Selecting Client Furniture

1. *Safety features* Furniture should be free of potentially harmful structures that could result in injury to the user.
   a. Furniture made of or detailed with metal or plastic should have no sharp edges or corners, and no burrs.
   b. Furniture made of wood or detailed with wood should be sanded and finished or sealed to be splinter-free.
   c. Nails or screws used in furniture assembly should be recessed, with no raised surfaces, and secured so that they cannot be easily removed.
   d. Furniture should be well balanced in design and strength to prevent easy tipping or collapsing.
2. *Durability* Furniture should require minimal maintenance and be of a quality that will withstand frequent usage.
   a. Table surfaces should be finished or constructed with hard-surfaced materials (i.e., formica), to minimize marring.
   b. Furniture details or ornamentation (i.e., plastic table edges) should be of the same quality as the furniture item to which they are affixed.
   c. If metal tubing is used on furniture, it should be of a good quality and not easily bent.
   d. Materials used in furniture assembly and method of assembly, (e.g., how table legs are secured to a table top), should be of a quality to prevent wobbling or loosening.
   e. Stain-free fabric or material treated with a stain-free sealer should be selected for furniture constructed with fabric.

3. *Flexibility* Furniture should be selected with flexible, practical, and space-saving features.

   a. Table and chair height dimensions should be compatible with each other.

   b. Whenever possible, multiple items (e.g., chairs of the same furniture design) should be selected to allow transfer of furniture items between clinic areas as needed (e.g., chairs moved from clinic treatment rooms for group meetings in larger rooms).

   c. Size and weight of furniture items should allow easy transportability by staff members and should fit various clinic rooms and areas (e.g., hallways).

   d. Whenever possible, furniture items should be stackable for storage or space-saving convenience.

   e. Furniture items constructed with adaptable features (e.g., adjustable table legs), have greater practicality than those with fixed features. Avoid furniture in which adaptability requires special tools or is difficult, however.

   f. Table shapes and sizes should be selected on the basis of use (e.g., small rectangular tables are practical for testing with preschoolers).

Whenever possible, specialized furniture should be color coordinated to increase attractiveness to children/adolescents and client families. In addition, furniture of advanced or unusual design should be avoided.

Specialized Equipment

Equipment may be either portable or nonportable. Nonportable equipment items are those affixed in some manner to the building structure and used in one area of the clinic, while portable equipment may be moved and used in a number of clinic areas. There are advantages to having both portable and nonportable equipment items. Portable equipment may be used in a variety of settings and stored out of the way when not in use. Nonportable items do not require storage or need to be tracked to prevent loss; these items are always in place and ready for use.

Specialized Portable Equipment Useful in a Clinic

Taping Equipment Audio cassette recorders and tapes can be used for taping client treatment sessions, dictating clinical reports and notes, recording client responses during assessments, and for supervisory purposes. Videotape equipment and tapes can be used for taping client treatment sessions, for evaluating client progress over time, and for client and staff training.

Biofeedback Equipment This type of equipment is useful for determining individual client physiological responses; for monitoring client physiological responses during relaxation training; and in teaching a client how to deal with various physical and psychosomatic complaints such as migraine and tension headaches, anxiety, bruxism, and asthma. Extensive information can be found in almost any bookstore on biofeedback, its application, and types of equipment available.

Biofeedback equipment useful in the child/adolescent clinic includes: a) EMG–electromyograph—an instrument that measures the amount of electrical discharge in muscle fibers and provides feedback on the measurement (e.g., with a child who grinds his teeth); b) EEG—electroencephalograph—an instrument that measures brainwave activity and provides feedback (e.g., in a child with seizures); c) Skin temperature feedback. Thermistors placed on skin surfaces can measure skin temperature and provide feedback (e.g., with a child with migraine headaches); d) Electrodermal feedback. This instrumentation measures changes in electrical characteristics of the skin to meaningful stimulation, and is used to provide feedback (e.g., with a child who is anxious); e) Blood pressure feedback. This instrumentation measures blood pressure and provides feedback (e.g., with a teenager who has high blood pressure); f) Heart rate. Instrumentation measures heart rate levels and changes in heart rate, and provides feedback (e.g., with a teenager who has an arythmia); g) Respiration feedback. Instrumentation measures respiratory processes and provides feedback on air flow (e.g., with a teenager who has asthma).

"Bug in the Ear" Devices   Devices of this type consist of a small microphone that can be placed in the ear to receive audio information transmitted from another room or location within a prescribed distance. Such devices can be useful for ''cueing'' either clients or staff during training sessions or when they are being supervised.

Computers and Computer Systems   Computers and computer systems are and will continue to be an integral part of the operation of most clinics for psychological and related services. The term *computer* applies to a vast range of equipment, from a single machine capable of handling huge amounts of data in a brief time span, usually housed in a large facility such as in industry, business, or government, to a piece of equipment with a much more restricted capacity, useful, for example, in homes or small clinics and often called the ''personal computer.'' The type of computer discussed in this guidebook is known as a ''minicomputer'' or a ''microcomputer'' and is suitable to perform desired operations for most clinics. Throughout this guidebook, and commonly elsewhere, the word *computer* is also used to describe a basic piece of equipment plus other equipment (e.g., keyboard, television, video display screen or monitor, printer, disk drives).

Last, the term *computer system* may be used to describe either a computer plus other equipment or a package of any number of software programs to be used with the computer, or both. For our purposes, *computer system* refers to: the computer, ancillary computer equipment, and software programs.

Word processing   Some general areas of clinic operation can be efficiently handled through computer systems. These include: a) word processing; b) business-related activities; c) clinical services–related activities; and d) public relations activities. In word processing, information is typed into a computer system and can be stored in that system. The typed copy may be simultaneously viewed on a video display screen. Corrections, changes, or modifications can be made easily in the text as it is typed or later on when the information is retrieved.

Table 2.4. Potential business-related activities for a computer system

Client billing (including third-party billing)
Accounts receivable and accounts payable
Cash receipts payments and payment information
Cash disbursements
General ledger
Payroll
Human services management (staff information and personnel records)
Financial reporting
Budgeting
Audit trails
Inventory control
Data base management

Thus, complete retyping of texts is unnecessary, saving clerical time and facilitating corrections. Word processing capability is useful for all reports and correspondence prepared in a clinic, as well as for preparing other written materials such as journal articles. For more extensive information on use of word processing in clinical applications, see Keller (1982) and Samuels and Herman (1982).

Business One of the best uses for a computer system in a clinic is for business-related activities such as inventory and accounting tasks and client billing. Table 2.4 lists business-related tasks that could be managed via a computer system. You may obtain software from commercial sources for specific business functions (e.g., billing) or for a complete management system (e.g., one consisting of numerous components designed for business management in human services organizations). Small clinics may find it more cost effective to develop their own programs for single operations. Administrators will need to take time to consult with computer experts and representatives of commercial sources before deciding on which business-related activities can be handled most efficiently and cost effectively in their clinic.

Service-related functions Another major use for a computer system in your clinic is for clinical services–related functions such as admissions/registration, client records, and clinical reports (preparation of assessment/evaluation reports using computers is discussed in Chapter 9).

A list of clinical services–related functions that could be processed by a computer system is provided in Table 2.5. In recent years software programs have become available through commercial sources for most, if not all, of the functions identified in the table. As previously mentioned, the extent to which computer-assisted programming can effectively increase the efficiency of data processing, provide convenience for staff, and reduce operational costs will vary from clinic to clinic, and will necessarily depend on the number of clients served and the extensiveness of services provided. Before deciding on whether to obtain software programs for clinical services–related activities in your clinic, you should spend time investigating what programs are available from commercial sources and consult with other clinic staff as well.

Table 2.5. Potential clinical services-related activities for a computer system

Clinic admissions/registration	Treatment planning
Appointment scheduling	Case review records
Client demographic data	Clinical reports
Clinical records	Indirect services information
Assessment/evaluation	
Test scoring/interpretation	
Diagnosis	

Biofeedback An interesting example of how a computer system can be used in client services is biofeedback training. As a client is being trained, client physiological data from one or several biofeedback instruments can be converted in a computer for digital readout by the trainer, as well as simultaneously converted to graph form for a video display that is shown to the trainee. This almost instantaneous conversion of physiological responses can provide feedback to both the trainee and trainer to allow for modification in training procedures or to alter or maintain client performance.

Confidentiality Some commercial suppliers of software packages build in safeguards for maintaining confidentiality of client data to prevent unauthorized access to client information. Usually, these safeguards involve the use of: a) a "log on" number, that is, a specified number that must be used to gain access to the system; b) a specific password assigned to each system user; and c) a functional control specification, that is, a specification allowing a user access to certain parts of a system and not others (i.e., when the system consists of multiple programs in both business-related and client services–related areas).

Other uses Other possible uses for a computer system in a clinic are for public relations and fundraising purposes. For example, fundraising can be a fairly easy task via computer when letters of appeal are to be addressed to numerous individuals, or when they are to be sent to a limited segment of the population, depending on the availability of computer-stored mailing lists, which can be cataloged as desired. Similarly, letters of acknowledgment can easily be dispersed to those who contributed to the fundraising effort.

Purchasing considerations Samuels and Herman (1982) have proposed three main factors that should be considered in purchasing a computer: a) how the computer is to be used in the clinic, b) how much technical sophistication is needed for computer operation, and c) economic considerations. Regarding the first factor, you should identify those clinic functions that could currently be handled most efficiently through a computer system, as well as those that could be incorporated in the near future. It is impractical to purchase a computer system with such limited capability that you will need to replace it after only a short time. In terms of factor *b*, you must also evaluate how much staff training is needed, and what level of competence is required for computer operators. The more complex and diversified the system, the greater the training and skills needed. Therefore, you will need to ascertain what training is included with the computer system purchase to initially implement the system, what consultation services will be available, and the cost, if any, of services after initial staff training. Regarding factor *c,* your selection of a computer system should be based on the overall cost, as well as the cost, availability, and reliability of maintenance and repair services. When a number of clinic operations are integrated into a computer system, the dependence on computer functioning increases. If the computer system requires frequent servicing and technical assistance to maintain efficient functioning, the cost in down-time could be a real problem within the clinic. Local service availability should be a high priority.

Storage of Specialized Portable Equipment

Ideally, a central clinic location that can be locked should be designated as a storage area for specialized portable equipment. Each equipment item should be marked or coded with a permanent marking (e.g., metal tag affixed), and the code entered on an equipment inventory. If multiple staff are to use equipment, checkout procedures should be developed so that responsibilities for equipment are clearly specified and so that equipment can easily be located in an emergency.

Specialized Nonportable Equipment Useful in a Clinic

Nonportable equipment is that which is affixed to some part of the clinic building structure. Each nonportable equipment item should be identified by a code number that is listed on an equipment inventory.

In clinics that have designated playground areas, either outdoors or indoors, playground equipment should be selected on the basis of safety features and durability, utilizing the standards discussed earlier in the "Specialized Furniture for Client Use" section of this chapter. Obviously in selecting such equipment, available funding will be a major factor. Some clinics have received local community organization support in equipping clinic playground areas.

Installation of nonportable video cameras in clinic rooms can be an asset in use of video equipment. When video cameras are permanently mounted, camera angle adjustments can be made by using controls in adjacent areas. There are several advantages to permanent video camera mounting: a) staff time is reduced in that moving and setting up equipment is not necessary; b) permanently mounted cameras are less obtrusive than mobile equipment and a video camera operator within the clinic room; c) picture clarity is improved over that obtained from a video camera focusing through an observation window if equipment is placed outside the clinic room.

Equipment Inventories

An inventory of clinic equipment should be kept up-to-date, for good business reasons (e.g., insurance, replacement values, tax deductions, and prevention of loss or theft). This is especially important in clinics where many different clinicians use equipment. The following information could be included for each item of equipment on inventories: a) date of purchase, b) where purchased and/or manufactured, c) purchase cost, d) model number, e) manufacturer's serial or identification number, f) clinic identification code or number (also to be engraved on equipment item), and g) warranty/guarantee information. All of this information can be stored on a computer disc for easy retrieval and update.

Equipment Maintenance

If maximum use is to be made of available equipment, then it must be maintained in working order. The best way to ensure this is to: a) provide staff with training in use of equipment, b) service equipment on a regular basis as recommended by manufacturers; and c) arrange for minor equipment repairs when problems occur. Depending on the number of equipment items, type of equipment, and level of clinic staff repair expertise, it may be practical to contract with equipment distributors for service. When there are a few equipment items, it may be more practical to obtain servicing on an as-needed basis.

Service maintenance records should also be maintained. These records can be useful when equipment replacement becomes necessary, since service costs and efficiency in service delivery should be an important consideration in selecting new equipment and in deciding when to replace existing equipment. Records of equipment service should include: a) dates of service, b) type of service or repairs completed, c) cost of service and parts, and d) time elapsed between requests for service and actual service call.

Specialized Materials

Both consumable and nonconsumable specialized materials are necessary in providing child/adolescent services. Consumable materials are not reusable, while nonconsumable materials may be used more than once.

Nonconsumable Materials

Tests The most common type of nonconsumable materials used in psychological clinics are tests. Tests are used in assessing client abilities and skills in most areas of psychological functioning. Different types of tests and their purposes are discussed in Chapter 6. Generally, the tests used in any one clinic will reflect clinic orientation, staff expertise, and types of client services offered. You may order most tests through test publishers or distributors such as the American Guidance Service (1985), Psychological Corporation (1985), and Western Psychological Services (1985–86). These suppliers will furnish catalogs upon request, and orders can be placed directly with them. It should be noted that some identical test materials are distributed by more than one supplier, and costs may vary. Therefore, it is wise to compare catalogs for their prices. Individual nonconsumable test items used in child and adolescent clinics may cost anywhere from $10.00 to $600.00.

Use of outdated tests or test information should not be allowed in any clinic. Thus, whenever tests are revised or when updated test information is available (i.e., new norm tables), outdated tests or test information should be replaced by the new materials.

Most tests are packaged in the form of test kits containing a variety of items for use in test administration. Also, some test items are arranged sequentially in test kits for use in testing, or are packaged within the kit for specific subtests.

Unless specific tests or test kits are assigned to clinicians on a somewhat permanent basis, it can be expected that tests will be kept in one central area and that clinicians will take tests from that area to clinical rooms. If so, a check-out system should be devised to ensure an orderly way of distributing materials and to maintain a record of where the materials may be found. Storage of tests is discussed later in this chapter.

It is essential that the test kits and contents be maintained in excellent condition and in readiness for clinician use. Worn or broken test items should be replaced. Replacement items for most tests can be ordered from distributors.

Maintenance of test kits is a major problem in clinics where there is frequent test usage and where they are used by different clinicians. A useful policy under these circumstances is to stipulate that each clinician using a test kit is responsible for returning it in a condition ready for future testing, and that the clinician must notify a designated staff member of broken, missing, or damaged test items. Even if this procedure is implemented, test kits should be checked periodically to: a) ensure that missing or damaged items are identified and replaced; b) make minor repairs (e.g., glue loose item pieces together), or c) arrange items in appropriate order (e.g., place all pieces of the same puzzle together). Whatever procedures are needed will be determined by the frequency of test use, number of users, and quantity of duplicate materials available.

Maintenance of test material inventories is a sound clinic practice. An inventory record should include: a) date of purchase, b) where purchased (e.g., publisher, distributor); c) cost of purchase; and d) clinic identification code or number (when items are duplicated).

Toys and Other Client Nonconsumable Materials A supply of toys and other nonconsumable materials for client use should be available within each child and adolescent clinic. It is anticipated that these materials will be used mainly in clinic waiting areas; however, some nonconsumable materials may also be used for evaluation or treatment purposes. Types of nonconsumable materials other than toys may be: books, magazines, video games or tapes, audio tapes, and film strips and film strip projectors. In selecting client-oriented nonconsumable materials, make sure that they are age appropriate. Selection of materials should also be based on other desirable aspects such as: a) safety, b) durability, c) minimal noise-producing features, d) washability, e) interest appeal or attractiveness, and f) educational or constructional aspects. Guidelines for toy selection categories are provided in Table 2.6.

It will be necessary to develop procedures for maintenance of nonconsumable materials. Certain general procedures should be implemented on a regular basis including:

1. Toys or materials used by infants and preschoolers should be cleaned after each use before being made available to another child. Toys or materials

used by older children should be cleaned on a periodic basis, or whenever handled by clients with colds or other health problems.

2. Toys should be checked regularly to determine if they have missing or broken parts, and should be discarded when they become potentially harmful or injurious.

3. Toy components in the same category (e.g., Legos, blocks), should be placed together after use in preparation for subsequent use.

4. Toys or other materials should be located on shelves or tables or in cupboards in the area where they are to be used, so that they are accessible to clients. Procedures for maintaining this area of the clinic should be developed.

Unless children and adolescent clients are supervised in the use of materials and in returning them to storage areas, a staff member should be assigned this responsibility or the responsibility rotated among staff members.

Consumable Materials

Assessment and Treatment Materials   Many materials used in assessment/evaluation of children and adolescents are not reusable. The most common of these are: a) test protocols; b) test profile and summary forms; c) questionnaires, inventories, checklists, and rating scales; and d) data collection forms.

Table 2.6.   Toy selection guidelines

Age range	Toy categories
Birth–3 years	Rattles Simple puzzles Ring stack toys Shape-sorting toys Early childhood educational toys
3–5 years	Construction toys, such as large Legos, Tinker Toys, Bristle Blocks, plastic straws Puzzles Small plastic animals Puppets Picture books Toy cars/trucks
5–9 years	Construction toys, such as Legos, Tinker Toys, Lincoln Logs, Blocks Puzzles Picture/early reader books Picture viewer Small plastic animals Puppets Toy cars, trucks
9–12 years and older	Puzzles of different kinds Books/magazines on nature, sports, teen issues and interests

A supply of consumable assessment and treatment forms adopted for use within each clinic must always be available. To ensure this, maintenance of an inventory of clinic materials and quantities should be a clinic practice so that replacements can be ordered in enough time. Depending on the types of assessments conducted at the clinic and the number of clients assessed, a minimum required number of test protocols and other consumable assessment instruments should be determined, and materials reordered or purchased whenever that number is exhausted. Obviously, the supply should be adjusted on the basis of experience.

Client-Consumable Materials Consumable materials may be used for clinical purposes with clients (i.e., drawing paper), or for waiting room activities. Some kinds of consumable materials for the latter purpose are: coloring books, educational workbooks, or recreational materials (e.g., puzzle books). In using these materials, clients also need to be furnished with drawing or writing implements, which could pose a problem with young children. (If not supervised, children might draw on walls or furniture.) It is recommended that only nontoxic and water soluble coloring, drawing, or writing instruments be purchased for client use.

Storage of Specialized Materials

Each clinic should determine the most practical and efficient means for storing materials within the facilities available. It is recommended that these materials be stored in an area that can be locked, since nonconsumable materials (e.g., test kits), represent a financial investment that needs to be protected.

Materials for Clinical Use Consumable and nonconsumable materials should be stored in a central location within the clinic where they are easily accessible to staff. Whenever more than one or two clinicians are to use the same materials, check-out systems should be developed to maintain an orderly procedure for sharing and use. The check-out system could be as simple as the placement of a sign-out board in the material storage area, or as elaborate as having one staff member assigned the responsibility for checking out materials.

An organized system for storing materials should be developed. For example, test kits could be placed on open shelving in alphabetical order. Test protocols could be placed in file boxes beside the appropriate test kit, or in a filing cabinet nearby.

Materials for Client Use Nonconsumable materials available for preschool or preteen clients in waiting areas should be easily accessible to them. Some guidelines for placement of these materials include:

1. Toys and other nonconsumable materials should not be placed above the eye level of clients who will use the materials. This is to prevent accidents from occurring when reaching for materials.
2. Heavier articles should be placed at lower levels than lighter articles for the safety of users.

3. Small construction toys and other nonconsumable materials (e.g., blocks) may be stored in plastic dishwashing pans at minimal cost. Materials can be separated by type into these colorful and durable containers, which will outlast original cardboard containers and allow for uniform storage. Materials stored in this manner are not only accessible to young children but also facilitate clean-up after use.

If consumable materials are used in waiting areas, they should be provided to individual clients by a staff member in the reception area. Writing or drawing implements should be collected by that person before the client goes to clinical rooms.

INSURANCE COVERAGE

The clinic administrator is responsible for arranging for the annual allocation of funds for insurance coverage for a number of clinic functions and assets. Insurance coverage is needed for: a) the clinic building and contents; b) liability insurance for accidents or injuries to staff, clients, and clinic visitors: c) medical and/or hospitalization group insurance plans for staff, and d) malpractice coverage for clinical staff unless clinicians are expected to maintain malpractice insurance coverage independently. You should consult with insurance specialists to determine the extent and type of insurance most applicable for your clinic. If clinicians are to maintain their own malpractice insurance, they should be so informed in writing, and a verification record of paid insurance should be retained in a file in the clinic.

SUMMARY

Marketing is a new, but critical, activity for professionals providing psychological and related services. It has become a central concern in assuring success as funding decreases while demand for services increases. Consumer needs must match services provided. In planning a clinic, attention must be given to availability of appropriate facilities, equipment, and materials for staff and for their use by, or with, the children, adolescents, and families served. Efficiency demands that computers be available and used as labor-saving devices for typing, budgeting, record keeping, and possibly in clinical application.

READER ACTIVITIES

Do you have a marketing plan for your clinic? If not, we suggest that one be developed. Furthermore, if you have a marketing plan but it is not current or suited to your needs, we suggest that it be revised. In your budget planning for the coming year, have you determined what new or replacement equipment, furniture, and materials will be needed and how to fund their purchase? If not, this may be the time to conduct a needs assessment with staff. If you have a computer system in the clinic, is it adequate and/or do your staff need inservice training in order to maximize use of this equipment? In addition, why not explore areas where the system could be expanded to increase usage? If you do not have a computer system, we suggest that you investigate whether or not a computer system would be useful in your clinic operation.

REFERENCES

American Guidance Service. (1985). *Instructional materials and tests catalog*. Circle Pines, MN: American Guidance Service.

American Psychological Association. (1981). *Ethical principles of psychologists*. Washington, DC: Author.

Christian, W. P., & Hannah, G. T. (1983). *Effective management in human services*. Englewood Cliffs, NJ: Prentice-Hall.

Drucker, P. F. (1954). *The practice of management*. New York: Harper & Row.

Guiltinan, J. P., & Paul, C. W. (1982). *Marketing management*. New York: McGraw-Hill.

Jain, S. C. (1981). *Marketing, planning and strategy*. Cincinnati: Southwestern Publishing.

Keller, P. A. (1982). Word processing for the clinical office. In P. A. Keller & L. G. Ritt (Eds.), *Innovations in clinical practice: A source book* (Vol. 1., pp. 194–198). Sarasota, FL: Professional Resources Exchange.

Klein, H. E. (1983). How to improve the marketing of therapy services. In P. E. Keller & L. G. Ritt (Eds.), *Innovations in clinical practice: A source book* (Vol. 2, pp. 233–241). Sarasota, FL: Professional Resources Exchange.

Kurtz, D. L., & Boone, L. E. (1984). *Marketing*. Chicago: Dryden Press.

Mancuso, J. R. (1985, May). What to name your company. *Success*, (pp. 9–11).

Psychological Corporation, The. (1985). *Tests and services for education*. Cleveland: Harcourt Brace Jovanovich.

Samuels, R. M., & Herman, K. (1982). Microcomputers in clinical practice. In P. A. Keller & L. G. Ritt (Eds.), *Innovations in clinical practice: A source book* (Vol. 1, pp. 199–209). Sarasota, FL: Professional Resources Exchange.

Seattle Mental Health Institute. (1984). *What's in your future? The steps in the development of a mental health long range plan*. Seattle: Author.

Serco. (1984). *Fighting the Stigma: An up-to-date pilot promoting mental health care*. Dayton, OH: Serco Marketing.

Western Psychological Services. (1985–86). *Catalog*. Los Angeles: Author.

3

Personnel Policies, Practices, and Procedures

After reading this chapter, you will be familiar with:
1. How to determine what personnel are needed
2. Skills needed by personnel of a comprehensive clinic that provides psychological and related services
3. The importance of staff comprehending clinic goals and staff rights and responsibilities
4. Components needed in written standard operating procedures and personnel policies
5. How dimensions of position assignments affect the psychological state of personnel
6. The impact of position enlargement, position enrichment, and change of position assignment on personnel
7. The purpose of well-developed position descriptions and responsibilities, and their relationship to staff evaluation
8. Staff motivation in program and client success

CHAPTER FOCUS

This chapter focuses on the core of any psychological service clinic: the clinic staff and the personnel procedures that govern staff behavior. Without appropriate personnel, accomplishment of the mission and goals of a clinic is doomed to failure; and without functional personnel procedures, personnel may get bogged down in petty day-to-day problems. Planning is needed to determine: a) the number of staff needed, b) the type of staff skills needed, and c) the procedures that will govern staff behavior. Planning, which is conducted by administrators, boards of directors, owners, staff, or a combination thereof, facilitates the establishment of a well-functioning and effective service clinic. The terms *personnel* and *staff* are used interchangeably throughout this guidebook. This chapter can only briefly consider major aspects of personnel procedures. For more extensive coverage you are referred to French, Bell, and Zawacki (1978) and O'Brien, Dickinson, and Rosow (1982).

CLINIC SERVICES DETERMINE PERSONNEL NEEDS

Determining Personnel Needs

In determining what personnel are needed, you must first "understand what you want to do" (Seattle Mental Health Institute, 1984, p. 2). You must consider all of the various psychological and related services you might offer to children and adolescents, and then outline in detail what would be ideal for your clinic. Goal setting as described in Chapter 1 is a must in this planning process. Planning should focus not only on immediate needs but should also include projections for 1, 3, 5, or even 10 years ahead. Such projections provide a direction for clinic growth. Staff and personnel procedures will be affected by decisions relating to the type of services to be offered. The questions that follow, although not exhaustive (see others in Chapter 1), are important to answer whether you are starting a new clinic or working in an existing clinic. They include:

1. What socioeconomic, ethnic, and cultural groups and age ranges does or should the clinic serve?
2. What are the most common referral problems for these groups and age ranges and what are the less common problems?
3. What kinds of services and staff skills are or would be needed to deal with each of these problems?
4. What other resources such as facilities, equipment, and assessment instruments are available or would be needed to deal with each referral problem? (See Chapter 2.)
5. What services are already available to the target clientele in the relevant geographic area that deal with the identified referral problems, and are there gaps in available services?
6. What type of clinic options are possible? Specialized, comprehensive, ideal? (See Chapter 1.)
7. Where in the geographic area should the clinic be located or relocated?

To answer these questions, administrators can contact community information sources such as the Chamber of Commerce; check community directories, such as the Yellow Pages of the telephone directory; read professional references on the topic; and possibly conduct surveys of psychological needs of children and adolescents among school personnel, parents, pediatricians, and other relevant groups.

Assessing Staff Resources

Assessing available resources in terms of facilities, funds, and equipment was discussed in Chapter 2. An evaluation of available staff resources is also critical and is considered here. The process starts by identifying the skills needed for the services to be provided.

Staff Skills Needed

After deciding what services are to be offered, it is important to determine the number of staff needed and what staff skills are necessary to provide the services. One approach to this task is to use already-published position descriptions that include the skills needed, modifying descriptors to fit the clinic's specific planned services. A *Dictionary of Occupational Titles* can be obtained for this purpose from a library (U.S. Department of Labor, 1977). The administrator can use it to prepare job descriptions by adding to or deleting the various skills included under relevant position titles. Some position titles might include: clinical child psychologist, intake worker, and family therapist. Care should be taken to cover the business aspects of the clinic by referring to position titles such as business manager, accountant, clerical worker, and secretary. The next step is to inventory staff skills.

Determining Staff Skills

In existing clinics, an inventory of the types of skills and degree of mastery of those skills for each staff member is useful in determining the skills needed to provide the services planned by clinic administrators. Identifying the skills and skill deficits of individual professionals can be a difficult and time-consuming task, but it is a necessary one for planning purposes. Supervisors may assess the level of specific skills by: a) using information they already possess about a staff member's performance, b) using information from staff members' résumés and transcripts, c) conducting individual skill interviews, and d) observing staff as they work with clients, using a form that lists the skills needed and rating the level of expertise for each skill. The information when combined with client satisfaction questionnaires and professional self-evaluation questionnaires, can be used to decide which master skill list items are in the repertoire of each staff member and the degree of mastery. A list of suggested skills for a psychologist is included in Table 3.1.

In conducting skill evaluations, it is important to inform staff that their purpose is to improve clinic services, and that such planning will in all probability benefit them. Having staff provide input about needed inservice and professional training makes them feel that they are a vital part of the organization, is a nonthreatening approach to planning, and should reduce job-related stress. Administrators must then take care to do what they say they will do (e.g., planning and proceeding with training) or they will quickly lose credibility with staff.

Once the lists of both current and needed staff skills have been compiled, the two lists can be compared to determine: a) if needed skills can be added via additional training for existing staff; b) if new staff with specific skills need to be hired; c) if some tasks should be subcontracted to others (e.g., accounting tasks); and d) if, as a last resort, some staff positions need to be eliminated because specific individuals do not possess relevant skills. If positions are to be eliminated, help should be provided in locating new positions for those individuals. They should also be given a reasonable amount of time to relocate. Not only is this an ethical administrative responsibility but it will also reassure other staff that administrators are interested in employees' welfare. For new clinics, the task of matching staff skills to specific services is one of developing appropriate job descriptions and then advertising and hiring individuals with the designated skills.

Table 3.1. Job description for a psychologist

General Summary Provides psychological services, both psychological assessment and psychotherapy, to children and adolescents. Provides consultation to other professionals regarding psychological aspects of children's behavior. Provides inservice education on psychological issues and supervises unlicensed psychology personnel.

Principal Duties and Responsibilities

1. Performs psychological evaluations of both children and adolescents using psychological tests, interviews, and questionnaires, as appropriate. Scores tests and interprets findings; makes recommendations; writes formal evaluation reports; interprets results and recommendations to parent/guardian: conveys results and recommendations to other appropriate persons (e.g., school psychologist); all within designated time interval.

2. Conducts appropriate and effective psychotherapy for children, adolescents, and/or their families. Intervention may be on an individual, family, or group basis. Formulates and records treatment plans, makes notes of treatment sessions, submits billing form and writes summary of course of treatment after termination.

3. Consults with school personnel as requested. Attends team meetings and case conferences; contributes opinions and recommendations regarding psychological aspects of patients' problems; evaluates team patients as requested; provides psychotherapy to clients as appropriate.

4. Covers emergency services on a 24-hour basis for 1 week, rotating with other staff members. During this time, stays within 30 minutes of the clinic, carries a pager, and responds to calls from the answering service. Evaluates the problem; consults with the psychiatrist on call; makes recommendations and follows up those recommendations when appropriate; writes opinion and recommendations in the client record on same-day basis.

5. Contributes to staff inservice training programs as requested.

6. Supervises unlicensed psychology personnel as requested. Reads, approves, and countersigns evaluation reports and emergency service notes; meets with employees to discuss clients and evaluates employees.

7. Serves on clinic committees as requested by clinic director.

8. Develops and maintains contact with a variety of community professionals in order to facilitate referrals, information exchange, and implement recommendations.

9. Meets with clinic director regularly to discuss assignments and to consult on selected problems.

10. Regularly presents cases for peer reviews.

11. Attends all staff meetings.

12. Maintains expertise by attending conferences and workshops and by reading current material.

13. Gives talks to community groups about clinic services and/or areas of expertise.

14. Assists in developing and implementing clinic policies and procedures. Assists director in developing plans and budgets as necessary.

15. Performs other functions as assigned by director.

Required Knowledge, Skills, and Abilities

1. A valid state license in psychology is required to legally perform the functions of a psychologist.

2. A doctorate in psychology is necessary to have accumulated the knowledge and skills needed to perform the functions of a psychologist.

3. Must possess knowledge of areas of psychology relevant to child/family assessment and child/family psychotherapy.

(continued)

Table 3.1 (continued)

4. Must possess skills in the areas of psychological assessment and psychotherapy.
5. Must possess the abilities necessary to apply psychological knowledge to particular client situations, assessing problems, making recommendations, formulating treatment plans, and carrying out effective interventions.
6. Must be able to write well-organized, coherent, relevant, and cogent evaluation reports, treatment plans, and treatment summaries.
7. Must possess interpersonal skills that facilitate interactions with patients, their families, staff, other professionals, and the public.
8. Must possess the skills needed to supervise clinic personnel in a constructive manner so that clinic standards are maintained and so that employee's performance improves.
9. Must possess the skills needed to execute the responsibilities of a psychologist independent of supervision.
10. Must adhere to the laws of the state, the regulations of the state board of psychology, and the code of ethics and of standards for providers of the American Psychological Association.

Working Conditions
1. Works in normal office conditions where there are minimal discomforts due to temperature, noise, and dust.
2. Work week consists of hours specified by the clinic director.

POSITION DESCRIPTIONS AND
THEIR RELATIONSHIP TO EVALUATION

Purpose of Position Assignment and Job Descriptions

Each clinic staff member should be informed of his or her position assignment and should have a position description that clearly defines job expectations, including the relationship of the position to the clinic's mission and goals. A good job description (see Table 3.1) allows each staff member to know: a) what is expected of him or her, b) the areas in which he or she will be evaluated (an evaluation should be based on how well an individual meets the job description), c) how to get reinforced within the system (e.g., to be eligible for merit pay or to attend conferences), and d) when to report problems (i.e., understanding the organizational chain of command) (Striefel & Cadez, 1983; see Figure 3.1 for a sample organizational chain of command).

Job Descriptions and Behavioral
Versus Outcome Measures in Performance Evaluation

Since it is to be used for performance evaluation, a well-developed job description should be worded so that either the behaviors or the outcomes of behaviors described are observable and measurable. In and of itself, outcome measurement is incomplete and can be misleading (Dickinson & O'Brien, 1982). Outcome measures of performance indicate whether a job is being done correctly, but they

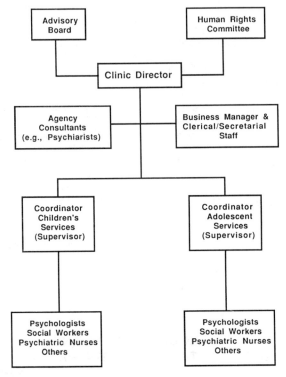

Figure 3.1.   Organizational chart showing chain of command

are only accurate and meaningful if the behaviors measured are critical to successful job performance. Thus, great care must be taken to develop appropriate job descriptions to assure that the responsibilities listed are, in fact, important to providing quality services. For example consider this statement: "The child psychologist will correctly administer: a) the Stanford-Binet Intelligence Test, b) the Wechsler Intelligence Scale for Children–Revised, or c) [list as many additional tests as desired], according to the standardized procedures in the test manuals." This behavioral measure allows a supervisor to observe and compare a staff member's performance according to the procedures specified in the test manuals, and thus rate the performance as, for example, "excellent," "generally as expected," "as expected," "below expectations," or "well below expectation." Whereas this is a well-written statement for a job description, it has drawbacks, however. Use of such behavioral measures requires the supervisor to make enough observations of the psychologist using different tests to obtain a representative sample of the psychologist's testing skills. Some clinics may wish to use such behavioral measures because they are more accurate than statements like the following: "The child psychologist will be able to administer all appropriate psychological tests correctly." Such descriptions may leave you in doubt concerning the meaning of "all appropriate psychological tests" and "correctly." Such confusion leads to difficulty in conducting a reliable performance evaluation. Next, contrast these behavioral statements with the outcome statement, "The child psychologist will assess all children referred to the clinic for testing, using tests appropriate to the child's age and the referral question." This statement would direct the supervisor to check the records for the number of children referred, to see if all were tested, and then to check test manuals to determine if tests used were appropriate to the child's age and the referral question. A performance evaluation could then be made. However, it should be noted here that this example includes nothing about the psychologist's behavior during testing, which is, in essence, the "behavior of testing." Some clinics might find this type of performance evaluation acceptable, especially if the supervisor has previously observed the psychologist's behavior on more than one occasion during which the psychologist administered tests according to the standardization procedures in the test manuals.

Our own preference is to develop job descriptions that include both behavioral and outcome measures. In some cases both components would be listed for a specific task and in others only the behavioral or only the outcome measure would be listed depending on what is judged to be the critical component. The example that follows includes both behavioral and outcome measures: "The child psychologist will assess all children referred to the clinic for testing, using tests appropriate to the child's age and the referral question, and will do so according to the standardized procedures described in the test manual for each test."

Measurement of personality traits or characteristics such as initiative and judgment have repeatedly been reported to be unsatisfactory; thus outcome measures are being suggested as the more definitive tool for evaluation (Cummings & Schwab, 1973; Dickinson & O'Brien, 1982, McMillan & Dorel, 1980). Administrators must strive continuously to improve the staff evaluation process. An explicit job description can then easily be converted into an evaluation form.

Converting Job Descriptions into Performance Evaluation Forms

Converting a job description into a format usable as an evaluation form requires nothing more than the creation of a Likert-type scale with numerical ratings (e.g., from 1 [excellent] to 5 [well-below expectation] or in percentages from 1 (100%) to 5 (below 70%) and a space for comments as shown in Table 3.2. The example shown in the table allows the supervisor to quantify the behavior and the outcome specified in the job description, thus providing a fairly objective means for performance evaluation. The statement could, of course, be worded differently in different clinics, depending on the performance to be measured.

A second, somewhat different, example is provided in Table 3.3, featuring outcome only. To evaluate the behavior of the clinician during face-to-face contacts specified in the table, the job description would need to include other behavior or outcome measures and an appropriate quantification scale. For example, the statement "The child psychologist provides services beneficial to

Table 3.2. Example of performance evaluation item

Statement The child psychologist will assess all children referred to the clinic for testing, using tests appropriate to the child's age and the referral question, and will do so according to the standardized procedures described in the test manual for each test.

Key behavior or outcome	Performance evaluation scale				
	Percentage				
All children assessed	1[a]	2[b]	3[c]	4[d]	5[e]
Used age-appropriate tests	1	2	3	4	5
Tests appropriate to referral question	1	2	3	4	5
Used standardized procedures	1	2	3	4	5
Comments: _____					

[a]100%.
[b]90%.
[c]80%.
[d]70%.
[e]Below 70%.

clients as determined by achieving ratings of beneficial services on 80% or more of client feedback evaluations,'' would be one way to evaluate clinician performance. The clinic director and other staff evaluators should take great care in deciding how staff performance is evaluated. Some clinics have chosen to use only one performance measure, concerning client satisfaction with the services provided. Such an evaluation is certainly simple, but it can also be problematic. For example, if a clinician gets several extremely difficult clients such as children with autism or with conduct disorders, or clients who are extremely critical of service providers, the clinician's client satisfaction ratings may be low, but not because of his or her skill. In addition, such an evaluation does little for the staff member in terms of providing the type of feedback necessary to improve performance in specific cases. The previous examples should provide you with sufficient information to develop, with proper input, job descriptions for all clinic staff members and then to convert these into evaluation devices.

Staff Improvement

A good job description is not the only requirement for effective performance evaluation. To be truly worthwhile, evaluations should be approached from the

Table 3.3. Example of performance evaluation item

Statement The child psychologist will spend 60% of his or her work time in direct contact with clients as determined from the weekly time log and billing sheets.

Key behavior or outcome	Performance evaluation scale				
	Percentage				
	More than 60%	50%	40%	30%	Less than 30%
Percentage of direct client contact	1	2	3	4	5

vantage point of being educative rather than faultfinding. The process requires, at a minimum:

1. Regular, ongoing feedback, in written form, whenever possible. The feedback should indicate what behaviors or outcomes are commendable, which are acceptable, and/or which need improvement. It should also indicate what corrective actions should be taken to improve performance, timelines for improvement, and whom to see if help is needed in applying corrective action. The written record provides a means of determining whether the person being evaluated is making progress in correcting areas identified as needing improvement. The feedback should focus on: positive rather than negative behaviors (Carlson & Sperduto, 1982); specific rather than general behavior; describing behavior rather than just labeling it; and it should be delivered as soon as possible after the faulty behavior has been noted. Again, all of the information on behavioral and outcome measurement already discussed in reference to the job description applies. A performance evaluation across staff can also be helpful in identifying deficits in the staff training and inservice program; in identifying strengths in some staff members that can be useful in training others; and in clarifying, revising, and improving the standard operating procedures of the clinic.

2. An annual performance evaluation. Such a work review may be more detrimental (Deming, 1983) than helpful if not properly conducted, because it may stress short-term rather than long-term thinking. But it does provide a formal means for an organization to make decisions concerning promotions, pay increases, reassignments, and termination. It is best to use it in conjunction with ongoing feedback.

Who Does the Performance Evaluation?

Several different types of performance evaluation can be used. These include: a) evaluation by the immediate supervisor, b) evaluation by the supervisor and selected peers, and c) evaluation by consumers (see Striefel & Cadez, 1983, for more information). The specific type of evaluation used is dependent on factors such as purpose of the evaluation, time available to conduct it, administrator's style, and staff preference. Clearly, evaluation by the immediate supervisor is the least time consuming type, but it is also the most subject to supervisor bias, especially if behavioral and outcome measures are not clearly written. Obviously, great care should go into developing staff evaluation policies.

Components of a Good Evaluation

A performance evaluation should involve:

1. Development of accurate, measurable job descriptions for all staff members
2. Determination of who will conduct evaluations (assignment of teams, if that is the mode used)
3. Development of a system for ongoing feedback

4. Development and implementation of a corrective action procedure that specifies, at a minimum: a) the behavior in need of change, b) the acceptable level of the target behavior, c) a plan for producing the desired performance change, d) a method for evaluating progress in achieving the specified change, and e) a timeline for completion
5. Development of a formal quarterly or semiannual performance evaluation and corrective action procedures
6. Updating of job descriptions at specified time periods (e.g., annually)
7. Review and revision of the evaluation procedure used, as necessary

Merit and Pay Increases

Part of the reason for staff evaluation is to collect information that an administrator can use in making decisions about merit and other pay increases. The more standardized the evaluation process, the easier it is to compare performance across employees, and thus to decide pay increases. Typical pay increases include merit, cost of living, and special increases that occur when the staff member changes positions within the organization, receives a state license or is recognized for some other accomplishment that makes his or her services more valuable to the clinic. The dollar amount of pay increases may be decided on the basis of a preestablished pay ladder (comprising steps and grades with dollar amounts attached), clinic income, the dictates of a larger parent organization, or purely at the discretion of the director. Written staff procedures should describe how pay increase decisions will be made.

STAFFING PROCEDURES

Hiring

The foregoing description of development of job descriptions is integral in preparing to hire staff. Job announcements can be placed in the classified ad sections of local newspapers or they can be sent to professional publications, for example the American Psychological Association's *Monitor*. Other possible sources for recruitment include university placement offices or affirmative action offices and your own professional colleagues.

Applications received must be screened to eliminate unqualified candidates. Generally a letter of interest, professional résumé (vita), and names of references are sufficient to provide initial information about candidates. Once the most promising applicants have been identified, it is generally useful to conduct telephone interviews with the top two or three before arranging face-to-face interviews. References can also be telephoned prior to face-to-face interviews, to compare their and the candidate's responses to questions about previous employers and colleagues. It is important to check with previous employers, colleagues, and possibly the State Abuse Register to rule out whether the person has any history of child abuse or neglect before hiring him or her to provide services to children and adolescents. Personal interviews can then be conducted with those candidates who appear the most qualified. We recommend face-to-face interviews at this stage, rather than hiring someone following only a telephone interview because telephone interviews have several drawbacks, including: a) they do not usually last long enough to get more than a general impression of an applicant; b) applicants might "role play" for a telephone interview, falsely claiming that they possess skills that they do not have; and 3) staff cannot provide an applicant with an opportunity to see the clinic, to meet him or her or assess how he or she would "fit in." A personal interview also allows for a more elaborate exchange of information and for more staff members to meet the applicant.

Termination of Employment

Staff should have available guidelines that specify the conditions and procedures that will be used to end employment. These include the length of notice given before termination becomes effective for: a) situations in which funding changes or reductions require a cutback in the number of staff (the longer the notice the better, but a minimum of 30 days); b) situations in which an individual staff member's overall performance is inadequate (e.g., 30 days); c) situations in which a violation of staff procedures is so severe as to require immediate action (e.g., sexual activity with a client). The procedure should also specify what behaviors are considered grounds for immediate termination. Behaviors commonly included in this latter category are sexual misconduct, violation of client confidentiality, serious infractions of the law, abuse of clients, and severe negligence in treating clients.

Grievance procedures must exist that allow an employee who is being terminated for cause to contest the decision. Such procedures usually consist of meeting with a grievance committee comprising an administrator and two or more peers. The committee's task is to "hear" both sides of the issue and to recommend to the clinic director a final decision. Employees who are voluntarily leaving employment for personal reasons or employment elsewhere should agree when initially employed to give written advance notice (e.g., 30 days) of their intent to terminate employment.

Orientation of Staff

A distressing problem faced by new staff members in clinics that have not instituted standard operating procedures is that of figuring out what is expected of them. As emphasized in Chapter 1, preparation of mission and goal statements and making this information available to staff can go far toward providing staff with some direction, particularly if activities needed to achieve the goals have also been planned. Clarifying expectations also means clarifying for each staff member what his or her job description is, how the job relates to achieving the clinic's mission and goals, and how his or her job responsibilities overlap with or differ from those of other staff members. Each of these items should be available in written form for staff use. As Shaw, Bensky, and Dixon (1981) and Striefel and Cadez (1983) pointed out, role clarity is essential for appropriate staff performance and is the most significant factor aiding stress reduction. Written role clarity also reduces supervisory time, procedural errors, and staff frustration.

Staff Rights and Responsibilities

It is vital that the rights of staff (professional, paraprofessional and clerical) also be defined. These rights include, at a minimum: a) the right to be treated as a professional and with dignity and respect, b) the right to a private life, c) the right to ongoing feedback concerning job performance, d) the right to voice dissenting opinions at the appropriate time and place, e) the right to information about job expectations in terms of job description and operating procedures, f) the right to inservice training, and g) the right to seek professional services to deal with personal problems that interfere with the quality and quantity of job productivity.

Just as staff have rights, they also have responsibilities. These responsibilities include, but are not limited to: a) abiding by the ethical and legal standards of one's profession and those established by the service clinic; b) performing the duties listed on one's job description; c) adhering to established personnel policies and clinic procedures; d) providing treatment to clients with at least ordinary care and skill: e) protecting the welfare and rights of clients; f) informing clients of treatment choices, risks, and expected benefits; g) not terminating treatment without mutual agreement with the client or provision of appropriate alternatives; and h) maintaining client files in accordance with clinic procedures.

Staff Motivation

Feedback

The more motivated staff are by virtue of the amount of positive feedback for their job performance, the more likely that their performance will be appropriate. It has been pointed out that money is neither the most desired nor the only reinforcer: in fact, it is more likely to be ranked third, fourth, or even fifth in importance by employees (Striefel & Cadez, 1983). What seems more important than money is the degree of freedom a person has to make decisions and carry out tasks, the diversity of tasks, whether the employee perceives the organization and the supervisor in a positive light, and whether the employee receives feedback indicating he or she is doing a good job and achieving successful outcomes for effort expended. For example, a major motivating factor for clinicians is seeing clients progress as a function of treatment provided. This allows not only personal satisfaction but also makes the clinician feel that he or she is contributing to the clinic's success by helping to accomplish its mission and goals. Provision of support by clinic administrators is very helpful in motivating staff, and thus directly affects morale (e.g., having work expectations adjusted when they are unrealistic).

Position Assignment and the Psychological State of Staff

Various factors affect morale in a clinic, including involving staff in team decisions and in team-building efforts, and affording regular opportunities for staff to voice concerns and to have these addressed by administrators. Additional factors are related to how closely an individual's skills complement his or her position assignments. If an assignment matches a staff member's skills, the staff member will be confident of his or her ability to do the job. Morale may thus initially be quite high. However, if the position does not allow for diversity, it can well become routine, and consequently boring to the individual. Alternatively, an individual assigned a job for which he or she is not qualified may find himself or herself presented with the dilemma of wanting to keep a job yet feeling stressed and unhappy about how to do the job properly. Morale can thus start low, but if the person is given the proper support and training, morale will rise. Suggested ways to improve staff morale include the following:

1. Offering job enrichment and job satisfaction, which basically means providing diversity in a job. For example, individuals assigned to provide psychological services to children or adolescents with whom little or no gains are expected, such as adolescents with chronic mental illness, may find that over time they become very dissatisfied with their job. They may begin to see the situation as hopeless and become more and more dissatisfied with their position. If staff are assigned to treat a diversity of clientele with different types of problems, including at least some with whom they have success, their job satisfaction is likely to be higher.
2. Involving staff in decision making. The more involved staff are in the decisions that affect them, the higher their morale should be.
3. Recognizing that job satisfaction and productivity are not necessarily related. One can be satisfied with a job and not be productive, or productive but not satisfied. The task of administrators is to help staff achieve both satisfaction and productivity.
4. Providing a comprehensive and explicit job description. A clear job description helps staff know what is expected of them, thus contributing to high morale.
5. Providing consultation, feedback, and support. The more support given staff in doing their job, the more positively they regard the organization and the more likely they are to work hard in its behalf. One form of support is consultation by an expert. A second is feedback on performance. A third is to have someone to talk to, in order to clarify ideas and expectations.
6. Improving communication methods. The most common and most detrimental problem for any organization is inadequate communication. Staff must have access to information about the organization, upcoming events; changes in procedures, policies, and practices: and feedback on performance. Administrators have a need for similar information. As organizations get larger, there is much greater chance that information will be dis-

torted or not communicated to all staff. Improved communication typically results in improved morale.

Involvement

Too much focus on task completion only, on satisfying staff needs only, can result in staff dissatisfaction on the one hand, lack of clinic income on the other hand, and extensive morale problems in general. The more that staff members are involved in establishing or reviewing the clinic's goals and updating them annually, the more they are involved in determining what activities will be needed to accomplish these goals, and the more they participate in developing and refining the ongoing procedures of the clinic, the better the clinic will operate. People are committed to the activities and programs that they help develop (Striefel & Cadez, 1983). If all of the goals and activities are determined by a clinic director who dictates these to the staff, problems will result. The director will be seen by staff as *the* person responsible for seeing to it that the goals are accomplished and for continually monitoring and policing the activities of staff. A "cat and mouse" game results that is totally unnecessary in a professional association. Staff turnover will be high among those with professional expertise and confidence in their skills, and the clinic could end up with staff who lack the skills and confidence to succeed on their own.

In caring for staff needs, it is important that morale problems be identified and dealt with as soon as possible. Morale problems can be determined by direct observation, by content of comments made in staff meetings, by formal questionnaires, by comments heard through the "grapevine," by turnover of staff, by client satisfaction/dissatisfaction, and by complaints received from others. Each problem that is identified needs to be addressed. The more it can be dealt with by the total staff, the better the outlook for staff morale. That is not to say that the clinic director should not make administrative decisions; this prerogative certainly remains with the person assigned the responsibility and authority for such activities. However, many decisions are more appropriately made by the various staff members who are directly affected by them. Clearly, leadership style has an impact on a clinic's functioning. Small clinics of less than 15 staff members can often outperform large clinics at fulfilling staff needs and assuring that communications are clear to all parties involved. The larger the staff, the more difficult it is to use a democratic team-building process to make decisions. If the mission and goals of the clinic have been clearly established, it is not extremely difficult to determine the kinds of personnel needed to accomplish these goals. A clinic director and all supervisors should learn all they can about team building, staff motivation, and leadership styles (Pfeiffer & Jones, 1971).

Communication

As previously mentioned, the availability of a procedural and policy handbook helps to eliminate some communication problems. In addition, regular staff meetings can provide an avenue for communication. Both supervisors and staff should have opportunities in staff meetings to discuss issues and problems, to exchange information, and to announce upcoming events. Such meetings can serve to make staff aware of each other's needs; can lend staff the genuine support needed by each team member (to offer support after a tragic incident, after a teenage client commits suicide); and can go far toward facilitating an efficient clinic organization. In short, staff are made to feel that it is enjoyable to be associated with the clinic. Other methods for improved communication include: a) a bulletin board for posting information (and having staff check it daily); b) an agreement with staff to request a meeting with their supervisor when there is evidence of conflicting communication (Christian & Hannah, 1983); c) distribution of written summaries of agreements reached at meetings; and d) use of interoffice memos.

Management

In order for a clinic providing psychological services to run smoothly, the clinic must implement an effective management system (Christian & Hannah, 1983). Increasing costs and government regulations combined with decreasing sources of public funds and escalating consumer demands (e.g., an increasing recognition that some children and adolescents need psychological services) make it imperative that clinic management be extremely efficient. To survive in the late 1980s and 1990s, human service clinics must be cost effective; good management is essential for this to happen. Other factors affecting cost effectiveness include: a) the level of psychological functioning of consumers (costs are higher for more difficult cases), b) the quality and quantity of administrative services and staff, c) management procedures, and d) program evaluation (Christian & Hannah, 1983). Management practices must assure that more and better services are provided at less cost.

Funding

To remain solvent, a human service clinic must strive to obtain funding from as many sources as possible, including: a) fees for services, b) contracts with health maintenance organizations, c) third-party payments, d) government funds, e) private contributions, and f) fees obtained from providing technical assistance in the form of workshops and consultations. Management will need to implement efficient procedures for collecting funds, and should constantly be alert to new or potential revenue sources.

Management Skills

Clinic management requires skills in program planning/organization; staff recruitment, training, and supervision; evaluation of programs and staff; quality control; management of materials, resources, and budgets; public relations; client advocacy, especially for children; implementing ethical and program standards; motivating the staff; and developing and negotiating grants and contracts. Because it is often difficult to find all of these skills in one person, the various responsibilities described may be divided among administrators. For example, a clinic director may be directly responsible for clinical areas while financial responsibilities are assigned to a business manager.

Supervision

Staff supervision is a complex task. A supervisor must be highly skilled if staff are to be motivated, loyal, and productive. A guiding principle is to "give to others what they need and they will give you what you need" (Conklin, 1979). Staff need to have supervisors who are concerned with helping them meet their needs for "feeling like a winner (Research Institute of America, 1984 p. 3), feeling important, and being treated like an individual. A supervisor should be aware that people: a) act in accordance with their image of themselves, and this image is affected by praise, appreciation, respect, promotion, raises, and other behaviors of the supervisor; b) react bitterly to attacks on their self-esteem (thus a good supervisor should avoid such attacks); c) react positively to positive direction such as "you are capable of doing better than this" or "you are good at dealing with problems"; and d) can positively surprise you if given the chance to do so and if creativity is expected of them (Research Institute of America, 1984). Success on the part of staff reflects positively on their supervisor, for it means the supervisor has also succeeded. A supervisor must delegate responsibility and allow staff the freedom needed to do the job. By knowing the level of responsibility a staff member can handle, a supervisor can delegate in ways that assure that staff succeed. Staff should be encouraged to bring ideas (e.g., a better way to treat a specific child's problem) and problems to their supervisors, who should listen carefully and take action that encourages continued open communication.

Task and Maintenance Functions

Supervisors should ensure that for every group activity, two major functions happen: a) the clinic's performance tasks are being carried out, and b) the needs of staff members are met. Supervisors must be cognizant of their roles and responsibilities in fulfilling the mission and goals of the clinic. An appropriate balance must be maintained between doing what the clinic should do (i.e., serve clients) and caring for the needs of staff. The primary role of a leader is to cue or prompt desired staff behavior (Mawhinney & Ford, 1977) while maintaining appropriate interactions and morale. In addition, supervisors need to have posted office hours or an open-door policy so that staff can both receive and provide information.

Consequences for Behavior

As mentioned earlier, stressing task performance by itself will often result in low morale unless the needs of staff members are also given appropriate attention. Staff need to have an opportunity to provide input, to feel supported by their supervisor, to feel that what they are doing is worthwhile, and to receive feedback. One of the best ways a supervisor can motivate staff is to arrange for appropriate consequences for behavior (Striefel & Cadez, 1983). In some cases, consequences that motivate staff are naturally occurring events (e.g., the progress of a child). In other cases, supervisors must arrange the consequences directly (e.g., by making positive comments about appropriate staff performance). Kornaki and Collins (1982) point out that without consequences (e.g., feedback, time off, increased pay, etc.) for performance of specific tasks, the performance of those tasks will be low. Pierce and Risley (1974) report that providing job descriptions increased performance so that 50% of expected tasks were completed; threats of "being fired" resulted in a temporary increase in performance; and receiving pay immediately after completion of specific tasks (consequence) resulted in a very durable increase in performance to near 100% appropriate performance. Information about expectations (antecedents) and consequences is often misunderstood because staff and supervisors do not understand the behavior principles involved in using antecedents and consequences effectively. Yet both antecedents and consequences are a natural daily occurrence. For instance, you do not answer the telephone unless it rings (antecedent event, e.g., job description) because there is no payoff (consequence—someone to talk to, e.g., feedback from supervisor). Supervisors must structure the service clinic environment so that staff know what is expected and then provide consequences for performance (e.g., positive consequences for appropriate performance and negative consequences for inappropriate performance [see O'Brien et al., 1982, for more specific information]).

STAFF INSERVICE TRAINING

The organizational plan should stipulate policies regarding the provision of inservice training (including both training provided within the clinic and that provided externally) for clinical staff, to include: frequency of inservice training sessions to be conducted, specific expectations of clinical staff members with respect to attendance at inservice (required or voluntary) training sessions and arranging and conducting inservice training sessions, how priorities for inservice training topics are to be determined, and resources in time and money that will be allocated for staff inservice training. A useful procedure is to schedule at least one inservice session per month (usually in conjunction with or in place of a regular staff meeting). A schedule of topics and presentors can be developed cooperatively by staff, supervisors, and administrators. It is useful to develop a schedule for 6 months to a year in advance. The schedule should remain flexible so unanticipated inservice opportunities and needs can be addressed.

PROFESSIONAL LIABILITY INSURANCE

Litigation is an ever-present problem for service providers. The director should arrange for appropriate liability coverage for staff members. In addition, individual staff members should obtain their own individual liability coverage. The best way to obtain adequate coverage is to discuss liability needs with insurance agents from several different companies and then make a decision based on the type of the coverage desired and the cost. The cost of liability insurance is rapidly escalating as more and more service providers are being sued. In addition, the dollar amounts awarded by courts are getting larger: thus, insurance coverage that was adequate last year will probably not be adequate this year.

One good source of liability insurance for individual professionals may be the national association for their discipline. For example, psychologists can obtain good liability coverage at a reasonable cost by buying from the insurance company that has an agreement with the American Psychological Association.

STANDARD OPERATING PROCEDURES

Standard operating procedures for a child and adolescent service clinic consist of a set of generally accepted policies and procedures for carrying out the specific operations of the unit. It is recommended that these be available to staff in the form of written policies. Written policies preclude problems in relaying information when new staff are hired: allow for revision and expansion of policies, as appropriate; and provide a format for communicating expectations to all staff from the director to supervisor, to direct care staff and clerical staff. The number of procedures that could be included in written personnel policies is endless and is up to the discretion of the director. Standard operating procedures include both day-to-day procedures and personnel policies.

Day-to-Day Operating Procedures

Specific day-to-day operating procedures should be developed for routine clinic operations for purposes of efficiency, for maximizing personnel time, and to ensure that requisite components are carried out. Routine procedures could be useful for such clinic functions as: a) client intake processing procedures, b) clinic recordkeeping, c) telephone usage, d) copying access, e) supervisor responsibilities, and f) clerical availability for professional staff. Later chapters of this guidebook cover procedures for some of the more salient clinic functions in greater depth. Some general comments are included here. Procedures developed should be based on such practical considerations as staff and resources available, client considerations, and in some areas, local circumstances. For example, procedures relating to the scheduling of appointments may be dictated not only by the number of staff available and staff case load but also by clinic location, client flow, and parking availability. Also, it may not be practical to schedule evening appointments if the clinic is situated in an unsafe area of the city or where parking is some distance from the clinic. As specified in Chapter 2, location selection thus becomes critical, since some child and adolescent clientele may only be available evenings, if both parents work.

Who should be designated to develop operating procedures for various clinic functions? In a smaller clinic, the clinic director may be solely responsible for generating these procedures, whereas in larger clinics, out of necessity, decisions on different aspects of clinic functioning will be made by individuals responsible for subunits of the clinic. Regardless of who is designated to develop operational procedures, procedures should be reviewed regularly (i.e., annually) and modified as needed to maximize their efficiency, ensure the best use of clinic resources, and to assure that client needs are met. An operational procedures review would ideally involve several staff members, particularly those most affected by the procedures.

Personnel Policies

Some major personnel policies that should be included are listed here. Most of these policies are discussed in detail in this chapter or elsewhere in this book. Written personnel policies should include but are not limited to: a) a clear program philosophy and mission statement (see Chapter 1), b) the goals and objectives of the clinic (see Chapter 1), c) the activities to be carried out to accomplish these goals (see all chapters), d) job descriptions and evaluation procedures for each individual (see this chapter), e) staff rights and grievance procedures (see this chapter), f) staff evaluation procedures (see this chapter), g) hiring and termination procedures (see this chapter), h) procedures for merit and pay increases (see this chapter), i) standards for service provision and ethics (see Chapter 11), j) the various forms needed and procedures for recordkeeping (see all chapters), k) procedures for establishing and maintaining morale (see this chapter), and l) procedures for evaluating program impact (see Chapter 7).

Standard Operating Procedures Format

If the clinic is to be operated efficiently and effectively, then standard operating procedures should be readily available to all staff involved. One of the ways this can be accomplished is through the preparation of an operating procedures handbook or manual. The handbook can be assembled in looseleaf binders containing typewritten material or can be in the format of a printed and bound book. We have found that typewritten material in looseleaf binders has distinct advantages over printed and bound books, not only because written procedures can be readily inserted and deleted using the looseleaf format, but sections can also be duplicated easily as needed. Furthermore, the initial cost of looseleaf handbooks is significantly less than typeset and bound books. A suggested table of contents for a clinic handbook is included in Table 3.4. In some clinics, handbooks may not be used: instead, operational procedures materials are contained in files and retrieved for specific purposes (e.g., intake procedures and report writing procedures).

Each staff member and clinic trainee should be expected to be familiar with the clinic operational procedures and the organizational plan. Christian and

Table 3.4. Sample of table of contents for clinic handbook

1. General Clinic Information
   a. Clinic Mission and Goals
   b. Admissions Criteria
   c. Fees and Billing Procedures
2. Client Confidentiality Policies and Professional Ethics Issues
3. Intake Procedures and Responsibilities
4. Follow-up Treatment Procedures and Responsibilities
5. Clinical Report Writing Procedures
   a. Outline for Client Contact Notes
   b. Outline for Comprehensive Evaluation Reports
   c. Outline for Single Discipline Assessment/Evaluation Reports
   d. Outline for Write-up of Home/School Visits
   e. Outline for Behavioral Observation Write-ups
   f. Sample Reports
6. Instructions and Format for Write-up of Treatment Program
7. Staff Job Descriptions
8. Intern Assignments and Responsibilities
9. Clinic Tests and Other Assessments and Information
10. Forms, Instructions for Completing Forms, and Form Letters for Clients

Hannah (1983) suggest that all staff be required to read the policies and procedures and to sign a statement indicating that they will adhere to them. The organizational plan describing the administrative structure and general clinic policies (see this chapter) may be incorporated into the same handbook as that containing the operational procedures. Alternatively, this information may be maintained in a separate file or handbook. We have found it useful to review at least yearly both the clinic organizational plan and operating procedures with staff (or subunits, if a full staff meeting is not feasible), to reacquaint them with essential information, and to introduce or discuss additions or modifications. An annual retreat may be a good time to conduct such a review.

In addition to the written information available to staff on clinic policies and operations, clinic staff will need to receive ongoing written communications about various situations that may relate to all staff members (i.e., inservice training sessions, workshops) or to specific staff members (i.e., specific case staffings, staff evaluation appointments). Each clinic will need to establish procedures on how information pertinent to staff will be disseminated. In many clinics, bulletin boards are placed in common areas such as lounges or hallways, where general announcements can be posted. In larger clinics, staff may be assigned mailboxes in a central area where they can receive information specific to them. Many clinics employ written memos for communicating among staff members. Some large clinics have also found that information to all staff can best be circulated through a newsletter that is compiled and distributed regularly.

Operational Practices and Procedures Revision

Inefficient or nonfunctional clinic practices and procedures should be changed or eliminated whenever identified or as a result of a regular review (e.g., annually).

Staff who find certain procedures cumbersome or impractical should bring their concerns to management. When this occurs, management should be responsive. Often minor changes can be made with little disruption to the clinic's operation. Whenever staff can be actively involved in planning and preparation activities, they are less likely to resist changing practices and procedures. At the least, staff should be prepared for any changes planned and should be informed of the reasons for the changes. According to Christian and Hannah (1983), the primary reasons for resistance to change are:

1. Lack of understanding of the rationale for change.
2. Lack of clarity as to what is involved in change.
3. Lack of understanding of the probable consequences of change.
4. Insufficient planning and preparation for change prior to implementation.

Christian and Hannah (1983) also suggest that staff resistance to change may be associated with a number of factors such as: a) fear of loss of autonomy, b) special interest group involvement, c) competition for limited funds, and d) territorial disputes. We have found, moreover, that staff resistance to change may be related to reluctance to alter familiar or comfortable patterns when the new procedures will require more individual effort, even though such changes may improve the clinic's overall efficiency. Sometimes, incentives can be identified that will spark enthusiasm for change with staff (i.e., a special holiday or staff party).

SUMMARY

Determination of the number and types of staff necessary to work at a clinic is directly related to the market segment to be served and their needs. Planning, development of job descriptions, and the evaluation of staff skills help assure that the needed services can be provided by clinic staff. The availability of such information is also useful to staff in knowing what is expected of them and in determining inservice needs. Attending to staff needs, involving them in the development of standard operating procedures, and providing them with ongoing feedback are all useful practices in motivating staff to be competent. In all personnel planning, it is vital to recognize and respect staff rights, while also stressing responsibilities.

READER ACTIVITIES

Do you have available in written form a set of standard operating procedures for use by staff? If not, develop and/or update them now. Do all staff have clearly defined and relevant job descriptions, and are staff evaluations related directly to these job descriptions? Review your staff job descriptions and evaluation procedures based on the information in this chapter. List three additional things you could do to improve staff motivation and morale or that your supervisor could do to improve your morale or motivation.

REFERENCES

Carlson, R. M., & Sperduto, W. A. (1982). Improving attendance and punctuality within a behavioral consultation model. In R. M. O'Brien, A. M. Dickinson, & M. P. Rosow (Eds.), *Industrial behavior modification: A management handbook* (pp. 209–223). New York: Pergamon.

Christian, W. P., & Hannah, G. T. (1983). *Effective management in human services.* Englewood Cliffs, NJ: Prentice-Hall.

Conklin, R. (1979). *How to get people to do things.* Chicago: Contemporary Books.

Cummings, L. L., & Schwab, D. P. (1973). *Performance in organizations: Determinants and appraisal.* Glenview, IL: Scott, Foresman.

Deming, W. E. (1983). Demings blames managers solely for economic decline. *Eccles Annual Review, 5*(1), 1–2.

Dickinson, A. M., & O'Brien, R. M. (1982). Performance measurement and evaluation. In R. M. O'Brien, A. M. Dickinson, & M. P. Rosow (Eds.), *Industrial behavior modification: A management handbook* (pp. 51–64). New York: Pergamon.

French, W. L., Bell, C. H., Jr., & Zawacki, R. A. (1978). *Organization development: Theory, practice, and research.* Dallas: Business Publications.

Kornaki, J., & Collins, R. L. (1982). Motivation of preventive maintenance performance. In R. M. O'Brien, A. M. Dickinson, & M. P. Rosow (Eds.), *Industrial behavior modification: A management handbook* (pp. 243–265). New York: Pergamon.

Mawhinney, T. C., & Ford, J. C. (1977). The path-goal theory of leader effectiveness: An operant interpretation. *Academy of Management Review, 2*(2), 398–411.

McMillan, J. D., & Dorel, H. W. (1980). Performance appraisal: Match the tool to the task. *Personnel, 57*(4), 12–20.

O'Brien, R. M., Dickinson, A. M., & Rosow, M. P. (Eds.) (1982). *Industrial behavior modification: A management handbook.* New York: Pergamon.

Pfeiffer, J. W., & Jones, J. E. (1971). *A handbook of structured experiences for human relations training* (Vol. 3). Iowa City: University Associates Press.

Pierce, C. H., & Risley, T. R. (1974). Improving job performance of Neighborhood Youth Corps aides in an urban recreation program. *Journal of Applied Behavior Analysis, 7*(3), 207–215.

Research Institute of America. (1984). *Personal report: Creating and motivating a superior, loyal staff.* New York: Author.

Seattle Mental Health Institute. (1984). *What's in your future? The steps in the development of a mental health long range plan.* Seattle: Author.

Shaw, S. F., Bensky, J. M., & Dixon, B. (1981). *Stress and burnout. A primer for special education and special services personnel.* Reston, VA: Council for Exceptional Children.

Striefel, S., & Cadez, M. (1983). *Serving children and adolescents with developmental disabilities in the special education classroom: Proven methods.* Baltimore: Paul H. Brookes Publishing Co.

U.S. Department of Labor. (1977). *Dictionary of occupational titles.* Washington, DC: U.S. Government Printing Office.

4

Client-Related Policies, Practices, and Procedures

The intent of this chapter is to provide you with information about:
1. How to publicize the clinic to prospective referrals
2. How clients are referred to the clinic and what client referrals should be accepted
3. Fees charged for services; billing; and fee collection procedures
4. Issues related to appointment scheduling and collection of preappointment information
5. First clinic appointment staff responsibilities
6. Courtesies to be extended to clients

MAKING THE CLINIC VISIBLE IN THE COMMUNITY

Without a sufficient number of clients, no clinic can exist for long. Certainly, clinic survival is directly associated with public awareness of what services are offered by the clinic and what constitutes an appropriate referral. As discussed in Chapter 2, a marketing plan is essential for new clinics or for clinics that are expanding their services. Well-established clinics should also ensue that there are ongoing activities to: a) maintain a positive public image, b) acquaint new community members with available clinic services, and c) reach public sectors that may not be well-acquainted with what the clinic has to offer. Some of the activities described in Chapter 2 for introducing new clinics or expanded clinic services to the community (e.g., use of brochures or pamphlets describing the clinic and its programs, and publication of news articles about the clinic) are also appropriate for maintaining or increasing public awareness of the clinic's operation and staff. Other activities that could be conducted on a regular basis include:

1. Initiation of direct contacts with community agency representatives and private professionals by clinic staff
2. Giving talks or presentations to local community groups (e.g., Parent-Teachers Association, service organizations)
3. Writing a regular column or articles for a local newspaper or other local publication on topics related to children, teenagers, and families

4. Sponsoring, or cosponsoring with other agencies, workshops on topics of local interest associated with children, youth, and family functioning
5. Giving interviews about the clinic or related topics on local radio or television

INQUIRIES ABOUT CLIENT SERVICES

Telephone or in-person clinic contacts are often initiated by prospective client families or interested individuals such as other human service professionals, in order to obtain specific information about the clinic such as: a) what services are offered, b) who can receive services, c) fees for services, d) whether a specific problem related to a child or adolescent is appropriate as a clinic referral, and/or e) availability of services (i.e., finding out when an appointment can be scheduled).

Some inquiries may be easily handled by providing responses to specific questions and/or by follow-up mailing of a clinic brochure or pamphlet. Other inquiries may require the provision of more extensive information. Clinic staff assigned to process inquiries should: a) be well acquainted with client admissions criteria, fees for services, services offered, and availability of services (waiting time, if any); b) be able to refer the caller to other community resources if it is apparent that the information sought is not pertinent to the clinic; c) know clinic emergency determination policies; and d) know whom to consult in the clinic (e.g., supervisors, clinic director) if questions are posed that they cannot answer. Be aware that an initial impression of the clinic, positive or negative, is projected by the manner in which staff respond to inquiries, impressions that may influence subsequent referrals. Clinic staff processing information inquiries should therefore have excellent interpersonal and communication skills. Information inquiries may be followed by a request for clinic services. Processing of referral requests is discussed later in this chapter.

CLIENT ADMISSION CRITERIA

Specific admissions criteria must be established for each clinic, in accordance with the clinic philosophy, mission, and goals. Definitive admissions criteria are necessary to ensure that a clinic accepts only those clients who can be appropriately served in terms of staff expertise, facilities, equipment, and materials. The more specific the criteria, the easier for those receiving referral requests to discriminate who are acceptable clients for the clinic. The following factors should be addressed in determining client admissions criteria:

1. Client characteristics: age range and sex of clients to be accepted
2. Type of referral problems or questions that will be accepted
3. Type of referral problems or questions that will not be accepted
4. Restrictions on services offered (e.g., problem severity, particular client disabilities or characteristics)

5. Clinic policies on parent/legal guardians' consent for services and participation in evaluation/treatment
6. Clinic policies on acceptance of adult substitutes for parents/legal guardians (e.g., case workers, court appointees)
7. Fee payment expectations

In some cases the prospective client will clearly meet the admissions criteria. At other times, particularly when multiple referral problems are described or unfamiliar referral problems are presented, decisions on accepting referral requests need to be determined on a case-by-case basis.

FEES FOR CLIENT SERVICES

Determination of Fees for Services

Regardless of the size or type of child/adolescent clinic, fees for clinic services must be established. Clinic management must determine fees for services and develop policies and practices related to fee collections. One way to arrive at an hourly client fee is by computing the difference between the total anticipated annual clinic operational costs and the total anticipated clinic income apart from client fees for a fiscal year, and then dividing the difference by the projected annual staff billable hours. For example:

1. $\dfrac{\text{Total anticipated}}{\text{clinic operational costs}} - \dfrac{\text{Total anticipated income}}{\text{(not including client fees)}} = \text{Difference}$

2. $\dfrac{\text{Difference}}{\text{Billable hours}} = \text{Estimated hourly fee charge}$

Once an estimated hourly fee is derived, the figure should then be compared with: a) the hourly rate charged by local clinics or professionals providing similar services; and b) average charges per visit to psychologists or psychiatrists within the region and in accordance with family income as reported by Taube, Burns, and Kessler (1984). Client hourly fees can also be figured on a sliding scale fee schedule. The fees for a sliding scale fee schedule may be derived from a formula such as a fixed decrease in hourly rate proportional to a fixed decrease in dollars of family income, utilizing the hourly rate determined through the method just described as the highest fee charged per hour at a particular income level cutoff (a sample of a sliding scale fee schedule is shown in Form 4.1). If a sliding scale fee schedule is adopted, a minimum hourly rate should be set so that clients are expected to pay some fee for services, no matter how small, unless special arrangements have been made.

Fixed or Flat Rate Fees

Clinic management may adopt a policy whereby fixed or flat rate fees for specific services are available, either in lieu of other fees charged or in addition to other

Sliding Scale Fee Schedule

EVALUATION:

Level 1: Evaluation will include psychoeducational, behavioral, or developmental (birth to 3 years) evaluation.

Sliding Scale

Income	Intake fee
$0– 5,000	$80.00
5–10,000	85.00
10–15,000	90.00
15–20,000	95.00
20–25,000	105.00
25–30,000	115.00
Above 30,000	125.00

Level II: Evaluation will include psychoeducational or behavioral at the Level I fee plus speech/language and/or motor evaluation fees.

Speech/Language Evaluation	$25.00
Motor Evaluation	$25.00

Medical evaluation is also available at an additional charge of $20.00–$50.00, depending on the extent of the evaluation.

Home or School Visit: A local home or school visit or contact may also be included as part of the intake evaluation at no additional charge as determined by the director of the _____ Clinic. If a home or school visit is needed outside of the local area, transportation and additional time charges will be made.

FOLLOW-UP TREATMENT: Clinical appointment or home and school visit fees are charged on an hourly basis and apply for all types of services.

Sliding Scale

Income	Intake fee
$0– 5,000	$10.00
5–10,000	15.00
10–15,000	20.00
15–20,000	25.00
20–25,000	30.00
25–30,000	40.00
Above 30,000	50.00

A transportation fee of approximately 28¢ per mile (or the current rate) round trip from the center will also be charged for home or school visits.

Telephone monitoring will be charged as follows:

1. Local calls: The hourly rate applicable to your situation will be charged for all local calls that exceed 5 minutes.
2. Long distance calls: The appropriate hourly rate will be charged in addition to the long distance telephone charge.

Please contact the clinic secretary or the clinic director for clarification or questions on fees for services.

fee schedules adopted (i.e., sliding fee schedule). For example, a standard fee may be set to cover a specific psychological test battery. This may be a practical arrangement for clients who contract for specific services for a designated time period (e.g., testing services for a school district).

Special Arrangements for Fee Reductions

Policies should be established for circumstances, if any, under which fees will be reduced or waived. For example, clinic policy may stipulate that clients who are unable to pay minimum fees may have fees waived if they can provide documentation of inability to pay. Psychologists are expected to donate a portion of their services for little or no remuneration as specified in their ethical principles (American Psychological Association, 1981).

Routine Procedures for Processing Service Charges

Routine procedures should be developed within each clinic for accurate record keeping of services provided to clients and fees charged. These procedures should be carried out by all involved clinic staff no matter what clinic billing system is adopted. One way to do this is to adopt a standard form to be completed by all clinicians after appointments, on which they record: a) date of service, b) type of service provided, c) time spent with client, and d) clinical signature. Before each appointment, the client could obtain the form from a receptionist and take the form to the clinician; or each clinician could have a supply of forms for this purpose (a sample billing form is shown in Form 4.2). Clinicians would then give completed forms to the individual responsible for billing. This could occur at the end of each session if it is clinic policy to collect fees at the time of services, or at the end of each working day if billing is to occur later.

Billing Practices

The most practical method of collecting fees is to make it clinic policy to collect fees at the time services are provided. Such a procedure eliminates the necessity for extensive bookkeeping and billing, as well as possible fee collection problems. This procedure is becoming common among other professions providing services (Faustman, 1982). Human service agencies have typically had inadequate fee collection practices, and clients have not been adequately informed of fee collection policies (Christian & Hannah, 1983).

In order to assure that income is not lost to a clinic, it is essential that management develop both clearly specified fee collection policies and routine procedures to carry out these policies. This needs to occur regardless of the type of billing system adopted. Individuals responsible for fee payment should be provided verbal information on policies and practices prior to the first clinic visit and given written information at their first clinic visit (Christian & Hannah, 1983).

FORM 4.2

Service and Billing Information

Date: _____

Client name: _____ Case no. _____

Responsible for payment: _____

Address: _____

Intake Evaluation: (to be completed by service provider; check appropriate items)

Charge (to be completed by Business Office)

_____ Psychological assessment $ _____
_____ Medical assessment   _____
_____ Educational assessment   _____
_____ Other (explain) _____ _____
_____ Other (explain) _____ _____

Follow-up treatment: (Check appropriate items.)	**Services Duration:** (hour/sessions)	**Charge**
_____ Child/adolescent individual treatment	_____	_____
_____ Child/adolescent group treatment	_____	_____
_____ Family therapy	_____	_____
_____ Parent/guardian consultation	_____	_____
_____ Other (explain) _____	_____	_____
_____ Home or school visit/ observation	_____	_____
_____ Travel expenses (List miles _____)	_____	_____
_____ Long distance phone rates Number called ( ) _____	_____ (length in minutes)	_____

TOTAL CHARGES: $ _____

Signed: _____
              (staff member)

Written Fee Collection Policies

Written fee collection policies provided to individuals responsible for payment should include: a) a clear statement of clinic policy for fee payment, b) specific instructions on clinic billing practices, and c) procedures that may be used by the clinic for nonpayment of fees. Both legal and ethical issues are involved in debt collection for psychological services (Faustman, 1982). Legally, written and verbal information should be provided and informed consent obtained from clients regarding actions that will be taken if their accounts are delinquent beyond a stipulated time period (i.e., collection agency involvement, interest charges). Ethically, it is only fair that payees be informed prior to receiving services that failure to pay clinical fees may result in release of their name and other relevant client information (a loss of confidentiality) to those assigned to collect fees (Faustman, 1982). Christian and Hannah (1983) also suggest that the written procedures include statements relating to any exceptions to the fee collection procedures described (e.g., not excluding anyone from services because of their inability to pay). Written procedures should be reviewed with the individual responsible for fee payment at the first clinic visit and then signed by this individual as an acknowledgment (informed consent) that the procedures have been reviewed and are understood. A sample of a written fee collection statement is shown in Form 4.3.

FORM 4.3

Fees for Services Agreement

Charges for services at the _____ Clinic are based on actual cost. Clients with insurance will be responsible for the total amount of the bill regardless of the amount reimbursed by the insurance company. The charges for clients without insurance or other third-party sources will be determined on the basis of a sliding fee scale according to annual gross family income. Actual cost to the _____ Clinic for services provided but not covered by the sliding fee scale must be obtained from other sources. Thus, payment of fees is critical.

Based on your gross income, and whether or not you have insurance, your personal fee for the intake and evaluation will be $_____ and for follow-up treatment services it will be $_____ per visit. You are expected to make a payment at the time of each visit or at least once every 30 days. If you cannot pay your complete bill at the time of the visit, arrangements for monthly payments must be made with the _____ Clinic secretary. Billing statements are mailed monthly.

I (We) have read and understand the information regarding fees and the rights of clients as explained in the Client Rights sheet attached. In addition, information has been explained to me (us) in detail. I (We) certify that the information that I (we) have provided regarding gross income and insurance coverage is accurate, and it is understood that failure to provide accurate information shall constitute valid grounds for refusal to provide services. I (We) also agree to provide verification of information upon request. I (We) understand that should an insurance claim be filed for services provided, permission is granted to the _____ Clinic to provide diagnostic information as requested. I (We) also understand that accounts may be referred to an outside collection agency or pursued in small claims court or other courts if they are delinquent over 60 days. In this case *delinquent* means not making payments in accordance with the agreement made with the _____ Clinic secretary. All court costs, attorney's fees, and collection costs shall be my (our) responsibility. It is also understood that interest at the rate of 1½% per month of the unpaid balance may be added to my (our) account if delinquent over 60 days. By signing below, I (we) certify that I (we) have read and understand this agreement and have full knowledge of its meaning and effect.

_____   _____
Witness   Signature of person responsible
                                       for payment

_____
Date

Credit Criterion Model

One fee collection model that has been adopted and found to be successful in some human service agencies is the credit criterion model (Christian & Hannah, 1983). In this model, the following procedures are implemented:

1. Individuals responsible for fee payment are provided a written billing policy at the first clinic visit, instructing them that cash payments are expected at each of the first three clinic visits in order to establish billing credit with the agency.
2. A financial interview is conducted with individuals responsible for fee payment to determine a sliding fee rate and to answer questions on the billing policy.
3. Clinic office staff verbally prompt the individual responsible for fee payment to pay fees after each visit.
4. If fee payment cannot be made after the first clinic visit owing to financial problems, a stamped envelope is provided to the individuals responsible for payment, and they are asked to mail the fee before the next clinic visit.
5. If payment is not made following the second visit, a meeting is arranged by appropriate clinic staff to discuss any problem that might be preventing fee payment.
6. When emergency treatment is needed, services are rendered, regardless of the extent of payment.

After billing credit has been established through the procedures described, the client may then be provided a monthly bill (Christian & Hannah, 1983). Monthly billing procedures then include:

1. Positive verbal feedback from clinic office staff for successful fee payment for the first three clinic visits.
2. Provision of a copy of the billing policy that states the option of paying cash at each clinic visit or receiving a monthly bill.
3. Following each monthly billing, at least 50% of the monthly bill should be paid.
4. If all or 50% of the monthly bill is not paid, the monthly billing option is removed and cash payments only are reinstated.
5. It is required that the balance of the monthly bill be paid in full within 3 months after termination of services.
6. In the event of unforeseen financial difficulties, the individual responsible for payment is to contact the clinic staff assigned to fee collection.

Third-Party Fee Payment

Third-party payments may be utilized to cover part or all of client service fees. Third-party payments may be issued through private insurance companies, government agencies, or credit card agencies. Clinic management should establish policies on whether the clinic will enter into third-party arrangements with clients, and if so, through what types of agencies and transactions. The clinic may either bill third parties directly for fee payments, or it may assist individuals responsible for the fee payments to complete the requisite reimbursement forms for fee payments made to the clinic. The reader is referred to Jones (1982) and Dorken (1983) for more extensive discussions on the pros and cons of third-party billing and for practical suggestions involved.

Third-Party Private Insurance Billing

Direct billing to private insurance carriers is not practical for all clinics for several reasons. First, clinic staff assigned to billing must be well acquainted with a wide range of billing procedures required by different insurance carriers (Jones, 1982). Second, insurance carriers frequently only pay a certain percentage of fees, with the percentage being different across insurance companies. If clients are to be billed directly for fees not reimbursed by insurance, careful record keeping would be necessary to ensure that clients are billed the differences. Third, different insurance carriers take varying time periods to process claims, which could result in a high accounts receivable figure for the clinic; this could be a problem if the clinic is dependent on regular income. Fourth, a number of insurance carriers require the signature of a licensed physician as verification of services rendered or as having provided services, which may limit psychological service fee collection if a psychiatrist or other medical professional is not affiliated with the clinic.

The most practical way for a clinic to deal with private insurance reimbursement is by making client families responsible for fees, but assisting them in completing forms that will allow them to collect reimbursement for fees already paid to the clinic. Even so, this can be a time consuming and inconvenient practice for clinic staff because most private insurance carriers require that: a) itemized bills be attached to insurance forms; b) standard procedural codes describing services provided be included on forms; and c) diagnostic codes be included from the *International Classification of Diseases, 9th Revision, Clinical Modification* (U.S. Department of Health and Human Services, 1980) or the *Diagnostic and Statistical Manual of Mental Disorders; DSM-II* (American Psychiatric Association, 1980). This third requirement poses several problems for clinic staff. First, diagnostic codes, when used, must be identified by the clinicians responsible for treatment. Second, diagnostic codes should only be seen as indicators of particular disorders, but not necessarily as a final statement of that disorder (Jones, 1982). Third, for some clinic services provided, diagnostic code assignment may not be appropriate or available.

Government Agency Billing

If the clinic pursues reimbursement for services through government agencies, there are usually some prescribed billing procedures to be followed: a) a service provider number must be obtained that is included on all billings submitted, b) billings are submitted on prepared forms furnished by agencies, and c) specific agency billing procedures must be followed. In addition, clinic management need to be aware that agencies may pay fees designated by them for specific services (i.e., a percentage of fees billed or on a fixed rate schedule). Before deciding on whether or not to provide services to clients that require fee collection from government agencies, clinic management should investigate the requirements and reimbursement schedules of agencies involved to determine whether it is a cost-effective pursuit.

Credit Card Billing

In recent years, client credit card use for payment of services has become available. This may involve use of nationally known credit cards; or, in some communities, local central credit card bureaus have been established for processing fees for medical and other professional services. Credit card billing assures that the clinic will be reimbursed, since once the credit card transaction has been processed the clinic is free of further billing or fee collection problems. Before adopting credit card billing as a clinic practice, however, clinic management should investigate the time interval between submission of credit card transactions and reimbursement. This may differ from one credit card company to another, and lengthy time delays could result in clinic budgeting problems.

Account Maintenance and Billing Procedures

If client accounts are to be opened within the clinic and periodic billings (e.g., monthly) submitted for charges incurred, an accounting system must be adopted and routine billing procedures established. Account record keeping and billings may be handled through: a) clinic office staff, b) a central business office in the same facility, or c) an outside agency specializing in this type of service. The sophistication of the accounting system and billing procedures adopted will depend on the resources available, number of clients served, and the flexibility of the clinic budget. Before setting up an accounting system or billing procedures, management should consult with business experts and/or business staff from other clinics providing similar services, to acquire information that will assist them in decision making.

Whenever client fees are to be billed after services have been provided, there is a potential fee collection problem. Even when those responsible for fee payment have been well informed about clinic policies and have signed a statement to this effect, there is no guarantee that fees will be paid. Fee collection may be facilitated if those responsible for payment complete a written agreement form that indicates how they intend to pay for fees charged (i.e., for the full amount or for specific payment amounts—a sample form is shown in Form 4.4). Such a procedure may prompt some individuals to make regular payments, since it is a form of commitment; however, it is probably not legally binding.

REFERRAL REQUESTS

Requests for referral may result from inquiries as discussed earlier in the chapter or they may be made by those already acquainted with the clinic.

FORM 4.4

Payment Agreement

I agree to make monthly payments of $_____ toward the fees for services provided by the _____ Clinic.

_____
Person responsible for payment

_____   _____
Witness   Date

Referral Sources

Although parents or legal guardians are the primary referral resources for children and adolescents, your clinic may also decide to accept referrals from agencies, community professionals, or professionals associated with other units or programs in your facility (i.e., from a pediatrician in a pediatric unit located in the same hospital as the clinic). You must establish policies on who can refer clients directly for services. If your clinic is to accept referrals from individuals or agencies in addition to parents and legal guardians, signed permission from parents or legal guardians for the referral should be provided to your clinic by those referral sources.

REFERRAL INFORMATION

As discussed earlier in this chapter, information about the client and the reason for referral needs to be obtained before a child or adolescent is accepted as a client, to ensure that the referral is appropriate. After it has been determined that the child or adolescent referred meets admissions criteria, further information should be obtained before the first clinic appointment is scheduled. Such information includes: a) demographic data pertaining to the client and client family, and b) specific information related to the referral question or problem. Sufficient information must be obtained about the referral problem to determine whether there is a need for emergency services versus regular appointment scheduling.

Agency Referral Form

If referrals are accepted from agencies, it is a good practice to provide agencies with some type of standard referral form. Agency referral forms should be completed by agency representatives and forwarded to the clinic with a signed acknowledgment from a parent or legal guardian granting referral permission. The use of standard agency referral forms facilitates the acquisition of pertinent information by your clinic (e.g., client birth date) and also serves as an indication

Form 4.5

Agency Referral Form

Date:_____

SECTION I

Client/student's name_____ Grade_____ Birth date_____

Name of parent
or guardian_____ Signature_____

Address_____ Telephone_____

Name and address of referring agency_____

or school district_____

School_____

Authorization_____
              (Signature of agency personnel)   (Title)

Note: Signatures by authorized agency personnel indicate the agency's responsibility for remittance regarding this referral.

Hours referring agency personnel can be reached for telephone consultation:

_____

Who initiated this referral?_____ Telephone_____

SECTION II

1. Please describe the problems of this client as you see them.

2. What information do you hope to obtain from this referral?

SECTION III

Indicate below any specific areas of assessment that are desired:

_____ I.Q. testing
_____ Achievement testing (academic grade levels, placement recommendation)
_____ Behavioral/emotional/social assessment
_____ Speech/language assessment
_____ Motor assessment
_____ Medical assessment
_____ Home or school observation

> Agency Comments:

SECTION IV

1. Previous testing results: *Test name*   *Date(s) given*   *Score*
   Intelligence:

   Achievement:

   Other:

(continued)

2. *Current* educational placement: Regular_____ Special Education_____

3. *Prior* educational placement (please check and explain in the space provided):

____Preschool (daycare/nursery)
____Special education services
____Regular classrooms
____Other—specify_____

Comments:

4. Possible contributing factors to client's problems (please check and explain in the space provided):

____Vision problem
____Hearing problem
____Speech problem
____Health—specify
____Motor: Fine____ Gross____
____Home problems
____Other

Comments:

of agency responsibility for fees for services unless otherwise noted. Form 4.5 is a sample of an agency form. Whenever an agency referral form is received, clinic staff assigned to process referrals should ascertain that the prospective client meets clinic admissions criteria before proceeding with further processing of the referral and scheduling of the first appointment.

Initial Contact Form

We have found it useful for all referrals who are accepted as clients to complete a standard initial contact form. This practice ensures that specific information is obtained for all clients, and the information included in the form can then be used in setting up a client file. A form of this type may be completed at the time the referral request is deemed appropriate for the clinic, or following receipt of a mailed referral form. It is suggested that the information on the initial contact form include: a) full name and birth date of referred individual; b) full names, addresses, and phone number of client family; c) names of referral agencies or parties if other than parents or legal guardians; and d) reason for referral or type of services requested. Regarding this last item, a checklist could also be included on the initial contact form for indicating what services are desired or areas of concern, or a space could be included on the form for a brief description of the referral problem. An initial contact form may also be used to record time and day of the first appointment scheduled, name of party responsible for payment, and any other information desired by the clinic. Form 4.6 is a sample initial contact form.

Client Family Information Forms

It is common practice in many child/adolescent service clinics to have parents or legal guardians complete some type of information form *before* the first clinic

FORM 4.6

Initial Contact Form

_____Clinic

File #_____   Party responsible for payment of
Client name_____   services_____
Birth date_____   Referred by:
Grade_____ Sex: M___ F___   ___Parent/legal guardian_____
Address_____   ___Physician_____
_____   ___Agency_____
Phone_____   Address_____
Parent/Guardian Father_____   Phone_____
                 Mother_____   ___Other_____
                                                      (Specify)
Date of initial contact_____
Type of initial contact: ___Letter ___Phone ___Person

Requests/Concerns

___Aggressive behavior (tantrums: physical, verbal, destructive)
___Social problems (lying, stealing, drug abuse, truancy, rebellious, sexual problem)
___Disruptive behavior (overactive, short attention span, out-of-seat behavior)
___Enuresis or encorpesis
___Health problems (sleep, eating, nutritional, frequent illness, somatic complaints)

___Sensory impairment (hearing, vision)
___Speech/language impairment
___Motor delays
___Neurological/convulsive disorder
___Placement recommendation
___Intelligence testing
___Academic problems (reading, math, spelling, handwriting, other)
___Other_____
Further information:

DEPOSITION OF CASE

___Emergency Intake
___Waiting List
___Scheduled for Evaluation
  / /   _____
mo. day yr.   Day of week
Time:_____

___Cancellation—No reschedule
___Cancellation—Rescheduled

  / /   _____
mo. day yr.   Day of week
Time_____   Overnight_____

visit. Information may be requested on client and family medical history; client developmental, personal-social, and educational history; previous assessments and evaluations completed; client school and home functioning; and referral question elaboration. Many service providers find client family information forms to be a time-saving approach, since clinical time does not have to be spent obtaining information directly that can be prepared in advance. Further, it is often easier for client families to more accurately report information via this approach than in an interview situation; that is, they have more time to recall pertinent information and may be able to refer to records at home for specific information (e.g., dates).

In addition to the type of information forms described, client families may also be provided rating forms or questionnaires to be completed by them and/or other relevant individuals such as teachers, on client functioning in one or more areas. This information can be utilized in conjunction with other assessments conducted in the clinic setting. (The use of rating scales, checklists, questionnaires, and inventories is discussed in Chapter 6.)

All information forms to be completed by client families may be assembled into one packet (which could also include other information about the clinic and the first visit appointment), and given to the client family at the time the first appointment is scheduled. Ideally, completed forms would be returned to the clinic before the appointment so that they could be reviewed by clinicians prior to meeting the client and client family. Although information forms are useful for service providers, it is very important that the client family not be overwhelmed with an abundance of forms to be completed, or with forms that are ambiguous or complex. Otherwise, forms may not be fully completed, or client families may lack the competency to provide information requested and will be discouraged before they arrive at your clinic. Also, many case files often contain vast amounts of paperwork that is rarely used or contains irrelevant trivia. If using information forms, you need to provide client families with forms that are clear and concise and that include requests for relevant information.

Information Interviews

In lieu of or in conjunction with written information to be provided by client families, other sources, telephone or in-person interviews may be conducted by clinic staff prior to the first clinic visit for the purpose of obtaining information related to the client and the referral problem. A standard form may be used for this purpose that can then be placed in the case record file for review by clinicians assigned to the case before they meet with the client. A sample form of this type is shown in Form 4.7.

Client Records from Other Sources

Copies of existing records of services provided by other agencies may contain relevant information with respect to the client and the referral problem. If at all possible, such records should be obtained prior to the first visit. Parents or legal guardians may be asked to have copies of pertinent written records sent or brought to the clinic before the first appointment, or they may be asked to give written permission for the clinic to request records. Records forwarded by other agencies may not reach the clinic before the first clinic visit if the client appointment is scheduled within a short time (e.g., a week) after the requests are sent. An interim of several or more weeks between requests of submission and receipt of records is not unusual. In addition, some agencies require a fee for fulfilling written record requests. If this is not known at the time of the request, records delivery may be delayed even further. When fees are charged for written records, fee coverage should be billed to the individual or agency identified as financially responsible for payment of clinic services.

Background Information

Date of interview: _____

Child/adolescent/client: _____ Birth date:_____

Information received from: _____

Relationship to client: _____

1. **FAMILY CONSTELLATION** (number of siblings and ages; parent information):

2. **BACKGROUND INFORMATION** (include motor, speech, health, medical, behavior, self-help skills, etc.):

3. **PARENTS' SPECIFIC CONCERN** (What do they consider a problem? What do they want from the evaluation?):

4. **SCHOOL:**

   Name of school: _____ Teacher: _____

   Address: _____ Phone: _____

   Grade: _____ Special Education: ____yes ____no

   Describe program:

   School adjustment (include social and academic):

5. **PREVIOUS EXAMINATIONS, EVALUATIONS, AND/OR TREATMENT** (When? Where? Results? What were parents told, etc.):

6. **OTHER:**

7. **CAN BOTH PARENTS/GUARDIANS BE PRESENT FOR THE INTAKE?**
   ____yes ____no

Information taken by: _____ Title: _____

Intake Coordinator: _____

EMERGENCY DETERMINATION

Every clinic must establish practices and procedures for identifying those clients who should be served on an emergency basis. If the clinic is set up only to handle routine cases, then arrangements should be made for referring emergencies to appropriate agencies or facilities, such as local crisis centers. Formal agreements with such agencies are critical for interagency cooperation. Screening to determine emergencies should be completed at the time of the initial contact with the parent or legal guardian. Some guidelines to be used in decision making on the need for emergency services include:

1. Is the potential client in immediate life-threatening danger from self? For example: Has the individual verbalized or attempted suicidal actions?
2. Does the potential client pose life-threatening danger or physical harm to others?
3. Has or is the potential client in physical or emotional danger from others? For example: Is there child abuse involved or is it imminent?
4. Is the referral problem of an intensity or has it increased to a degree where delayed action could result in harm to the potential client or others?
5. Are there legal or other factors that require immediate action?

In some clinics, any suspected or identified emergency may be referred to the director of outpatient services, the clinic director, or a supervisor or other staff member designated to decide whether the situation warrants emergency action, and if so, how it will be handled. In other clinics, the staff member involved in the initial contact may assign the client to the next available open appointment time slot, or schedule an appointment no later than 24 hours after contact has been made. It may also be clinic practice that the staff member then be required to notify a designated staff member (e.g., clinic director) of the action taken. In other clinics, emergency situations may be referred directly to other identified agencies. Emergencies can also arise at any time during contact with a client/client family, and, thus, procedures for dealing with such emergencies must be in place. In most clinics, staff rotate responsibility for emergencies during times when the clinic is closed. An emergency number can be made available that will place the caller in contact with the emergency worker almost immediately. Battery-operated beepers are carried by the emergency worker so that contact can be made easily and promptly.

CLIENT APPOINTMENT SCHEDULING

Each clinic will also need to establish procedures for scheduling regular or nonemergency client appointments and for waiting list arrangements in the event of service overload. Because of the demands for services, some clinics may need to schedule appointments several or more weeks after the initial contact. This is not a desirable situation, but may be impossible to circumvent because of staff size and case loads. If it is necessary to schedule appointments beyond a week or two in advance, parents/legal guardians should be informed of other resources where earlier services may be obtained, or informed that they will be on a waiting list for openings that may arise before the scheduled appointment. It is standard practice in some clinics to schedule the parent/guardian for an intake interview within a short time after the initial contact, while the child/client family appointment is scheduled for a later time. A determination may then be made by the staff member conducting the interview (e.g., intake officer) to refer the client elsewhere, to assign the client to a cliician for an appointment within a short time (i.e., a week), or to place the client's name on a waiting list if no clinicians are currently available to provide services.

The major responsibility for scheduling appointments for all staff members is generally assigned to a receptionist, although it could be assigned to another staff member such as a social worker or intake officer. The same individual involved in the initial contact with the parent or legal guardian may be the individual assigned to schedule appointments, or it may be the responsibility of another staff member. In a facility where a number of staff are available representing multiple disciplines, appointment scheduling can be a complex procedure if coordinated by one individual. Another option is to have individual staff members arrange their own appointment schedules independently, either directly or through a secretary, after initial contact/referral forms have been completed.

Centralized Appointment Scheduling

A centralized appointment scheduling procedure, manual or computerized, may be utilized in your clinic for scheduling all appointments. If such a procedure is followed, service providers will need to be informed of appointments scheduled for them. Advantages of using a central appointment scheduling procedure are that: a) the clinician's time can be reserved primarily for services rather than being involved in the administrative task of arranging individual appointments, b) clinic/observation rooms that need to be used by multiple staff can be more efficiently scheduled, and c) administrative and supervisory staff can have access to all current clinic appointments and scheduling. Disadvantages of using a central appointment scheduling procedure are that: a) individual clinicians may prefer or find it more convenient to manage their own schedules, and b) individual clinicians must be careful to inform the staff member assigned to scheduling of any changes or subsequent appointments made by them. Despite these disadvantages we believe that the advantages of maintaining a central appointment scheduling procedure of some type in clinics with more than one or two staff members outweighs the disadvantages.

Parental Information to Be Provided

The parent/legal guardian should be provided with some information on clinic policies, practices, and procedures before the first clinic visit. The extent of information to be provided will vary for each clinic, depending on the number of clients and what specific information is considered necessary. You may want to provide your client families with information such as: a) directions on how to reach the clinic, particularly if it is located in a large city or a large hospital complex; b) available parking and any specific procedures related to parking (e.g., parking ticket validation process); c) where to go once inside the clinic and whom to ask for; d) expected time duration for the appointment; e) purpose for the appointment (e.g., parent intake interview, child assessment); f) whether the child or adolescent client is to be brought to the clinic; g) clinic policies on attendance of children who are not identified as clients (e.g., availability of child care); h) preparation of the child or adolescent client for the appointment; i) what records should be brought to the appointment (e.g., test reports, medical records); and j) clinic policies related to parents or legal guardians observing assessments being conducted. Whatever information is to be provided to client families may be communicated by either telephone or letter. We have found it useful to provide client families with general information at the time the first clinical intake appointment is scheduled, followed by a letter containing more specific information, including appointment date and time and enclosures (e.g., a brochure describing the clinic, a map showing clinic location, any forms to be filled out in advance of the appointment). It is advisable that a letter of this type be sent approximately one week before the scheduled appointment, particularly if the appointment has been scheduled for a date far in advance of the initial contact. The letter then serves as a reminder of the appointment date and time as well as providing other needed information.

Preparation of the Client

Preparation of the child or adolescent client for coming to the clinic should be discussed with parents or legal guardians when the first appointment is made, and certainly before the first clinic visit. This can be accomplished via telephone or letter. Clearly, client families have the right to provide their child or adolescent with whatever information they feel should be communicated about why they are to be at the clinic. Some client families do not know how to approach this situation, however, and clinic staff can provide valuable guidance in this area. We believe that, whenever feasible, school-age children and adolescents should be informed of the appointment and its purpose before being brought to the clinic. For example, the child may be told that he or she will be seen at the clinic in order to help the child and his or her family deal with problems the child may be having in relationships with other family members. Despite the fact that some school-age or adolescent clients may react negatively to news of an upcoming clinic appointment, we feel it is their right to know in advance about their potential involvement in clinic activities. Further, advance notice allows the client's family time to discuss undue anxieties and subdue unnecessary fears. The situation with preschool-age clients is less clear-cut. For some children, advance information about a clinic appointment may have little or no meaning. If the preschool child has adequate comprehension skills, however, prior preparation may result in less anxiety than for them to arrive at a new and strange facility peopled with unknown adults. Those children with extensive and sometimes aversive medical histories (e.g., shots) may become anxious on arrival if not prepared in advance, because they may think that they are to be treated medically.

How far in advance should children and adolescents be told about the appointment? Usually 1–3 days' advance notice is sufficient. The client family is generally able to predict their child's reaction to the appointment information. For example, if the child or adolescent is being brought to the clinic because of extreme worrying or anxious behavior, it would probably be in the child's best interest to tell him or her about the appointment no more than one day beforehand, to minimize the buildup of possible stress. Little research is available on issues related to informing children and adolescents of the purposes for intake, evaluation, or testing, of what may occur during the evaluation, or when notices of scheduled appointments should be given. Clinic staff will need to establish procedures for helping client families deal with these issues.

ADMINISTRATIVE TASKS PRIOR TO THE INITIAL APPOINTMENT

Case Assignments

Once the first appointment has been scheduled, assignment of appropriate clinic staff is necessary. Case assignments for staff may be the responsibility of one person (e.g., clinic director, clinic supervisor, or full-time intake coordinator), or the responsibility may be rotated among other clinic staff. In larger clinics, intake assignment teams may review intake information and make assignments to clinicians according to their areas of expertise and availability. In a clinic facility where only a few staff members are available to provide services or where clinicians are assigned clients on an as-available basis, case assignments will be somewhat easier, but as the number of staff members and disciplines increases, the task may be more complex. Clinician assignments are discussed more fully in Chapter 8.

When more than one staff member is to be assigned to one client, there are two options on how cliet interactions will take place: a) all clinicians involved may meet with the client and client family as a team and carry out assessments in a team approach (an interdisciplinary team approach), or b) each team member may meet individually with the client and client family for independent assessment/evaluation (a multidisciplinary approach). There are, of course, possible variations (i.e., two of the team members may conduct assessments together while a third team member conducts independent assessments). Whatever the types of teams, team members should have opportunities to meet as a team after conducting assessments, in order to integrate information obtained. (This is discussed more fully in Chapter 6).

Whether a clinic is staffed with only one interdisciplinary or multidisciplinary team, or teams are assigned from a clinical pool, team assignments may be rotated among clinicians. Further, depending on the services needed, not all disciplines need to be assigned to every case. When teams are assigned to cases, team leaders may be chosen either by those making team assignments or by team members. Some teams operate without a team leader; if so, another clinic staff member should be assigned to coordinate team functioning and serve as a liaison between the client family and the team.

Clinicians' Preappointment Responsibilities

Before the first client appointment, clinicians assigned to provide client services should review the information contained in the client case record file, including any client data that has been collected. Whenever an interdisciplinary team has been assigned to provide services, it is advisable for the team to meet to plan the first appointment after each team member has had an opportunity to review the client file. A case supervisor may also be included in team meetings. In addition to allocating specific team member responsibilities at a team meeting, decisions may be made on what assessments and assessment approaches are to be used.

Scheduling of Clinic Rooms

Prior to the first client visit, service providers need to schedule shared clinic rooms or offices for use (i.e., whenever clients are not to be seen in private offices or treatment rooms designated for use by individual clinicians). Ideally, clinicians would be assigned to individual offices and treatment areas, but this is not usually the case when there are more than a few clinicians in the clinic. If a number of clinicians are on staff and providing services within the same time periods, and there are limited clinic treatment rooms, room scheduling may be accomplished by use of a reservation schedule placed in a central area. Alternatively, room assignments could be made by a staff member who has access to a central appointment schedule or who is responsible for appointment scheduling.

Clinic Intake Schedule

Preparation of a clinic intake schedule (e.g., weekly or monthly), may be useful in clinics staffed by more than one or two clinicians. An intake schedule could be in the form of a master schedule maintained in a central area, such as an appointment book. In a large facility, copies of the schedule could be distributed to clinicians and other appropriate staff members (e.g., supervisor). Because of the need to protect client confidentiality, it is recommended that client names only be included on the master schedule and not on any intake schedules distributed to clinic staff. Instead, client file numbers or a type of coding system should be used. An advantage of disseminating individual copies of an intake schedule to clinicians is that it provides them with both information on their case assignments as well as those of other clinicians, making it easier to arrange conferences or meetings and to schedule clinic rooms. A sample intake schedule form is shown in Form 4.8.

Tasks and Procedures to Be Conducted with Client Families

Before a child or adolescent client is seen by a clinician, the client family needs to be involved in certain tasks and procedures. These will usually take place during the first appointment, but some tasks may be completed prior to that time.

1. It is essential that the parent or legal guardian sign a consent for the clinical services to be provided to the child or adolescent. No services should be provided unless this consent has been obtained. A copy of a form for this purpose is shown in Form 4.9.
2. Other forms deemed necessary for the clinic should be obtained, including: a) requests for release of records from other sources, b) requests for release

Intake Schedule

Week of: _____

Date	Time	Client	Age	Case coordinator	Team members	Suggested assessments	Referral source	Room number

FORM 4.9

Consent for Clinical Evaluation-Treatment
Services/Release Information

Having been informed about the testing, diagnostic, and clinical services provided by the _____ Clinic, I _____ hereby consent for _____ to receive all those services deemed necessary to the clinical staff. I understand and agree that such services will be undertaken within the guidelines of ethical standards established for such services.

I have also been informed and understand that the results of the evaluation and/or treatment will be used to provide assistance to better understand and meet his or her needs. I therefore consent to releasing the results of the evaluation to authorized persons at the Clinic. I also consent to releasing the evaluation results to a referral agency representative or to the referral agency _____ if that agency has made the referral for evaluation and is assuming responsibility for fee payment.

Date: _____   _____
                                                   Signature

                                                   _____
                                                   Witness

of records or information from the clinic to other sources, c) billing payment agreements, and d) background information forms.

3. A clinic staff member should verbally review a client rights agreement with the parent or legal guardian, and also with the child or adolescent client under certain circumstances (see Chapter 11 for a fuller discussion of client rights).

CLIENT-RELATED ISSUES

Client Perceptions of the Clinic and Staff

The clinic setting is ''home territory'' for clinic staff, but not so for clients. In a sense client staff may be seen as hosts, and clients as guests. Client perceptions of the clinic and staff may be greatly influenced by the way procedures are introduced and clarified by staff and by courtesies extended to them. It is important that all staff realize how their interactions with clients and their families may affect the entire clinical process. In situations where clients are routed to a number of different individuals for screening and administrative purposes, clients and their families will have formed some opinions of the clinic operation before ever meeting a clinician.

Client families and clients who have had few or no experience with psychological services or facilities are likely to be quite apprehensive about what will be expected of them and what will be involved in the clinical process. Child and adolescent clients are particularly vulnerable in this respect. Initial positive interactions with clinic staff can help to reduce client and client family apprehension.

Meeting the Clinician

Clinicians assigned to clients may not be involved in procedures associated with initial contact, acquisition of preliminary referral information, or other administrative tasks. If not, their first meeting with children/adolescents and parents/legal guardians will follow clinic admissions procedures either on the same day or on another day. Introductions to clients may be made by the clinicians themselves if clients have been directed to their offices or treatment rooms, or if it is clinic practice to have clinicians greet clients in waiting room areas. Otherwise, clinicians may be introduced to clients by receptionists or secretaries.

The initial meeting of the clinician and parent or legal guardian may or may not include the child or adolescent child (this issue is also discussed in Chapter 6). Inclusion of the child or adolescent at this first appointment may be decided on the basis of: a) standard clinic practice, b) a case-by-case basis appraisal, c) clinician preference, or d) client family request.

If the child/adolescent is not to be included in this first meeting he or she may either: a) not accompany the family to the clinic on the day of the meeting, b) be involved in assessment procedures with other clinicians as an alternative, or c) be placed under supervision of other clinic staff and provided with play or reading materials.

Client/Client Family Courtesies

Setting the Stage for Professional Relationships

The way individuals are introduced and how they address one another often defines their relationships. Thus, adult friendship is more likely fostered with the use of first names, while professional relationships often involve the use of titles and last names between adults. How should this be handled in a clinic setting?

Clinicians usually have a preference for how they would like to be addressed. Client family members have preferences also. Usually, both adult client family members and clinical staff will initially refer to one another by titles and last names (e.g., Dr. Smith, Mrs. Jones). We prefer this approach, as it seems to set the stage initially for the purpose of the appointment, that is, the professional business at hand. Less frequently, all adults present in a clinic setting may address one another on a first-name basis at the first meeting. If the relationships continue over an extended period of time, however, first name usage may or may not become the usual way of referring to one another. Then, too, some clinicians prefer to address adult client family members by their first names, yet wish to be addressed themselves by title and last name. This approach tends to suggest bilevel status that may not be conducive to communication. Typically, clinicians address the child or adolescent client by their first name, even though it may be expected that the child or adolescent client will address them by their title and last name. Similar identification practices may be followed by all clinic staff in one clinic, or the practices may vary among clinicians, depending on personal preference. Thus, clinicians set the stage for relationships with clients and their families by the way they handle initial introductions.

Client/Family Comfort

Another area requiring clinician sensitivity pertains to the physical comfort of clients and their families. Clinical staff should be alert to the affect that room temperature, room lighting, and seating accommodations and arrangements may have on clients and their families, and should correct uncomfortable situations whenever they occur if at all possible, not only as a courtesy to clients but to minimize potential distractions from clinical issues. Frequently, only minor changes can bring about a maximum comfort level. For example, we have often observed that in a winter climate client family members may not remove their coats and gloves while in the room with a clinician until invited to do so. If clinicians do not extend this courtesy, clients may become overheated and distracted from clinical issues. Physical discomfort may also occur for some clients if they are: a) seated directly facing windows, so that they experience glare from outside light, b) seated in a draft, or c) straining to hear a clinician because of extraneous noise factors such as a room air conditioner. These and other clinic situations that could produce discomforts for clients and their families may be easily eliminated or reduced by action taken by the clinical staff.

Break Needs

Another courtesy that should be extended to clients by clinical staff is attention to break needs (e.g., for drinks, toileting, or "to stretch their legs." Breaks are particularly important for children and adolescents, and staff should be alert to signals from clients that breaks may be needed. Parents/legal guardians also should be informed of clinic facilities available near the clinical intake areas (e.g., restroom locations). When younger children are involved in the clinical intake, parents/legal guardians should be asked to inform the clinical staff when their child may need breaks.

Communication with Client Families and Clients

Clinical staff often overlook the need to inform clients or client families about clinical procedures. Ongoing communication with clients by clinical staff can prevent or minimize uncertainties about the procedures being followed or mistrust of the clinicians. For example, a written negative evaluation by a parent of a clinic experience referred to "secretive staff interactions" observed by the parent during her child's evaluation. The "secretive" interactions actually involved a trainee being asked by a supervisor to leave the observation room where the parent was observing, so that the trainee could be given instructions. In this situation, the parent assumed that the supervisor and trainee were discussing her child negatively. Misinterpretation of such a situation could have been avoided if the parent had been informed prior to the assessment that supervisor-trainee interactions might occur during the assessment and the purpose and format for such interactions.

SUMMARY

This chapter has included guidelines for maintaining clinic visibility in the community and for processing inquiries and client referrals. Suggestions were included for establishing client admissions criteria, client fees, fee collection practices, and other administrative tasks preparatory to initial client appointments. Other client-related issues were also covered, including client preparation and courtesies.

READER ACTIVITIES

We suggest that you volunteer and arrange to carry out one of the marketing activities provided in this chapter to maintain or expand clinic visibility. You could also plan a week of marketing activities with other staff members if you are in a clinic with a large staff.

In order to find out how much time and effort is involved for parents/guardians to complete preappointment information forms requested by your clinic, try completing a set of forms yourself. If your clinic does not use such forms, obtain them from other sources and review them to see which forms you might wish to adopt or modify for your clinic.

It is also suggested that you set aside some time to review your client fee schedules and fee collection practices to determine whether or not these should be updated and/or revised. You could obtain current fee schedules from other local clinics and private practitioners for comparison purposes.

REFERENCES

American Psychiatric Association. (1980). *Diagnostic and statistical manual of mental disorders: DSM-III*. Washington, DC: Author.

American Psychological Association. (1981). Ethical principles of psychologists. *American Psychologist, 36*(6), 633–638.

Christian, W. P., & Hannah, G. T. (1983). *Effective management in human services*. Englewood Cliffs, NJ: Prentice-Hall.

Dorken, H. (1983). Health insurance and third party reimbursement. In B. D. Sales (Ed.), *The professional psychologist's handbook*. (pp. 249–284). New York: Plenum.

Faustman, W. O. (1982). Legal and ethical issues in debt collection strategies of professional psychologists. *Professional Psychology, 13*(3), 208–214.

Jones, S. E. (1982). How to collect insurance reimbursement. In P. A. Keller & L. G. Ritt (Eds.), *Innovations in clinical practice: A source book* (Vol. 1, pp. 184–193). Sarasota, FL: Professional Resources Exchange.

Taube, C. A., Burns, B. J., & Kessler, L. (1984). Patients of psychiatrists and psychologists in office-based practice: 1980. *American Psychologist, 29*(12), 1435–1447.

U.S. Department of Health and Human Services. (1980). *International classification of diseases: 9th revision: Clinical modification*. Washington, DC: Author.

5

Family Involvement in Assessment/Evaluation, Treatment, and Training

The purpose of this chapter is to provide you with information on:
1. The importance of psychological services and related services to children and adolescents
2. The family of the client as active participants in client assessment/evaluation and treatment
3. Family issues pertinent to children and adolescents
4. Child/adolescent issues that affect the family
5. Client family training and consultation

DEFINING THE CLIENT'S FAMILY

In this chapter the term *client's family* is used to describe: a) one or more adults who are legally responsible for the child or adolescent client; b) those adults not legally responsible for the client, but who are directly involved in interactions with the client in a home setting; and c) those individuals of minor age who live in the same residence as the client.

It is no longer relevant or realistic to view the family of the client as a unit composed only of biological parents and siblings from the same set of parents. Instead, today's family structure encompasses a wide diversity of family constellations and role functions, an issue discussed more fully later in this chapter.

THE FAMILY AS A SOCIAL SYSTEM

Levant (1984) describes the family as a social system, generally the first social system to which an individual is exposed. A child learns to act and react within the context of the family social system. Each family establishes its own communication system and expends extensive energy to maintain it. Clinicians should learn as much as they can about family systems and their effect upon individual members. Doing so will not only help you understand the origin of many problems of children and adolescents and the role of the family in these problems and may also suggest potential intervention strategies. Levant (1984) provides extensive information on different theories about how families are organized, how they contribute to pathology in children and adolescents, and how to assist them to produce positive changes.

THE IMPORTANCE OF PSYCHOLOGICAL SERVICES

The importance of psychological and related services to children and adolescents cannot be overemphasized in terms of facilitating these individuals' optimal development and adjustment to the family and to daily living. Problems of children and adolescents are typically identified early, but appropriate services may not be identified, provided, or even available (Knitzer, 1984). It is estimated that from 1 to 33 out of every 100 children and adolescents have some type of psychological maladjustment (Gelfand, Jenson, & Drew, 1982). The President's Commission on Mental Health has estimated that 5% to 15% of all children and adolescents need some type of mental health service (Knitzer, 1984). Yet, only one in three children identified as exhibiting serious emotional disturbance is receiving mental health service (National Council of Community Mental Health Centers, 1986).

The problems encountered by children and adolescents as they develop today are much more complex than in the past. Until the last 25 years, the typical family in this country had two parents and several children, and provided its members with affection, status, education, religious orientation, protection, recreation, and economic status (Olson & Habenstein, 1983). With time, the traditional concept of the family changed as industrialization and changing social standards decreased family control. In addition, today one in two marriages ends in divorce; and one in two children is being raised in a single-parent home or in a reconstituted family as parents remarry or live with other partners. One of every two children is also being raised in a family where both parents are working (Bernard, 1981), and the number of working mothers is rapidly increasing (Smith, 1979). Nor are closely knit extended families common (Olson & Habenstein, 1983). Often the nearest relative is hundreds of miles away and is not available for support and help. Thus, many families have become more isolated (Bronfenbrenner, 1980).

In sum, today's families are experiencing increased stress as a result of many factors including disintegration of the extended family, increased mobility, mothers who are working, high divorce rates, changes in childbearing practices, and loss of paternal power (Olson & Habenstein, 1983). These factors combined can result in immense psychological pressures on children and adolescents—for instance, coping with the absence of one parent while the other parent works and while also adjusting to a new neighborhood. Family stresses may lead to child abuse and neglect, lack of parent availability for support and training, dissonance in the family, increased childhood loneliness and isolation, and lack of personal guidance. Eisenberg (1979) points out that socially isolated children are more likely to become emotionally disturbed or physically ill than are children from intact families, and Patterson (1977) notes that children with inadequate family support systems are less effective in coping with life stresses. Due to these conditions, the need for psychological services has increased dramatically in the last 20 years (Olson & Habenstein, 1983). The types of services needed have also become more complex. Many children are dealing with problems associated with factors such as joint custody in which they live alternately in two homes and are interacting with stepparents and/or individuals not directly related. Such alternative life-styles and divergent family types, in addition to the complexity of problems faced by children and youth, require that service providers be trained to deal with a wider range of concerns than in the past. Providers must strive to provide comprehensive quality services with existing resources. The needed services may often involve individuals from several disciplines or agencies; thus, coordination becomes increasingly important. Service providers must be prepared to conduct interviews and assessments and to design, implement, and evaluate individualized treatment programs for a diversity of problems ranging from simple temper tantrums, to psychosis, to child custody, to extreme aggression and destruction of property, to a search for a "direction" in life. The task faced by the practitioner can seem mind boggling. Sales (1983) points out that to deliver psychological services today, it is no longer sufficient simply to be a competent professional. Additional information is needed in many areas including: a) standards of professional practice, b) operation of professional organizations such as the American Psychological Association, c) current professional developments, d) laws affecting professional practice, e) legal regulations related to the business aspects of service delivery, f) legal regulations of one's own profession, g) regulation of clients, h) managerial and business skills, i) values and interests that affect professional decision making, and j) political processes (Sales, 1983).

THE FAMILY AS ACTIVE PARTICIPANTS

Involvement in Client Referral

As discussed in Chapter 4, parents or legal guardians are usually the primary referral agents for child/adolescent clients. A difficult task for most parents/guardians is deciding when to seek psychological assistance for their child or the family. Reluctance to seek services may be related to a number of factors, including: a) most parents/guardians have not had prior contact with psychologists or clinics that provide psychological and related services, b) there continues to be a stigma attached to seeking assistance for psychological or mental health problems, and c) parents/guardians may not know what is normal child/adolescent behavior or what behaviors indicate the need for professional intervention. Some guidelines for use with parents/guardians in seeking psychological assistance are presented in Table 5.1.

Involvement in Assessment/Evaluation

Families of clients are primary sources of information about the referred clients. Their involvement is also ethically and legally mandatory (see Chapter 11 for more on this issue). Although the parent usually most actively involved in the

Table 5.1. Indications for parents seeking assistance

1. When the child appears to be unhappy and/or moody most of the time. This is often expressed by the child crying, not being interested in engaging in activities, and/or sleeping excessively.
2. When the child cannot seem to make or keep friends.
3. When the child is having ongoing problems at school.
4. When the child goes from one activity to the next, never completing a task, and never attending to anything or anyone for more than a few seconds.
5. When the child deliberately destroys property, hurts others, and breaks known rules.
6. When the child seems to live in a world of his or her own and is not responsive to others or is overly attached to someone.
7. When the child has uncontrollable temper tantrums or fits of anger.
8. When the parent does not know how to manage the child's behavior.
9. When the parent has or feels like abusing the child.
10. When the parent is having problems that interfere with family harmony.
11. When the parent has difficulty showing love and affection to the child.
12. When the parent does not understand the behavior of the child or questions if certain behavior is normal.
13. When the parent has difficulty communicating with or deciding what are realistic expectations of the child.
14. When the parent realizes that the child has a problem but the child is unwilling to discuss it with the parent.

assessment/evaluation has traditionally been the client's mother or individual assuming this role, there has been a trend in recent years toward increased involvement of fathers (both biological and adoptive—e.g., stepfathers). Other family members are also often active contributors to the evaluation, and should be included whenever: a) referral concerns are directly associated with general or specific interpersonal conflicts, b) the client's problems appear to be associated with problems in family functioning or dynamics, or c) it is anticipated that such individuals may need to be included in the treatment to be provided. The degree of involvement of family members in the evaluation and the specific techniques used with them is dependent on their individual competencies and capabilities. For example, if a child is referred because of concerns about apparent hyperactive behavior, it may not be necessary to include other children in the family in the evaluation, unless they have relevant information to offer (i.e., they feel that the problem is disruptive in their lives).

Involvement in Treatment

Active involvement of the client's family may occur in one of the following ways: a) by providing direct treatment to the client, b) by participating in treatment with the client, or c) by providing support to the client while treatment is provided by professionals.

Providing Direct Treatment

Parents and other significant adults are often designated to be direct treatment providers when asked to implement treatment in the home or other environmental settings. Whenever parents are to provide direct treatment to children, the service provider functions mainly as a consultant, providing training to the parent prior to treatment implementation, modifying treatment procedures as needed, and monitoring treatment implementation on a regular basis. The direct treatment model is used primarily when changes in the provider's behavior are being implemented in conjunction with the referred client's behavior change. In essence, parent behavior needs to change if child behavior is to change relative to the parent. For example, a parent may be trained to increase a child's compliant behavior by providing positive consequences for instances of desired behavior in addition to receiving training in how to deal with noncompliant behavior.

Participation in Client Treatment

Family members of clients are often included either throughout treatment or at various times during its course. Any and all family members might be included. For example, some therapists with a psychodynamic orientation prefer to involve family members of all ages in therapy sessions. On the other hand, therapists utilizing a behavior contracting approach would likely include only those family members (e.g., parents and teenagers) who have the ability to comprehend what they are agreeing to in accepting contract terms. In general, involvement of family members occurs through: a) participating in therapy sessions (e.g., family therapy, dyadic therapy); b) participating in contracting arrangements (see Chapter 7 for an extensive discussion of this treatment approach); and c) assisting in client training (e.g., assertiveness training, *in vivo* phobia sessions). The involvement of relevant adult family members in actual treatment has some advantages such as: a) maintaining client compliance during treatment, b) improving communication among client and family members, and c) not pinpointing the client as the sole target problem.

Pinpointing Support during Client Treatment

If family members of clients are not directly involved in providing direct treatment or participating in treatment (e.g., when a client is receiving individual psychotherapy), they can still be effective in supporting the client during treatment. This can be done by: a) visiting the client if hospitalized (e.g., following a suicide attempt), b) being sensitive about the client's problems (e.g., not teasing the client about a bed-wetting problem, c) communicating caring to the client in small ways, (d) encouraging client participating in treatment, and e) acknowledging positive efforts and changes exhibited by the client even for minor improvements. Clinicians can assist individual family members in identifying specific ways they may be supportive of the client's treatment and of the client directly during treatment.

FAMILY ISSUES THAT AFFECT THE CHILD/ADOLESCENT

As part of a family constellation, children and adolescents are affected by circumstances or events that occur within the family, or to the whole family or its members. They are particularly vulnerable to situations or factors that have a negative impact on their ability to function in their daily lives. The more directly they are personally affected, the greater the impact on their lives, especially if singled out as a target for negative action. Of all family issues that may affect a child or adolescent, child abuse from other family members can be one of the most damaging psychologically.

Child Abuse

Whether or not the incidence of child abuse has increased in the United States, the problem has become a national concern as individual cases have received prominent publicity. The reported experience by several clinics is that many children and adolescents referred for psychological services are present or past victims of some form of child abuse. Only too frequently the abuse has been perpetrated on them by parents or other family members. The term *child abuse* is now mainly considered to involve either or both aggressive or violent action resulting in inflicted physical damage to the child or adolescent or their involvement in sexual activity initiated by others.

Clinical Management

Clinicians may become involved with children or adolescents who are child abuse victims in at least two ways. First, a client may be referred because of other problems, and during clinical interactions it is revealed that there is ongoing child abuse. Second, clients may be referred to the clinic after having been identified as child abuse victims, either of recent or past occurrence. If child abuse is identified during clinical interactions, clinic staff have no alternative than to report abuse to appropriate authorities (see Chapter 11 for more specific information). This could preclude further interactions between clinicians, client, and client families, depending on: a) whether an agreement can be negotiated with legally responsible authorities for the clinic to provide services (e.g., family therapy, as needed); b) whether the referral was initiated by an agency or parent (e.g., if by a parent, the referral may have been initiated so that the problem could be brought into the open, whereas, if by an agency, there may be parental anger toward the clinician or clinic for reporting the child abuse); c) subsequent actions taken by the legal authorities involved (e.g., removal of the child or adolescent from the home environment); or d) whether the parents were informed at the outset of intervention on the limits of confidentiality, including reporting requirements in the case of child abuse (see Chapter 11 for more information). Clients who have been abused, physically or sexually, may be referred to the clinic for: a) individual treatment to help them deal with negative psychological reactions that may be interfering with current functioning, and b) family therapy with other family members to restructure family dynamics.

Other Family Issues

A number of other circumstances that affect the family negatively from within or without also may affect the child or adolescent's mental health. At the same time, some adverse conditions may affect adult family members to the point that child abuse ensues. Among these family issues are:

1. Changes and adjustments in family constellation or in extended families, including parent separation or divorce, death, birth of a new family member, or additions or deletions of individuals to the family (e.g., new stepparent, grandparent coming to live with the family, or older child moving out of the home)
2. Anticipated or real changes in physical or mental status of family members, including terminal illness and accidents or disabilities to family members or to the referred client
3. Environmental changes, including family move to new location, school changes, parent who did not work previously taking employment, or new child care arrangement
4. Economic changes, including parent's loss of employment, increased expense burden (health problems, child going off to college), decreased income
5. Communication problems, including parental overuse of "you messages" (e.g., "Why did *you* drop that egg?) instead of "*I* messages" (e.g., "I like it when you are careful putting the eggs away") (Gordon, 1981) or lack of/or inconsistent house rules and expectations
6. Poor parenting, including parents who are overly restrictive or overly permissive, parents who do not attend to positive behavior but do attend to negative behavior, and parents who lack behavior management and nurturing skills
7. Stressed families, including those in which a parent is an alcoholic, is drug dependent, is mentally ill, or where a child has a handicap (e.g., autism)

The degree to which any single or multiple family issue that is perceived as negative directly affects the function of minor-age clients is dependent upon: a) how directly the clients' own lives are affected, b) how aware they are of the impact on other family members, c) how other familiy members deal with issues, d) how helpless they feel about alleviating family stress, and (e) what access they have to other resources. How any, or a combination of these and other factors, may be associated with child or adolescent problems is unclear. Yet children and adolescents do not live in isolation and so must develop coping strategies, not always positive, to deal with issues that surround them. Clinicians need to be informed of family circumstances that may be having an impact on their clients in order to properly weigh results obtained during assessment/evaluation and treatment.

CLIENT/ADOLESCENT ISSUES THAT AFFECT THE FAMILY

Just as the child or adolescent may react to family issues, family members may be affected by problems of the minor-age client whether resulting from single events (e.g., teenage pregnancy revelation), ongoing circumstances (e.g., child hyperactivity), or temporary situations (e.g., adjustments to short-term placement of an adolescent in a residential setting). The degree to which family members may react to a child or adolescent's problems may be influenced by one or more of the following factors: a) the severity of the child's problems and prognosis for change; b) the longevity of problems, c) family disruption and disharmony, d) respite or support from other family members or from outside the family, e) coping strategies of individual family members, and f) financial resources available. Information on family functioning is useful to the clinician in order to determine who is, or are, the primary clients, and to evaluate possible treatment alternatives (see Chapter 7 for discussion of this issue).

A sensitive issue for clinicians concerns being a bearer of unwelcome news. It is not unusual for clinicians to discover or have revealed to them by the minor-age client information about the client that will potentially adversely affect the client's family or individual members. Aside from issues related to revealing confidential communications (see Chapter 11), clinicians must at times impart information to family members that may result in strong emotional reactions (e.g., sadness, anger). There is no one, or easy, way to do this, but it is helpful if clinicians can be direct, but not blunt, in conveying the information, as well as supportive of family members' reactions by allowing them to express their feelings. Probably one of the most difficult tasks for service providers in child/adolescent clinics is to reveal information to family members about their child that has long-range effects for the child as well as the family (such as a diagnosis of mental retardation or autism).

ROLES OF THE PRIMARY CAREGIVER AND CHILD/ADOLESCENT

Clinicians need to have a concept of what the role of a primary caregiver should involve in order that: a) they may assess the adequacy of the child/adolescent client's parent/guardian functioning, and b) they may determine whether family training should be provided. The child/adolescent has a right to expect the following from his or her primary caregivers:

1. To receive at least the minimal level of physical comforts (e.g., food, shelter, and clothing)
2. To receive at least the minimum level of nurturance (e.g., love, affection, and acceptance)
3. To be taught at least the minimal level of rules necessary to function in society (e.g., right from wrong, respecting the rights and property of others, do unto others as you would have them do unto you)
4. To have limits set and enforced that will protect them (e.g., not allowing playing in busy streets or going off with strangers)
5. To have fostered the development of a positive self-concept by receiving attention to and comments about their positive attributes and behavior rather than always focusing on negatives (e.g., ''John, you sure can run fast.'' or ''Susie, that's a nice picture you drew.'')

6. To understand and have communicated realistic expectations of them and for those expectations to change appropriately as a child grows older (e.g., expecting a child to make a bed may be unrealistic at 3 years of age, but not at 12 years of age; expecting a child of 6 to be in bed at 8:00 P.M. may be realistic, but not one who is 12)

Clinicians also need to know what parents/guardians have a right to expect from their child in a normally functioning household. Such awareness provides a frame of reference for determining the extent of client deviance from fulfillment of an appropriate child role. Primary caregivers should realistically expect the child to:

1. Contribute to the physical well being of the family within his or her means (e.g., assume responsibility for chores around the home)
2. Contribute to the emotional and psychological well-being of the family (e.g., show affection—requires modeling of similar behaviors by parents)
3. Learn to follow the rules of society (e.g., not break things that belong to others)
4. Adhere to limits set by parents and learn to negotiate new limits as he or she grows older
5. Become the best person possible by thinking and speaking well of himself or herself (e.g., learning that self-talk often determines how one feels about oneself)
6. Adhere to realistic expectations and negotiate when expectations seem unfair, realizing that everyone must do some things in life that they would prefer not to do (e.g., making one's own bed at a certain age)

Many psychological problems in children and adolescents are the result of a breakdown in the child's or parents' ability to perform properly their respective roles. For example, a parent who does not provide for the physical comforts of a child can lose the child to state jurisdiction via neglect laws, which can result in problems for the child when placed in a foster home. Likewise a child who does not adhere to the rules of society (e.g., destroying property), can find himself or herself isolated from others.

TRAINING FOR THE CLIENT'S FAMILY

Family members may be given individual or group training in order that: a) they may interact more effectively with their child or adolescent, b) they may, in turn, provide training to the child or adolescent, (c) family functioning may be improved (i.e., communication skills training), and d) their own interpersonal skills are improved (e.g., assertiveness training). Training differs from therapy in that participants are provided instruction on a selected topic, usually involving a sequence of tasks or skills to be learned. Training also typically involves practice in both the instructional setting and in other environmental settings.

The type of training that may be offered in a clinic depends on:

1. Training topics of interest or need
2. Size of staff and staff expertise
3. Capabilities and competencies of trainees
4. Alternative training options or resources
5. Time and cost factors

Individual Family Training

Training provided to one or more members of a family group is advantageous in that: a) it can apply directly to issues of primary importance to trainees, b) it may be modified in order to adapt to changes occurring during training, c) the arrangements for training sessions can be somewhat flexible (i.e., different family members involved at different times, sessions increased as needed or time intervals between sessions increased), d) trainees receive the full attention of trainers during training sessions, and e) home practice assignments can be individualized.

Group Training

The introduction of family members into a group training situation has advantages for both the clinician and family members, including: a) staff time can be more effectively used across individuals, b) costs for group training sessions can be lower than for individual sessions, c) family members benefit from hearing about similar problems in other families and solutions or coping strategies used to deal with them, d) group members provide support and approval to other members in acquiring and using training techniques, and e) training may be enhanced by having enough group members to practice with one another. Obviously, some of the advantages of group training would be disadvantages in individual training and vice versa. However, there are some potential disadvantages in group training that would not need to be addressed in individual training such as: a) maintaining regular group attendance, b) differences among group members in acquisition of skills, c) group personality differences and possible friction or tensions, and d) confidentiality of information about group members. Each of these issues can be detrimental to training. For example, absentees miss segments of training that may preclude them from advancing in their training unless there are opportunities for make-up sessions. Otherwise, group members may be delayed in their training while earlier training content is repeated. Also, there are more demands on the trainer in group training to ensure that all group members have equal time. Frequently, some group members are more verbal than others which may result in group disharmony. A team of trainers (e.g., two per group) is invaluable in addressing such issues.

Training Topics

A variety of training topics would be suitable for training family members and/or clients. Probably the one most frequently covered with parents and legal guardians is behavior management, possibly because often a preferred treatment strategy for many referral problems (e.g., hyperactivity, conduct problems) requires that family members change their behavior (see also Chapter 7). A number of other topics would also be appropriate for training, such as problem-solving skills, communication, family negotiation, and contracting.

Training Programs

Commercial training programs are available that are suitable for clinic use. Commercial programs not only save staff time in preparing and assembling training materials but can be reused repeatedly. The only expense for reuse of some programs is that of replacing consumable materials, usually at a minimal cost. Although initial costs of some commercial programs represent a major investment, this can be offset by their reusability. Many commercial programs include a variety of teaching aids (e.g., videotapes, films, audiotapes, as well as instructor manuals and printed materials). Some examples of programs available are: a) *Communication Workshop for Parents and Adolescents* (Brownstone & Dye, 1973), b) *Systematic Parent Training* (Miller, 1975), c) *The Art of Parenting* (Wagonseller & McDowell, 1977), d) *Teaching Involved Parenting (TIP)* (Wagonseller & McDowell, 1982), e) *Assertion Training Series* (Guerra, Cotler, & Cotler, 1976), f) *Helping the Noncompliant Child* (Forehand & McMahon, 1981), g) *Parent Effectiveness Training (PET)* (Gordon, 1970), h) *Winning!* (Dangel & Polster, 1979, and i) *Systematic Training for Effective Parenting (STEP)* (Dinkmeyer & McKay, 1976).

Clinics that serve only a limited number of clients may not want to invest in commercial programs, preferring to develop their own instead. Training programs can be developed by staff on topics that satisfy client need or interest and can be reused or modified as necessary for use with other client family members. In fact, many commercially available training programs originated in clinic settings and were later published for a wider audience. One advantage of developing in-house training programs is that they can incorporate skill training specifically appropriate to the recipients. A common question is: How can program developers know where to begin training? That is, at what level would training be appropriate for trainees? One way to determine this is to give trainees pretests on the training topic. Other ways are through: a) role play situations, b) interviews, and c) *in vivo* observations.

Training Evaluation

Training effectiveness can be evaluated by: a) readministration of the pretest following training to determine gains, b) reviewing assignments given to trainees to be completed outside of the training sessions, and c) trainee demonstration of skills acquired in training sessions.

Individual Consultation

Family members may participate in individual consultations with clinicians without the child/adolescent client present. Consultation may occur for a number of reasons, including: a) to provide family members with support while the child or adolescent is receiving ongoing treatment (e.g., individual therapy), b) to help family members cope with new problems as they arise, c) to acquaint family members with client progress during treatment, and d) to help family members deal with their personal problems or as follow-up counseling on an as-needed basis after the client treatment has been terminated. The counseling format differs from the training format in that it does not typically involve the teaching of skills through a didactic or systematic approach.

Psychiatric Consultation

If a part-time psychiatrist is available to the clinic (i.e., there are no full-time psychiatrists on staff), arrangements may be made for family members to consult with the psychiatrist about their child's psychiatric problems, particularly when medication has been prescribed. Such consultation is also useful if the child has a medical problem, such as asthma or seizures, in addition to psychological problems.

SUMMARY

Children and adolescents both affect and are affected by the family social system; thus, clinicians should understand family systems. Since children and adolescents do not often seek psychological services on their own, family members, particularly parents, are the most common referral source. Service providers should see family members as both a source of information and a resource for effective intervention. Parents and other family members, as appropriate, should be involved in assessment and intervention services to children and adolescents to the degree that it is beneficial to client progress. Often parents will receive training and will implement intervention programs in the home with support services provided to parents by the therapist. A variety of different family interventions is possible and appropriate. To change child and adolescent behavior, parents must often first change their own behavior.

READER ACTIVITIES

Describe the communication system of your family of origin. Now describe that of a client you have recently served. How do the two compare? List three family training procedures that you have found useful in working with clients. Which of these approaches might have been useful for the parents of one of your clients? Describe five ways families cause psychological difficulties for their children and adolescents and three ways children and adolescents cause stress for their families.

REFERENCES

Bernard, J. (1981). The good provider role. *American Psychologist, 36*(1), 1–12.

Brofenbrenner, U. (1980). On making human beings human. *Character, 2*(2), 1–7.

Brownstone, J. E., & Dye, C. D. (1973). *Communication workshop for parents and adolescents.* Champaign, Ill: Research Press.

Dangel, R. F., & Polster, R. A. (1979). *Training parenting specialists.* Arlington, TX: American Children's Foundation.

Dinkmeyer, D., & McKay, G. D. (1976). *Systematic Training for Effective Parenting (STEP).* Circle Pines, MN.: American Guidance Service.

Eisenberg, L. (1979). A friend, not an apple a day, will keep the doctor away. *The American Journal of Medicine, 66*(4), 551–553.

Forehand, R., & McMahon, R. J. (1981). *Helping the noncompliant child: A clinician's guide to parent training.* New York: Guilford Press.

Gelfand, D. M., Jenson, W. R., & Drew, C. J. (1982). *Understanding child behavior disorders.* New York: Holt, Rinehart & Winston.

Gordon, T. (1970). *PET: Parent Effectiveness Training.* New York: Peter H. Wyden.

Guerra, J. J., Cotler, S. B., & Cotler, S. M. (1976). *Assertion training series.* Champaign, IL: Research Press.

Knitzer, J. (1984). Mental health services to children and adolescents: A national view of public policies. *American Psychologist, 39*(8), 905–911.

Levant, R. F. (1984). *Family therapy: A comprehensive overview.* Englewood Cliffs, NJ: Prentice-Hall.

Miller, W. H. (1975). *Systematic parent training.* Champaign, IL: Research Press.

National Council of Community Mental Health Centers. (1986). Problems, services for teens, focus of mental health month. In *National Council News* (pp. 1–2). Rockville, MD: Author.

Olson, R., & Habenstein, R. (1983). Families and children in history. In C. E. Walker & M. C. Roberts (Eds.), *Handbook of clinical child psychology* (pp. 3–25). New York: John Wiley & Sons.

Patterson, S. (1977). Toward a conceptualization of natural helping. *Arete, 4*(3), 1–11.

Sales, B. D. (1983). The context of professional psychology. In B. D. Sales (Ed.), *The professional psychologist's handbook* (pp. 3–15). New York: Plenum.

Smith, R. E. (Ed.). (1979). *The subtle revolution.* Washington, DC: Urban Institute.

Wagonseller, B. R. & McDowell, R. L. (1977). *The art of parenting.* Champaign, IL: Research Press.

Wagonseller, B. R., & McDowell, R. L. (1982). *Teaching Involved Parenting: (TIP).* Champaign, IL: Research Press.

6

Assessment/Evaluation Practices and Procedures

The intent of this chapter is to provide you with information on:
1. Strategies commonly used in child and adolescent assessment and evaluation
2. Guidelines for selecting appropriate evaluation batteries
3. Integration of evaluation results and decision-making issues
4. Communication of assessment/evaluation results and recommendations.

Many excellent materials have been published on assessment of children and adolescents and issues related to assessment (Anastasi, 1976; Gelfand, Jenson, & Drew, 1982; Goldman, L'Engle Stein, & Guerry, 1983; Mash & Terdahl, 1981; Ollendick & Hersen, 1984; Sattler, 1982). Some of these publications have focused on specific areas of assessment such as intellectual assessment (Sattler, 1982), assessment of childhood behavioral disorders (Gelfand et al., 1982; Mash & Terdahl, 1981) or on single test instruments (Kaufman, 1979), while other publications have addressed both general issues in child or adolescent psychological assessment and specific assessment instruments (Goldman et al., 1983).

Other published materials contain descriptors and critiques of assessment materials and tests (Buros's *Mental Measurement Yearbooks,* 1938–78; Buros's *Tests in Print,* 1974). This chapter contains an overview of child and adolescent assessment/evaluation practices and procedures for use in clinics.

DEFINITIONS

The terms *assessment* and *evaluation* are used interchangeably in this chapter to describe processes used to obtain information on an individual's abilities and skills for an identified purpose or purposes. Gelfand et al. (1982) concluded after reviewing a number of published definitions of the term *assessment* that most of the definitions referred to a two-part process: a) the acquisition of information in an objective manner, and b) decision-making based on the information gathered. The term *evaluation* is defined in this chapter as a process involving "systematic assessment" (Nay, 1979).

Specific procedures used in conducting either an assessment or evaluation have been defined or described by different authors as "strategies" (Ollendick and Hersen, 1984), "approaches" (Kaufman & Reynolds, 1984), "methods" (McMahon, 1984), or "techniques." All of these terms are used interchangeably in this chapter.

PURPOSES FOR ASSESSMENT/EVALUATION REFERRALS

Children and adolescents are referred for assessment or evaluation by adults who are concerned about some aspect of functioning of the referred minor and are seeking guidance on future action. Some specific reasons for referral of children and adolescents to a clinic include: a) to determine the need for treatment or intervention services, b) for diagnosis or classification of a disorder, c) for school or residential placement and programming recommendations, or d) for child custody determination. The type of the assessment/evaluation is therefore largely influenced by the referral question or concern. For example, if the reason for referral is to obtain recommendations about the need for special education in a school placement, the assessment procedures selected by professional staff will be those most suited to provide information about abilities and skills associated with academic achievement in order that appropriate recommendations may be made. Although the focus of the assessment/evaluation process is primarily directed toward resolution of the referral question(s), it is not uncommon for professionals to identify other client-relevant issues that should also be addressed or that may even supersede the referral question issue (i.e., need for involvement of other disciplines, or other psychological problems such as depression). If other problems are identified, ethical considerations for the primary client's welfare may result in a shift of focus during the assessment/evaluation process.

Another major purpose for assessment/evaluation (discussed in Chapter 7) is that of determining treatment progress and success. Similar strategies used in initial assessment/evaluation may also be used to determine treatment progress or outcome.

ASSESSMENT/EVALUATION STRATEGIES

Numerous assessment strategies are available for acquiring information relative to the referral problem or question and to other relevant concerns. The following strategies are reviewed in this chapter:

1. Interviews (adult and child)
2. Rating scales, checklists, questionnaires and inventories
3. Self-report and self-monitoring
4. Tests (standardized and nonstandardized)
5. Behavioral observation techniques
6. Projective assessment
7. Physiological assessment

Use of multimethod assessment strategies provides the clinician with the best information on which to base recommendations (Goldman et al., 1983; Mash & Terdahl, 1981; Ollendick & Hersen, 1984). However, assessment/evaluation selection is often influenced by four major factors, discussed here first.

1. Clinic philosophy and policies
2. Professional staff expertise
3. Client characteristics
4. Availability of assessment materials

Clinic Philosophy and Policies

The clinic's philosophy and policies (discussed more fully in Chapter 1) directly influence not only the choice of assessment strategies but the ways in which strategies are used. For example, a clinic based on psychoanalytic philosophy would be unlikely to advocate use of specific behavioral observation techniques derived from a behavioral psychology orientation. Clinic policy might also dictate the use of particular assessment instruments or techniques to the exclusion of others. For example, it may be clinic policy not to use screenig tests in place of comprehensive tests.

Professional Staff Expertise

It is essential that clinicians use only those assessment tools or strategies that they have been trained to use. To do otherwise would be unethical (see sections on "General Information about Tests and Other Assessment Strategies" in this chapter, as well as Chapter 11, for further discussion of this issue). If the clinician responsible for a client is not qualified to use a particular assessment tool or strategy of choice, then other clinicians within the clinic with the necessary qualifications should be involved. Otherwise, it may be necessary to arrange for the assessment to be conducted by trained clinicians outside of the clinic. In such cases, arrangements should subsequently be made for one or more clinicians to receive training in the use of the specific assessment strategy so that future clients do not have to be referred elsewhere.

Client Characteristics

Only those assessment strategies and tools that are appropriate for use with the client should be selected. That is, selection of assessment tools should be based on client characteristics such as: a) age, b) developmental level, c) skill/ability levels, and d) socio-cultural backgrounds. Also, the necessary involvement of parents or relevant adults in the evaluation process mandates that any assessments conducted with them be compatible with their individual characteristics (e.g., educational level, cultural background, and familiarity with the client's functioning).

Availability of Assessment Materials

Selection of specific assessment tools is also influenced by tools that are available to the professional staff. Each clinic should make a concerted effort to have available the materials typically needed for the types of service to be provided. Trained staff will generally be familiar with the resource materials needed to conduct specific assessments and can recommend those that should be available for clients to be served. To ensure that appropriate and current materials are available, staff should review new assessment instruments, read current literature concerned with assessment, and have access to test catalogs from test distribution companies as well as reference books such as Buros's *Mental Measurement Yearbook* (1978). In deciding whether appropriate assessment instruments are available, a clinician can ask himself or herself questions such as: a) What information do I need to obtain for this client? b) What tests or other materials are most appropriate to provide that information? c) Which tests or other materials are available, and which of these would be most suitable for this client? d) Will it be necessary to enlist other resources, within or outside of the clinic, to obtain necessary information?

If proper assessment materials are not available, it may be possible to borrow materials from other clinics or professionals. Ultimately, however, outdated materials must be replaced and testing resources expanded so that appropriate materials are available. The more extensive the inventory of materials in the clinic, the better.

SPECIFIC ASSESSMENT/INTERVENTION STRATEGIES

Interviews

Based on the premise that the evaluation process involves the acquisition of information relevant to the referral question, the interview is considered the single most important assessment strategy. The interview is a highly popular assessment approach among professionals because it provides opportunities for the development of clinician-client relationships, which may facilitate other assessments, and also allows response elaboration that may be more restricted in other assessment approaches (Gelfand et al., 1982). The interview has been described as a situation where ''one person assumes responsibility for directing and maintaining the activity'' (Goldman et al., 1983) during an exchange of verbal material. Goldman and associates differentiate the interview from other exchanges of verbal material (i.e., social conversation), in that the interview is conducted mainly to elicit and appraise information rather than for other communication purposes.

Although most interviews will involve verbal exchange in the same language, interview situations may require an interpreter (for a client whose primary language is not English) or if the interview is nonverbal (e.g., whenever the client communicates mainly through signing or gestures). Frequently, a family member can serve as an interpreter. If not, perhaps another staff member can assist at these times. The need for an interpreter should be determined in advance, preferably when the intake appointment is scheduled.

Parent/Legal Guardian Interviews

A face-to-face initial interview with a parent/legal guardian may be conducted for one or more purposes such as: a) clarification or elaboration of information provided on forms completed before the interview; b) obtaining of developmental, social history, or other background information, either not obtained on forms or in addition to that provided on forms; c) elaboration of the reason for referral provided at the time of the initial clinic contact; d) obtaining of information pertinent to the referral question or problem. While conducting an initial interview with the referral party(ies), the clinician will also likely be engaged in: a) establishing rapport with the interviewee(s); b) developing tentative hypotheses relating to the referral question; and c) considering other assessment strategies to be pursued following the interview.

The child/adolescent client may or may not be included either during part of the initial interview or the entire interview. The advantages of including the child or adolescent client are that: a) the client hears all information provided by the adult interviewee, possibly preventing any suspicion of a conspiracy among adults that could interfere with later treatment; b) areas of agreement and disagreement between adults and minor-age clients could be ascertained (Gelfand et al., 1982); c) interactions between the adults and child or adolescent may be observed; and d) the interviewer is given an opportunity to establish a relationship with all individuals present. Disadvantages for inclusion during the entire interview are that adult interviewees: a) may be inhibited from expressing negative feelings or concerns about the child or adolescent, b) may not reveal sensitive information relevant to potential treatment, c) may be reluctant to discuss specific details concerning the referral problem, or d) may express concerns that could upset the child/adolescent client. In addition, under certain circumstances, friction between parents and the primary client may be so great that the interviewer gains little specific information.

Guidelines for Inclusion of Clients in Initial Interviews

Since little empirical data are available, we have developed, through trial and error, the following guidelines for inclusion of children and adolescents in the initial interview with parents/legal guardians. Each clinic should develop a set of guidelines appropriate for its clients.

1. Both the child/adolescent client and parent/legal guardian come to the clinic together for the first appointment, during which the initial interview is conducted.
2. Unless requested otherwise by the parent/legal guardian (because of sensitive information to be provided), the child/adolescent is included in the

part of the interview where background information (e.g., developmental, social history) is obtained or reviewed (from forms completed earlier).

3. Preschool children then remain in the room for the rest of the interview unless their behavior is so disruptive that the interview cannot be productive. They are provided with quiet play materials for self-entertainment.
4. Children from 5 to approximately 12 years of age are usually taken to another room before the referral problem is discussed, unless their presence is desired by professional staff or is requested by the parent/legal guardian.
5. Adolescents (from approximately 12 years upward) are usually present throughout the entire interview unless the parent/legal guardian requests otherwise, or unless the professional staff feel it would be inappropriate for them to remain.

Of course, unusual circumstances or situations will warrant modification of the adopted guidelines, and professional staff should make exceptions to clinic guidelines when appropriate. Even when clinic guidelines are followed, there may be times during the interview when changes are needed. For example, if during the interview, a parent shows open hostility toward the child or adolescent client, this may put undue stress on that person, and it might then be advisable to meet with the parent and child/adolescent separately. It would be important to handle this situation carefully so that rapport with both the child/adolescent and parent is not impaired.

Whether parents/legal guardians and primary clients are interviewed together at the time of an initial interview, most clinicians agree that they should be seen together at some point during the assessment/evaluation process as well as seen separately (Gross, 1984).

Interviews with Persons Other Than Parents/Legal Guardians

During the evaluation process, adults other than parents/legal guardians should be interviewed (after requisite written permission has been obtained—see Chapter 11) when they can provide relevant information about the referral problem. Those adults most likely to have such information are teachers or other school personnel, case workers, physicians, or other professionals. Interviews with these individuals may often be conducted by telephone rather than in person, thus saving staff time. Also, it is usually most efficient to conduct such interviews after initial interviews with parents/legal guardians and after other preliminary assessments with the primary client have been conducted so that questions may be geared to areas where information is desired.

For some referral problems (e.g., family conflicts), interviews may be conducted with other family members (e.g., siblings), or through group interviews with a family constellation.

Adult Interview Formats

In general, the interview structure will reflect the interviewer's psychological orientation and interviewing expertise as well as be influenced by the referral question or concern. For example, if the referral concerns problem behavior exhibited by the child/adolescent, the clinician with a behavioral orientation is likely to direct the interview content to the problem behavior and its associated antecedents and consequences.

Some clinicians have found it helpful to prepare for interviews by use of structured interview formats or by predetermining content areas or questions they intend to cover that will provide them with pertinent information. Other interviewers would prefer o "play it by ear." Whenever it is anticipated that information in a number of areas of functioning will be sought during an interview, or when novice interviewers are involved, written guidelines for the interview can be useful. A comprehensive interview guideline is shown in Form 6.1. All or selected segments of this guideline could be used on a case-by-case basis, depending on the extent of interview information desired.

Child and Adolescent Interviews

Independent interviews should be conducted with child and adolescent clients who have requisite communication skills. This activity is particularly important if clinicians are to honor the rights of child and adolescent clients (see Chapter 11). Kanfer, Eyberg, and Kahn (1983) suggest that children 6 years and older are able to provide content information of relevance to referral concerns. Interviews with preschool-age children may also be productive if the interviewer is adept in communicating in a manner appropriate for the developmental level of the child and understands the child's possible verbal liitations. There are a number of advantages in interviewing children or adolescents apart from adults, including: a) the interviewer may obtain information on the child or adolescent's perceptions of the referral concerns that may or may not agree with adult perceptions; b) clinician and client can begin to establish rapport that may lead to later treatment cooperation, a relationship of central importance in traditional child therapies (Kanfer et al., 1983); c) the client may be less inhibited than when in the presence of the referring adults, and will disclose more essential information relative to the referral question than would otherwise be the case. Wolberg (1977) has indicated that a good client/clinician relationship depends upon a clinician who: a) clarifies and removes misconceptions about what will occur during the interactions, b) convinces the client that the therapist understands the problem and is capable of helping, c) defines the objectives of each session, and d) motivates the client.

LaGreca (1983) proposes that adults who have referred children for assessment usually expect clinicians to interact with their children and so are not opposed to the practice of interviewing the child/adolescent alone. We have found, however, that frequently parents are apprehensive about interviews conducted by clinicians solely with their children. Such apprehensions may be due to concerns that: a) the parent(s) may be negatively portrayed by the child or adolescent, b) possible family "secrets" or details would be revealed, c) incongruencies may surface between information provided by parents and that

FORM 6.1

Guidelines for Intake Interview

Date of Interview: _____

Interviewee: _____

Interviewer: _____

Client: _____ Client File #_____

I. **REFERRAL CONCERNS**

   Problems at Home

   What kinds?

   Describe examples:

   Onset of problems:

   Frequency of occurrence:

   Duration of occurrence:

   Intensity:

   Under what conditions do problems occur?

   How are problems handled?

   Are problems handled the same way by both parents?

   Problems at School

   What kinds?

   Describe examples:

   Onset of problems:

   Frequency of occurrence:

   Duration of occurrence:

   Under what conditions do problems occur?

   How are problems handled?

II. **DEVELOPMENTAL**

   Child adopted?_____(yes/no) If adopted, when?_____

   Pregnancy Information

   Any difficulties?_____(yes/no) If yes, what?

   Accidents:

   Medication/alcohol usage:

   Compare to other pregnancies if any:

   Delivery/Birth Information

   Delivery complications?_____(yes/no) If yes, what?

   Premature_____ (yes/no) If yes, how early?_____

   Compare to sibling delivery if any:

   Special treatment provided in hospital:

   Physical Development/Health History

   Usual childhood illnesses/diseases:

   Any others:

   Complications of any illnesses/diseases:

(continued)

Ear infections history (frequent, treatment):

Medications (past/present):

Physical growth/any concerns:

Medical examination history:

Current family physician:

Date of last physical exam:

Date of last visual exam/results:

Date of last hearing exam/results:

Accident history (ages/reasons/treatment):

Hospitalizations (why/length of time):

Family Health History

Family health history/any problems:

Natural mother/premenstrual syndrome (PMS):

Parent learning problems:

Siblings/relatives with developmental disabilities:

Speech and Language Development/Skills

Age babbled:

Infant vocalizations:

Age first words:

Age two-word combinations:

Any speech or language concerns (before 3 years of age):

Any speech or language concerns (after 3 years of age):

Current speech/language concerns:

Speech intelligibility (history/current status):

Speech fluency (history/current status):

Speech/language special services received (where, when, what):

Motor Development Skills

Gross Motor

Infancy/Preschool Development

Age sat up/any concerns:

Age turned over/any concerns:

Age crawled/any concerns:

Age walked/any concerns:

Age ran/any concerns:

Compare child to peers/siblings in infancy/preschool age development:

Compare child/youth to peers/siblings since preschool age:

Current sports activities:

Current problems/concerns:

Any special gross motor services received (where, when, what):

Fine Motor

Infancy/Preschool Development

Age reached for small objects/any concerns:

Age small objects held/manipulated/any concerns:

(continued)

Preschool toy/object/crayon manipulation/any problems:

Current eating utensils used/any problems:

Handwriting status/any concerns:

Tool/object manipulation/any concerns:

Any special fine motor services received (where, when, what):

Social/Behavioral Development/Skills

Infancy/Preschool

Age first smiled:

Responsiveness to others during first year/any concerns:

Play interactions with other children/any concerns:

Compliance with parental requests/any concerns:

Responsiveness to home/preschool roles/standards:

Attention span/any concerns:

Other problems/concerns:

School-age Youth Skills

Relationships with peers or siblings/any concerns:

Responsiveness to school standards/roles:

Compliance with teachers' requests/instructions:

Leader/follower in peer group situations:

Feeding/Eating and Sleeping Behaviors

Feeding/Eating

Infancy/preschool/any feeding problems:

Infant colic:

Food allergies:

Current eating problems, if any:

Sleeping

Infant/preschool sleeping patterns/any concerns:

Current sleeping patterns/any concerns:

Bedtime problems:

Self-Help Skills

Current dressing/undressing skill levels:

Current grooming/bathing skill levels:

Current toileting—bladder control (day/night):

Current toileting—bowel control (day/night):

Day toileting problems (what kind, related details):

Night toileting problems/bed-wetting (frequency, treatment, effort, medication):

If toileting problems, toilet training history:

Home chores assigned/any problems:

Other self-help competencies in repertoire (cooking/sewing):

Compare to other same-age children:

Any self-help deficits:

(*continued*)

III. SCHOOL EXPERIENCES

Preschool/Day Care

    Dates of enrollment(s):

    Type of setting (private preschool/Headstart):

    Schedule (daily/2 × weekly/all day/morning):

    Reports of strengths/problems:

    Teacher or day care provider:

Public/Private School

Kindergarten

    Where:

    Strengths:

    Problems:

    Interpersonal relationships (classmates/teacher):

    Special education services (what, how often):

Elementary Grades Attended (list each grade and relevant information for each grade):

    Where:

    Reading skills acquisition/any problems:

    Any reading program interventions (Title I or Chapter 1):

    Other academic subjects (math, written language)/any problems:

    Special education services (what, how often):

    Strengths:

    Problems:

    Interpersonal relationships (classmates/teachers):

Secondary Grades Attended (list each grade and relevant information for each grade):

    Academic performance:

    Strengths:

    Problems:

    Interpersonal relationships (classmates/teachers):

IV. PSYCHOEDUCATIONAL EVALUATION/TREATMENT HISTORY

Previous Educational Testing

    Where:

    When:

    Results:

    Recommendations:

Previous Psychological Counseling/Therapy

    Where:

    When:

    Why:

    Individual:

    Group:

(continued)

FORM 6.1 (*continued*)

V. FAMILY SITUATION

Who lives at home:

Sex and ages of siblings living in home:

Family/parent interactions:

Family/parent stresses:

reported by the primary client, or d) the parents feel "in the dark" about what the clinician may ask the child or adolescent. Adult apprehensions may be relieved if the clinician informs parents of the purposes for the separate interview and reviews the interview format with the parents prior to the child or adolescent interview. At times parental fears may be justified in that children or adolescents may indeed reveal information damaging to the parent, especially in cases of parental child abuse. It is essential that each clinic establish specific policies regarding the confidentiality of information provided by the child/adolescent client during interviews with clinicians. Since parents/guardians hold the legal right to confidentiality, an agreement must be negotiated with them. This issue is discussed in depth in Chapter 11. Clinicians conducting child and adolescent interviews must adapt interview styles and formats to the ability and skill levels of the individual child or adolescent interviewed. Kanfer et al. (1983) suggest that interviewers can alter their style in three major areas to accommodate client age differences:

1. Using vocabulary and sentence structure appropriate for the age and verbal skills of the client.
2. Minimizing silence intervals (a technique common in adult interviewing but which appears to be aversive to children in verbal interactions with adults and may lead to client resistance)
3. Introducing or including conversational topics not directly related to the referral problem such as current age-associated fads, hobbies, television programs, popular toys, books

Preschool or preteen client interviews may be facilitated by incorporating other materials or procedures (e.g., puppets for preschoolers, drawings). For example, a child who is reluctant to respond to direct questions from the interviewer may respond to the same or similar questions when presented via hand puppets. Preteen children may also become more involved in an interview situation as a result of a discussion of drawings they have produced (i.e., pictures of them, their families, their friends, or familiar situations). The skilled interviewer may need to be creative at times in using supplemental materials to elicit client verbalizations.

In addition to obtaining content information during a child or adolescent interview, Kanfer et al. (1983) contend that there are ongoing process goals being pursued throughout the interview that involve establishment of rapport and maintenance of communication. Five basic communication techniques are identified by Kanfer et al. as useful in achieving these goals:

1. Use of descriptive statements or comments on the child's appearance, demeanor, and nonnegative behavior. For example: "That's a pretty blouse you are wearing today."
2. Use of reflective statements, involving almost the same words used by the child, or elaborations or interpretations of the child's statements.
3. Use of praise statements denoting approval of specific actions or behavior exhibited by the child to signify to the child what is acceptable and pleasing to the clinician. Praise statements should vary according to age and should be less frequently used with adolescents, who may perceive such comments as patronizing or insincere.
4. Establishment of ground rules (i.e., what behaviors are appropriate during the interview at the beginning of the interview), to minimize the possible need for critical statements about the adolescent's behavior ("stop" commands) for inappropriate behavior. Such responses can result in an unproductive interview if viewed as signifying adult disapproval by the child, particularly younger children.
5. Use of open-ended questions involving "What" questions whenever possible. It is also suggested that "Why" questions be avoided with children; such questions tend to increase defensiveness because of frequent use by caregivers in their interactions with children.

Interview Information

Some of the types of information to be elicited in the child/adolescent interview include the client's: a) perceptions of the problem and related areas; b) concerns about other problem areas, feelings, and mood states; c) perceptions of who needs help and what form it should take; d) perceptions about interactions with parents; and e) concerns about the interview and intervention process.

You are also referred to articles by Kanfer and associates (1983) and LaGreca (1983) for more detailed information on how to conduct child and adolescent interviews.

Even when a child/adolescent interview has been conducted as an initial step in the evaluation process, this assessment strategy may be used again at other times during the evaluation for purposes of: a) clarifying other assessment information that has been obtained (e.g., responses on certain projective instruments such as sentence completion tests), b) reviewing previous interview information for validation, or c) obtaining more detailed or other information once client trust has been established.

Rating Scales, Checklists, Questionnaires, and Inventories

The use of prepared forms such as rating scales, checklists, questionnaires, and inventories is another assessment approach, which may be used: a) to identify "narrow-band" behavior syndromes (e.g., hyperactivity, social withdrawal), b) to obtain general information on child/adolescent problem behavior, c) to obtain information on a specific area of functioning (e.g., fears/phobias), or d) to obtain a broad view of functioning across different areas (e.g., communication, motor, personal-social). The advantages of this approach include: a) forms are easily administered; b) information collected on some forms can be scored quantitatively; c) on some forms scores may be compared to normative groups; d) information may be obtained that is not shared or covered in face-to-face interviews; e) information may be obtained from relevant individuals not available for face-to-face interviews; f) information from the forms may corroborate that obtained in other approaches, or if it does not, further exploration of a problem may be warranted; and g) information obtained may be used as a basis for employment of assessment strategies. Other assessment devices in this category must be administered in face-to-face presentations and so are like structured interviews. Some well-known instruments in this approach include: Child Behavior Checklist (Achenbach, 1981) and Personality Inventory for Children–Revised (Lachar, 1984).

Disadvantages of this assessment approach are that: a) items typically included on the devices are often only global descriptors that are open to various interpretations; b) respondents completing these devices independently must have adequate reading skills to comprehend the language used; c) the reliability and validity of many devices in this category may be nonexistent or highly questionable; d) different devices designed to assess the same area (e.g., hyperactivity) may not be interchangeable owing to differences in the kinds of items included or the score values assigned.

The majority of commercial instruments available in this category incorporate the term *Rating Scale, Checklist, Questionnaire,* or *Inventory* in their title, although some similar devices use the word *"Scales"* or *"Index."* Such devices are assumed to have the same characteristics as those already described; that is, they require the respondent to identify items that best describe the individual or behaviors exhibited by the individual for whom the device is being completed.

A comprehensive review and critique of the literally hundreds of instruments available to rate virtually all aspects of child and adolescent behavior (McMahon, 1984) would be impossible in this book. Many devices were initially developed for use in research projects (Goldman et al., 1983), and have since been modified for clinical application. A number of such devices are available through commercial sources (e.g., psychological test distributors) or may be used with written permission from their developers. Not uncommonly, clinicians or clinics also develop their own devices or modify existing ones for specific purposes. Probably no other assessment approach includes such a variety or array of devices. Furthermore, reliability and validity concerns associated with these devices have been much discussed in the literature. For more extensive information on these assessment devices and related issues see Goldman et al.; McMahon; *Journal of Psychopathology and Behavioral Assessment;* Sattler

(1982). Other resources that include examples of these assessment devices are those by Cautela, Cautela, and Esonis (1983) and Mash and Terdal (1981).

Guidelines for Selecting Checklists, Rating Scales, Questionnaires, and Inventories

The following considerations should be taken into account in selecting devices for this assessment strategy:

1. *Relevance of device to the purpose for referral.* Devices should be selected that include items related to acquisition of information most pertinent to the referral question or problem. For example: If a client has been referred for determination of mental retardation, it is essential for classification purposes that an adaptive behavior measure be obtained in conjunction with a standardized intellectual assessment (Grossman, 1983).

2. *Reliability and validity.* Preferably, devices should be selected with established reliability and validity. Results of devices without adequate reliability or validity should be interpreted cautiously.

3. *Client characteristics.* Whenever devices have been designated by developers for specific client characteristics (e.g., age, sex), the selection of such devices should be limited to clients with those similar characteristics. This is particularly important when information obtained is to be compared with reference groups.

4. *Language included on devices.* Whenever respondents are asked to complete this category of assessment devices independently, it should be predetermined that the devices are: a) at an appropriate reading and vocabulary level for the respondent, b) as free as possible from ambiguous wording, and c) free from technical terms or jargon. Some devices include "anchors" (e.g., behavioral examples) to assist respondents in completing the information.

5. *Number of items included.* Devices included in this assessment approach may contain anywhere from 10 to 600 items. There is little research indicating the optimum number of items that should be included in any one device. McMahon (1984) reports some evidence that on problem behavior checklists, at least 50 items on various behaviors should be included if "narrowband syndromes" are to be identified from the total conglomerate of items. Several factors need to be considered before selecting a device for a respondent to complete: a) how much information is desired about a particular area of functioning? b) how comprehensive a view of the primary client's function is derived? c) what are the time constraints for respondents (what are their attentional abilities)? There is no point in asking respondents to complete lengthy devices that include items not relevant to the referral problem. On the other hand, brief devices may serve no purpose other than to stimulate an interview direction. Clinical judgment must be used.

6. *Specific respondent forms.* Some devices in this category are designed specifically for completion by educators (e.g., classroom teachers, special

educators), and should be used by them only. Other devices include forms that differ slightly to accommodate the roles of the respondents (e.g., both the primary caregiver and classroom teacher).

Checklists, Rating Scales, Questionnaires, and Inventories for Adult Use

Most frequently, adults who are asked to complete these assessment devices are the primary caregivers (e.g., parents) and teachers of the referred client (McMahon, 1984). Whenever feasible, however, this approach should involve acquisition of information from several adult sources, that is, teachers and other professionals as well as parents, in order to: a) ascertain whether different adults have similar perceptions of the primary client, b) determine whether referral problems are present across situations, c) determine problem intensity difference in various settings and with different individuals, and d) detect unusual or specific negative or positive biases toward the primary client. Only those adults well acquainted with the functioning of the child or adolescent in the areas where information is sought should be asked to complete devices included in this assessment strategy. Indeed, some manuals of commercially available materials specifically state that respondents should have had an opportunity to observe the individual on whom they are completing a device over a minimum time period (e.g., 30 days), before completing the device (Walker Problem Behavior Checklist—Revised, 1983).

Although most devices in this assessment category are designed for respondents to complete items independently of an interviewer, other devices require a face-to-face interview (e.g., Vineland Adaptive Behavior Scales—Interview Form 1984). Depending on which device is used, face-to-face presentations may be conducted either in a highly structured manner, with standard questions or items presented in specified sequences, or informally by allowing the presenter to explain or elaborate on items presented. If respondents are to complete instruments independently, we recommend that the respondent be instructed to place question marks by any items that are unclear or ambiguous or that they feel unable to answer. Following the independent completion of items, the professional can review questionable items with the respondent and clarify any confusion. Even if respondents complete all items without asking for assistance or noting questions, a brief review of the completed form with respondents is often quite useful to clarify: a) contradictory items; b) unusual ratings (e.g., when low ratings are made on specific problem behaviors, when the referral concern relates to those problem behaviors); or c) unmarked items.

Checklists, Rating Scales, Questionnaires, and Inventories for Child/Adolescent Self-Report

Fewer devices in this assessment approach are available for use by children and adolescents than for adults for several reasons. First, as indicated earlier, respondents must have requisite reading skills (including comprehension skills) for independent self-reporting on written forms. This usually requires reading skills at least at the third- or fourth-grade level or higher. A second reason for the limited use of self-report instruments with children and adolescents has been the assumption by many professionals that minor-age individuals are not skilled observers of their own behavior or feelings, and that they therefore provide less reliable and valid information than could be obtained from adults. A third reason has been the assumption that minor-age children are more susceptible to the ''demand characteristics,'' that is, the tendency to respond in response patterns, or to provide socially acceptable or desirable responses in order to please adults. In recent years, however, it has been indicated that child and adolescent self-report information can be useful in determining treatment goals and procedures, and that the omission of such self-report data can have a deleterious effect on treatment effectiveness (Finch & Rogers, 1984; Mash & Terdal, 1981).

The most commonly used materials developed for use by children and adolescents have been designed to assess anxiety, fears, depression, anger, assertiveness, self-concept, and locus of control (McMahon, 1984). Normative information is available for some of these devices so that comparisons can be made with reference groups of individuals with similar characteristics (e.g., sex, age range), to determine whether clients' self-perceptions reflect problem areas. Other materials are available for the purpose of obtaining idiosyncratic responses in a specified area. For example, a fear inventory listing a number of possible fearful objects or events can be given to an adolescent to rate on an intensity scale. Ratings are then ranked by a clinician to determine the greatest to least fears. Writing on child assessment, Finch and Rogers (1984) describe in some detail a variety of instruments that have been developed for use with children and adolescents to assess anxiety, depression, anger, and locus of control. You may refer to this source and others for more in-depth critiques and descriptions of devices that can be used by child/adolescent clients.

Checklists, rating scales, and questionnaires have also been designed to elicit information from children or adolescents on preferred activities or desired objects that could be potential reinforcers for use in behavioral programming (see Chapter 7, for a discussion of behavioral programming).

Information obtained on checklists, rating scales, and similar devices that are completed by child/adolescent clients should be interpreted with caution, for the reasons already mentioned (e.g., social conformity responses, lack of discriminative skills in identifying feelings). Information provided through child and adolescent self-report should be supported by other assessment information whenever possible and should not be used as an exclusive assessment approach.

Standardized and Nonstandardized Tests

In a clinic setting, the testing strategy typically involves one-to-one professional interaction with the child or adolescent client for the purpose of eliciting information on a selected instrument(s). Sometimes, however, the child/adolescent may be asked to respond to test stimuli independently, that is, to provide written responses for specific tasks (e.g., mathematics problems). It is expected that in the near future computer-assisted assessment may supplant at least some face-to-face professional-client assessment interactions. Except for very young children who may not separate easily from a parent or legal guardian, the clinician and the primary client usually participate in this assessment approach apart from parents or other adults.

Two general categories of assessment instruments are used in this assessment approach: standardized and nonstandardized tests. For our purposes, standardized tests are defined as those instruments that: a) are individually administered, b) are administered similarly to all examinees in accordance with test developer specified procedures, and c) provide data to allow comparison of examinee scores with those of appropriate reference groups that were included in standardization of the test administered. Standardized tests are also described frequently as norm referenced tests (Guion, 1983). Nonstandardized tests are defined in this book as those instruments that: a) are individually administered, b) do not require strict adherence to specific administration procedures, and c) are not used for comparison of individual scores with specific reference groups (although some instruments provide general guidelines for interpretation of performance—e.g., approximate grade level). For more elaborate definitions and descriptions of standardized and nonstandardized test categories, you are referred to other sources such as Goldman et al. (1983), Salvia and Ysseldyke (1981), and Sattler (1982).

Both standardized and nonstandardized tests are available that allow for nonverbal, verbal, or both verbal/nonverbal administration and examinee responses. Few tests have been specifically developed for children/adolescents with handicaps, but some have been developed for specific populations (e.g., those with hearing impairment).

Standardized Tests

In recent years, there has been a great deal of controversy on the use of standardized tests and testing. Several central issues have been addressed: a) the appropriateness of using standardized tests identified as "intelligence" tests to assess children and adolescents from minority populations or cultural or ethnic backgrounds different from those individuals included in reference sample groups (that is, Caucasians with "middle-class" socio-economic status), b) the question of how useful or relevant standardized test information is in determining intervention or programming needs of the individual assessed, and c) the claim that certain tests are based on underlying personality theories assessing personality characteristics or traits. Each of these issues has been debated extensively in public forums and in numerous publications, and it is beyond the purpose of this book to explore these concerns in-depth. We believe that there is a place for standardized testing in the child/adolescent clinic if the professionals using the testing materials select, use, and interpret the results in an ethical manner—that is, in accordance with national standards—and provided the professionals are cognizant of test limitations and the rational criticisms levied by opponents (Kaufman & Reynolds, 1984).

Standardized Ability Tests Hamill (1985) has described ability tests as those instruments used to assess performance areas (e.g., learning aptitudes) that are common across all individuals. The most frequently used ability tests in the assessment of children and adolescents are those identified by test developers as assessing "intelligence," "cognitive functioning," "mental processing," or "learning aptitude." Despite the difference in terms used by test developers and professionals to describe an area of individual functioning, a general assumption underlying most of these tests is that each individual has some capacity, fixed or flexible, for acquiring information obtained through inheritance or environmental experiences or by a combination of both. This chapter does not seek to discuss the pros and cons of ability tests of this type, but to examine issues related to their use.

Why are ability tests used so frequently with children and adolescents? First, they have been found to be fair predictors of academic achievement if there are no other complicating factors (e.g., conduct disorders, attentional problems). Second, a number of instruments of this type have established statistics on reliability and validity (Gelfand et al., 1982; Sattler, 1982). Third, eligibility for special education services in the United States is partially determined by performance scores obtained on standardized tests of intellectual abilities. Fourth, entry into specialized programs (e.g., gifted and talented), if not governed by rules and regulations for special education, may be dependent on specific performance ability scores. Fifth, intelectual ability test scores may be used to ascertain the degree to which an individual may be expected to benefit from certain treatment approaches when treatment options are available (Kaufman & Reynolds, 1984). For example, an adolescent with limited intellectual functioning (e.g., IQ of 58) may not benefit from participation in individual psychodynamic or cognitive behavior therapy, but, instead, should be offered an alternative approach.

Although there are no universal guidelines for selecting the most useful test of intellectual aptitude for each client (Goldman et al., 1983), the most popular tests of this type are the Stanford-Binet Intelligence Scale and the Wechsler Scales (Gelfand et al., 1982). Sattler (1982) and others provide in-depth information on each of these tests. Both are comprehensive assessments of this type, meaning that a number of behaviors of verbal and performance ability are sampled, in contrast to screening tests, such as the Slosson Intelligence Scale, that sample fewer items. The Wechsler Intelligence Scale for Children, the Wechsler Adult Intelligence Scale, and the Stanford-Binet Intelligence Scale have been revised over the years. Other newer ability tests have also been published that are purported to test mental processing functions (e.g., Kaufman Assessment Battery for Children, 1983). As in other assessment strategies, the selection of an ability test of intellectual functioning must be based on: a) client characteristics (e.g., age, verbal, and other skills), and b) the information needed to address the referral question. Other factors should also be considered:

1. Would assessment information from a screening test be sufficient as opposed to that provided from a comprehensive test? For example, if the referral concern is an emotional problem and it will be adequate to ascertain an estimate of the client's intellectual ability, a screening test would be more cost effective to administer than a comprehensive test (i.e., 30 minutes compared to an hour or hour and a half). On the other hand, for educational placement resolution, screening test information is less widely accepted as providing acceptable support for some classifications (e.g., persons with intellectual handicaps).

2. Would one test provide more information on different aspects of functioning than another test? For example, until the recent revision of the Stanford-Binet Intelligence Scale (1986), some professionals preferred using the WISC–R to assess school-age children, because separate verbal and performance ability scales were included on the latter.

3. Would a short form of a comprehensive test provide sufficient information versus the longer form? On certain tests, developers have identified abbreviated formats that can be used in lieu of administering the complete test. Selection of an abbreviated form should be made on the basis of adequacy of information obtained for resolution of the referral question, as well as technical information available on such a form. The abbreviated form of a test may be useful with younger children or with children who have attentional problems (i.e., difficulty remaining on-task for extended time periods).

4. Which test is most suited to the client? That is, what test best fits client characteristics (e.g., interest level, communication skills, motor skills, attentional skills)? For example, a child with limited verbal skills could be expected to perform better on a nonverbal intellectual test, such as the Leiter International Performance Scale (1948) or the Matrix Analogies Test (Naglieri, 1985) than on a test requiring verbal skills.

A listing of standardized ability tests is provided in Table 6.1.

Traditionally, the psychologist or psychometrist has been designated as the best trained specialist to administer and interpret tests of intellectual functioning. Kaufman and Reynolds (1984) point out that "knowledge and skill in psychometrics and measurement are requisite to intelligent testing" (p. 202). These authors and others (Gelfand et al., 1982; Goldman et al., 1983; Sattler, 1982) also stress that extensive training must be a prerequisite for those administering tests of intellectual functioning such as the Wechsler series or the Stanford-Binet Intelligence Scale. With the recent publication of other ability tests, test developers have either new or revised editions; some specifically indicated that test administrators of their instruments should have had psychological test training. They do, however, advise that test administrators should be well trained.

Standardized Achievement Tests Hamill (1985) has described achievement tests as those used to assess performance or skill areas not necessarily in the repertoire of all individuals (e.g., reading skills). Further, Kaufman and Reynolds (1984) indicate that academic attainment is crucial in the evalua-

Table 6.1.   Standardized ability tests

Detroit Tests of Learning Aptitude–II
Kaufman Assessment Battery for Children (K-ABC), Mental Processing Section
Leiter International Performance Scale
Matrix Analogies Test
McCarthy Scales of Children's Abilities
Slosson Intelligence Test
The Stanford-Binet Intelligence Scale: Fourth Edition
Wechsler Adult Intelligence Scale–Revised (WAIS-R)
Wechsler Intelligence Scale for Children–Revised (WISC-R)
Wechsler Preschool and Primary Scale of Intelligence (WPPSI)

tion of children, especially since school-aged children spend a significant amount of time acquiring academic skills. Sattler (1982) also suggests that the results obtained on achievement tests are more reflective of learning experiences acquired at home or in school than results obtained on intelligence tests, and, as such, achievement tests appear to be more culture bound and do not assess the breadth of areas of functioning, but, instead, mastery of factual information. Therefore, the use of standardized achievement tests in the child/adolescent clinic is of particular importance in the evaluation of school-age clients. Standardized achievement test materials for prekindergarten children are almost nonexistent, probably because there has been little need for such tests, and because preschool children are not universally exposed to formal learning situations.

Usually, standardized tests selected for assessment of client achievement skills in a clinic will be those considered to be somewhat general in nature, rather than diagnostic or highly specific (Goldman et al., 1983). For most purposes in the clinic setting, it will be sufficient to sample academic skills in such areas as reading, mathematics, and written language, in order to ascertain the level of the client's skills, rather than to determine specific academic strengths or weaknesses in these areas (Goldman et al., 1983). Thus, results from a general achievement test can be used to make educational placement recommendations or to determine whether or not a client is delayed in academic areas relative to a grade placement. There may be times, however, when it is desirable to identify particular academic strengths and weaknesses, so that specific recommendations can be made to address problem areas, especially when school-age clients have been referred because of learning problems. Standardized tests can be administered for this purpose, depending on the type of clinic and the clinicians' expertise in educational assessment and programming. Often, school-age clients will have recently been given individual achievement tests in the school setting by special educators, school psychologists, or other educational specialists before the clinic referral. If so, assessment results could be obtained and may preclude further educational assessment. It is cautioned, however, that reliance on information obtained in assessments administered by unknown professionals may be unwise and not in the best interest of the client. Further, test results from group

Table 6.2. Standardized achievement tests

General tests
  Kaufman Test of Educational Achievement (K-TEA), Brief and Extended Forms
  Kaufman Assessment Battery for Children (K-ABC), Achievement Section
  Wide Range Achievement Test–Revised
  Woodcock-Johnson Psycho-educational Battery, Tests of Achievement, Part II

Specific content area tests
  Key Math Diagnostic Test
  Woodcock Reading Mastery Tests

testing conducted in the school setting are not usually as reliable as results from individually administered tests, and so should not be used in place of such test information, or should be verified by further testing.

A number of factors should be considered in selecting achievement tests appropriate for a clinic:

1. What assessment information will be most useful and cost effective (i.e, a test used to assess one academic area versus one designed to assess several academic skill areas)? It can be expected that a test assessing one academic area will cover that area more thoroughly than one that covers several areas. When test funds are limited, however, it is more practical to purchase tests than incorporate several academic areas.

2. How appropriate is the instrument for the client (e.g., age, grade level, communication required, estimated skill functioning level)?

3. How adequate and appropriate are the psychometric properties of the test (e.g., reliability, validity, normative data)? For example, a number of achievement tests have poor standardization and normative data (Goldman et al., 1983).

Table 6.2 provides a list of standardized achievement tests that could be useful in a clinic setting.

Standardized Tests in Other Areas   Standardized tests are available for assessment of other areas of child and adolescent functioning apart from academic achievement and intellectual functioning. These areas include: visual motor coordination, visual and auditory discrimination and processing, speech and language skills, and motor functioning. Some instruments of this type do not require strict adherence in wording of instructions given to examinees while others do, yet informative data are available so that individual performance may be compared to reference groups.

Nonstandardized Tests

As noted in the definition provided earlier in the chapter, nonstandardized tests are those used to assess an examinee in one or more areas of functioning where the information obtained is not used to compare the performance of the individual assessed to that of other individuals. Instead, individual content referenced test scores are interpreted on the basis of performance on a continuum defined by the instrument used (Guion, 1983). Educators often refer to such tests as criterion- or domain-referenced tests, that is, referenced to specified criteria or standard performance. Guion (1983) has pointed out, however, that the 1974 American Psychological Association (APA) Standards define criterion-referenced instruments as those that allow score interpretation in relation to an external criterion, a definition somewhat different from that used by educators, and thus leading to confusion between educators and psychologists. For the purposes of this book, the nonstandardized tests discussed include those instruments that are based on a continuum of skills.

There may be a number of advantages for using nonstandardized tests in a clinic, such as: a) in seeking in-depth analyses of client strengths and weaknesses in academic or academically related areas after preliminary information has been obtained on a standardized instrument, b) as a substitute for standardized tests whenever comparison with a reference group is not needed or desired, c) in lieu of standardized tests if the client's characteristics do not "fit" or "match" reference groups on standardized tests available, d) for obtaining information on the client's functioning in areas not covered on standardized tests, and e) for acquiring more specific information for treatment recommendations that can be obtained from general standardized tests administered.

At times, it may also be advantageous to use standardized tests or test items in nonstandardized ways (Barkley, 1981) (e.g., allowing pantomimed responses if the client is unable to provide oral or written responses). Of course, such uses would preclude the use of the normative data available except for an estimated performance level. The use of nonstandardized tests is limited, however, because: a) reliability and validity data reported on instruments are limited or unavailable, and b) most tests of this type are designed to assess academic skill areas.

Projective Assessment

Projective assessment involves the use of techniques (e.g., drawings, tests, stories) designed to elicit information on nonovert aspects of functioning (e.g., personality characteristics and motivators, private feelings and perceptions). Gelfand et al. (1982) and Goldman et al. (1983) propose that most or all projective techniques have been derived from a "projective hypothesis," an underlying assumption that psychological forces within the individual directly influence "the content and style of that person's perceptions" (Goldman et al., 1983) and that the individual is driven by such psychological forces as sexual and aggressive urges (Gelfand et al., 1982). Further, specific projective techniques reflect the theoretical orientation of their developers (e.g., psychoanalytic).

There has been a great deal of disagreement among professionals about the usefulness of projective assessment. Controversy has centered on two major issues: a) the acceptance or reflection of the underlying assumptions of projective techniques, and b) whether the criterion measures used are less well defined than in other areas of assessment (Goldman et al., 1983). For extended discussions on these and other issues, you are referred to sources such as: French, Graves, and Levitt (1983), Gelfand et al. (1982), and Goldman et al. (1983).

Whether projective techniques are seen as a viable assessment approach depends largely on the training and psychological orientation of the professionals involved in assessment. In addition, specific techniques are preferred by some clinicians and not by others. Descriptions of some general classes of projective techniques follow:

1. *Design or picture cards.* This technique involves the use of a series of designs or pictures that are presented to the client. The client is asked to verbally respond to each item by: a) telling a story about what is portrayed, or b) describing what the design represents. Some of the best known techniques of this type are the: Rorschach Inkblot Test (1941–1945); Thematic Apperception Test (Murray, 1935–43), designed for use with those 14 years old and older; Childrens' Apperception Test (Bellack and Bellack, 1949–74), for use with children 3–10 years old; and the Symond's Picture-Story Test (Symonds, 1948), for use with adolescents. A number of variations on this technique have also been developed, such as: The Hand Test–Revised (Wagner, 1983), where pictures of hands in different positions are presented and the client is asked to describe what the hands are doing; and the Mutual Story Telling Technique (Gardner, 1971), where children pretend they are on an imaginary television quiz show and are asked to provide words or statements that fit into introduced phrases or sentences.

2. *Completion techniques.* The client is presented with a series of incomplete items, usually sentence stems, and is asked to write or verbalize information to complete the items. There are many variations of this technique, including those designed for different age groups, that are used to elicit information on various aspects of the client's life (e.g., school situations, home environment). One of the most popular is the Rotter Incomplete Sentences Blank–High School Form (Rotter, 1950).

3. *Client-production.* This technique requires that the client be presented with one or more materials (i.e., usually a blank sheet of paper and a pencil) and is asked to create a product. The best-known use of this technique requires clients to draw one or more pictures of persons, frequently of themselves, and/or family members. Numerous variations are suggested for objects or situations to be drawn (e.g., animals, homes, trees, unpleasant situations). Other variations in this technique have involved the use of different materials (e.g., finger painting, clay, or sand). A major advantage to this technique is that the client does not have to provide verbal responses in order to complete the task. If clients have verbal skills, however, clinicians sometimes use the client production as a basis for client interviews or for eliciting verbal elaboration from the client about his or her productions.

For more extensive discussions of specific techniques described here, as well as more detailed information on specific instruments, you are referred to reviews by Buros's *Mental Measurement Yearbooks* (1938–78); French et al. (1983), Gelfand et al. (1982), and Goldman et al. (1983).

Several other types of assessment devices could be categorized as projective techniques if used for interpreting information based on "the projective hypothesis" described earlier. These include: a) puppets used by children for telling stories or interacting in role-play situations, b) card sort activities in which the client arranges cards depicting pictured situations or printed materials in preferred orders, and c) self-report personality inventories. In the latter category, the most widely used instrument with adolescents is the MMPI, Minnesota Multiphasic Personality Inventory (Hathaway & McKinley, 1967). The utility of this instrument has been evaluated in numerous publications (French et al., 1983). Problems discussed earlier in this chapter with respect to self-report instruments in general (e.g., social desirability, response bias), also apply to self-report personality inventories.

Physiological Assessment

Physiological assessment requires the use of specialized equipment (as described in Chapter 2) to assess physiological processes (e.g., heart rate, muscle tension, brain activity). In addition to the instrumentation, specialized training and collaboration with physicians may be needed. To date, this assessment strategy has had limited clinical use with children and adolescents (Gelfand et al., 1982), except by those working with medically related problems such as asthma, headaches, or muscle retraining. For particular referral problems, direct assessment of physiological functioning can yield valuable pretreatment information and can be used to monitor changes during treatment (see Chapter 7).

After conducting a search of current books relating to physiological assessment *with children and adolescents,* we were not surprised to find relatively few references on this little used assessment strategy. Information on physiological assessment, however, can be obtained from reviews or articles on treatment of specific problem areas (White & Tursky, 1982). Finley (1983) also offers a useful review on biofeedback training for children. Moreover, there are many published materials on assessment of physiological processes with adults, especially in books and articles on biofeedback. Some general guidelines for using this assessment strategy include:

1. Whenever possible, two or more physiological processes should be assessed simultaneously to determine interrelationships or discriminant processes. For example, while finger temperature is being measured with a temperature indicator, forehead muscle tension could also be assessed at the same time through electrodes connected to an electromyograph (EMG). The most preferred approach is to conduct what is known as a stress profile. In this process, sensors from as many psychological instruments as are available are attached to the child (e.g. heart rate, respiration, skin temperature, electromyograph, and electrodermal). A resting baseline is collected for 5– 10 minutes and then the child/adolescent is exposed to some form of stress.

For example, the child/adolescent might be asked to talk about the problems he or she is experiencing that resulted in coming to the clinic, or is asked to count backward from 10,000 by subtracting 7s. During exposure to the stress situation, the clinician keeps track of which physiological parameters are outside the normal range, and which respond the most during stress. When the stress situation is removed, the clinician notes which physiological functions recover the quickest and how long recovery takes. Each of these factors provides diagnostic information on the level of the child's stress. Such information can be quite useful in treating phobias, headaches, asthma, and general anxiety.

2. Preschool-age children may be less suitable candidates than school-age children and adolescents for involvement in this assessment strategy because: a) they are more likely to be frightened by the equipment or to resist being "hooked" up to the instruments; b) developmental factors may preclude obtaining reliable or interpretable assessment information from younger children (that is, there is greater variability and change in some physiological processes), and c) fewer preschool children are referred for problems that would suggest use of this assessment strategy (i.e., childhood migraine headaches, which usually are reported by children from 6 to 10 years of age [Finley, 1983], with the incidence increasing with age.

3. Because of the physical contact necessary in attaching measurement devices to the client, it is recommended that another adult be present in addition to the clinician while the assessment is conducted. One adult person should be the same sex as the client (i.e., this does not have to be another clinician but could be another staff member, or parent, unless assessment results would be adversely affected by the parent's presence).

4. Before measurements are taken for assessment purposes, clients should be given a short time period (e.g., 5 minutes) to adjust to the situation after the equipment sensors have been attached.

5. Whenever feasible, measurement of the same physiological processes (e.g., muscle tension) should be taken from different body areas, (e.g., measure of arm tension as well as forehand tension).

6. Medical clearance and collaboration is essential. One would not want to assess and plan a psychological intervention for a physical problem (i.e., pain reduction for a brain tumor that should be removed).

Behavioral Observation

This section of the chapter provides an overview of both structured direct observation techniques that have been developed primarily by psychologists and others with a behavioral orientation, as well as the use of more informal behavioral observation methods. For more extensive discussions on structured direct behavioral observation techniques and procedures, see Barton and Ascione (1984), Gelfand and Hartman (1984), LaGreca (1983), and Striefel and Cadez (1983).

Structured Behavioral Observation Purposes

Information obtained from this strategy can be very useful not only for assessment but also for determining treatment progress (see Chapter 7). Barton and Ascione (1984) describe this strategy as "the core of child behavioral assessment" (p. 167) and Gelfand et al. (1982) refer to it as "the most direct form of assessment" (p. 392). Structured direct behavioral observation requires that there be: a) explicit descriptions of behaviors to be observed, b) a predetermined behavior observation technique or format, c) specification of observational settings and times, and d) a record of identified behavior during observation time periods. The use of this strategy has a number of advantages: a) subjective reports of behavior can be confirmed or refuted; b) information obtained is less influenced by subjective evaluation or interpretation than some other assessment approaches; and c) this strategy is more applicable for certain clients (e.g., those with overt problem behavior) than other approaches, or with clients who have limited functioning skills (e.g., verbal skills that would preclude the use of other strategies such as interviewing).

Despite the potential applicability of this strategy in assessment, it has had limited use in many clinics because: a) it has been highly identified with a behavioral orientation to child psychology and may be less well accepted by providers who do not agree with that orientation; b) the best data collection is associated with the use of trained observers, which requires time and effort; c) more than one observation is needed; d) if information is obtained within a clinic setting, it may not accurately reflect what goes on in the natural environment; e) it is often not practical or feasible for clinicians to observe clients and client families in the natural environment (LaGreca, 1983); and f) "true" behavior patterns may not be seen because if the child or adolescent is aware of being observed, the targeted behaviors for observation may not be exhibited.

Selection of Behaviors to Be Observed

In using this assessment strategy, the clinician must first select behaviors to be observed before deciding on a specific format for observation. Barton and Ascione (1984) suggest some ways to identify behaviors of interest: a) by selecting behaviors that are directly related to the referral problem; b) by noting differences between a client identified as exhibiting a problem behavior and a reference group who do not exhibit similar problem behavior; and c) through subjective ratings from others, that is, a form of social validation. Barton and Ascione also suggest that information obtained through a "narrative recording" technique can be useful in identifying behaviors for further observation. A "narrative recording" technique requires that an observer maintain an ongoing written or dictated record of behavior over a prescribed time period. Thus, antecedent and consequent events associated with the behavior observed may also be recorded. An analysis of narrative recording information can then be used to assist in identifying the behaviors of interest. After such behaviors are identified, they must then be described, so that as Striefel and Cadez (1983) point out, for a behavior to be observable, "it must be seen, heard, or felt" (p. 152).

Structured Behavioral Observation Techniques

Determination of an appropriate technique for observing and recording the behaviors of interest should be based on the characteristics of the behavior(s) to be observed as well as on the technique that will provide the most useful information. For example, certain behaviors occur at such a high frequency that counting them as they occur would be impossible. Other factors also need to be considered: a) qualifications of the observer and training required, b) situations in which the observations are to be conducted, and c) obtrusiveness of the recording system. Practically speaking, the rigor of structured behavioral observation required for research purposes and program evaluation is not a standard that can be used in many applied settings, particularly when parents are assigned to be the primary observers of behavior in the natural environment, which is frequently the way observations are handled. Every effort should be made, however, to obtain the most objective data possible, and this frequently requires that the simplest observational technique be employed that will result in useful information.

Some of the most common techniques that have potential utility for direct structured behavioral observation are described briefly here. For more extensive descriptions and discussion of the techniques' advantages and disadvantages, you may refer to the sources identified earlier.

1. *Frequency/event/tally* This observational technique requires that the observer count each occurrence of the behavior(s) of interest during a specified time period. This is one of the easiest observational techniques to use when the behaviors: a) have a distinct beginning and end, b) occur over approximately the same length of time, and c) occur at not too rapid a rate.

2. *Duration* This observational technique requires that the observer use a timing mechanism (e.g., stopwatch, clock) to record the length of time of each occurrence of the behavior(s) of interest. It is best suited for use when the behaviors: a) have a distinct beginning and end, b) occur during variable periods of time, and c) last for more than a few seconds.

3. *Latency* This observational technique requires that the observer use a timing mechanism to record the length of time between the occurrence of a preliminary cue (e.g., instruction) and a subsequent behavior.

4. *Interval* This observational technique requires that the observer record the occurrence/nonoccurrence of behaviors of interest at equal time intervals. It is most useful when information is desired on multiple behaviors or if more than one individual is to be observed. It is not as practical as other techniques, since it requires more sophisticated training as well as a cueing system.

5. *Momentary time sampling* This observation technique requires that the observer note whether the identified behavior(s) is/are occurring at specified

observation periods, either fixed (e.g., every 30 minutes) or on an intermittent schedule.

Other Structured Observation Formats

LaGreca (1983) has described assigned situation formats to be used in clinics for observing parent and child interactions related to behaviors of interest. Formats have been designed by a host of clinicians to assess: compliance, anxiety, activity level, and social skills. The most structured situational format involves the use of role-play techniques. As LaGreca (1983) has pointed out, simulated observations in the clinic are practical in that they save time for clinicians and clients and also provide clinicians with an opportunity to observe behaviors of interest for some problem behaviors when observations in the natural setting are not possible or feasible. Drawbacks to the use of standard situation formats, however, are that they are simulations of real life experience, and may not reflect actual situations.

General Comments on
Structured Direct Behavior Observation

Proponents of structured direct behavior observation call attention to potential problems (Gelfand & Hartman, 1984), such as: a) the possibility of upsetting children when they are aware they are being observed; b) observations are less useful when children are inhibited or distracted by attending to observers; and c) bias on the part of the observer, particularly if that person is the primary caregiver. Other areas that need to be addressed involve interobserver agreement and validity considerations. Interobserver agreement and validity issues in structured behavior observation are discussed in detail by a number of other authors (such as Barton & Ascione, 1984; Gelfand & Hartman, 1984; Striefel & Cadez, 1983), and should be referred to for more specific information.

Unstructured Behavior Observation

Unstructured behavioral observation information can also be utilized for assessment purposes. Unstructured behavior observations are those made incidental to other ongoing activities (e.g., testing, waiting room behavior, and parent-child interactions). It is impossible for clinicians to avoid making these observations throughout the evaluation process, but clinicians need to be aware of how subjectively influenced such observations can be by: a) clinicians' prior experiences with other clients, b) clinicians' orientation and beliefs about child and parent behavior, and c) other unidentified factors (e.g., biases) and responses to certain personality types. For example, the idiosyncratic observance of hand tremor exhibited by the primary client during standardized intelligence testing may indicate a neurological problem that should be investigated medically.

Despite these drawbacks, valuable information about the primary client may be observed that has either a direct or indirect association with the referral problem. The value of the unstructured behavioral observations can be increased when other professionals who are assigned to the case or invited to observe also concur on observations made.

General Information about Tests and Other Assessment Strategies

Whatever assessment strategies are used in a psychological clinic, clinicians should abide by professional standards that have been developed (American Educational Research Association, American Psychological Association, and National Council on Measurement in Education, 1985) in selecting, administering, scoring, and interpreting results of these strategies. Guion (1983) describes "test users" as those who "make decisions about tests and other measuring procedures, who interpret test scores, or who make decisions or prescriptions affecting the lives of others on the basis of measures obtained" (pp. 130–131). The following guidelines should be adhered to by "test users" (Guion):

1. The user should accept responsibility for understanding the validity of any intended interpretations.
2. A test user needs to recognize his or her qualifications, as well as limits, for particular kinds of measurement activities.
3. Procedures followed by test users should be consistent with the standardized procedures used in the reported evaluation research.
4. Test security should be maintained.
5. Tests should be accurately scored.
6. Tests users should be careful and thoughtful in interpreting individual test scores.
7. Interpretations, not merely numbers, should be reported when the results of measurement are reported to examinees or other interested persons.

Furthermore, it cannot be overemphasized that clinicians must ascertain the level of visual functioning and hearing acuity of child/adolescent clients before attempting to conduct assessments. If it is unclear whether or not there are visual or hearing problems, the child or adolescent should receive examinations in these areas of functioning prior to the evaluation.

SELECTION OF ASSESSMENT/EVALUATION STRATEGIES

Current practice widely advocates that child and adolescent assessment/evaluation should be accomplished through a multimethod approach, that is, the use of multiple measures, in order to obtain the most reliable and valid assessment information (Gelfand et al., 1982; Goldman et al., 1983; Mash & Terdal, 1981; Ollendick & Hersen, 1984). Also, many clinicians emphasize the practicality of incorporating initial assessment strategies that may later be used to evaluate treatment effectiveness (Bornstein, Bornstein, & Dawson, 1984). Several models for multimodal assessment have been proposed for use in clinical behavior therapy (e.g., Behavioral Assessment Grid [Cone, 1978], BASIC ID

[Lazarus, 1973]; Multimethod Clinical Assessment [Nay, 1979]) that could be adapted for other more traditional approaches to assessment.

Although professionals generally concur in the need for a multimethod approach, clinicians have few empirically based guidelines for determining: a) how many different strategies should be employed; b) the extent of assessment/ evaluation necessary within each strategy; or c) which instruments, devices, or techniques will yield the best information. It is frequently assumed that as the expert, the clinician will recognize when he or she has sufficient assessment/ evaluation to answer the referral question and to arrive at appropriate recommendations. Thus, clinical professional judgment sets the standard for ''sufficient'' measurement, and clinicians with adequate training and experience should be able to make such judgments.

The following are suggested general guidelines in the form of a 10-step sequence for conducting child/adolescent evaluations. The chapter sections immediately following these guidelines provide more specific evaluation guidelines on some of the most common child/adolescent problems referred to a clinic.

A Ten-Step Sequence for
Conducting Child/Adolescent Evaluations

1. Conduct parent/guardian interview
2. Conduct child/adolescent interview
3. Have checklists, rating scales, inventories, or questionnaires completed by client families and clients, where applicable
4. Administer standardized and nonstandardized tests
5. Administer other relevant assessments (e.g., projective techniques, physiological measures)
6. Conduct in-clinic structured behavioral observation
7. Obtain client information (e.g. interviews, questionnaires) from relevant sources other than parent/guardian (e.g., teachers, physicians, family members)
8. Conduct out-of-clinic behavioral observations (e.g., school/home, where applicable)
9. Obtain pertinent client records from other sources
10. Review evaluation information and conduct additional assessments if needed

Evaluation Placement for Common Referral Problems

Educational Placement and
Academic Learning Problems Evaluated

As noted by Stetson (1983), the selection of assessment strategies for classification of school-age students for special education services is largely determined by standards established by state departments of education and local school districts. Indeed, many state boards of education specify that certain instruments, (e.g., tests) and procedures be used. Stetson proposed that assessments be conducted in the areas of academic achievement, intellectual functioning, language adequacy, adaptive behavior, and cognitive learning style. Stetson has also proposed that one of two levels of evaluation be conducted: a) Level I–Screening, or b) Level II–Diagnostic. Level I is identified as a screening level, since it is used primarily for determining student qualification for special services. At this level, the student is administered standardized intellectual and general achievement tests, usually including skill assessment in reading, mathematics, and written language, to ascertain how scores obtained meet state standards for special services. As noted earlier, an adaptive behavior measure must also be obtained if the client's IQ score falls in the intellectually handicapped range in order to classify the client as an intellectually handicapped student. We also suggest that some assessment of behavior may be advisable for students with average or somewhat higher intelligence scores, since concerns about acting out or withdrawal may be contributing factors to learning problems.

Stetson (1983) describes a Level II educational evaluation as diagnostic; that is, the assessment battery is conducted to identify specific academic strengths and weaknesses for remedial programming recommendations. Level II also includes assessment in other areas (e.g., language adequacy and cognitive processing). At this level, both standardized and nonstandardized tests would be used. In the Stetson model, language adequacy is mainly determined through performance on verbal items on intelligence tests. Other aspects of language (e.g., grammatical competencies, articulation) require the use of tests designed to assess language, some of which would be appropriate for a trained psychological clinician to administer. Otherwise, the student should be referred to a qualified speech and language pathologist for evaluation.

Stetson (1983) also proposes that the student's cognitive processing be assessed through auditory and visual processing and visual-motor integration. This area has been controversial, as there has been little research to support many of the theoretical positions that attempt to explain causes for learning problems, or that contend that academic skills have improved indirectly as a result of specific modality training. Despite the disagreement, information obtained through assessments in these areas does yield evidence of deficits that may be directly addressed (i.e., recommending coping strategies that the student and/or teacher can employ), while still recommending specific academic remediation for academic deficits.

Educational assessment batteries may also include the following, in addition to standardized/nonstandardized tests:

1. Checklists/rating scales, inventories
2. Teacher/parent/student interviews
3. Structured classroom behavioral observations

For further and more detailed information, you are referred to Stetson (1983) and Sattler (1982).

Evaluation of Attentional Problems and Hyperactivity

Evaluation for diagnosing attentional deficit disorder with or without associated hyperactivity typically involves the use of the following assessment strategies:

1. Interviews with relevant adults (e.g., parents) and clients, if age and skill appropriate.
2. Completion of written report forms (e.g., rating scales, checklists designed for identification of problems in this area of functioning) by significant adults such as, parents, teachers.
3. Objective observations of behavior in the clinic setting (Barkley, 1981), and, where feasible, in the home and classroom settings. Goldman and associates (1983) consider this area of assessment as providing "critical evidence" for evaluating hyperactivity.
4. Standardized testing (e.g., intellectual and academic).
5. Medical evaluation, including a neurological screening, if there is a psychiatrist, pediatrician, or physician with expertise in attention deficit disorder on staff. If not, it would be appropriate to refer the child to a medical professional for such an evaluation.

If the clinician seeks to establish a specific diagnosis of attention deficit disorder in accordance with the *DSM-III* definition, then all of the strategies identified would be appropriate. Academic achievement testing is recommended, as a large percentage of school-age children and adolescents with attentional deficits (whether associated with hyperactivity or not) also have learning disabilities.

Conduct Problem Evaluation

Evaluation of clients referred because of overt conduct problems (e.g., non-compliance, oppositional behavior, aggression) typically encompasses the following strategies: a) interviews with parents, teachers, significant others, and the client, if appropriate; b) completion of written report measures (e.g., checklists, rating scales); and c) direct behavioral observation when feasible and appropriate (Atkeson & Forehand, 1981; Gelfand & Hartmann, 1984; Goldman et al., 1983). The evaluation of conduct problems focuses on the acquisition of specific information related to both the problem behavior(s) of concern as well as antecedent and consequent events. As an adjunct to those assessment strategies already identified, screening tests of intellectual ability and academic achievement skills are useful, as poor school performance is frequently associated with conduct problems. For more detailed information on evaluation of conduct problems, see Atkeson and Forehand, Doke and Flippo (1983), Gelfand and Hartmann, Gelfand et al. (1982), and Striefel and Cadez (1983).

Social/Emotional Problems Evaluation

Problems associated with social or emotional areas (e.g., phobias, depression, and social withdrawal) are evaluated through a variety of assessment strategies.

Most clinicians would include interviews with significant adults and the client, where appropriate, as a primary assessment strategy.

Kennedy (1983) proposes that evaluation of phobias include the following strategies: a) questionnaires and inventories for the child/adolescent and parents to complete; b) development of a phobia hierarchy; c) projective assessment; and d) situational or *in vivo* assessment, where the client is exposed to varying degrees of the fear-producing situations in real or representational situations.

Evaluation of childhood and adolescent social isolation, withdrawal, or avoidance has been approached from several directions (Pretti, 1983): a) sociometric measures by peer rating, b) direct behavioral observation of social interactions, and c) teacher nomination of ratings. In contrast, the evaluation of childhood and adolescent depression has mainly focused on: a) the use of self-report inventories, rating scales, or checklists; b) interviews; and c) unstructured clinical observations of the client's demeanor and affect.

Since problem concerns in the social/emotional area usually result in treatment following the initial evaluation, it is also important for the clinician to know the child's capability to participate and benefit from various interventions. Therefore, it is appropriate to administer a screening or full scale test of intelligence as well. Also, academic assessment may provide useful information.

Neuropsychological Evaluation

A neuropsychological evaluation is conducted to determine indications of brain damage or dysfunction (Goldman et al., 1983). This specialized evaluation involves measurement of more than one psychological process or content area (Boll, 1983) (e.g., memory, sensory, motor, language, cognitive) and consists of the use of standardized tests and interviews as the primary assessment strategies. Sattler (1982) points out that this type of evaluation is a complement to a neurological examination and is often conducted as an adjunct to medical testing. Although some tests used in the neuropsychological evaluation are similar to those used in evaluations conducted for other purposes (e.g., intelligence tests), the way test results are analyzed may differ; that is, patterns of responses may be a focus of interpretation. Specialized test materials are also usually administered (e.g., Halsted Neuropsychological Test Battery for Children [for use with children 9–14 years of age], Reitan-Indiana Neurological Test Battery for Children [for use with children 5–8 years of age]). For more detailed information on this type of evaluation and specialized test batteries, see Boll (1983), Goldman et al. (1983), or Sattler (1982).

Evaluations for Other Referral Problems

Children and adolescents are referred to a clinic for evaluation for a number of reasons apart from the general areas already described, including: sleep and eating disorders, suicidal intent or attempts, identity and gender problems, psychotic behavior, enuresis/encopresis, elective mutism, and gifted/talented identification. It is beyond the scope of this chapter to describe which assessment strategies should be employed for evaluating each of these and other problems. Such information is available in a number of books and professional journals, including Mash and Terdal (1981), Ollendick and Hersen (1984), Sattler (1982), and Walker and Roberts (1983).

Special Needs Evaluations

Although the same general assessment strategies are used to evaluate children and adolescents with developmental disabilities, or those from minority or ethnic groups, only instruments or techniques that are appropriate for these clients should be used. Reference to this point was made earlier in the chapter, but it bears reemphasis here. Assessment tools are available that have been developed specifically for use with special populations (e.g., nonverbal tests for those with hearing impairment), and should be used in place of less appropriate instruments.

OTHER ASSESSMENT/EVALUATION ISSUES

Administration of Tests and Report Instruments

Much has been written about administration of assessment instruments to children and adolescents (Goldman et al., 1983; Mash and Terdal, 1981; Sattler, 1982), including information discussed in this and other chapters. Therefore, only an overview of the following selected issues is included here: a) gaining and maintaining cooperation of the child/adolescent; b) importance of familiarity with instruments used; and c) administration accommodations for clients with developmental disabilities.

Gaining and Maintaining Client Cooperation

Some children and adolescents who have been brought to a clinic for assessment/evaluation are unwilling participants (Goldman et al., 1983). This may stem from a number of factors: shyness, anxiety, defensiveness, anger, or rebelliousness. Some clients experiencing negative or fearful feelings may still cooperate on assessment tasks if approached in a positive manner, if the purpose for assessment is described to them, and if they are prepared for what will be expected of them. In addition, there are clients who either deliberately refuse to engage in tasks or do so with a minimum of effort. Skillful administrators often are able to overcome client resistance or refusal through a variety of means, including: a) offering opportunities for the client to engage in a more preferred activity in exchange for cooperation (with younger children this may involve presentations of a sample of the activity in advance), b) encouraging the client to talk about why they are refusing or reluctant to cooperate before trying to do more formal testing, c) negotiating with the client for a shorter assessment session than planned, or d) giving the older client an opportunity to reschedule the assessment. The clinician and client family must both recognize that the client has the ultimate control in this situation, and that reliable assessment is dependent on this factor. Clinicians confronting a resistant client must be creative in eliciting cooperation. Negative approaches are not only ill advised but would be unethical, and also would probably impair any future rapport with the client. If none of the methods attempted is successful, the clinician may need to terminate a session and talk with the parents about the usefulness of rescheduling for a later attempt (Goldman et al., 1983).

After gaining initial cooperation from the client, clinicians must maintain the client's attention to tasks and cooperation throughout the session. For many clients this is difficult (e.g., with younger children or clients with attentional problems). Clinicians should modify the length of the assessment sessions to fit individual client capabilities so that performance on assessment instruments remains at an optimum level. There are no hard and fast rules on how long assessment sessions should last. Some younger children may be able to stay on-task for 1–2 hours with little difficulty; others find it difficult to remain on-task for periods of longer than a quarter hour. Those children can be given short breaks at frequent intervals (e.g., 15 minutes), in order to maintain their attention. Adolescents and children from 6 to 12 years of age are usually able to attend during 2–2½ hour testing sessions, but they should be given at least one break during sessions of that length, and more frequent breaks if needed. Even during short testing sessions, some clients are easily distracted from test tasks (i.e., they may be distracted by extraneous objects or noises). Other clients may be easily discouraged by being presented with items they perceive to be difficult or overwhelming, or by a series of successive item failures. Clinicians may be able to maintain on-task behavior through a variety of means such as: a) providing verbal praise for their effort or appropriate behavior; b) providing social acceptance (e.g., smiling) for on-task behavior; c) not making critical statements or comments; d) recognizing and acknowledging that items may be increasing in difficulty; e) providing tangibles (e.g., colorful stickers, or opportunities to play with a small toy car for one minute), after a certain number of tasks are completed. At no time, however, should responses to test tasks be commented on or treated by any of the methods described.

Preschool children are often some of the most difficult clients to assess (Sattler, 1982), for several reasons, including: a) usually, it is difficult to maintain preschoolers' interest in assessment, b) they may be impulsive in responding, c) they are often not responsive to the same approaches that work with older children, and d) they are more likely to express strong emotion (e.g., cry). Sattler describes a number of activities or arrangements that can be used to enhance the assessment of preschool children, including: a) have test materials available and systematically arranged; b) adjust the speed of item presentation to the child's attention level; c) be alert to signs of restlessness, boredom, or emotional stress, and take action before they disrupt testing. Nevertheless, it is not uncommon for preschoolers to suddenly terminate assessment with little warning (i.e., after initial cooperation, they may suddenly refuse to cooperate further).

Familiarity with Assessment Instruments to Be Used

As noted elsewhere in this chapter, it is essential that clinicians administer only those assessment instruments that they are trained to use and feel competent to administer. If a service provider has not had recent practice in administration of an instrument, even though trained at some point in the past, then the assessment should not be administered until he or she has had sufficient practice.

Administration Accommodations with Clients with Developmental Disabilities

Child or adolescent clients with developmental disabilities (e.g., those with hearing impairment) may need to be assessed with instruments developed specifically for use with them. If available, assessment instruments of this type frequently were normed on a similar population. Often, however, specific assessment instruments have not been developed. Assessment instruments that were standardized on nondevelopmentally disabled individuals may be used or adapted, but the normative information available may not be applicable. Therefore, any estimates or conclusions about results obtained should be interpreted very cautiously, and supported by a variety of assessment strategies.

Scoring Procedures

Clinicians are ethically bound to score test protocols and other assessment devices (e.g. inventories, rating scales) in an accurate manner. Because of the scoring complexities on some instruments, as well as the inclusion of items that ultimately force subjective conclusions (even though guidelines may be provided), scoring at times may be inaccurate despite the best of intentions. Ways to avoid scoring inaccuracies are: a) rechecking scoring at another time or on another day (since scoring inaccuracies may be due to fatigue or pressure factors), or b) having a colleague or supervisor double-check scoring.

Scoring should also be rechecked whenever incongruencies in assessment results are found after all assessment results from various instruments and strategies have been compiled. Sattler (1982) also stresses that test scorers need to be familiar with research results on possible scoring biases, halo effects, common test scoring errors, and the scoring criteria for each instrument used.

INTEGRATION AND INTERPRETATION OF ASSESSMENT FINDINGS

The more extensive the evaluation, the more complex the task of integrating the information obtained in the process. Practicality demands that a systematic method be used for assembling the puzzle pieces into an organized whole. Some clinicians may have access to computer programs where one can input the numerical results (e.g. raw score) from various instruments administered and receive not only transformed scores (e.g., standard scores, percentiles, age/grade equivalents) but limited interpretation of results as well. As more complicated computer programs are available in the future, greater use of this technology will result in considerable time savings for clinicians and, perhaps, serve as a way of confirming clinical judgment. At this time, however, interpretation of assessment information is still primarily the task of one or more clinicians.

It is helpful for clinicians to prepare some type of organized compilation of specific assessment information (e.g., test data) for review, to assist in arriving at interpretive conclusions. Use of assessment data forms such as Stetson's (1983) Psychometric Data profile are aids to this process. When assessments have been conducted by representatives of different disciplines, each clinician may compile data from his or her assessments that can then be integrated onto one form. Otherwise, information can be integrated at a summary staff conference (discussed later in this chapter).

Review of the compiled assessment information can lead directly to a series of summary statements or conclusions (i.e., "The evaluation results clearly support a *DSM-III* diagnosis of attention deficit disorder with hyperactivity"). Summary statements drawn from an evaluation profile or data form should: a) address referral questions or concerns, b) address incongruencies or discrepancies, and c) identify strengths and weaknesses. When evaluation information is organized as described, consultation provided by other clinicians will be based on the same information (not from a potentially biased verbal explanation) and can be reviewed by them independently and quickly.

A common complaint of consumers and clinicians alike is that there is a tendency among a sector of clinicians to overinterpret results and draw conclusions from limited findings, or make inferences from results obtained on instruments not designed for the areas in question. Any clinician doing so is not only unethical but will lose the respect of other professionals. More on this topic is included in Chapters 9 and 11.

COMMUNICATING ASSESSMENT/EVALUATION RESULTS

Staff Conferences

Before assessment/evaluation results are presented to client families or agency representatives, all clinicians involved should meet to share and integrate findings. It is recommended that this meeting also include a supervisor or colleague who has not been directly involved, since this individual can view the results from a different perspective and may be able to offer useful input on the interpretation of results or need for further assessment. Advantages of staff conferences held for this purpose are: a) data gaps may be identified where further assessment is indicated; b) contradictory findings may be resolved or dealt with; c) an outline may be prepared for how and what information is to be communicated to client families and agency representatives; and d) preliminary recommendations may be generated, or integrated.

Client Family/Agency Representative Meetings

It is customary to provide parents or legal guardians with a verbal summary of assessment/evaluation findings and to discuss preliminary recommendations with them. Whenever possible, if both parents are living in the home, meetings should be scheduled at a time when both can attend. This is particularly important if treatment is to be provided to the child/adolescent client, and parents are expected to be active participants in that process (e.g., family therapy). When agencies have been the direct referral source, it is a courtesy to provide agency representatives with an opportunity to receive verbal information after an assessment/evaluation has been conducted, particularly if actions need to be taken by the agency prior to receipt of a written report. In some instances, it is appropriate for agency representatives and client families to meet at the same time; otherwise, a separate meeting is needed. This should be decided on a case-by-case basis, but one meeting is more efficient in terms of staff time and client dollars.

Several issues need to be resolved prior to meeting with client families or agency representatives:

1. Who will represent the clinic in the meeting? When only one clinician has been involved, this question is easily answered. If more than one clinician has been assigned, one or more of these must be delegated. In interdisciplinary team evaluations, it is not unusual for each team member to be present to provide a summary of his or her evaluation findings. This, however, is a costly process in terms of staff time. It is usually more practical in team evaluations to assign one person to meet with the client families (e.g., team coordinator, social worker).

2. How are the assessment/evaluation results to be presented? When an outline has been prepared in advance (i.e., at a staff conference), a sequence has already been established. If not, a sequence needs to be prepared. Further, the degree of specificity in reporting results should be considered. There are distinct advantages in providing general information at the summary meeting instead of highly specific information. First, the family of the client can more easily attend to significant information provided, rather than being distracted or overwhelmed by less significant details. Bombarding parents with details (e.g., specific test titles) may not only result in loss of their attention but could lead to confusion. Second, a written report of the assessment/evaluation process, containing more specific information, will be submitted to parents/agencies after the summary meeting, thus negating the need for detailed information at the verbal summary meeting (written reports are discussed in Chapter 9). Third, when less specific details are described, more time is available for questions to be raised and answered, and for discussion of recommendations.

3. Is the child or adolescent client to be included throughout or for part of meetings held with parents or legal guardians and agency representatives? Some issues discussed earlier in this chapter in the interview section also pertain to decisions made at this point (e.g., age of client, referral problem). Whereas initial meetings focus on obtaining information, the purpose of evaluation summary meetings is to disseminate information. Therefore, the content of that information should to a great extent influence decisions on the advisability of child or adolescent presence. That is, decisions should be

made on a case-by-case basis and not in accordance with a standard clinic practice (e.g., that all minor-age clients are not allowed at evaluation summary meetings with adults).

The following factors should be considered in reviewing whether the child or adolescent should be present at the adult summary meeting: a) Of what benefit will it be to the minor-age child? b) How will it affect open and direct communication between clinicians and client family members? c) How may it inhibit client family members from expressing emotional reactions to findings (e.g., sadness, fears)? d) Are there pros and cons of future considerations to be discussed that could be upsetting to the child (e.g. possible residential placement), and should these issues be resolved before the child is presented with information? In general, children under the age of 5 usually do not benefit from being included in the verbal summary meeting, as often the information communicated is not meaningful for them. Further, children tend to be distractors at such meetings, and sometimes even disruptive. Also, children and adolescents with limited comprehension skills are often disinterested in such adult meetings. However, it can be very useful to include children and adolescent clients in the verbal summary meeting whose comprehension skills are adequate and whose behavior will not be disruptive. If minor-age clients are to be present, however, clinicians should at all times include them in the communication interchanges and not talk about them as if they were not present.

Child and Adolescent Summary Meetings

If minor-age clients are excluded from the adult verbal summary meetings, they have a right to an independent verbal summary meeting apart from their families. The content included should be determined on the basis of: a) the client's comprehension skills, b) the client's emotional and maturity level; and c) the client's need for information. Again, there are no rules available to guide clinicians. At times, summary meetings with children or adolescents may only involve: a) praising them for their cooperating during the evaluation, b) identifying strengths revealed in the evaluation process, and/or c) giving encouragement for future endeavors. On a continuum, however, there will be times when adolescents may be given the same or almost the same information that was provided their families. Clinicians must be careful not to overwhelm minor-age clients with unnecessary details, and to ensure that information communicated has been understood. Many children and adolescents are not as likely as adults to raise questions or seek clarification.

SUMMARY

Child and adolescent assessment and evaluation may be conducted through a variety of approaches. Our purpose in this chapter has been to present an overview of strategies most commonly used in clinics for children and adolescents.

We have identified and discussed the strategies of interviewing, standardized and nonstandardized ability and achievement tests, behavioral observation, projective assessments, rating scales and devices of a similar nature, in addition to other strategies. We have also provided guidelines for evaluation of some specific child/adolescent problem areas and a discussion of various issues related to assessment/evaluation.

READER ACTIVITIES

If you would like to expand your repertoire of skills, we suggest that you schedule time in the near future to become acquainted with and practice the administration of an unfamiliar, revised, or new test designed for use with children or adolescents. When you have mastered this skill, you could then arrange to provide a demonstration to a group of professionals.

As a clinician, you could be a valuable resource to those interested in developing or revising assessment instruments. Try to list ways a test or other assessment device that you are familiar with could be improved or modified to increase its usefulness. You could then offer your suggestions to the developer or publisher.

If your clinic accepts referrals of preschool-age children, we suggest that you review published structured behavior observation formats that have been developed for observation of parent-child interactions. See if any would be useful in your clinic and arrange with the developers for their use or modification to suit your clinic's clientele.

We suggest that you prepare or locate an assessment data form or summary form for use in compiling data obtained on all of the assessments conducted for one client. If you already have such a form, compare yours with forms that you have found through other sources (e.g., other clinics, private practitioners, psychological assessment books). Find out if there is a better way of presenting the data for visual inspection than the form you have prepared or currently use.

We suggest that you plan a way (e.g., meeting, evaluation questionnaire) to find out how clinical staff view the current practices and procedures for handling and storing assessment instruments. Involve clinic staff in any modifications that may need to be made to increase convenience for staff and cooperation among staff members. You may find it useful to conduct a survey with clinical staff to determine what assessment instruments or devices need to be updated or acquired in the next year so that you may budget accordingly.

REFERENCES

Achenbach, T. M. (1981). *Child behavior checklist*. Burlington: University of Vermont.
American Educational Research Association, American Psychological Association, and National Council on Measurement in Education. (1985). *Standards for educational and psychological testing*. Washington, DC: American Psychological Association.
Anastasi, A. (1976). *Psychological testing* (4th ed.). New York: Macmillan.

Atkeson, B. M., & Forehand, R. (1981). Conduct Disorders. In E. D. Mash & L. G. Terdal (Eds.), *Behavioral assessment of childhood disorders* (pp. 185–219). New York: Guilford Press.

Barkly, R. A. (1981). Hyperactivity. In E. D. Mash and L. G. Terdal (Eds.), *Behavioral assessment of childhood disorders* (pp. 127–184). New York: Guilford Press.

Barton, E. J., & Ascione, F. R. (1984). Direct observation. In T. H. Ollendick and M. Hersen (Eds.), *Child behavioral assessment* (pp. 166–194). New York: Pergamon.

Bellak, L. (1947–1973). *Thematic Apperception Test (TAT)*. New York: Psychological Corporation.

Bellak, L., & Bellak, S. (1949–1974). *Children's Apperception Test*. New York: Psychological Corporation.

Boll, T. J. (1983). Neuropsychological assessment of the child: Myths, current status, and future prospects. In C. E. Walker and M. C. Roberts (Eds.), *Handbook of clinical child psychology* (pp. 186–208). New York: John Wiley & Sons.

Bornstein, P. H., Bornstein, M. T., & Dawson, B. (1984). Integrated assessment and treatment. In T. H. Ollendick & M. Hersen (Eds.), *Child behavior assessment* (pp. 223–243). New York: Pergamon.

Buros, O. K. (1974). *Tests in print*. Highland Park, NJ: Gryphon Press.

Buros, O. K. (Ed.) (1978). *The eighth mental measurement yearbook*. Highland Park, NJ: Gryphon Press.

Cautela, J. R., Cautela, J., & Esonis, S. (1983). *Forms for behavior analysis with children*. Champaign, IL: Research Press.

Cone, J. D. (1978). The behavioral assessment grid (BAG): A conceptual framework and taxonomy. *Behavior Therapy, 9,* 882–888.

Connolly, A. J., Nachtman, W., & Pritchett, E. M. (1976). *Key Math diagnostic arithmetic test*. Circle Pines, MN: American Guidance Service.

Doke, L. A., & Flippo, J. R. (1983). Aggressive and oppositional behavior. In T. H. Ollendick & M. Hersen (Eds.), *Handbook of child psychopathology* (pp. 323–356) New York: Plenum.

Finch, A. J., & Rogers, T. R. (1984). Self-report instruments. In T. H. Ollendick and M. Hersen (Eds.), *Child behavioral assessment* (pp. 106–123). New York: Pergamon.

Finley, W. (1983). Biofeedback with children. In C. E. Walker & M. C. Roberts (Eds.), *Handbook of clinical child psychology* (pp. 1050–1068). New York: John Wiley & Sons.

French, J., Graves, P. A., & Levitt, E. E. (1983). Objective and projective testing of children. In C. E. Walker & M. C. Roberts (Eds.), *Handbook of clinical child psychology* (pp. 209–247). New York: John Wiley & Sons.

Gardner, R. A. (1971). *Therapeutic communication with children: The mutual story-telling technique*. New York: Jason Aronson.

Gelfand, D. M., & Hartmann, D. P. (1984). *Child behavior analysis and therapy* (2nd ed.). New York: Pergamon.

Gelfand, D. M., Jenson, W. R., & Drew, C. T. (1982). *Understanding child behavior disorders*. New York: Holt, Rinehart & Winston.

Goldman, J., L'Engle Stein, C. L., & Guerry, S. (1983). *Psychological methods of child assessment*. New York: Brunner/Mazel.

Gross, A. M. (1984). Behavioral interviewing. In T. H. Ollendick & M. Hersen (Eds.), *Child behavioral assessment* (pp. 61–79). New York: Pergamon.

Grossman, H. J. (Ed.). (1983). *Classification in mental retardation*. Washington, DC: American Assocation on Mental Deficiency.

Guion, R. M. (1983). Standards for psychological measurement. In D. B. Sales (Ed.), *The professional psychologist's handbook* (pp. 111–140). New York: Plenum.

Hamill, D. D. (1985). *Detroit Tests of Learning Aptitude (DTLA-2)*. Austin, TX: PRO-ED.

Hathaway, S. R., & McKinley, J. C. (1967). *The Minnesota Multiphasic Personality Inventory manual–revised*. Minneapolis: MN: Interpretive Scoring Systems (NCS).

Jastak, S., & Wilkinson, G. S. (1984). *Wide Range Achievement Test–Revised (WRAT-R)*. New York: Psychological Corporation.

Kanfer, R., Eyberg, S. M., & Kahn, G. L. (1983). Interviewing strategies in child assessment. In C. E. Walker & M. C. Roberts (Eds.), *Handbook of clinical child psychology* (pp. 95–108). New York: John Wiley & Sons.

Kaufman, A. S. (1979). *Intelligence testing with the WISC-R*. New York: John Wiley & Sons.

Kaufman, A. S., & Kaufman, N. L. (1983). *Kaufman Assessment Battery for Children*. Circle Pines, MN: American Guidance Service.

Kaufman, A. S., & Kaufman, N. L. (1985). *Kaufman Test of Educational Achievement*. Circle Pines, MN: American Guidance Service.

Kaufman, A. S., & Reynolds, C. R. (1984). Intellectual and academic achievement tests. In T. H. Ollendick & M. Hersen (Eds.), *Child behavioral assessment* (pp. 195–220). New York: Pergamon.

Kennedy, W. A. (1983). Obsessive-compulsive and phobic reactions. In T. H. Ollendick and M. Hersen (Eds.), *Handbook of Child Psychopathology* (pp. 277–291). New York: Plenum.

Lachar, D. (1984). *Personality Inventory for Children—Revised*. Los Angeles: Western Psychological Services.

LaGreca, A. M. (1983). Interviewing and behavioral observations. In C. E. Walker & M. C. Roberts (Eds.), *Handbook of clinical child psychology* (pp. 109–131). New York: John Wiley & Sons.

Lazarus, A. A. (1973). Multimodal behavior therapy: Treating the "BASIC ID." *Journal of Nervous and Mental Disease, 156,* 401–411.

Leiter, R. B. (1948). *The Leiter International Performance Scale*. Chicago: Stoelting Co.

Mash, E. J., & Terdal, L. G. (Eds.), (1981). *Behavioral assessment of childhood disorders*. New York: Guilford Press.

McCarthy, D. A. (1972). *McCarthy Scales of Children's Abilities*. New York: Psychological Corporation.

McMahon, R. J. (1984). Behavioral checklists and rating scales. In T. H. Ollendick & M. Hersen (Eds.), *Child behavioral assessment* (pp. 80–105). New York: Pergamon.

Murray, H. A. (1935–43). *Thematic Apperception Test (TAT)*. New York: Psychological Corporation.

Naglieri, J. A. (1985). *Matrix Analogies Test*. Columbus, OH: Charles E. Merrill.

Nay, W. R. (1979). *Multimethod clinical assessment*. New York: Gardner Press.

Ollendick, T. H., & Hersen, M. (1984). An overview of child behavioral assessment. In T. H. Ollendick & M. Hersen (Eds.), *Child behavior assessment* (pp. 3–19). New York: Pergamon.

Pretti, T. A. (1983). Depression and withdrawal in children. In T. H. Ollendick & M. Hersen (Eds.), *Handbook of Child psychopathology* (pp. 293–321). New York: Plenum.

Rorschach, H. (1941–45). *Rorschach technique*. New York: Psychological Corporation.

Rotter, J. B. (1950). *Rotter Incomplete Sentences Blank*. New York: Psychological Corporation.

Salvia, J., & Ysseldyke, J. E. (1981). *Assessment in special and remedial education* (2nd ed.). Boston: Houghton Mifflin.

Sattler, J. M. (1982). *Assessment of children's intelligence and special abilities* (2nd ed.). Boston: Allyn & Bacon.

Slosson, R. L. (1981). *Slosson Intelligence Test (SIT)*. New York: Slosson Educational Publications.

Sparrow, S. S., Balla, D. A., & Cicchetti, D. V. (1984). *Vineland Adaptive Behavior Scales*. Circle Pines, MN: American Guidance Service.

Stetson, E. (1983). Educational assessment of the child. In C. E. Walker & M. C. Roberts (Eds.), *Handbook of clinical child psychology* (pp. 158–185). New York: John Wiley & Sons.

Striefel, S., & Cadez, M. J. (1983). *Serving children and adolescents with developmental disabilities in the special education classroom: Proven methods*. Baltimore: Paul H. Brookes Publishing Co.

Symonds, P. M. (1948). *Manual for Symonds Picture-Story Test*. New York: Teachers College Press.

Thorndike, R. L., Hagen, E. P., & Sattler, J. M. (1986). *The Stanford-Binet Intelligence Scale: Fourth edition*. Chicago: Riverside Publishing Co.

Wagner, E. E. (1983). *The Hands Test, Revised*. Los Angeles: Western Psychological Corporation.

Walker, C. E., & Roberts, M. C. (Eds.). (1983). *Handbook of clinical child psychology*. New York: John Wiley & Sons.

Walker, H. M. (1983). *Walker Problem Behavior Checklist–Revised*. Los Angeles: Western Psychological Services.

Wechsler, D. (1967). *Wechsler Preschool and Primary Scale of Intelligence*. New York: Psychological Corporation.

Wechsler, D. (1974). *Wechsler Intelligence Scale for Children–Revised*. New York: Psychological Corporation.

Wechsler, D. (1981). *Wechsler Adult Intelligence Scale–Revised*. New York: Psychological Corporation.

White, L. & Tursky, B. (1982). *Clinical biofeedback: Efficacy and mechanisms*. New York: Guilford Press.

Wolberg, L. R. (1977). *The technique of psychotherapy: Part 1*. (3rd ed.). New York: Grune & Stratton.

Woodcock, R. W. (1973). *Woodcock Reading Mastery Tests*. Circle Pines, MN: American Guidance Service.

Woodcock, R. W., & Johnson, M. B. (1977). *Woodcock-Johnson Psycho-educational Battery*. Allen, TX: DLM Teaching Resources.

7

Developing, Implementing, and Evaluating Treatment

At the end of this chapter you will be able to:
1. Select a treatment plan format
2. Use appropriate forms for treatment plans, follow-up contact notes, and staffings
3. Develop treatment goals and a treatment plan
4. Understand the various considerations involved in implementation
5. Establish rapport with a client
6. Define *treatment*
7. Monitor treatment progress
8. Understand and be able to plan for generalization and maintenance of treatment goals
9. Evaluate the quality of a treatment plan and determine client satisfaction

This chapter assumes that readers have knowledge of content in their particular areas of specialization; thus, the focus here is more heavily on process.

DECIDING WHO IS THE CLIENT

The extent to which family members are interested in the problems of their children depends on many factors, including the age of the child, the nature of the problem, the degree to which the child is "legally responsible," and the degree to which the problem is aversive to the parents (Feldman & Peay, 1982). When a child, adolescent, or any other person is brought to a clinic for treatment, the therapist will want to know: "Is there a problem, and if so, who has it?" (Feldman & Peay, 1982, p. 235).

Deciding whether a problem exists depends on who raises the question. Therapists are inclined to accept the existence of a problem whenever someone is concerned enough to seek assistance for themselves or someone else. In some cases the solution appears to be as simple as providing factual information. For example, a mother of a 6 month old, who is concerned because her child is not yet toilet trained, can be reassured that children are not physically ready for toilet training at that age. In addition, the issue of an overconcerned or uninformed parent is raised, which might require additional interventions. In most cases, the pinpointing of the specific problem and its solution are more complex.

Since children and adolescents seldom seek treatment on their own, the next concern after agreeing that a problem exists becomes, "Is it the child's problem or that of the parent or teacher who complains about the child's behavior? In issues involving children and adolescents, there is usually more than one client. Feldman and Peay (1982) label the person who is suffering because of the receipt of aversive consequences or the absence of positive ones, the *initial client*. Anyone else who is affected by the problem or who needs to be involved in its solution is also considered to be a client (*consequential client*). In situations in which a child is enjoying life but his or her behavior causes problems (pain and suffering) for the parent(s), it is the parent(s) who is/are the primary client. The parents' behavior needs to change in order for the child's behavior to change. Ideally the change should remove the aversive consequences for the parent(s), while increasing or maintaining the positive consequences of behavior for both the child and the parent(s). A good example of such a case involves a child who makes a mess (smearing food, dropping paper, etc.) wherever he goes, but the mess is only of concern to the parent. At the opposite end of the continuum is the situation in which the child is experiencing pain (lack of positive consequences or receipt of negative consequences) that is not also affecting the parent. In such situations the child is the primary client but other family members may need to be involved in the treatment process in order for positive changes to generalize to, and be maintained in, the child's daily environment. An example of such a problem would be a child who interacts appropriately with his family but lacks the skills needed to establish or maintain peer friendships. Many child and adolescent referrals involve situations in which both the parent(s) and child are suffering and both must be treated as clients.

ESTABLISHING THERAPEUTIC RELATIONSHIPS

Therapeutic interventions consist of a process in which a client seeks to change his or her behavior, thoughts or feelings, or those of his or her child, and in which a clinician/therapist (the terms are used interchangeably here) tries to facilitate that change (Shelton & Levy, 1981). Successful intervention depends on a good working relationship between the client/family and the clinician. Ideally the relationship is one in which the client feels warmth, trust, acceptance, and understanding that may seldom be experienced elsewhere (Wolberg, 1977). The development of a proper working relationship between the client/family and the clinician is the major purpose of the first phase of treatment. The therapist must engage in interaction-enhancing activities that encourage liking, respect, and trust (Shelton & Levy, 1981). These may result in improved communication with the client and an openness and flexibility on his or her part that lead to positive behavior changes. If a good working relationship does not exist, the client is unlikely to make progress, may be dismissed from treatment as "unsuitable" (Wolberg, 1977), or may terminate treatment because the therapist "doesn't understand." A clinician must be able to provide the client with options for a new way of life. Resistance to change must be overcome, and this seems best accomplished via the establishment of a good working relationship, or what is often called "rapport." Establishing rapport begins with the first contact with the client and maintenance of rapport continues until case termination.

Clients may have any of a variety of needs, including: a) the need to be dependent, b) the need for unqualified understanding and acceptance, c) the need to express painful ideas and feelings, d) the need for factual understanding, e) the need for a transference relationship, and f) the need for a cooperative human relationship (Wolberg, 1977). The therapist must find ways to deal with these needs while establishing and maintaining rapport.

Pacing

Lankton (1980) argues that "resistance," "transference," and "counter-transference" are not a demonstration of a client's difficulty, but rather of the therapist's limited range of responses. Establishing rapport requires the therapist to be adept at utilizing numerous strategies for dealing with different situations. One useful skill for establishing rapport is pacing (Charny, 1966; Lankton, 1980). Pacing involves meeting the client at his or her representation of the world and establishing a relationship with him or her. This is accomplished by matching the client's verbal and nonverbal behavior, in essence, by mirroring the client's behavior. One can pace a client by matching his or her voice tone and tempo, breathing, body posture, gross or minute muscle movements, and so on (Lankton, 1980). In some cases the pacing is indirect (e.g., tapping one's foot to the rhythm of the client's breathing). Speaking "the same language" and having common experiences to share are good methods of pacing. With children, participating in a common play activity is often useful.

Once the therapist has paced the client, he or she can attempt to change the pace and lead the client elsewhere. Effective pacing depends on: a) establishing a feedback loop (client can see some of his or her own behavior being modeled by the therapist as the behavior is occurring with the client, and b) the occurrence of a subjective sense of rapport that the client reports. The following example of pacing will help to illustrate these points. Haley (1973, p. 199) reports a case in which Milton Erickson, an expert at pacing, worked with a disturbed child. The child was lying on the floor yelling and when he stopped to catch his breath Dr. Erickson let out a yell (pacing). This startled the child and so Dr. Erickson told him, "It's my turn," and then said, "Now it's your turn." After taking a few turns (pacing), Dr. Erickson indicated they could continue to take turns yelling, but that he (Erickson) would rather sit in a chair, and pointed out a chair for the child to sit in (leading). The child sat down in the chair. A level of rapport had been established and therapy progressed from there.

Other Factors

Other factors important in establishing a working relationship include knowledge of interviewing techniques, appropriate facial expressions, gestures and subvocal utterances (after pacing). All are means for expressing attention, acceptance, and interest. Objectivity, asking direct questions, restating, and summarizing what has been said are also helpful in communicating to the client an understanding of the problem. With children or adolescents this must be addressed at a level appropriate to their level of understanding. Wolberg (1977) indicates that a therapist must be trained to avoid: a) exclamations of surprise, b) expressions of overconcern, c) moralistic judgments, d) being punitive, e) criticizing the client, f) making false promises, g) personal references or boasting, h) threatening the client, i) burdening the client with the therapist's difficulties, j) displays of impatience, k) political or religious discussions, l) arguing with the client, m) ridiculing the client, n) belittling the client, o) blaming the client for his or her failures, p) rejecting the client, q) displays of intolerance, r) dogmatic utterances, s) premature deep interpretations, t) dogmatic analysis of dreams, u) probing traumatic material when resistance is too great, v) flattering and praising the client, and w) unnecessary reassurance. He goes on to say that the therapist should: a) reassure the client when necessary; b) express open-mindedness, even toward irrational attitudes; c) respect the client's right to express values different from those of the therapist; d) clarify the purpose of the interview as often as necessary; and e) make sympathetic remarks where appropriate. All of these ideas are useful. At times, employing one or more of the items Wolberg says to avoid can be very useful therapeutically, if planned and executed correctly, especially with children. For example, sometimes compliments can be very appropriate for bolstering a client's satisfaction with a change in clothing or appearance, while simultaneously showing how attentive to detail the therapist has been. The compliment should be genuine. As a therapist you must have available a wide variety of responses for dealing with situations that arise, and for selecting the response choice that seems most therapeutic at the time. For example, when a child has a temper tantrum in a session, the clinician can: a) ignore the child, b) pace by also having a tantrum, c) continue as if nothing happened, or d) do something new or different.

TREATMENT

Defining Psychological Treatment

Defining *psychotherapy*, which is one major form of psychological treatment, is at best difficult. A comprehensive definition seems both desirable and useful in order to provide a context here for the information that follows. "Psychotherapy is the treatment, by psychological means, of problems of an emotional nature in which a trained person deliberately establishes a professional relationship with the patient with the object of (1) removing, modifying, or retarding existing symptoms, (2) mediating disturbing patterns of behavior, and (3) promoting positive personality growth and development" (Wolberg, 1977, p. 3). Thus, psychotherapy covers a broad spectrum of psychological treatment methods. Psychotherapy is probably not the treatment of choice for most child and preadolescent clients. It becomes more relevant in later adolescence, when clients have well-developed verbal skills.

Other equally important psychological treatment methods for use with children and adolescents include, but are not limited to, behavior therapy, play therapy, family therapy, educational, casework, and counseling. Regardless of the form of intervention, the goal of all psychological treatment is the development or enhancement of effective self-management in so far as possible. The role of the clinician is that of guiding and educating clients (children, adolescents, and families) in areas in which they are experiencing difficulties in self-management. This guidance and education should be based on the most effective and efficient intervention techniques available for achieving the particular goal(s) of the client, by using methods the client finds acceptable (Feldman & Peay, 1982). Before therapy can begin, a decision needs to be made concerning "Who is the client?"

Experimental Foundation

Treatment should be based on a theoretical or practical foundation that can be verified experimentally so that treatment techniques can be developed, assessed, and improved. Only by adhering to such approaches can we utilize the tools and procedures of research psychology (Levis, 1982). An experimental foundation can help protect against claims of incompetence while simultaneously demonstrating accountability. Self-management steps can be verified experimentally and are useful with children and adolescents.

Steps for Effective Self-Management

The steps for effective self-management include (Lee, 1978):

1. Identification and specification of treatment outcomes (goals)
2. Development of the intervention activities (treatment plan)
3. Implementation of the treatment plan
4. Review of goal achievement and client performance
5. Revision of goals and plans

The process of carrying out these five steps is not necessarily sequential, in that planning, review, and implementation are ongoing. There is more to developing a treatment plan than writing realistic goals and a feasible plan, and than making the plan operational. Of the many activities in the process, one of the most important is that of deciding what the treatment plan is to include. A good place to start this discussion is with information about goals.

Goal Selection

The establishment of goals begins during the intake interview. Goals are revised, prioritized, and changed, as necessary, throughout treatment. It is important that goal selection be considered within the context in which the behavior occurs (Bernstein & Ziarnik, 1984). Some factors to consider are listed in Table 7.1.

Table 7.1. Factors to consider in goal selection

1. The ultimate goal of therapy is usually some type of improvement in the client's self management.

2. Goals are really just a series of behaviors that, when combined, result in the ultimate treatment outcome.

3. A therapist must be able to translate referral problems into goals that meet the criteria specified on the Goal Evaluation Checklist (see section on "Development of the Treatment Goals and Plan" and Form 7.2 in this chapter).

4. Treatment should be performance based, so the therapist can evaluate and provide evidence of changes in performance to the client and his or her family. The client or parent should be involved in the development and evaluation of goals.

5. Therapists may hesitate to admit that they have been unable to identify the problem they are treating. Rather, they believe what they are doing is correct, helpful or useful. Clearly specified goals, decided mutually, help alleviate this problem.

Difficulties

Some difficulties in formulating goals have been specified by Krumboltz and Thoresen (1969) and are listed in Table 7.2.

Goodness of Goals

A goal might be considered "good for the client" (Burns, 1972) if the specified behavior:

1. Is meaningful or useful
2. Is enjoyable
3. Is necessary later
4. Has a high vocational utility
5. Is easy
6. Is something the client was successful with (learned)
7. Is culturally applicable
8. Is considered good by experts (i.e., professionals in the appropriate topic area)
9. Is considered good by the average person—sounds good to others
10. Is frequently required in life

Once treatment goals have been selected, the activities of a clinician shift to the development of treatment plans.

Treatment Plans

In simplified terms, a *treatment plan* consists of a written formulation of the desired treatment outcomes (goals) and of the activities the therapist, client, and significant others will engage in to achieve those goals. The goals and activities are usually developed in conjunction with the client and/or significant others (e.g., parents), within the framework of ethical and legal guidelines.

Purposes

Treatment plans may serve diverse purposes. First, the availability of a written plan is an ethical requirement for most professional associations (American

Table 7.2. Difficulties in formulating goals

1. The problem presented by a client is attributed to someone else, (e.g., a parent comes to a psychologist complaining of his or her son's behavior). It is the parent who is the primary client; thus, the therapist must structure the situation so the client accepts responsibility for engaging in behavior that will remedy the situation.

2. The problem is expressed as a negative feeling (e.g., "I feel unliked"). The therapist must reflect and clarify the problem(s), determine an action that is incompatible with the negative feeling (e.g., What could you do that would make at least some people like you?), and establish more realistic standards to compare feelings.

3. The problem is the absence of a goal (e.g., the parents have negative feelings about the child but cannot identify what they want to change).

4. The problem is that the desired behavior is undesirable (e.g., the teenager wants to achieve a goal that the therapist is unwilling to help him or her achieve).

5. The problem is that the client does not know his or her behavior is inappropriate. The client's perception may be inaccurate, and so information given to the therapist is inaccurate (e.g., a girl whom adolescent males date only once or twice may engage in behavior that threatens them, but she is unaware of this).

6. The problem is a choice conflict (e.g., a client has two desired alternatives that are incompatible, such as wanting to date two people at the same time).

Psychological Association, 1981). Second, a treatment plan can enhance the setting of clear, realistic goals and plans for their achievement, thus providing direction for treatment. Third, a plan may cue an individual therapist that he or she needs peer consultation in cases where development of the treatment plan proves difficult. Fourth, a plan provides a clear record for the file for purposes of clinic administration, peer review, litigation, third-party payer requirements, and supervision. Fifth, the treatment plan provides a means to monitor and evaluate treatment outcome, in terms of goal achievement and treatment efficacy and efficiency. In addition to specifying the problem to be treated, the treatment outcome sought, and the way the outcome is to be achieved, the client and therapist should specify a method to monitor how well those outcomes are being achieved. A treatment plan is not static but flexible, changing as required by the availability of additional information and by the client's progress or lack of progress. Achievement of the goals necessitates active client involvement, to overcome: procrastination, perfectionism, irrational fears, pervasive negativism, avoidance of unpleasantness, habitual behavior, and the dread of overwhelming tasks (Lee, 1978).

Treatment Plan Format

Purposes

As in other clinics, clinics providing psychological and related services to children and adolescents should strive for one uniform treatment plan format, for several reasons (Striefel & Cadez, 1983). First, a common format assures that in the absence of one therapist due to illness or vacation, or in the case of staff turnover, another therapist can review a client's file and readily understand the treatment goals to be worked on and the progress to date, and can continue treating the client as prescribed, with minimal disruption. Second, a common format makes the task of a supervisor and peer review team easier when reviewing the quality of a treatment plan or evaluating staff performance, because they will already be familiar with the format. Third, a uniform plan assures that an agency has incorporated those elements that might be necessary in a client's file in order to respond to an outside peer review by, for example, an insurance company (guidelines may be obtained from the insurance company). Fourth, availability of a format makes training of new staff easier, because examples and experience with the format are common to all clinical staff. Thus, individuals other than the supervisor can provide training. Fifth, a common format provides a method to assure that all staff have considered specific items in developing the treatment plan for each client.

Format

We believe that each clinic should develop a specific treatment plan format. This form should specify all of the necessary components for each treatment plan, to ensure that an extremely busy therapist does not, in the crunch of time, short-circuit the planning and monitoring purpose for which the treatment plan was initially developed. At a minimum, the treatment plan format should specify: a) what the presenting problem is, and its dimensions; b) what the individual client's strengths and weaknesses are in reference to the presenting problem; c) the treatment outcome agreed to by the client/family and therapist; d) how this outcome will be achieved; and e) how progress will be measured. Treatment plan formats can be quite simple, an approach that provides an efficient use of time but carries the danger of overlooking important information in the planning process. At the other extreme, treatment plan formats can be extremely complex and time consuming. A compromise between simple and complex formats would seem most desirable. The treatment program format shown in Form 7.1 has served our clinic extremely well and incorporates all of the components that we think are essential.

Advantages

The advantages of a treatment plan format as shown in Form 7.1 are that: a) it clearly specifies all of the parameters necessary for treatment; b) it clearly outlines who is responsible for specific activities (this is especially important when parents are involved in carrying out a majority of the treatment of their own child in the home setting); c) it specifies how the client's progress will be monitored; d) it provides an excellent tool for training new staff or interns and practicum students to meet a minimal standard; e) it provides a good record of what was being attempted; f) it provides information that can be used to provide feedback to staff on their performance; g) it provides for uniformity of information kept on file; h) it ensures that some planning goes into the development of treatment plans and that such information is available for future purposes—for example, for peer review; i) it assures that accurate records are kept; and j) it provides

FORM 7.1

Treatment Plan Format

Client:_____   Approved by:_____
                                          Client
File #:_____
                                          _____
Case coordinator:_____   Parent/guardian

                                          _____
Date of implementation:_____   Therapist

                                          _____
            Date approved:_____   Supervisor (if appropriate)

PRESENTING PROBLEMS:

TREATMENT (in measurable terms, including timelines and criteria for success):

GENERAL PROCEDURES:
____Individual child therapy
____Individual parent counseling/therapy
____Individual parent training and home programming
____Marital counseling
____Family intervention
____Group parent training
____School programming
____Motor therapy and/or programming
____Self-help programming
____Speech and language therapy and/or programming

PERSON(S) RESPONSIBLE FOR TREATMENT (and areas of responsibility):

_____

_____

Treatment Plan ____

SPECIFIC PROCEDURES:

EVALUATION PROCEDURES:

DATA COLLECTION RESPONSIBILITIES:
Client/family:

Therapist:

Procedures:

REVIEW DATES AND INITIALS: FREQUENCY OF APPOINTMENTS:

guidance to staff on what is expected in treatment plans. The treatment plan format can be put on a computer disk, as can a specific treatment plan. As such, changes can be made more efficiently.

The disadvantages of this treatment program format are that: a) it takes time to include all of these components, and time is often at a premium for clinicians; b) plans may need to be changed frequently as treatment progresses and new information is obtained; and c) the typing load will increase if plans are typed.

DEVELOPMENT OF THE TREATMENT GOALS AND PLAN

In addition to establishing a treatment plan format, a clinic must also provide guidance to staff on the sequence of steps to follow in developing treatment goals and the overall treatment program. Treatment plans seem to be guided more by specific excesses and deficit behaviors of an individual than by diagnostic labels (Leitenberg, 1976) attributed to a client as a function of intake and assessment procedures.

Treatment Plan Development—Step 1

General Questions

Treatment plan development typically begins with an intake interview and assessment (see Chapter 6) in which the therapist seeks to answer a number of general questions such as those listed in Table 7.3 (Lazarus, 1981). Gambrill (1977) lists additional information that is helpful in selecting the potential target behavior. That information is shown in Table 7.4. The answers to these general questions are obtained through a process of specific questioning as outlined in the following paragraphs. The process should clarify the presenting problem, the dimensions of that problem, the strengths and weaknesses of the particular child or adolescent, and possibly the effects on the family.

Goal Evaluation Checklist

Treatment goals should be developed by the therapist in conjunction with the family, based on the information obtained during the process outlined in Step 1. Goals can be short-term (per session) or long-term, and can be physiological, psychological, or symptom reduction (behavior). These treatment goals should meet the criteria specified in the "Goal Evaluation Checklist" featured in Form 7.2. To determine if a goal meets the criteria, a clinician would answer each question in the checklist and revise the goal if any item received a "no" answer. The goal could be written on the checklist sheet in the appropriate space, or the checklist could be used in conjunction with a goal written elsewhere. The goals must be agreed to by the client/family, and multiple goals must be listed in order of priority.

Table 7.3. General questions for the therapist to answer in developing a treatment plan

1. What maladaptive behaviors need to be eliminated, and what adaptive behaviors need to be acquired?
2. Can a mutually satisfying work relationship be established, or should the client be referred elsewhere?
3. Can you describe the patient's appearance in terms of grooming, physical characteristics, motor activity (e.g., rigid posture, fidgeting, ticks), manner of speaking, and attitude (e.g., friendly, hostile)?
4. Did you notice any thought disorders (e.g., looseness of association, flight of ideas, blocking)?
5. Were there any incongruencies of affect (e.g., the inappropriate laughter, anger, or tears)?
6. Did you hear or observe information concerning the presence or absence of self-recrimination, suicidal thoughts, obsessional trends, delusions, hallucinations, or morbid fears?
7. Have you decided whether the client will respond more appropriately to a directive, nondirective, or other approach, and have you decided at what pace therapy should proceed?
8. Do you know what the client/family wish to achieve by therapy?
9. Did you provide the client/family with legitimate reasons for hope during this session?
10. Do you understand what or who is maintaining the client's deviant behaviors?

Specific Questions

One process for developing the goals with clients is outlined by Schwartz and Goldiamond (1975). It includes a combination of explanations and questions that help clarify desired outcomes. The questions can be asked of the child (if old enough), the parent, the adolescent, or all relevant parties. The sequence for the therapist would approximate that shown in Table 7.5.

Treatment Plan Development—Step 2

The second step in treatment plan development centers around using the assets and deficits of the client (Shelton & Levy, 1981), client family, and the environ-

Table 7.4. Additional information for selecting target behaviors

1. How much annoyance does the current situation pose for the client and his or her family?
2. What danger, if any, does the current situation pose for the client or others?
3. What interference does the current situation impose on the life of the client and/or on his or her family?
4. What is the probability that a desired outcome will be achieved with intervention?
5. How central is the problem within the complex of problems present?
6. How accessible is the problem?
7. What is the probable cost of intervention, in terms of time, money, energy, and resources?
8. What is the relative frequency, duration, and severity of the problem?
9. How acceptable, ethically, is the outcome to the clinician?
10. What is the likelihood that behavior change will be maintained after treatment ends?

Goal Evaluation Checklist

List goal here:

For each item, check either yes or no, as appropriate:

____ Yes ____ No   1. Is it a goal desired by the client? A goal should be something desired by the client (child, adolescent, family), not just what the therapist would like for the client (e.g., clients seldom come to a therapist asking for "self-actualization").

____ Yes ____ No   2. Is the therapist willing to help the client achieve this goal? The goal should not be one the therapist finds unethical or outside his or her area of expertise.

____ Yes ____ No   3. Does the goal statement identify what the client will do or say in specific behavioral (measurable) terms? Learning and recognizing are not examples of behavioral terms, but listing and pointing are. A goal must be stated from the viewpoint of the client, rather than that of the therapist.

____ Yes ____ No   4. Does the goal describe how well the client must perform the behavior to achieve the goal? For example, how often, at what rate or intensity, or how many times?

____ Yes ____ No   5. Does the goal specify one or more of the following: the setting in which the behavior will occur; the people, materials, or resources needed to accomplish the goal? It should do so.

____ Yes ____ No   6. Is the goal worded so that the client and professionals from the same and/or different professions can understand what it means? It should communicate clearly to anyone who reads it.

____ Yes ____ No   7. Is the goal specified in terms that will help the therapist select the intervention technique(s) to use?

Table 7.5.   Specific questions for goal selection

I am going to ask some questions to find out what it is that you would like to see happen. The questions have three purposes:

First, for me to get to know you.

Second, for you to learn things about me and my approach to problems.

Third, to find out how we're doing. To do this, we need records of what things are like now and how they change. Please answer the questions as completely as you can.

Area 1. Goals/Outcomes   Let's start by finding out what you want to change.

Function	Question
a. Goal/outcome	a. What would you like to see change?
b. Observable outcome	b. What would others see after the change occurred?
c. Present state	c. How is this different from how things are now? Give me an example of two.

(continued)

Table 7.5. (continued)

Area 2. Changed and Unchanged Behaviors Next, let's find out which things in your life are going well and which are not.

Function	Question
a. Unchanged behaviors	a. What's going well for you now? What areas of your life would not be affected by our program?
b. By-products	b. What behaviors, other than those we work on directly, would change?

Area 3. History The next questions give us a history of what you have done to change things.

Function	Question
a. Present attempt	a. Why start now?
b. First attempt	b. When did you first decide to try to change? What was going on? What did you do? What happened?
c. Intervening attempts	c. What did you do next? What was going on? What happened? (Series continues up to present situation.)

Area 4. Assets and Strengths Now, let's find out what you have that we can build on. Everyone starts with something.

Function	Question
a. Related skills	a. What skills and/or strengths do you have that are related to what you'd like to change?
b. Other skills	b. What other skills do you have?
c. Environmental control	c. Are there times or situations in which the present problem is not a problem?
d. Relevant problem-solving repertoire	d. In the past, what related problems did you tackle successfully? How?
e. Other problems solved	e. What other problems did you tackle successfully? How?
f. Past control	f. Did you ever control the present problem? If so, when and how?

Area 5. Consequences Next let's find out about outcomes produced, and outcomes you'd like to produce.

Function	Question
a. Secondary gain	a. Has your problem ever produced any special advantages for you? Can you give me some specific examples (in school, job, at home)?
b. Symptom negatives	b. As a result of your problem, have you been excused for things—or from things—that you might not be otherwise?
c. Symptom cost	c. How is your present problem a drag, or how does it jeopardize you? (Omit this question if answered in 3a.)
d. Potential positives	d. What do you really like to do, or would you like to do?
e. High probability positives	e. What do you find yourself doing instead (or getting instead)?

ment that are germane to the treatment process in developing the actual plan. Many of these assets were determined via the questions asked in the preceding section. The information can be summarized into answers for the two questions that follow: Does the client (client family) have skills that can be used in treatment? Does the environment include factors or people that can be used in treatment?

The written treatment plan uses the plan format chosen by the specific clinic. It should also include a clear specification of the outcomes expected and the time anticipated to achieve these outcomes. In choosing an intervention strategy, the clinician may wish to classify the intervention into one of four broad types (Shelton & Levy, 1981) that either: a) provide the client/client family with new information, b) enable the client/client family to alter the physical environment, c) alter the existing reinforcers, or d) allow the client/client family to learn new skills or extinguish old ones. The process of developing a written treatment plan would occur after the treatment methods have already been discussed verbally with the parents and/or the child/adolescent. Such discussion should cover the particular treatment recommended, the rationale for selecting the treatment, its advantages and disadvantages, and alternative treatments that might be available.

Considerations

A variety of factors must be considered by the therapist in selecting the appropriate treatment strategy, including: a) What is the problem and how severe is it? b) What is the treatment of choice in the existing literature? c) What is the skill level of the particular therapist or other staff members in implementing the treatment of choice? d) What are the ethical and legal considerations? e) What other resources are available in the immediate area? f) What considerations revolve around the family, their situation, their value system, financial resources available, and other family problems? g) What are the client's individual characteristics? and h) How "good" is the relationship between the clinician and the client? (Shelton & Levy, 1981).

In this process the therapist should consider whether what is being recommended is the treatment of choice for the particular presenting problem. If it is not, a clear explanation and rationale must be available to the client for defending that choice, should one's peers later question the treatment methodology selected. In some cases, the rationale is simply that the treatment of choice is complex, the therapist and other members of the clinic are not trained to provide it, and the client does not wish to be referred elsewhere.

The Written Plan

After the treatment plan has been agreed to verbally, it should be put into written form. Signatures should be obtained from the appropriate parties indicating that they agree to the plan. Such a procedure increases the likelihood that all parties understand what will constitute treatment. A treatment plan should be reviewed on an ongoing basis, with a specified, formal review at least once a month. The treatment plan can be revised as necessary, dependent upon the degree of progress made, other probles that occur, or changes in the client's situation. Internal client staffings or peer reviews are very useful in helping therapists justify the selection of their treatment approach and in receiving recommendations for possible needed changes. These can then be discussed with the particular child or adolescent and his or her family.

Planning for Generalization and Maintenance of Treatment Goals—Step 3

It cannot be assumed that a treatment outcome will be maintained once treatment is terminated or the conditions of treatment change (Prater, Wolter, & Clement, 1982; Striefel & Cadez, 1983; Striefel & Owens, 1980; Whitney & Striefel, 1981). Thus, it is essential that therapists build procedures into treatment plans to ensure that treatment outcome generalizes to the daily living environment and that the behavior can be maintained within that environment. This is certainly one of the advantages of having the treatment plan carried out by the parent in the home, or by the teacher in the school, in that more relevant variables are being dealt with in the environment in which that behavior would naturally occur. If new behaviors are being established in an individual child or adolescent's repertoire, care should be taken to ensure that the behavior will occur in the presence of different people, across time, in different locations, and in various situations. This type of generalization can be accomplished by the implementation of the process specified in a matrix such as the one shown in Figure 7.1, which includes people, time, situations, and settings.

Transfer across Therapists

Procedures established and utilized by one clinician/teacher/parent in one setting to establish a specific new behavior for the child or adolescent can sometimes be transferred to other people, settings, times, or situations by using a procedure such as that developed by Sanok and Striefel (1979). Sanok and Striefel trained a selectively mute child to respond verbally in one setting and then programmed for generalization to other people and settings. A discrete trial behavioral training program was employed to establish verbal responding. A combination of probes and training in other settings was then used to produce generalization to new settings. To obtain generalization across people, the following sequence occurred:

1. The original therapist presented 16 trials and reinforced correct responses, while a second trainer observed.
2. The original therapist presented 16 trials, but correct responses were reinforced by the second trainer.
3. The second trainer presented 16 trials and reinforced correct responses, while the original therapist observed.

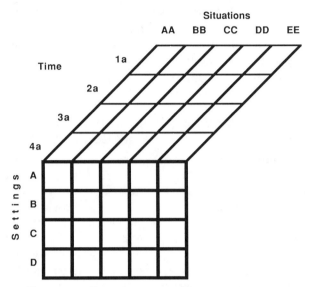

Figure 7.1. Generalization matrix for a treatment plan.

4. The original therapist left the room, and the second trainer conducted 16 trials and reinforced correct responses.
5. Steps 1–4 were repeated with a third trainer and so on.

The time needed to transfer responding from the original therapist to the next trainer was only 20 minutes. Such procedures can be highly effective in producing generalization of self-management skills acquired in therapeutic settings. Such a procedure, of course, is not appropriate to all treatment plans, nor is sufficient research data available to know the limitations of the procedure.

Other Techniques

Other techniques can be used to foster generalization and maintenance and can be incorporated into program implementation, including: a) homework assignments that are relevant to treatment outcomes, including the keeping of diaries or other self-monitoring data, or the keeping of such data by parents or teachers (Shelton & Levy, 1981); b) treatment structured to occur at various times, places, and with different people in the course of normal living (Ayllon, Kuhlman, & Warzak, 1982; Striefel & Cadez, 1983); c) self-monitoring, verbalization, and reinforcement (Prater et al., 1982); and d) planned practice of new behaviors in different situations.

Therapists who want to eliminate dysfunctional behaviors in children and adolescents and also obtain generalization should consider the same factors. It is essential to identify behaviors that are incompatible with the dysfunctional behavior and that can be taught to the client as substitutes for the inappropriate behavior(s). In essence, it is a process of teaching the client a behavior that is incompatible with the one that is undesirable, but one that will allow the client to achieve the same ends. For example, a young child who knows no other way to get attention other than to be aggressive could readily be taught that when you want something from someone else, you ask instead of hitting. This example may be oversimplified, but in many cases the elimination of inappropriate behaviors is, in fact, that simple. Generalization training would consist of teaching the child to ask for what he or she wants in a variety of contexts, at different times, and with different people.

Methods for Implementation

Implementation of treatment plans for children and adolescents is often quite different from implementing those dealing with adult problems. With children and adolescents, one must decide who will implement the particular treatment procedures. The treatment approach appropriate for dealing with child and adolescent problems generally includes some form of behavioral management techniques in which events preceding a particular behavior (antecedents) or following a particular behavior (consequences) are changed. For adults and older adolescents, many forms of therapy involve verbal exchanges with the adult, rather than a manipulation of the variables surrounding the adult's behavior. With children and young adolescents, the presenting problem often occurs either in the home or in the school, and thus the best place to change that behavior is in that setting within the natural environment (Tharp & Wetzel, 1969).

The Triadic Model

Treatment plans are often developed for implementation by parents at home or by teachers in school. We recommend the Triadic Model (Tharp & Wetzel, 1969), in which the clinician trains the parent or teacher, who then works directly with the target client. This model presents a unique but not uncommon set of problems. One problem is the time needed by the parent or teacher to implement the program. The parent or teacher must also possess reinforcers (payable to the client for good behavior), and must be able to deliver them contingently (Tharp & Wetzel, 1969). In addition, the intervention program must be very simple, easy to understand, and easy to implement.

In the development of treatment plans to be implemented in other locations, it is often helpful if the therapist or designated paraprofessional can visit the location to make naturalistic observations in that setting (Goldfried, 1982) that can aid in the development of the plan, its implementation, and monitoring. The information to be collected includes: a) general information about the environment; b) the frequency, severity, and so forth, of the target behavior; c) events that precede the occurrence of the target behavior; and d) events that immediately follow the occurrence of the target behavior. Before a treatment plan is given to a parent or teacher to implement, it is very useful if the therapist has field-tested the plan by implementing it himself or herself in the clinic or other environment, thereby eliminating any potential problems that exist and facilitating the parents' task of teaching it. A clinic field test provides a situation in which: a) the therapist can model the program, b) parent(s) can ask questions concerning implementation, and c) parent(s) can practice implementing the program while receiving immediate and direct feedback from the therapist.

In some cases, implementation of treatment in the therapist's office or clinic will not be possible because the specific behavior occurs only in specific environments and the cost of having the therapist go to those environments is prohibitive (e.g., when the family lives in another community). Wherever possible, however, it is recommended that the therapist go into the home or school setting and implement the treatment plan there to determine whether it considers all of the necessary variables in that environment. Once the therapist has tested the treatment plan, he or she should be able to sow the parent, teacher, or other agent how to implement it. In some settings it may even be possible for the therapist to videotape the treatment implementation for parental review, if they cannot be present for a "live" demonstration. As mentioned previously, a useful training sequence is for parents to: a) observe the therapist carrying out the necessary procedures; b) try the procedures themselves, receiving feedback on what they are and are not doing correctly; and c) practice the program in the natural environment (home), with the therapist available as needed by telephone or weekly follow-up sessions.

Client Treatment

When a teacher or parent is unable or unwilling to participate in the implementation of the treatment program, or the problem is too complex for their implementation, the task for the therapist becomes more difficult and may be more expensive for the family. In such cases, it may be necessary to rearrange natural environments or set up artificial ones to enable interaction for the child or adolescent's particular problems. This includes play therapy, group treatment, placement in special environments, or changes in the child's school placement, to expose him or her temporarily to an environment conducive to behavior change. None of these alternatives is as desirable as treating the child within the environment in which the problem has occurred, because the more that treatment is removed from the natural environment, the more difficult it is for behavior to generalize to that environment (Baer, 1981).

Hospitalization

For some types of problems (e.g., anorexia nervosa) it may be necessary and appropriate to have a child or adolescent hospitalized for a period of time, during which a treatment plan is implemented and tested. After discharge, the procedures that were included in the development of the plan for programming, maintenance, and generalization of treatment outcomes can be implemented.

Who Will Provide Treatment

Factors to consider in deciding who will implement a particular treatment plan include: a) location in which the problem occurs, b) amount of time it would take to implement treatment, c) distance involved, d) available resource alternatives, e) skill levels of the individuals in the location where the problem occurs, and f) potential reinforcers available. Assessing whether parents are capable of being a change agent for their own child can be facilitated by having them complete a Parenting Stress Index (Abidin, 1983), which provides information on the stress experienced by particular parents and helps determine how these stresses contribute to dysfunctional parenting skills.

Individual versus Group Treatment

In working with children and adolescents, it is often useful to consider whether or not treatment can best be implemented working alone with the client or placing him or her in a group. In large part, deciding to conduct groups will depend on the skills of the individual clinician and on factors such as the advantages and disadvantages of groups for dealing with specific problems. The advantages of group treatment include: a) a clinician can see more clients in the same amount of time, thus the cost to the client/family is lower per session; b) homogeneous groups enable a client/family to realize they are not the only ones experiencing a specific problem; c) by putting children/adolescents into groups with other parents and vice versa, each member of a client family is provided an opportunity to view the problem from another family's perspective; d) groups provide an opportunity to learn about self-management by learning from the experience of others; e) group support can help reinforce individual progress; f) group members tend to "tune in" to faking, and usually someone confronts that person; and g) some problems (e.g., social skills) require the presence of others.

The disadvantages of group treatment include: a) there is less time for each member in the group to discuss problems; b) confidentiality is more difficult to maintain; c) it is difficult to monitor and maintain records of individual client progress; d) an immense amount of energy and skill is needed to conduct group sessions so that all participants gain from the experience; and e) conflicts unrelated to the group's goal often arise, and valuable time must be spent resolving them.

Contracting

The success of treatment depends heavily on the activities the client engages in when not with the therapist (Shelton & Levy, 1981). One way to try to arrange the occurrence of several activities is to use contracts; another is to assign "homework." Both methods accelerate progress toward achievement of treatment goals, increase generalization and maintenance of behavior change, and allow the client to work on problems in which the therapist's presence would be awkward (Shelton & Levy, 1981). Contracts are particularly useful between parents and adolescents.

Contracting is the structuring of all the necessary elements of the intervention process so clearly and explicitly that they can be written into an agreement for behavioral change that is acceptable and understandable to everyone involved. A contract is a written copy of that agreement.

Parts of a Contract   A contract should include the following components:

1. Date agreement begins, ends, and/or is revised
2. Behavior(s) targeted for change
3. Type and amount of reinforcer (reward) to be used
4. Reinforcement schedule
5. Time schedule for review of progress
6. Bonus clause for sustained or exceptional performance
7. Statement of penalties to be imposed if specified behavior is not performed
8. Signature of all involved (client/parents/therapist)

Form 7.3 provides a sample of a contract form.

Uses of a Contract   A contract serves a number of purposes, including:

1. To specify clearly what the therapist and client or parent and adolescent each agree to do
2. To specify in written form an effective behavior change process in order for all persons involved to receive a reciprocal exchange of reinforcers
3. To provide administrators with evidence to justify the effectiveness of their programs to funding sources within the limits of confidentiality
4. To provide supervisors with a method to determine the need for additional staff training or increased case supervision
5. To provide a focus for individual therapy sessions

FORM 7.3

Contract Form #1

1. Effective dates from _____ to _____
2. Revision dates _____
3. Target behaviors
   a.
   b.
4. Reinforcers and schedule
   a.
   b.
5. Progress review date _____
6. Bonus
7. Penalty
8. Signatures

   _____
   Client

   _____   _____
   Parent   Therapist

---

6. To provide a method for determining the effectiveness of the intervention and to avoid wasting time
7. To provide a record for planning for other similar cases
8. To provide the therapist with a method of defusing faultfinding and name calling during treatment sessions

Steps in Contracting in Conjunction with the Client Following are steps in contracting:

1. Select the one or two behavior(s) to be changed first (try to select behaviors that will be functional for obtaining an increase in the frequency of natural reinforcers).
2. Describe the behaviors so they can be observed and counted. They should meet the criteria listed on the Goal Evaluation Checklist (see Form 7.2).
3. Identify the reinforcers that will motivate the target client to do well.
4. Identify other individuals in the client's environment who can monitor the client's behaviors and who can deliver the reinforcers. This person should: a) be seen by the client often, b) be someone the client looks up to and respects, and c) be consistent in carrying out the role specified in the contract.
5. Write the contract in simple terms so everyone can understand it.
6. Collect data.
7. Troubleshoot if the behavior does not change.
8. Revise the contract, as necessary.
9. Continue to monitor, troubleshoot, and revise, as necessary, until behavior(s) change.
10. Select the next behavior to modify.

Considerations Kanfer (1975) and Homme, Csajyi, Gonzales, and Recks (1969) specify some factors to consider in developing contracts. These are provided in Table 7.6.

Monitoring Treatment Progress

Categories

The monitoring of treatment progress can be difficult, but is an essential component of any treatment plan. Funding by third-party payers (insurance companies) is becoming more and more dependent on accurate assessment, availability of written treatment plans, and the availability of systematic information on client progress. Decisions should be made by the clinic staff concerning the types of monitoring that will occur. Monitoring can be divided into several categories. The first is essential and involves treatment of the client in which the therapist monitors progress informally on an ongoing basis and also conducts formal reviews. In the second category the clinic conducts staffings (internal peer reviews) in which there is an opportunity for input, assessment, and change. In the

Table 7.6. Factors to consider in developing contracts

1. The contract payoff should be arranged so the consequence is delivered immediately after the specified behavior occurs. With children the specific behavior must be simple and easy to identify.

2. The initial contract should call for and reward small approximations of the target behavior. This requires that the behavior be broken down into its component parts (e.g., the different elements that, when combined, make up a behavior class called "room clean").

3. The rewards should be frequent and the size of reward should be adjusted to avoid satiation (e.g., in using food).

4. The contract should reward accomplishments that the child can determine without the need for an adult being present.

5. The performance should be reinforced (a payoff) after the behavior occurs. Avoid "paying off" for a behavior that is to occur in the future.

6. The contract should be fair. It is important that the client accept the contract conditions, and a balance must exist between the magnitude of reinforcement and the required behavior.

7. The contract should be clear so the client knows how much performance is required and what kind of payoff he or she can expect.

8. The contract should be honest, which means the reinforcement must be delivered whenever the client engages in the specified behavior.

9. The contract should be positive. The basic message to the client should be that fulfillment of the contract represents a positive contribution to the client's growth and development, rather than a threat of punishment.

10. Contracting should be used systematically. This means that the contract should be used 24 hours a day, 7 days a week, and should not be reversed just for special occasions. As much as possible, the contracting conditions should be adhered to without exception. In fact, the contract uses self-management techniques that should become the rule for everyday conduct.

third category the supervisor monitors client progress as one way to keep informed of therapist performance. An outside consultant can also be hired for this purpose, in which case the review must be conducted in accordance with more stringent ethical guidelines (see Chapter 11).

Data Collection

If a treatment plan has been clearly formulated in accordance with the guidelines provided here, it will include methods for collecting data to determine the progress made. The type of data collected determines, in large part, how to monitor the client's progress and helps to clarify how often monitoring must occur.

The types of data that can be collected include: a) direct observation data in naturalistic settings (e.g., the child at home); b) observations of responses in situations contrived by the clinician (e.g., the child in a playroom); c) responses that are manifest in role-playing situations (e.g., the child pretending to be the parent); d) the individual's own self-report of behavior (e.g., the Fear Inventory [Cautela, Cautela & Esonis, 1983]); e) the clinician's subjective assessment of performance (e.g., how depressed a child is on a scale of 1 to 10); f) parental report; and g) the information obtained from standardized (e.g., the Minnesota Multiphasic Personality Inventory [MMPI]) and criterion-referenced assessment devices (Goldfried, 1982, data types a–d just mentioned). Monitoring of client progress can be fairly objective if the therapist employs direct observation techniques such as counting the frequency of a specific behavior, or recording the duration of a particular behavior, the rate of the behavior, or the latency of events. Or, it can be subjective. Whatever choice is made concerning data collection, it should be based on the factors relevant to the specific problem being treated. Data collection techniques and assessment were covered to some degree in Chapter 6. Additional information can be found in references by Goldfried (1982) and Striefel and Cadez (1983).

Progress Considerations

Data collected prior to the onset of treatment can serve as a baseline against which to measure the impact of the treatment program by continuing to collect the same type of data and then comparing that data with the baseline. If a client does not make progress one must reconsider whether: a) the goals are appropriate, b) the treatment program is appropriate, c) the program is being implemented as designed, d) there are positive payoffs for the client in achieving the treatment goal outcomes, e) there are secondary gains (e.g., by having an asthma attack, a child can control his or her parents' behavior whereas successful treatment of the asthma could result in a loss of this control) that are larger than what would be available to maintain or establish a new behavior, f) the treatment program is appropriate for the problem as defined, g) the focus of treatment has changed, h) the appropriate type of data is being collected, and i) consultation should be sought.

Client Contact Notes and Case Staffing Reports

Client contact notes, also called treatment progress reports or session notes, are prepared to describe the content of what happened in each client treatment session. Case staffing reports describe the decisions that take place in a case staff meeting. Both types of reports should be signed or initialed by all clinicians involved in the particular interaction. Client contact notes and case staffing reports serve many of the same purposes as the treatment plan format form. Both are used to assess progress in meeting treatment goals. Both types of reports are maintained primarily for use by clinicians and supervisors, and copies are not provided to individuals outside of the clinic. The specific uses of these reports include:

1. To provide a record of the most recent client contact or staff review of client progress
2. To provide supervisors and other relevant clinic staff with case information
3. To assist clinicians in recall of previous client interactions
4. To prompt clinicians on future appointments or action to be taken during subsequent treatment sessions
5. To stimulate clinicians to consider changes in the treatment approach if progress is not occurring

Table 7.7. Treatment content report critique guidelines

1. Is the client and client-related identifying information accurate (e.g., correct client file number, date of client interaction)?
2. Has the type of client interaction been identified (e.g., phone contact, clinic appointment)?
3. Does the language used provide a clear explanation of the interactions that have occurred?
4. Has objective data been included or attached to support subjective clinical impressions or a subjective progress report by client or parent/legal guardian?
5. Have clinician responsibilities that are to be taken care of between appointments been identified and listed (e.g., needed preparation of materials for parent training)?
6. Have future appointments (e.g., date and time) been indicated?
7. Has the clinician noted treatment tasks to be addressed at the subsequent appointment?
8. Have previous and future client and client-related homework assignments been reported?

6. To provide an ongoing record of client-related interactions and decisions during treatment

The content of contact notes and case staffing reports can be simple or complex, dependent on the needs of each clinic. Some guidelines for critiquing treatment report content are presented in Table 7.7. The forms for treatment progress reports range from a narrative account of client interaction to a more structured form that includes specific areas to be completed. Forms 7.4, 7.5, and 7.6 feature the sufficient components. Client contact notes have frequently been used by clinicians as a way of recording their impressions, inferences, or speculations about a client, or associated factors in the treatment being provided. Clinicians sometimes write observations that they would not want to share with

---

FORM 7.4

Client Contact Note

Name of client:_____Date of birth:_____

Contact person:_____

Parents:_____

Address:_____

_____

Phone:_____

Date:_____

FOCUS OF SESSION:

INTERACTION:

HOMEWORK ASSIGNMENTS (new and review of previous assignments):

FORM 7.5

Progress Notes

(Alternate Client Contact Form)

Client identification _____ Therapist's name _____

Date of contact _____

PROBLEMS DEALT WITH:

SUBJECTIVE INFORMATION (what client or others say of problem):

OBJECTIVE (what is observed or recorded):

EVALUATION (what you, the therapist, think is going on with each problem):

FUTURE PLANS (What homework assignments were given? What has therapist agreed to do?):

DATE PROBLEM RESOLVED:_____

---

clients or their families, and have at times considered their notes sacrosanct. Current client legal rights specify that clients (or their guardian in the case of minors) must be given access to all information in the client's file; thus, clinicians should be circumspect in deciding what to record in contact notes.

Evaluating the Quality of the Treatment Plan

The evaluation of the quality of the treatment plan can be based on a number of factors, including: a) the degree to which the treatment goals have been achieved, b) client satisfaction with treatment outcome, c) whether the treatment plan includes the seven points (specified earlier, see Form 7.2) for establishment of treatment goals and accomplishment of generalization and maintenance, d) the satisfaction of the other family members and the community with treatment outcome, e) peer reviews, and f) therapist satisfaction with the plan. Although therapist satisfaction was listed last, it is not the least important. Evaluation of the quality of treatment plans is important if professional staff members who implement the plan are to continue to improve their skills. Evaluation data should be discussed with the client/family and appropriate changes made in the plan.

Client Satisfaction and Termination

Satisfaction

How to decide if the client is satisfied or dissatisfied with treatment is problematic for most clinicians. First, the client must be given an opportunity to

Case Staffing Report

Date:_____ File #:_____

Client:_____

CASE DISPOSITION:

TREATMENT PLAN CHANGES RECOMMENDED:

(Use back of page if necessary.)

CASE REVIEWED OR STAFFED BY:

_____

(name, title and discipline)

_____

(name, title and discipline)

_____

(name, title and discipline)

_____

(name, title and discipline)

indicate whether or not he or she is satisfied with progress and be given information on how the therapist sees the client's progress. Any data that has been collected should be shared with the client/family. If the goals of the treatment plan have been achieved and the client and family are reporting satisfaction, the case can be terminated in such a manner that if future problems occur the door is open for the client to return for additional treatment. In addition, it is useful to provide some follow-up monitoring on a periodic basis before the case is totally terminated—in essence, a phase-out period.

If a client expresses the desire to end treatment but goals have not been achieved, the therapist is faced with a difficult decision. Perhaps appropriate goals were not set at the outset, or there may be secondary reasons why this client would like to terminate. A direct discussion with the client (if old enough) and the client's parents may readily clarify this issue. The more information the therapist can gain, the easier it is for the therapist to evaluate the situation and recommend the appropriate next step. In any case, termination should occur when it is agreed to by the client, the family, and the therapist. It often occurs by default when the client fails to attend several scheduled sessions, and attempts have been made to do a follow-up with no response. It can occur when all treatment goals have been achieved, and it can occur when no progress has occurred. If no progress occurs, the therapist is obligated not to abandon the client but, rather, to refer him or her to other appropriate services. Nonabandonment means that the therapist must ensure that the client has been given the

---

FORM 7.7

Client Satisfaction Questionnaire—Form A1

Agency:_____ Client:_____

Agency address:_____

Person completing form:_____

1. Please list things you were specifically *satisfied* with in terms of services provided.

2. Please list things you were specifically *unsatisfied* with or on which our agency could improve.

---

information necessary to receive services elsewhere in what may be a more appropriate treatment facility. Sometimes this includes arranging an appointment with another professional. In some cases, when progress cannot be made by one therapist within a clinic, other staff members may have skills that are more appropriate to treat the client. In such cases, it may be desirable to transfer this client to another therapist, but a case staffing or consultation should occur first.

A Follow-up Form

In addition to a treatment format, a client progress note form, and a staffing report, a clinic may want to have available a form for doing a follow-up after termination at 1-month, 6-month, and 12-month intervals to determine client satisfaction, to determine whether the goals of treatment have been maintained, and to provide feedback to staff on the appropriateness of the treatment procedures used (Lazarus, 1981). Form 7.7 provides a sample of a Client Satisfaction Questionnaire. A cover letter should accompany the form, specifying the purpose of the follow-up (e.g., to evaluate services provided so that services can be improved).

Case Closure

The client record should always indicate when a client's file is closed (case terminated) and the reason for it. Accurate information concerning termination is maintained for possible future reference. Many clinics have a special form for this, which includes a summary of what occurred with the case (see Chapter 8 for more detailed information).

SUMMARY

Whereas treatment planning and implementation are complex processes, they can be simplified by using systematic procedures such as rapport building, a structured interview, goal selection procedure, a treatment program format, contact notes, client involvement, and planning for generalization and maintenance of treatment outcomes. Each step in this process provides a clinician and clinic with several alternatives. Each alternative, in turn, has advantages and disadvantages; thus prior planning is essential to maximize advantages and minimize disadvantages. A useful sequence for plan development and implementation was provided and discussed.

READER ACTIVITIES

List the advantages and major components of a treatment plan format form. How does the format form suggested in this chapter compare with what you are using? Define *pacing,* and list as many different ways of pacing as you can. Which of these do you use with clients, and which would be useful for you to learn to use? Write three treatment goals for clients you are currently serving. Then compare them with the items in the Goal Evaluation Checklist (Form 7.2) and rewrite the goals as needed to comply with the checklist. Could your goal writing skills be improved by using the checklist regularly? List the topics you typically address in progress notes. Now compare them with Form 7.5 on progress notes. Are you including enough information in your progress notes to protect yourself in the case of litigation?

REFERENCES

Abidin, R. R. (1983). *Parenting Stress Index.* Charlottesville, VA: Pediatric Psychology Press.
American Psychological Association. (1981). *Standards for providers of psychological services.* Washington, DC: American Psychological Association.
Ayllon, T., Kuhlman, C., & Warzak, W. J. (1982). Programming resource room generalization using Lucky Charms. *Child & Family Behavior Therapy, 4*(213), 61–67.
Baer, D. M. (1981). *How to plan for generalization.* Lawrence, KS: H & H Enterprises.
Bernstein, G. S., & Ziarnik, J. P. (1984). Training behavior change agents in outcome selection. *Behavior Therapist, 7*(4), 103–104.
Burns, R. W. (1972). *New approaches to behavioral objectives.* Dubuque, IA: W. C. Brown.
Cautela, J. R., Cautela, J., & Esonis, S. (1983) *Forms for behavior analysis with children.* Champaign, IL: Research Press.
Charny, J. (1966). Psychosomatic manipulations of rapport in psychotherapy. *Psychosomatic Medicine, 28*(4), 305–315.
Feldman, M. P., & Peay, J. (1982). Ethical and legal issues. In A. S. Bellack, M. Hersen, & A. E. Kazdin (Eds.), *International handbook of behavior modification and therapy* (pp. 231–261). New York: Plenum.
Gambrill, E. D. (1977). *Behavior modification.* San Francisco: Jossey-Bass.
Gelfand, D. M., Jensen, W. R., & Drew, C. J. (1982). *Understanding child behavior disorders.* New York: Holt, Rinehart & Winston.
Goldfried, M. R. (1982). Behavioral assessment: An overview. In A. S. Bellack, M. Hersen, & A. E. Kazdin (Eds.), *International handbook of behavior modification and therapy* (pp. 81–107). New York: Plenum.

Haley, J. (1973). *Uncommon therapy*. New York: W. W. Norton.

Homme, L., Csajyi, A. P., Gonzales, M. A., & Recks, J. R. (1969). *How to use contingency contracting in the classroom*. Champaign IL: Research Press.

Kanfer, F. H. (1975). Self-management methods. In F. H. Kaufer & A. P. Goldstein (Eds.), *Helping people change* (pp. 309–355). New York: Pergamon.

Krumboltz, J. D., & Thoresen, C. E. (1969). *Behavioral counseling: Cases and techniques*. New York: Holt, Rinehart & Winston.

Lankton, S. (1980). *Practical magic*. Cupertino, CA: Meta Publications.

Lazarus, A. A. (1981). *The practice of multi-modal therapy*. New York: McGraw-Hill.

Lee, W. (1978). *Formulating and researching goals*. Champaign, IL: Research Press.

Leitenberg, H. (1976). Behavioral approaches to treatment of neuroses. In H. Leitenberg (Ed.) *Handbook of behavior modification and behavior therapy* (124–167). Englewood Cliffs, NJ. Prentice-Hall.

Levis, D. J. (1982). Experimental and theoretical foundations of behavior modification. In A. S. Bellack, M. Hersen, & A. E. Kazdin (Eds.), *International handbook of behavior modification and therapy* (pp. 33–56). New York: Plenum.

Prater, J. S., Wolter, C. F., & Clement, P. W. (1982). Setting generalization during self-reinforcement with educationally handicapped children. *Child and Family Behavior Therapy, 4*(4), 25–39.

Sanok, R. L., & Striefel, S. (1979). Elective mutism: Generalization of verbal responding across people and settings. *Behavior Therapy, 10*(4), 357–371.

Schwartz, A., & Goldiamond, I. (1975). *Social casework: A behavioral approach*. New York: Columbia University Press.

Shelton, J. S., & Levy, R. L. (1981). *Behavioral assignments and treatment compliance: A handbook of clinical strategies*. Champaign, IL: Research Press.

Striefel, S., & Cadez, M. J. (1983). *Serving children and adolescents with developmental disabilities in the special education classroom: Proven methods*. Baltimore: Paul H. Brooks Publishing Co.

Striefel, S., & Owens, C. R. (1980). Transfer of stimulus control procedures: Applications to language acquisition training with the developmentally handicapped. *Behavior Research of Severe Developmental Disabilities, 1*(2), 307–331. (Reprinted from *Gedrag, 8*(1), 34–56).

Tharp, R. G., & Wetzel, R. J. (1969). *Behavior modification in the natural environment*. New York: Academic Press.

Whitney, R., & Striefel, S. (1981). Functionality and generalization in training severely and profoundly handicapped children. *Journal of Special Education Technology, 4*(3), 33–39.

Wolberg, L. R. (1977). *The technique of psychotherapy: Part 1*. (3rd ed.). New York: Grune & Stratton.

8

Additional Assessment and Treatment Information and Issues

After reading this chapter, you should understand:
1. Some of the practicalities of the assessment/evaluation and treatment processes and strategy selection
2. Some specific treatment processes and strategies
3. How to determine what resources are available and what is needed for specific problems
4. Individual versus group treatment
5. Differences in providing service in a clinic versus in a hospital or in the home
6. Telephone versus live follow-up
7. Expectations of clients/client families during assessment and treatment and of clinicians
8. Problem solving when treatment is not effective
9. Adjusting treatment to individuals on the basis of relevant factors
10. Strategies and resources for the 10 most common child/adolescent problems

UNDERSTANDING DEVELOPMENT

A clinician providing psychological services to children and adolescents should be aware of his or her assumptions concerning physical and psychological development. Wood (1975) reported such a set of assumptions and implications for treatment. These have been modified slightly and are provided in Table 8.1. The assumptions and implications listed in the table are not all-inclusive, nor are they "sacred." You should read them and compare them with your own assumptions, and modify or add additional assumptions, as appropriate. In addition, you should critically examine your assumptions to see if they are supported by existing data.

Table 8.1. An illustration of assumptions about development

Assumptions	Implications
1. Psychological problems of children and adolescents are interwoven with normal functioning and are difficult to separate out. Normal functioning is often overlooked or interpreted as atypical.	1. Assessments conducted and treatment plans and goals should incorporate both normal and problem behaviors. Doing so takes advantage of a child's strengths to facilitate progress and helps avoid an overemphasis on deficits and problems.
2. Physical and psychological development follow a general sequence that is well documented in the literature.	2. This sequence results in behavior change during growth in both normal and disturbed children and adolescents. Such growth can produce many new behaviors in a short period of time. Clinicians can anticipate some of these changes by being aware of normal development and can incorporate such changes into treatment plans.
3. Normal growth is predictable and yet uniquely individual, and is affected by biological, environmental, and experiential factors.	3. The normal sequence of development should be taken into consideration in selection of assessment and treatment, as well as the client's developmental status and strengths and weaknesses.
4. A child/adolescent's knowledge of himself or herself, level of self-confidence, and willingness to take risks are affected by the positive and negative experiences he or she has.	4. Assessment/treatment should include experiences that allow for some success, and these should be pointed out to the client. The assessment and treatment experience must be pleasant for the client if learning is to be maximized.
5. Children and adolescents learn and progress more by what they experience than by what they are told. Experience provides meaning and skill.	5. Treatment should provide experiences for clients that help them deal with their lives. What is learned in treatment must be associated with the client's world so that the skills transfer to daily activities.

PRACTICALITIES OF THE ASSESSMENT AND TREATMENT PROCESS

Children and adolescents are referred for psychological services for a variety of reasons including: excessive anxiety, psychotic symptoms, aggression, acting out, depression, sleep disturbances, school problems, and a host of other concerns. These concerns can be conceptualized as a "range of psychopathology" (Wright, 1982). Regardless of the problem concern, a psychological service clinic for children/adolescents should be equipped to provide treatment. Given a range of problems, there also needs to be a range of interventions varying in approach, intensity, length, and cost (DeLeon, VandenBos, & Cummings, 1983). Consumers, legislators, and professional groups are becoming increasingly aware and concerned that treatment should be efficacious, safe, and appropriate.

Assigning Clients

In providing psychological and related services to children and adolescents in a clinic setting, the administrator must make a number of practical decisions concerned with the assessment and treatment process. One of these decisions is how to assign clients to individual therapists. A common procedure in clinics with a number of clinicians is to assign clients on a rotational basis, so that each therapist takes a turn receiving clients as they enter the service system. Such a procedure helps keep the number of clients each therapist serves about equal. Although on the surface this may appear to be an equitable method, it has drawbacks. One is that it is very possible that a therapist, by the "luck of the draw," will get several clients who are much more difficult to deal with than those assigned to other therapists, and will become overloaded. Second, it is also likely that a particular therapist will be assigned a client who has a presenting problem that could be dealt with better by another staff member. Most well-trained clinicians can be helpful with most client problems, but some staff possess extraordinary in-depth expertise in one or more areas (DeLeon et al., 1983). Such expertise should be applied to clients in need and should also be used to improve the skills of other staff members. Third, an ethical issue arises, at least for psychologists, if they are assigned to treat a problem with which they have no experience. Psychologists are ethically bound to "only provide services and only use techniques for which they are qualified by training and experience" (American Psychological Association [APA], 1981, p. 634). In order to provide service in an area in which they are not trained, psychologists need to receive training and close supervision. This can present a major problem for clinics with only one or two staff members.

In large clinics where an intake worker screens all clients, the problem of rotational assignment could be prevented by a weekly team meeting to decide how to most equitably distribute the clients who have come through intake in the past week, accounting for various staff members' expertise and case loads. In clinics that do not have a large staff, it may still be possible for a supervisor to keep track of client load for different staff members and to allocate cases accordingly. It is important that a clinic establish a procedure for client assignment and that this procedure be flexible enough to allow for internal shifts when an inappropriate assignment has been made. Factors that come into play in making therapist assignments include items such as those shown in Table 8.2.

Treatment of Choice

An important point to remember is that many, if not most, therapists, are not familiar with the treatment of choice for all of the various problems coming into a particular clinic. This is owing, in part, to professional disagreement on what the treatment of choice is for particular problems, to a lack of information on what the treatment of choice is, and to rapidly changing procedures for dealing with specific problems. As a clinician, however, you may be familiar with treatment approaches that work or that, in the past, were the treatment of choice for a

Table 8.2. Therapist assignment considerations

1. What is the client's presenting problem?
2. Would a male or a female therapist be best for this particular case? For example, for female clients who have been sexually abused, it may be most appropriate and even essential that a female therapist provide services rather than a male.
3. Can this problem be dealt with better in individual therapy or in a group? For example, a child who lacks social skills might best be taught those skills within a group context.
4. How frequently does the problem behavior occur? What is its variation? When did the problem start? Was it present at birth or occur thereafter? The longer a problem has been in existence, the more resistant it will be to change, which means that the skills of the therapist must be more highly honed in order to deal with such a problem.
5. What is the treatment of choice according to the published literature, and what reality factors must be addressed by the particular clinic? Does someone on the clinic staff have the expertise needed to implement the treatment of choice? If not, should this client be referred elsewhere, or is there an alternative available that also has a high probability of success and that protects the rights of the client to have the most efficient, effective treatment provided?
6. What is the current skill level and case load of each clinician?

particular problem. Any clinic that expects to remain solvent may out of necessity try to treat problems for which its staff may not be fully qualified to provide the treatment of choice. Competence and ethical concerns must be balanced with this reality to ensure that the client's needs are met in the most efficient way possible. A failure to do so raises ethical, as well as legal, concerns.

At times, a client will need to be served by a clinician who is not competent to deal with a specific problem, thus violating the APA principle on competence. Failure to serve the client may be an even bigger disservice. For example, in rural or remote areas, if the clinician does not attempt to treat a problem such as aggression toward others, a child may go untreated because of a lack of resources and may even be injured severely by a beating from an angry parent. In cases where a clinician treats a client whose problem lies in an area in which the clinician is not competent, appropriate supervision must be obtained, even if via long-distance travel or telephone. In addition, case consultation or a peer review should be obtained to help decide what types of treatment and supervision are appropriate.

In small communities offering only one clinic or professional service group, or in instances where it would be a hardship for the client to travel long distances to receive other therapy, the decision to serve the client is generally made. In such cases a pointed discussion with the client/family is in order, and a reduced fee might even be negotiated. In a large community where there are many therapists to choose from, it is more difficult to justify serving a client in an area in which the clinician is not competent. However, it is also easier in such locations to obtain training and supervision to become competent.

Legal factors may also be relevant. For example, if staff are totally untrained in any of the methods for treating a particular problem and they attempt to treat the client without informing him or her of the alternatives, the clinic could very possibly face a negligence lawsuit. The best "rule of thumb" is that the client should be involved in the decision-making process if possible. At minimum, the parents of the child or adolescent should be involved in the process. In addition, clinicians should be aware of their own professional limitations and the strengths of other clinicians in their geographic area so that clients receive competent services.

Individual, Group, and Family Therapy

Another consideration in dealing with children and adolescents is whether to provide individual therapy to the child, to provide therapy to the parents and the child, or to provide family therapy including all family members. This decision, touched upon earlier in Chapter 7, will depend upon many factors, the most critical of which are the skills of the therapist, the presenting problem, and whether the therapist is trained to do individual and family therapy.

Whose Problem Is It?

A useful step in deciding whether to treat a child or an adolescent alone, to treat a family, or to treat some portion of the family is to clarify who "owns" the presenting problem. To determine problem ownership you can start by asking the question, "Whose problem is it?" (see Chapter 7 for more information). For example, when a child is doing fine at home but is having difficulty getting along with peers in school, family therapy may not be useful. It will be much more effective to provide individual training to this child on how to get along with others and to help facilitate use of these new skills in school and neighborhood settings. However, if the problem were one in which an adolescent boy has difficulty with his father and mother concerning what are realistic expectations of work to be completed and the time at which the child should be home, then intervention with both parents and the adolescent would be the intervention of choice, since a difference in value systems must be resolved.

Cost Effectiveness and Efficiency of Group Interventions

In deciding whether to use individual versus group training, one must ask the question, "What is the most cost effective and efficient use of resources with the specific client's problem(s)?" If several individuals can be served in a group by one staff member, it is probably more cost effective in time and effort for a clinic to provide service to a group. Some groups can be organized that are beneficial in resolving family difficulties. For example, three groups could be formed, each consisting of equal numbers of parents and adolescents, but with no two members of the same family in the same group. This allows the teenager to gain a perspective on how other parents see his or her particular problem, and allows parents to see how other adolescents and parents deal with specific presenting concerns. In addition to time and cost efficiency, this can be a worthwhile method for providing parents with a reasonable amount of exposure in a non-threatening way. As mentioned in an earlier chapter, groups can certainly present their own problems. For instance, individuals may not attend all sessions, and their absence and later return may cause some disruption. Also, family members must be willing to participate in a group for group therapy to be a realistic choice.

Age and Severity

For children under age 6, it often helps for the parents to receive assistance and training so that they can improve the child's behavior (Furman, 1957). This assumes, of course, that the therapist agrees with the family that the child's behavior is inappropriate and should be altered in the direction desired by the parents. Specific guidelines to help parents work with their own child are found in Furman, Patterson (1971), Walker and Roberts (1983), and Wright (1978a).

For children over 6 years of age and for adolescents, there is a difference of opinion on the best way to treat psychological problems. Reisman (1973) views psychotherapy as most effective with the mild to moderate problems of childhood. Routh (1981) emphasizes behavioral approaches; Zimmerman and Sims (1983) stress family therapy. The approaches a clinician uses depend upon his or her theoretical orientation and training. Psychotherapy relies heavily on a model in which a therapist works directly with the target child using play and verbal behavior to accomplish therapy goals (Freedheim & Russ, 1983). Individual psychotherapy often occurs in conjunction with school consultation, family therapy, parental guidance, or group therapy.

The behavioral approach has been reported to be the most beneficial treatment for persons with moderate and severe retardation (Finch & Kendall, 1979), and some believe it is the way to treat all child problems. It certainly has been effective with severe problems such as conduct disorders and autism (Gelfand, Jenson, & Drew, 1982). Effective treatment also requires consideration of a number of principles to which the therapist must adhere. These are discussed next.

Therapist Principles

Reisman (1973) has listed seven principles to which most child therapists adhere regardless of theoretical orientation. These include:

1. The therapist assesses the child before therapy and as an integral part of ongoing therapy.
2. The therapist listens to the child and allows the child to express feelings and beliefs.
3. The therapist communicates understanding, respect, and a wish to help.
4. The therapist negotiates goals with the child.
5. The therapist clarifies what is unusual in the child's behavior, beliefs, and feelings.
6. When dealing with behavior supported by a system, such as the family, the therapist may modify the behavior by negotiating with the system.
7. The therapist negotiates treatment termination with the child when those advantages outweigh those for continuation.

Each of these seven principles would generally be applied in a similar manner by a behavioral psychologist, a family therapist, or a child psychotherapist. The behaviorist may, however, differ from the family therapist and the child psychotherapist in his or her view of the mechanisms that account for changes in behavior. The family therapist and child psychotherapist would probably agree with Freedheim and Russ (1983) that the mechanisms of change are:

1. Catharsis and the labeling of feelings
2. Insight in dealing with problems
3. The occurrence of corrective emotional experiences
4. The learning of alternative problem-solving techniques and coping strategies
5. The development of internal structures of self-control
6. A variety of nonspecific variables, such as the child not considering himself as being alone or recognizing that the problem is being addressed.

A behaviorist would be more inclined to believe that the major mechanisms of behavior change are change in events that immediately precede (antecedents) or follow (consequences) a behavior, and would largely ignore the first three items just presented (Feldman & Peay, 1982).

Practice Limitations

Clearly, if no staff member in the particular clinic is trained in a particular intervention approach (e.g., family therapy), then that approach will not occur. If a clinic finds that there is a recurring need for this approach among its clientele, then the clinic director should consider adding a staff member with that orientation. Thus, the professional training and orientation of staff members will, in large part, dictate what type of intervention is considered most appropriate for the presenting problems.

If only one child in the family is initially identified as the presenting problem, then it is important that the family not bring other children to the treatment sessions (see Chapter 6). Clinic staff must be sure to inform families that it is best not to bring children other than the client to the sessions, thus preventing additional costs to the family for child care at the clinic, if available. In addition, parents' full attention can be directed to the child with the presenting problem.

As discussed early in this book, there must also be an appropriate waiting area for clients and their families. This area should be well lighted, should include books and other materials to occupy individuals who are waiting, and should include a space where individuals can complete forms as necessary (e.g., personal history).

Hospital versus Home Program versus Clinic

The best place to address a problem is in the setting in which it occurs. However, that is not always feasible because of factors such as the presenting problem and its severity, the resources available, the cost, skills of the parents (if they are to be involved in the treatment) and the physical space for providing treatment.

Hospital

Certain severe problems such as anorexia nervosa, which is increasingly common with teenage girls, can probably best be treated initially in a hospital setting where numerous variables can be controlled and where the child can be force fed if necessary to preserve life. Problems that require major medication adjustments (e.g., controlling seizures) can also be effectively handled in a hospital setting. Other problems that might be dealt with in a hospital setting include: preparation for surgery, preparation for death, preparation for major life changes precipitated by loss of limbs, psychosis or complete disorientation, and so on.

Home

The home is an ideal place to treat many of the problems that children and adolescents experience, particularly if they involve other family members or complaints by the parents. However, the home would not be the ideal place to attempt to resolve a problem that is brought to the attention of the family by the school system and that is only a problem in the school setting. In such a case, one would hope to treat the problem in the school setting. Some common problems to be treated in the home include behaviors such as enuresis, temper tantrums, noncompliance, aggression against siblings, destructive behavior, and withdrawal.

Clinic

The clinic is a useful place to treat problems that cannot be readily treated in other situations. It is often a good place to initiate treatment. In later stages, positive changes that have occurred in the clinic are generalized to the home, school, and other daily environments. Almost every conceivable child/adolescent problem has been seen at one time or another in a clinic setting. Unfortunately, in many cases no provisions were made for generalization of treatment gains to the rest of the world, so that the program was not successful overall.

Live versus Telephone Follow-up

Live

Regrettably, research on the relative effectiveness of live and telephone treatment follow-up is largely nonexistent. Having families, an adolescent, or a child return to the clinic on an ongoing basis is a very useful method of monitoring progress. For programs that are implemented in the clinic, it is the follow-up of choice. It allows the therapist to observe the individual client to see if changes are readily apparent, but it is also more costly for the family.

Telephone

Telephone follow-ups allow a family or school that is implementing a treatment program developed by a therapist to contact the therapist as needed to raise questions and resolve issues. In some cases, the family may be asked to mail data sheets to a therapist to report progress on a particular program, such as a program to increase a child's compliance with instructions given in the home setting. The family could also be instructed to call in the data on a daily basis. A combination of live and telephone follow-up is probably preferable. The telephone can be used as a bridge between sessions for exchanging information or dealing with questions or problems. It is also a useful way to maintain contact during the period when therapy is being faded out.

Where distances are great, the telephone may be the only realistic way to monitor an ongoing program implemented by a parent at home. So long as progress occurs and the parent and child are satisfied with that progress, this is certainly an acceptable alternative. If problems arise that cannot be resolved over the telephone, then it may be necessary to arrange for a face-to-face interaction, allowing for a direct interchange of information and direct observation.

A clinic must have a clear policy regarding charges for therapist telephone time, and be sure that the client is aware of it. The most typical arrangement is that the same rate will be charged as for an office visit, except that the charge will be prepared on the basis of time used. There will usually be an additional fee for long distance telephone charges.

OTHER SOURCES OF INFORMATION

You are referred to Wolberg (1977) for in-depth information about psychotherapy; Leland and Smith (1965) for information on play therapy; Chapter 5 for information on parent training; Walker and Roberts (1983) for information on treatment content; Bandura (1973) for information on social learning theory; Bijou and Baer (1961) for information on the operant approach; Mahoney (1974) and Meichenbaum (1977) for information on cognitive behavior modification; Franks, Wilson, Kendall, and Brownell (1982), Leitenberg (1976), Wilson and Franks (1982), and journals such as *Behavior Therapy* and the *Journal of Applied Behavior Analysis* for information on behavior therapy.

DETERMINING RESOURCES AVAILABLE

Internal Resources

Although time consuming, a determination of resources available in the clinic is important and is increasingly beneficial as time goes on. It will be useful in assignment of staff to specific problems, and in determining gaps in service patterns that can be remedied by hiring new staff. A good way to start is to examine the orientation, training, and skills of staff currently employed by the clinic. By listing staff and theoretical orientations on one axis and common problem areas seen by the clinic on the other axis, you can complete a chart (see Form 8.1) that clarifies what specific problems that staff is prepared to treat. This information can be used to make decisions on additional training needed by

FORM 8.1

Resource Chart

Staff and orientation	Problems			
	Aggression	Depression	Neuroses	Hyperactivity
Person A Cognitive behavioral	X	X	X	X
Person B Family therapy	X	X	X	
Person C Play therapy			X	
Person D Psychodynamic			X	

current staff, on which kinds of problems might best be referred elsewhere if that is feasible, and/or on what other staff are needed.

External Resources

A second task that administrators might conduct is to contact other professionals in the geographic area who provide psychological services, to discover what their specialties are, what kinds of clients they feel most comfortable treating, and which kinds of clients they do not wish to see. This information can be put on a chart. The Yellow Pages of the telephone directory, word-of-mouth referrals, and professional organizations are good sources for such professionals. It is useful to keep track of comments one hears in the community about the skills and services of these other professionals. Are they praised in the areas in which they are comfortable and criticized in other areas? When referring a client elsewhere, it is best, for reasons of legal protection, to give clients a list of choices rather than to make a referral to a specific party. If a clinician makes a referral to a specific source, and that person engages in a behavior detrimental to the client, the clinic could be sued for having made a referral to a negligent source. If, however, a client is given multiple choices, you are not accountable for the client's choice. It is to be expected that a client would never be referred to a source whose qualifications and skills are questionable. Clinicians can get to know the various other providers in the area on a personal and professional basis by arranging luncheon dates, joint meetings, exchanging inservice training activities, and so forth. Doing so may well establish relationships that will facilitate referrals to or from the clinic, as well as clarify what resources are available.

EXPECTATIONS OF CLIENTS AND CLINICIANS

Client Expectations

A client and his or her family have a right to expect that the clinician will provide assessment and treatment with at least ordinary care and skills in an effort to help the client accomplish agreed-upon goals, while protecting the client's and family's welfare and, within legal bounds, ensuring confidentiality. Moreover, they have a right to know what the therapist's background and training are; to know whether he or she has ever treated a problem such as theirs before; to change therapists if they are not satisfied with the particular therapist; to be informed of the type of treatment and the risks and benefits involved; to expect treatment to continue until goals are achieved, or an alternative treatment is arranged, or a mutual agreement to terminate is achieved; to have specific goals and a treatment plan agreed upon by the client/family and therapist; to have accurate, non-speculative contact notes recorded on file (see Sales, 1983, p. 488); and to have the therapist maintain the structure of treatment.

Therapist Expectations

The therapist has a right to expect that the client will be courteous; that he or she will be on time for appointments; that appointments will be cancelled at least 24 hours in advance; that the client will carry out all homework assignments; that the client will be honest and not withhold information from the therapist that is needed in order to make decisions that concern treatment; that treatment will be paid for as agreed upon at the outset of treatment; that the client/client family will discuss with the therapist concerns about treatment; and that the client/family will accept the fact that their symptoms may in some way be a result of their living patterns.

PROBLEM SOLVING WHEN TREATMENT IS NOT EFFECTIVE

The most critical aspect of determining whether or not treatment is effective is to document what did or did not occur. The primary reason for measurable and outcome-oriented goals is to allow evaluation of progress. Objective data such as that obtained by parents counting the number of times a child responds to specific requests, or subjective data reported by the client ("I think I am doing better," "I think I am less depressed," "I am at a 4 now rather than a 10 so far as my subjective impression of how depressed I am") can be useful. Subjective impressions of the therapist, a report by the parents on the child's behavior, checklists, rating scales, or information obtained from a home or school visit are also helpful (see Chapter 6). When a determination has been made—either through subjective or objective means, or a combination of the two—that progress did not occur, several questions need to be answered. These include, at a minimum:

1. Is the treatment program appropriate for the particular problem?
2. Was the problem clearly defined?
3. Is the program being carried out as specified?
4. Are other options available?
5. Are there factors related to this problem that have not previously been identified that interfere with accomplishment of the treatment goal?

6. Has good rapport been established with the client and the client's family?
7. Is the client/client family confident of the therapist's ability?
8. Is there any transference or resistance occurring, and if so, surrounding what issue?

By systematically answering each of these questions, the area of difficulty that interferes with effective treatment should be identified. Consideration can then be made of what changes are appropriate. When a problem has occurred during treatment or progress has not occurred, the case should be discussed by the clinic staff to obtain input from others to ensure that the therapist is not overlooking the obvious. Peer reviews of this nature (see Chapter 11) are extremely beneficial to all parties concerned and help indicate when a problem needs referral elsewhere, in what ways the program needs to be changed, or when the individual might better be treated by another staff member.

ADJUSTING TREATMENT TO THE INDIVIDUAL CLIENT

During the time treatment is provided, it is not unusual for changes to occur in the client's situation: a) new data may become available, b) the clinician may become familiar with newer or different intervention techniques, and/or c) other clinic staff members may provide worthwhile input. For these reasons, the treatment program must be flexible enough so that it can be changed to best benefit the client. Some of the specific factors that a clinician should be alerted to include:

1. Changes in client/family motivation can affect performance. Unless motivation is maintained within certain boundaries, it will interfere with treatment. If it is low, the client/family will fail to carry out homework assignments, may be late for or miss sessions, and in general will not perform therapeutically relevant tasks. If motivation is too high the client may try too hard, which could interfere with performance. The Yerkes-Dodson law (Olton & Noonberg, 1980) states that the relationship between motivation and performance is complex and looks like an inverted U. With no motivation there is no performance. As motivation increases, so does performance, up to some optimal point, after which motivation interferes with performance. A lack of motivation can be due to a belief that treatment will not succeed or produce change (Stroebel & Glueck, 1973), or to ambivalence about eliminating a problem.
2. Failure to monitor home practice carefully can result in a lack of progress for the client (Gaarder & Montgomery, 1977). If homework assignments are important, then the client/family must understand their importance and their contribution to achievement of treatment goals. One way to monitor home practice is to question the client/family carefully concerning: Was the homework assignment carried out? What data are available to support verbal claims? How, when, and how often was the homework assignment carried

out? What problems arose? If questioning does not occur, the therapist does not know if adjustments in the assignment need to be made. A failure to monitor homework assignments may give the client/family the impression that they are not important.

3. There is a natural tendency for clients to resist giving up their symptoms (Gaarder & Montgomery, 1977), because to do so would require a readjustment in their life-style. The therapist must stress the importance of change and that it will require effort on the part of the client for a substantial period of time.

4. The occurrence of self-fulfilling prophecies can occur (Gaarder & Montgomery, 1977). If a child or adolescent has become conditioned by failure to expect to fail again, he or she may not try or may give up easily if things do not change rapidly for the better.

Overcoming each of these difficulties requires that the clinician attend to details, encourage the client, keep close track of difficulties, have alternative interventions available, deal with the client's feelings, seek professional consultation if necessary, and keep informed on current findings in the literature related to the problem area.

Family support factors in the home that contribute to successful treatment include: a) stability, b) realistic and relaxed attitudes toward treatment, c) an intact extended family, d) a positive self-concept on the part of parents, and e) the ability to balance the child's need for growth and independence with the dependency fostered by the problem (Kenny, Bergey, & Young-Hyman, 1983). Unfortunately, these factors are seldom all present.

COMMON CHILD AND ADOLESCENT PROBLEMS

Similarity of Problems

Many presenting psychological problems of children and adolescents are similar. They may be expressed in the same manner at different ages, or they may be expressed differently over time owing to additional experiences, changes in expectation, or different environmental factors. For example, young children tend to be physically aggressive when they have a disagreement with another child. Older children tend to express their aggression verbally, although there are exceptions. Problem behaviors may be due to having learned inappropriate behaviors, to not having acquired a behavior at all, or to not having acquired a behavior to a degree sufficient for the behavior to be functional. These deficits and excesses are best dealt with early in life, by exposing the child to acceptable alternatives. For example, if a young child is spanked when he or she is physically aggressive with other children, he or she may learn not to be physically aggressive; or he or she may just as readily learn not to be aggressive in the presence of the person who does the spanking; or, indeed, to behave more aggressively because aggression (in the form of spanking) has been modeled.

Table 8.3. Common problems of children and adolescents

Problem	Sample causes	Age of onset	Potentially effective treatment	References
1. Asthma, anorexia nervosa, migraines, and other psychosomatic conditions	Family rigidity, overprotectiveness, overinvolvement with other family members, lack of conflict resolution, and use of client's symptoms to avoid conflict	Any age	Family therapy, behavior therapy (classical conditioning, disensitization, etc.), biofeedback	Kenny, Bergey, & Young-Hyman (1983); Wright (1978b)
2. Depression	Insufficient body contact and nurturing, separation from primary caregiver, loss of love object, feeling unloved or rejected	Rare before age 10, common after age 14	Behavior therapy, teach alternatives for getting attention, family therapy	Cantor (1983); Toolan (1978); Kaslow & Rehm (1983)
3. Aggression	Frustration, learned behavior, normal behavior to some degree	Any age	Timeout, response cost, overcorrection, modeling appropriate behavior	Johnson & Fennell (1983); Kazdin & Frame (1983)
4. Hyperactivity	Neurological pathology, advanced motor system, learned behavior, diet	Usually early in life	Medication, contingency management, cognitive behavior modification, relaxation/biofeedback	Franks (1982); Kerasotes & Walker (1983); Striefel & Baer (1980)
5. Neuroses: a. Obsessive-compulsive	Family rigidity, overprotectiveness, overinvolvement with other family members, failure to resolve family conflicts	Any age	Psychodynamic therapy, behavior therapy, (contingency management, implosive therapy, symptom interruption), play therapy	Adams (1973); Dollinger (1983); Milby, Wendorf, & Meredith (1983)
b. Phobias and fears	Parent worrying about something, classically conditioned, imagination, modeling another's	Any age	Behavior therapy (systematic desensitization, participant-modeling, stimulus facing, self-con-	Dollinger (1983); Miller (1983); Morris & Kratochwill (1983b)

	fear, defense against unconscious impulses		trol); educating child about the reality of the danger, dynamic therapy	
6. Psychosis: a. Autism	Organic defect	Before 30 months of age	Play therapy, drugs, behavior therapy, special education	Dawson & Mesibov (1983)
b. Childhood/adolescent schizophrenia	Genetic predisposition and environmental stress	Seldom before age 10	Behavior therapy, special education, social skills training, individual and family therapy, drug therapy	Dawson & Mesibov (1983); Weiner (1983)
7. Sleep disorders	Daily stress, overstimulation, diet, depression, medical problems	Any age	Behavior therapy (progressive relaxation, stimulus control), drugs	Ware & Orr (1983)
8. Tics, habits, and mannerisms	Stress, increased attention, conflict	Any age, but tics most common ages 8–12	Operant conditioning, negative and massed practice, self-monitoring, habit reversal, family therapy and play therapy, extinction, reinforcement of incompatible responses, relaxation	Corbett, Matthews, Connell, & Shapiro (1969); Matthews, Liebowitz, & Matthews (1983)
9. Sex role identity and other sexual problems	Birth defects, hypocritical attitudes, delayed puberty, sexual abuse	Any age	Play therapy, nonaversive behavior therapy, family therapy, sex education	Haroian (1983); Kaplan (1979)
10. Toileting problems (enuresis, constipation and encopresis)	Lack of proper training, physiological, psychological trauma	Training not expected until 24–36 months	Azrin & Fox program (enuresis), diet (constipation), suppository and enema procedure (encopresis), wet alarm (nighttime enuresis), medical collaboration	Azrin & Fox (1974); Christophersen & Rapoff (1983)

(continued)

Table 8.3. *(continued)*

	Problem	Sample causes	Age of onset	Potentially effective treatment	References
11.	Eating problems (obesity, pica, rumination, food obsessions)	Behavioral management, neuromotor problems, mechanical obstructions	Any age	Reinforcement, timeout, extinction, shaping, fading, family intervention, stimulus control	Linscheid (1983)
12.	Developmental disabilities of all types	Genetic, trauma, illness, nutrition	Any age	Behavioral intervention, family therapy (for rest of family), special education	Cleland (1983)
13.	School problems (learning problems, school phobia, conduct disorder, social withdrawal)	Developmental disabilities, environmental, behavioral mismanagement	School years (some start at birth and some extend beyond school years)	Behavioral intervention, pharmacological, psychodynamic, humanistic special education, family therapy	Durlak (1983); Neeper & Lahey (1983); Phillips (1983)
14.	Teen-parent problems (acting out, withdrawal)	Separation issues (parent too close or too distant)	Teen years most common (can occur in childhood)	Parent and adolescent intervention, behavioral contract	Krug (1983); Rae (1983)
15.	Puberty and adolescent adjustment problems	Normal development, abnormal development, psychogenic, genetic	Teen years	Education, behavior therapy, psychodynamic therapy	Rekers & Jurich (1983)
16.	Career choice	Individual experiences, attitudes, values, self-concept, family pressure	Teen years	Education and exposure to choices, family therapy, individual vocational counseling	Banikiotes & Bartlett (1983)

Parents often use aggressive techniques such as spanking exclusively, with minimal or no training provided to the child on acceptable alternative behaviors. When spanking does not eliminate the aggressive problem, parents may seek professional assistance. A clinician should be prepared to help parents identify and train acceptable alternative behaviors. Unless a child learns acceptable alternatives, the problem will likely persist through childhood and adolescence, resulting in many negative experiences for both the child/youth and their family.

Common Problems and Causes

Some of the more common problems of children and adolescents, along with suggested interventions (reported in the literature as useful) and references for further information are presented in Table 8.3. (Ollendick & Hersen, 1983, is also a good source of information.) The causes of some of these presenting problems can be readily identified through the collection of a good personal history (e.g., the death of a parent may lead to depression). In other cases it is difficult, if not impossible, to pinpoint the exact cause of a problem (e.g., autism). Some of the common causes of psychological problems for children include:

1. Child abuse (both physical and sexual)
2. Divorce or separation from parent
3. Death of a loved one
4. Punitive experiences
5. Lack of reinforcement and feedback
6. Physiological trauma or infection
7. Relocation
8. Family pathology
9. Lack of social skills
10. Developmental disabilities

SUMMARY

A variety of problems result in referrals for treatment. Clinicians must understand their own philosophical position in terms of child and problem development. In addition, many practical issues are related to successful operation of treatment services, including assignment of clients, choices of treatment modality, deciding who the client is, what the problem is, what intervention will be most effective, and how to conduct follow-ups. Therapists must proceed logically in addressing these issues and adhere to principles associated with effective intervention services. An accurate assessment of resources available in a clinic and the strengths of staff and different treatment approaches is quite useful in addressing many of these issues.

READER ACTIVITIES

Do you have an equitable way of assigning clients that also takes into account therapist skills and client needs? If not, develop one now. List the "treatment of choice" for each of the most common problems referred to your clinic. Now discuss these with all of your service providers to see if they agree, and also check to see if these "treatments of choice" are in fact being used with clinic clients. If not, inservice training and/or more staff discussion is needed. If you have a waiting list, could you reduce it by having appropriately trained therapists provide more family or group therapy? Have you developed a policy on charges for telephone contacts with clients? If so, is it used by all staff? As a clinician, what policy would you propose to assure that clinicians are not assigned clients in areas where the clinician is not competent? List your expectations of a good client.

REFERENCES

Adams, P. L. (1973). *Obsessive children: A sociopsychiatric study.* New York: Brunner/Mazel.

American Psychological Association. (1981). Ethical principles of psychologists. *Ameican Psychologist, 36*(6), 633–635.

Azrin, N. H., & Fox, R. M. (1974). *Toilet training in less than a day.* New York: Simon & Schuster.

Bandura, A. (1973). *Aggression: A social learning analysis.* Englewood Cliffs, NJ: Prentice Hall.

Banikiotes, P. G., & Bartlett, W. E. (1983). Career choice: Problems and issues. In C. E. Walker & M. C. Roberts (Eds.), *Handbook of clinical child psychology* (pp. 833–852). New York: John Wiley & Sons.

Bijou, S. W., & Baer, D. M. (1961). *Child development I: A systematic and empirical theory.* New York: Appleton-Century-Crofts.

Cantor, P. (1983). Depression and suicide in children. In C. E. Walker & M. C. Roberts (Eds.), *Handbook of clinical child psychology* (pp. 453–471). New York: John Wiley & Sons.

Christophersen, E. R., & Rapoff, M. A. (1983). Toileting problems in children. In C. E. Walker & M. C. Roberts (Eds.), *Handbook of clinical child psychology* (pp. 593–615). New York: John Wiley & Sons.

Cleland, C. C. (1983). Mental retardation. In C. E. Walker & M. C. Roberts (Eds.), *Handbook of clinical child psychology* (pp. 640–659). New York: John Wiley & Sons.

Corbett, J. A., Matthews, A. M., Connell, P. H., & Shapiro, D. A. (1969). Tics and Gilles de la Tourette's syndrome: A follow-up study and critical reviews. *British Journal of Psychiatry, 115,* 1229–1241.

Dawson, G., & Mesibov, G. B. (1983). Childhood psychosis. In C. E. Walker & M. C. Roberts (Eds.), *Handbook of clinical child psychology* (pp. 543–572). New York: John Wiley & Sons.

DeLeon, P. H., VandenBos, G. R., & Cummings, N. A. (1983). Psychotherapy—Is it safe, effective, and appropriate? *American Psychologist, 38*(8), 907–911.

Dollinger, S. J. (1983). Childhood neuroses. In C. E. Walker & M. C. Roberts (Eds.), *Handbook of clinical child psychology* (pp. 524–542). New York: John Wiley & Sons.

Durlak, J. A. (1983). Providing mental health services to elementary school children. C. E. Walker & M. C. Roberts (Eds.), *Handbook of clinical child psychology* (pp. 660–679). New York: John Wiley & Sons.

Feldman, M. P., & Peay, J. (1982). Ethical and legal issues. In A. S. Bellack, M. Hersen, & A. E. Kazdia (Eds.), *International handbook of behavior modification and therapy* (pp. 231–261). New York: Plenum.

Finch, A. J., & Kendall, P. C. (1979). *Clinical treatment and research in child psychotherapy.* New York: Spectrum.

Franks, C. M. (1982). Behavior therapy with children and adolescents. In C. M. Franks, G. T. Wilson, P. C. Kendall, & K. D. Brownell (Eds.), *Annual review of behavior therapy* (Vol. 8, pp. 273–304). New York: Guilford Press.

Franks, C. M., Wilson, G. T., Kendall, P. C., & Brownell, K. D. (Eds.). (1982). *Annual review of behavior therapy* (Vol. 8). New York: Guilford Press.

Freedheim, D. K., & Russ, S. R. (1983). Psychotherapy with children. In C. E. Walker & M. C. Roberts (Eds.), *Handbook of clinical child psychology* (pp. 978–994). New York: John Wiley & Sons.

Furman, F. (1957). Treatment of under 5's by way of parents. *The psychoanalytic study of the child* (Vol. 12, pp. 312–322). New York: International Universities Press.

Gaarder, K. R., & Montgomery, P. S. (1977). *Clinical biofeedback: A procedural manual.* Baltimore: Williams & Wilkins.

Gelfand, D. M., Jensen, W. R., & Drew, C. J. (1982). *Understanding child behavior disorders.* New York: Holt, Rinehart & Winston.

Haroian, L. M. (1983). Sexual problems in children. In C. E. Walker & M. C. Roberts (Eds.), *Handbook of clinical child psychology* (pp. 573–592). New York: John Wiley & Sons.

Johnson, J. H., & Fennell, E. B. (1983). Aggressive and delinquent behavior in childhood and adolescence. In C. E. Walker & M. C. Roberts (Eds.), *Handbook of clinical child psychology* (pp. 475–497). New York: John Wiley & Sons.

Kaplan, H. S. (1979). *The new sex therapy: Vol. II. Disorders of sexual desire.* New York: Brunner/Mazel.

Kaslow, N. J., & Rehm, L. P. (1983). Childhood depression. In R. J. Morris & T. J. Kratochwill (Eds.), *The practice of child therapy* (pp. 27–85). New York: Pergamon Press.

Kazdin, A. E., & Frame, C. (1983). In R. J. Morris & T. J. Kratochwill (Eds.), *The practice of child therapy* (pp. 167–192). New York: Pergamon Press.

Kenny, T. J., Bergey, S. F. A., & Young-Hyman, D. (1983). Psychosomatic problems of children. In C. E. Walker & M. C. Roberts (Eds.), *Handbook of clinical child psychology* (pp. 437–452). New York: John Wiley & Sons.

Kerasotes, D., & Walker, C. E. (1983). Hyperactive behavior in children. In C. E. Walker & M. C. Roberts (Eds.), *Handbook of clinical child psychology* (pp. 498–523). New York: John Wiley & Sons.

Krug, R. S. (1983). Substance abuse. In C. E. Walker & M. C. Roberts (Eds.), *Handbook of clinical child psychology* (pp. 853–879). New York: John Wiley & Sons.

Leitenberg, H. (1976). *Handbook of behavior modification and behavior therapy.* Englewood Cliffs, NJ: Prentice-Hall.

Leland, H., & Smith, D. E. (1965). *Play therapy with mentally subnormal children.* New York: Grune & Stratton.

Linscheid, T. R. (1983). Eating problems in children. In C. E. Walker & M. C. Roberts (Eds.), *Handbook of clinical child psychology* (pp. 616–639). New York: John Wiley & Sons.

Mahoney, M. (1974). *Cognition and behavior modification.* Cambridge, MA: Ballinger Publishing Co.

Matthews, L. E., Liebowitz, J. M., & Matthews, J. R. (1983). Tics, habits, and mannerisms. In C. E. Walker & M. C. Roberts (Eds.), *Handbook of clinical child psychology* (pp. 406–436). New York: John Wiley & Sons.

Meichenbaum, D. (1977). *Cognitive behavior modifications: An integrative approach.* New York: Plenum.

Milby, J. B., Wendorf, D., & Meredith, R. L. (1983). Obsessive-compulsive disorders. In R. J. Morris & T. J. Kratochwill (Eds.), *The practice of child therapy* (pp. 1–26). New York: Pergamon Press.

Miller, L. C. (1983). Fears and anxiety in children. In C. E. Walker & M. C. Roberts (Eds.), *Handbook of clinical child psychology* (pp. 337–380). New York: John Wiley & Sons.

Morris, R. J., & Kratochwill, T. J. (1983a). *The practice of child therapy.* New York: Pergamon Press.

Morris, R. J., & Kratochwill, T. J. (1983b). *Treating children's fears and phobias.* New York: Pergamon Press.

Neeper, R. S., Lahey, B. B. (1983). Learning disabilities of children. In C. E. Walker & M. C. Roberts (Eds.), *Handbook of clinical child psychology* (pp. 680–696). New York: John Wiley & Sons.

Ollendick, T. H., & Hersen, M. (Eds.). (1983). *Handbook of child psycho-pathology.* New York: Plenum.

Olton, D. S., & Noonberg, A. R. (1980). *Biofeedback: Clinical applications in behavioral medicine.* Englewood Cliffs, NJ: Prentice-Hall.

Patterson, G. R. (1971). *Families.* Champaign, IL: Research Press.

Phillips, B. N. (1983). School problems in adolescence. In C. E. Walker & M. C. Roberts (Eds.), *Handbook of clinical child psychology* (pp. 813–832). New York: John Wiley & Sons.

Rae, W. A. (1983). Teen-parent problems. In C. E. Walker & M. C. Roberts (Eds.), *Handbook of clinical child psychology* (pp. 725–740). New York: John Wiley & Sons.

Reisman, J. (1973). *Principles of psychotherapy with children.* New York: John Wiley & Sons.

Rekers, G. A., & Jurich, A. P. (1983). Development of problems of puberty and sex roles in adolescence. In C. E. Walker & M. C. Roberts (Eds.), *Handbook of clinical child psychology* (pp. 785–812). New York: John Wiley & Sons.

Routh, D. (1981). Child treatment citation classics. *Professional Psychology, 11,* 901–906.

Sales, B. D. (1983). *The professional psychologist's handbook.* New York: Plenum.

Striefel, S., & Baer, R. (1980). Biofeedback applications with handicapped children and youth. In D. A. Sabatino & L. Mann (Eds.), *Fourth review of special education* (pp. 175–198). New York: Grune & Stratton.

Stroebel, C. F., & Glueck, B. C. (1973). Biofeefback in medicine and psychiatry: An ultimate placebo? In L. Birk (Ed.), *Biofeedback: Behavioral medicine* (pp. 19–33). New York: Grune & Stratton.

Toolan, J. M. (1978). Therapy of depressed and suicidal children. *American Journal of Psychotherapy, 32*(3), 243–251.

Walker, C. E., & Roberts, M. C. (1983). *Handbook of clinical child psychology.* New York: John Wiley & Sons.

Ware, J. C., & Orr, W. C. (1983). Sleep disorders in children. In C. E. Walker & M. C. Roberts (Eds.), *Handbook of clinical child psychology* (pp. 381–405). New York: John Wiley & Sons.

Weiner, A. S. (1983). Emotional problems of adolescence: A review of affective disorders and schizophrenia. In C. E. Walker & M. C. Roberts (Eds.), *Handbook of clinical child psychology* (pp. 741–755). New York: John Wiley & Sons.

Wilson, G. T., & Franks, C. M. (1982). *Contemporary behavior therapy: Conceptual and empirical foundations.* New York: Guilford Press.

Wolberg, L. R. (1977). *The techniques of psychotherapy: Part 1.* (3rd ed.). New York: Grune & Stratton.

Wood, M. M. (1975). *Developmental therapy*. Baltimore: University Park Press.
Wright, L. (1978a). *Parent power: A guide to responsible childrearing*. New York: Psychological Dimensions.
Wright, L. (1978b). Assessing the psychosomatic status of children. *Journal of Clinical Child Psychology, 7*(1), 94–112.
Wright, L. (1982). Rethinking psychology's turf. *Clinical Psychologist, 35*(1), 3–4.
Zimmerman, J., & Sims, D. (1983). Family therapy. In C. E. Walker & M. C. Roberts (Eds.), *Handbook of clinical child psychology* (pp. 995–1025). New York: John Wiley & Sons.

9

Functional
Clinical Reports

In this chapter, you will be informed about:
1. Purposes of written clinical reports
2. Different types of clinical reports and their components
3. Prevention of problems in writing clinical reports
4. Use of computers for clinical reports
5. Review and critique procedures for clinical reports
6. The value of clinical reports for clinic public relations

DEFINITION

A clinical report is defined as a written record that contains pertinent information relating to a client or client-related contact(s) and recommendations or information about future client or client-related contacts.

PURPOSES OF WRITTEN CLINICAL REPORTS

Clinical reports are written for various purposes:

1. To communicate assessment/evaluation information and recommendations
2. To serve as a permanent written record
3. To provide a diagnosis or classification of the client served
4. To provide a summary for use in peer or human rights reviews

TYPES OF FUNCTIONAL
CLINICAL REPORTS AND THEIR COMPONENTS

Two general types of clinical reports are discussed in this chapter: a) the assessment/evaluation clinical report, and (b) the case summary report. Treatment contact progress reports were discussed in Chapter 7.

Assessment/Evaluation Clinical Reports

Reports of this type may originate from a representative of a single discipline, or the report may be a comprehensive integration of information from more than one discipline involved (i.e., psychological and speech/language).

Single Discipline Reports

Frequently in multidisciplinary clinic settings, team members from different disciplines will prepare independent assessment/evaluation reports. Such reports are then distributed to relevant parties either in one package or separately. This practice is efficient for team members because they: a) can focus on their own contribution and discipline, and b) can prepare reports on their own time schedules. This practice makes each team member equally responsible for report preparation. For report recipients, however, particularly nonprofessionals, it is often overwhelming to receive a sheaf of independent reports that may be written in different styles, using different forms, requiring the reader to integrate all information received into a meaningful whole. Further, report recipients may at times be faced with contradictory comments, findings, or recommendations, or, of lesser importance, the information may be redundant. Some of these problems can be resolved by: a) adopting a standard report format for use by all team members, b) having all reports reviewed before they are disseminated, and/or c) distributing a summary of findings and recommendations from all separate reports to recipients.

Comprehensive Team Reports

A comprehensive evaluation report incorporates assessment information and recommendations from two or more disciplines into one document. It is usually prepared in settings where interdisciplinary evaluations are conducted, that is, where most or all team members have frequent interactions in the course of the client evaluation. Typically, one or two team members are designated to assemble the assessment/evaluation information from the separate disciplines involved into one integrated report, which is then disseminated to report recipients. Comprehensive reports are valued by report recipients because information is combined into one document. If the report is well-prepared, contradictions are addressed and redundancies eliminated. Furthermore, evaluation results and recommendations are integrated into a meaningful instrument.

Disadvantages for the comprehensive report practice include: a) added staff time involved in integration of evaluation information into one report, b) unequal staff responsibilities, in that designated report writers have more responsibility for written report preparation than other team members, c) designated report writers may lack training or skill in interpreting technical terminology or information pertinent to other disciplines, and d) the staff writing the reports may inadvertently misinterpret or omit essential information other team members wish to communicate.

Components of Assessment/Evaluation Reports

Although there are no rigid rules about clinical reports, and forms and styles may differ (Goldman, L'Engle Stein, & Guerry, 1983; Sattler, 1982), the components of assessment/evaluation reports for children and adolescents are fairly similar.

The following items are typically included in such reports, even though descriptor headings and presentation formats may vary among professionals:

1. Personal data
2. Dates of evaluation
3. Tests/assessments administered
4. Reason for referral
5. Background information
6. Observations of client
7. Assessment results obtained
8. Summary of report contents
9. Recommendations

A sample evaluation report outline and examples of components are shown in Form 9.1. You may also wish to consult other sources for sample outlines and guidelines (such as Goldman et al., 1983; Sattler, 1982).

Each clinic should adopt procedures for clinical staff to follow in preparing written assessment/evaluation reports, including report outlines to be used and descriptions of what information is to be featured in each component of the reports.

Case Summary Reports

Whenever a client treatment is terminated, a final case summary report may be written. This report may be as brief as one typewritten page describing the reason for referral and who initiated it, the number of treatment sessions conducted, the time frames during which treatment was provided, general treatment procedures used (e.g., parent training and behavior management, individual counseling), and treatment outcome (e.g., data collected). Or, the report can be a fairly extensive document that not only elaborates on the areas just noted but also summarizes any assessments or evaluations that may have been conducted prior to case termination. Within each clinic, the content of reports may differ depending on the services provided. Also, independent reports may be filed from several different clinicians if a client has received treatment across several disciplines; or the report may be a single document integrating all treatment, treatment results. and recommendations provided in the clinic. The advantages/disadvantages for single discipline versus comprehensive reports discussed in the assessment/evaluation report section of this chapter apply also to case summary reports. These reports are frequently provided to identified report recipients (e.g., parents, referral agency representatives) in accordance with ethical standards (see Form 9.2 for a sample case summary report form).

PREPARATION OF WRITTEN ASSESSMENT/EVALUATION AND/OR TREATMENT CLINICAL REPORTS

The issues discussed in this section of the chapter focus primarily on written clinical reports that are to be disseminated outside of the clinic, although some

Comprehensive Evaluation
Report Outline and Component Examples

1. **Personal Data**

   Client: full name

   > Age: years and months
   > Birth date:
   > Grade: (If client is school age, give grade and school year [i.e., 1985–86 school year].)

   Parents/Legal Guardians: full names

2. **Date(s) of Assessment/Evaluation:** Include all dates pertinent to the assessment or evaluation.

3. **Assessment(s) Administered:** Provide complete and accurate titles of tests or other assessments administered. List in alphabetical order.

   Example:

   Audiometric Screening
   Brigance Diagnostic Comprehensive Inventory of Basic Skills
   Bruininks-Oseretsky Test of Motor Proficiency
   Child Behavior Checklist
   Developmental Test of Visual-Motor Integration
   Expressive One-Word Picture Vocabulary Test
   Peabody Picture Vocabulary Test–Revised, Form L
   Test of Language Development–Primary
   Vineland Adaptive Behavior Scale, Classroom Edition
   Wechsler Intelligence Scale for Children–Revised

4. **Reason for Referral:**

   Include *who* referred the client, (e.g., Mrs. John Thomas, Joe's mother) *for what purpose* the referral was made (e.g., for a comprehensive evaluation) and *what prompted the referral* (e.g., because of behavior problems exhibited in the home). It may also be appropriate to indicate the expectations of the referral party of the evaluation (e.g., Joe's mother would like recommendations on how to manage Joe's behavior more effectively).

   The referral party is the person or agency (or agency representative) identified as responsible for payment of services. Provide the full name, title, and relationship to client (where appropriate) of the referral party.

   Examples:

   a. Bill was referred for evaluation by his parents because of behavioral problems that are disruptive to family functioning, such as noncompliance and aggression toward siblings and family pets.

   b. Mr. John Jones, pupil personnel director, Washington School District, Lincoln, Utah, referred Mary to the clinic for evaluation because of withdrawal behavior exhibited at school and indications of depression.

5. **Background Information:**

   Relevant information about the client obtained through interviews or from reports of other agencies should be summarized in this section. This should include information obtained by *all* members of the evaluation team.

   a. The introductory paragraph of this section should include the names, relationships, and titles (where appropriate) of those who accompanied the client to the first or subsequent evaluation appointments and who provided client and referral question information.

(continued)

FORM 9.1 *(continued)*

b. Following the introductory paragraph, the next paragraph(s) should usually summarize information provided that is directly relevant to the reason(s) for referral. A clear and concise description of current and past events, issues, or situations related to the referral question should be communicated.

c. Other areas that may be included in the background section (e.g., depending on the age of the client or referral question) are:

Developmental history
Educational history
Medical/health history
Job history
Social/emotional/behavioral history

Each area of functioning may be summarized in separate paragraphs, or certain functioning areas may be combined (depending on how much information is available or pertinent). Information should usually be presented in chronological order, giving dates (i.e., month and year) and locations. Reports will differ as to the emphasis and extent of the summaries included. The variation among reports is somewhat dictated by the referral question and the amount of information acquired.

d. Use separate paragraphs for information provided from different sources. For example: Do not report information obtained from a teacher in the same paragraph as that provided by a parent. Also, attribute information obtained to the individual who provided the information (e.g., Mrs. Smith reported that Janie . . .). Avoid the use of quotes unless there seems to be no better way to rephrase the information given.

Example: [All names used in this report, and subsequent examples, are fictitious.]

The following is a summary of information provided by school staff of the Happy Valley County School District and Jeff's parents, Mr. and Mrs. Carson, who accompanied Jeff to the clinic.

Jeff was enrolled in the Happy Valley County School District as a kindergarten student in the fall of 1983. In the kindergarten placement, Jeff's interaction with peers was minimal. He rarely initiated social peer interactions and tended to be somewhat socially isolated. He was also delayed in communication skills and in academics. Although Jeff was advanced to first grade in the 1984–85 school year, social problems identified in kindergarten increased. He made continued efforts to isolate himself from classmates and the teacher (e.g., turning away from them and hiding his face). In addition, increases were noted in Jeff's academic deficits and in nonproductive classroom behavior.

Jeff was tested by school staff last February 1985, and was found to have average intellectual functioning on a verbal test, but below average academic and language skills. One week prior to the clinic intake, Jeff was placed in a behavioral adjustment class. The teacher of this class reported to Mr. and Mrs. Carson that Jeff has had no adjustment problems after being placed in the class.

According to information provided by Jeff's parents, he first attended preschool at age 3. Teachers in that setting reported that Jeff's behavior was atypical in that setting. For example, he did not participate in group activities, did not relate or interact with peers, and he appeared to be "in his own world." Due to a family move, Jeff was placed in a new preschool setting. According to teacher report, he did not adjust easily to the new placement. Other children in his class were learning to read while he was still acquiring readiness skills (e.g., learning colors and the alphabet). Jeff often refused to cooperate in that setting. The family then moved to their current location where Jeff participated in a preschool program on a part-time basis. He continued to exhibit communication problems and social interaction difficulties in that program.

Mr. and Mrs. Carson reported that, currently, Jeff seems to have adequate

(continued)

FORM 9.1 *(continued)*

gross-motor skills, (e.g., can keep up with peers on playground activities and can ride a two-wheel bicycle). His parents' only concern regarding his gross-motor development is that he does not catch a ball well. However, the parents expressed greater concern about Jeff's fine-motor development. For example, he has difficulty achieving uniform size and spacing when he is printing. Jeff reportedly can manipulate a pencil and scissors to perform assigned tasks, but is somewhat slow and clumsy with them. Jeff's parents also reported that he is independent in feeding and is able to perform all dressing skills without assistance, including shoe tying. Also, he is independent in bathing, teeth brushing, and toileting.

At present, Jeff reportedly is able to express his needs and desires and appears to utilize a large vocabulary and complex sentence construction. However, although Mrs. Carson was unable to provide an example, she reported that he uses some improper grammatical structures. Both parents expressed concern that Jeff sometimes exhibits speech dysfluencies (i.e., stuttering), characterized by repetitions of single words and parts of words. Mr. and Mrs. Carson reported that speech and language testing by school staff within the past 4 months revealed that Jeff has some speech dysfluencies (i.e., stuttering, uses improper grammar, and has difficulties in expressing himself spontaneously). It was further reported by Jeff's parents that they have no concerns regarding Jeff's ability to hear, since he responds to whispers, conversations, and environmental sounds without difficulty.

Mrs. Carson reported that she had no difficulties during her pregnancy with Jeff and that he was delivered without complications. His Apgar scores were 8 and 9. Both of Jeff's parents reported that Jeff's motor development proceeded normally and that he acquired gross and fine motor skills during preschool years at expected ages. During infancy and early preschool years, Jeff also appeared to be acquiring speech and language skills as expected (e.g., first word spoken at 1 year, three- to four-word phrases produced after 2 years of age. Currently, Jeff's speech and language skills are delayed in comparison with a younger sister's acquisition of skills in this area.

6. **Observations of the Client**
   a. This section should include specific behaviors of the child/adolescent client that are observed during contacts with the client (e.g., behavior observed during interview, testing behavior).
   b. Do not include inferences or speculations of "why" the client behaved in the manner observed.
   c. *Avoid overworked words or phrases* such as *cooperative* or "Mary was pleasant to work with." Whenever possible if overworked words are used, describe overt behavior exhibited as examples.
   d. Do not describe the client's physical appearance (e.g., well-groomed) unless the description is significant to the assessment/evaluation and will later be discussed in the summary section of the report.

Examples:
   a. During the initial testing session, Carl entered the testing room independently and responded to the examiner's questions, although he rarely initiated conversations. After 15–20 minutes, he asked for his mother and began to cry. When his mother joined him for the remainder of the test, he sat close to her and laid his head on her lap at times. Carl did not respond readily to items toward the end of the session. The provision of stickers or the presentation of tasks as "games" was sometimes effective in eliciting responses. In a subsequent assessment session held on another day, Carl did not resist being separated from his mother to go with staff for testing in another room. Carl was easily distracted from tasks and also attempted to manipulate test materials before receiving instructions.

(continued)

FORM 9.1 *(continued)*

b. Ellen participated in all activities presented to her by staff. In between test tasks, she volunteered information about herself and her family and responded to staff questions without hesitation. It was noted that she gave up quickly on items she perceived to be difficult unless verbally encouraged to continue to complete tasks.

7. **Assessment or Test Results:** (whichever is most appropriate)

   a. A separate paragraph should be written for each test or assessment administered. Clinic Test Descriptors should be used whenever appropriate. In dictating or writing rough drafts of the report, the test can be identified by name only and the test descriptor paragraph printed out on the rough draft copy with blanks for scores or other necessary information that can be filled in by the report writer. Clinic Test Descriptors should be modified whenever appropriate to individualize the descriptor for a particular client.

      If Clinic Test Descriptors are not available for specific tests or assessment procedures, the report writer will need to write a descriptor for each test or assignment given. Test descriptors should include the complete and accurate name of the assessment instrument, a brief description of what the instrument is purported to assess, and how the information is obtained (e.g., what and how instructions are given and what the client is asked to do). Assessment results should be reported along with any particular outstanding strengths or weaknesses identified.

   b. Whenever more than one assessment instrument is administered in the same areas of functioning (e.g., intellectual), provide an explanation for why this occurred (e.g., because of concerns that the child's language impairment could have resulted in deflated scores).

   c. Whenever informal assessments are conducted, they should be so identified. Further, the procedures used should be described and specific responses reported if obtained. Include qualifying statements about the results being estimates of functioning.

   d. It is the clinic policy not to report specific IQ scores in written reports. Instead, range functioning should be reported (e.g., Mary's performance on this test places her within the average range of intellectual functioning). This procedure should be modified only when contractual or other arrangements are made to the contrary. The director of the clinic will provide such information to the report writer.

   e. In reporting projective test results, preface your interpretation with a statement indicating that such results may be interpreted in different ways and that the interpretation to follow is that of the examiner. Whenever possible, support your interpretations with observable behavior noted. Avoid ambiguous terms and professional jargon.

Examples of Test Descriptors:

The Leiter International Performance Scale was administered to Sally. This individually administered test of intellectual abilities is given without verbal instructions and does not require verbal responses from the individual taking the test. Instead, instructions are given through visual examples, gestures, and mime, and the respondent places small wooden blocks with response choices into slots in a tray. On this test, Sally completed tasks that represent performance in the average range of intellectual functioning, with an IQ of 104.

The Burk's Behavior Rating Scale was completed by Jeff's parents and teacher. The scale requires that respondents read a list of behaviors and rate the degree to which those behaviors are observed in the child. Responses are compiled into 18 basic areas. The frequencies reported by the respondents (i.e., the degree to which parents and teacher have noticed a behavior) allow for judgments about the magnitude or significance of what could potentially be problem

(continued)

behaviors. Examination of Mrs. Carson's responses indicate that Jeff does not behave in a problematic manner in the majority of areas. "Significant" ratings were found in only two categories: excessive self-blame (e.g., "upset if he makes a mistake") and poor anger control (e.g., "becomes angry quickly"). Mr. Carson's responses indicated that Jeff behaves in a problematic manner "significantly" in five categories: excessive self-blame, excessive withdrawal (e.g., "is shy," "prefers to work by self"), poor academics, poor attention and excessive sense of persecution (e.g., "complains he never gets his fair share of things"). Ratings by Jeff's teacher indicated "very significant" problems in two areas: poor attention and poor anger control.

8. **Other Component Areas That Could Be Included:**

School Contacts:

This section of the report should be included whenever a contact (telephone school visit) is made on behalf of the client. It should feature a summary of information obtained during this contact that is relevant to the referral question. Identify the date of contact, type of contact (e.g., phone or school visit), and the individuals contacted by name and title. If several individuals have been contacted (i.e., regular classroom teacher, resource room specialist), use separate paragraphs for summarizing their input.

Home Visits:

If a home visit is conducted as part of the intake evaluation, this section of the report should be included. Provide a summary of that visit, describing specific observations made, areas discussed, etc. Identify date and time of visit, those present, and the situation in which the visit occurred (e.g., during dinner hour).

9. **Summary and General Recommendations:**
   a. This section is probably the most difficult for the report writer. If the report reader were to read this section of the report only, he or she should be able to determine why the child was referred, general evaluation findings, and what is suggested for resolution of the referral question.
   b. *All* information you have obtained about the client (e.g., assessment results, input from parents and others, behavior observed at the clinic, etc. should be integrated in this section), but should not be a reiteration of previously stated information.
   c. DO NOT repeat all of the specific test results. Briefly state client strengths and weaknesses.
   d. Be certain that the referral question has been addressed and that evaluation results are discussed relevant to the referral question. Discuss all information relevant to specific recommendations that are made.
   e. It may also be appropriate to include a prognosis statement(s) in this section of the report.
   f. After writing this section, review and reflect on how it will sound to parents, administrators, teachers, and others who will read it.

Example:

Summary:

Scott was referred to the clinic by his parents because he engages in activities typically defined as feminine. Mr. and Mrs. Wiggins provided a history of the feminine behaviors engaged in by Scott. The results of the evaluation indicate that Scott exhibits a childhood gender identity disorder according to the criteria outlined in the *Diagnostic and Statistical Manual of Mental Disorders—Third edition (DSM-III)*. The DSM-III is a widely used manual by mental health professionals that specifies guidelines for diagnosing clinical disorders. According to this manual, three criteria must be met before a diagnosis of childhood gender identity disorder can be made for a male child. Those criteria are: a) the

(continued)

FORM 9.1 *(continued)*

presence of a strongly and persistently stated desire to be a member of the opposite sex, or insistence that the child is a member of the opposite sex; b) either a persistent rejection of male anatomy or a decided preference for activities usually engaged in by the opposite sex and cross dressing; and c) onset of the disturbance before puberty. It is the professional opinion of clinic staff that those three criteria have been met.

Other assessments conducted indicate that Scott has average intellectual ability and does not exhibit significant behavior problems in the home.

According to *DSM-III* information, social conflict tends to become a major problem for children diagnosed as gender disordered at about age 7 or 8. If Scott were to experience such a social conflict, it may be difficult for him to establish and maintain positive peer relationships with other boys. And although there is still a lack of consensus as to the relation between childhood gender identity disorder and adult homosexuality, it has been reported in the literature that perhaps ⅓–½ of children diagnosed as gender disordered in preadolescence later become aware of a homosexual orientation during adolescence.

Based on the assessment findings, parental concerns about cross gender behavior, and information available through the DSM-III and other sources reported in the literature, it is the opinion of clinic staff that intervention service would be appropriate for Scott for the gender identity disorder, since this is in accordance with parental request. It is the expectation that intervention will be mainly conducted with Scott's parents rather than with Scott, and will focus on increasing options for gender appropriate behavior in his environment. Although it is staff opinion that Scott should still be encouraged to be kind, nurturant, and caring, he can be encouraged to express those behaviors in what are typically considered to be masculine ways.

10. Specific Recommendations:

    a. Typically, the clinic reports include a statement following this major heading such as "It is recommended that:" with specific recommendations then listed below the statement.

    b. If more than one recommendation is to be provided, number recommendations (e.g., 1, 2, 3), placing them in order of priority according to their relevance to the referral question.

    c. Recommendations should be brief statements, including who will be expected to take responsibility for carrying out recommendations, and when or under what circumstances the recommendations should be carried out.

    d. No recommendation should be included in this section unless there has been prior reference to the problem or area in the summary section of the report.

    e. Include *all* recommendations that are related to the referral questions, as well as recommendations that may have resulted from the evaluation (e.g., visual examination).

    f. Where appropriate, provide resource information. For example: "Additional testing can be obtained through a clinic offering this service or a private practitioner." Always include more than one resource if available. Do not list or provide names of private practitioners.

Example:

It is recommended that:

1. Jeff's educational placement be determined through mutual agreement with school district staff and Mr. and Mrs. Carson, utilizing the information provided in this report.

2. Jeff's individual educational plan include steps for mainstreaming into the regular classroom. Programming for independent skills would be particularly important preparation for mainstreaming. Initially, positive consequences

(continued)

Form 9.1 (*continued*)

should be provided for completion of brief tasks. The length of the tasks should be systematically increased once Jeff is successful at the independent completion of shorter tasks.

3. Jeff's academic programming focus on readiness skills.

4. Jeff receive motor services to improve his balance, fine-motor speed and dexterity, and eye-hand and bilateral coordination. Treatment should emphasize activities such as weight bearing on upper and lower extremities, reciprocal use of arms and legs together, and visual-motor tasks. Programming should be developed and implemented by registered occupational/physical therapists.

5. Speech and language training be initiated, including:

   a. Daily stimulation training for vocabulary and language development within the classroom setting. This programming should be developed and closely monitored by a qualified speech and language pathologist.

   b. Mainstreaming into activities for normal peer interactions and exposure to age-appropriate language models throughout his daily educational routine.

6. Jeff participate in a social skills program in a small group setting. The training should focus on basic interaction skills such as making eye contact, replying to questions, and making requests. Steps in this training should include a verbal description of the desired response, modeling of presocial behaviors, rehearsals via role-playing, and reinforcement for appropriate behaviors. Involvement of students with adequate social skills would be a helpful component of this training. More specific information on social skills training is available through a number of commercial programs.

7. Jeff and his parents participate in family therapy on a regular basis to resolve family conflicts in the home. These services can be obtained through the clinic.

Form 9.2

Summary Report Form

Client name:_____ Date:_____

Presenting problem:

Referral source:

Summary of treatment:

Treatment outcome:

Reason for termination:

aspects of the discussion pertain to in-house written reports (e.g., treatment progress reports).

Methods

The clinical report writer may use one of several approaches during the actual clinical report preparation. A first draft of the report may be: a) dictated into a dictation machine, b) handwritten or typewritten by the report writer, c) transcribed by a trained assistant or secretary from the clinician's notes, d) dictated directly to a secretary (this procedure is somewhat outdated), or e) typed directly into a computer (see following section regarding computer use). Although the novice clinical report writer will need to develop skills in use of dictation equipment, once these skills are obtained, dictation is one of the most efficient ways to prepare clinical reports. Clearly, if use of dictation equipment is adopted as a clinic practice, it will be necessary for clinicians to have easy access to dictating equipment or to be assigned dictation instruments.

Timing

Whenever possible, the clinical report writer should prepare the clinical report immediately after client interactions. This procedure is more feasible when the report is a treatment progress report or single discipline report, or when one phase of an evaluation has been completed (e.g., developmental interview). If time restrictions do not allow for report preparation directly after client interaction, it is a good practice for the clinician to dictate or write brief notes regarding the client interaction. Such notes could then be referred to when the first draft of the functional clinical report is prepared.

Comprehensive Reports

When the clinical report is to include the integration of evaluation information from an interdisciplinary team, the preparation of such a report could be the task of one or two team members (as noted earlier) or a team operation. In a total team approach, team members would meet to prepare a rough report, each team member contributing information for each section of the report or reaching an agreement on what is to be included in the report. A standard format (e.g., form including subheadings and blank spaces) could be used for this process. One team member or a secretary could be assigned the task of completing the form during the meeting, or the rough report preparation session could be taped and one individual assigned to write the report from the tape.

An alternative to this approach is to have team members write their sections of the report independently, including their recommendations. One team member would then be assigned to integrate these separate reports. This procedure may be practical when it would be difficult to schedule all team members for a joint report preparation meeting.

Report Revision

The printed first draft of the functional clinical report should be reviewed by the report writer and appropriate error corrections, additions, deletions, or modifications noted, either by redictating the report (which can be time-consuming) or by handwritten report changes on the draft copy itself. If numerous changes are necessary, a second draft may be prepared for review. Otherwise, a final report may be prepared. The corrected first or second report draft may be submitted to a supervisor or colleague for review before the final report is prepared (review and critique of clinical reports is discussed in another section of this chapter). Once the final report has been printed, it should be proofread by the report writer to ensure that all revisions and corrections have been made, that the content is appropriate, and that the report is ready for dissemination. The signing of the report by the report writer represents an acknowledgment that the report has been proofread and approved. This *should not be* a rubber stamp procedure. Signatures on a report have legal implications in terms of responsibility for the report's content. One quality control procedure is to have a supervisor review all reports and sign off when he or she is satisfied that the report is acceptable for dissemination.

Practicalities

The clinical report writer will need appropriate materials and equipment to prepare clinical reports, and (if he or she does not have a private office) should have access to a private area where the reports can be written or dictated with minimal disruptions. The report writer may also find it useful to maintain a log of reports due, including dates of first draft submissions, report revisions submitted, and final report release dates. Maintenance of such a log provides the report writer with an accessible record of the status of clinical reports for which the clinician is responsible. It also provides a method for supervisory control and staff performance evaluation on report writing activity.

Functionality

Clinical report writers should be guided by the term *functional* when making decisions on what is to be included in the report. To a degree, the writer is guided by clinic standards. Even so, a great deal of information is usually obtained during an evaluation that may or may not be included in the written report. This is especially true when multiple interviews have been conducted with the parents and various sources (e.g., referral agency representatives). In culling information for the report, it is helpful for the writer to systematically question the potential usefulness or practicality of including specific information in the report. The writer should consider the primary purpose(s) of the report, as well as the potential responses of those recipients likely to use the clinical report contents for the welfare of the primary client.

Communication

Once decisions are made on what is to be included in the report, the report writer must communicate that information clearly and concisely. This is often easier said than done. In reviewing a number of surveys conducted between 1950 and 1970 with readers of psychological reports, Tallent (1976) concludes that several major problem categories could be identified: a) impracticality or uselessness of report content, b) report orientation overly theoretical, and c) report content too abstract. Sattler (1982), Tallent, and other professionals discuss a number of specific "problems of communication" and "pitfalls" that can interfere with the communication of information in clinical reports. The writer of functional clinical reports needs to be aware of these potential communication inhibitors and to consciously endeavor to avoid them when writing clinical reports. Some of these inhibitors of communication are discussed next.

Potential Communication Inhibitors

A major communication problem found in clinical reports is the use of technical vocabulary or jargon that is familiar or well known to a limited set of professionals. To be as functional as possible, the information contained in a clinical report must be understood by all recipients, particularly those who will likely use it in making decisions about the client. If it is certain that a clinical report will be received and read only by another member of the same or related discipline, and if the writer is confident that the technical vocabulary or jargon will be understood by the reader, then there is no problem in using professional terminology, and can, indeed, be a time-saving "shorthand" for the writer. At the same time, in clinical reports prepared for readers with diversified experiences and education, it may be unrealistic to avoid use of all technical vocabulary, and, indeed, to advocate doing so might be considered by representatives of some disciplines as an infringement on their professional rights. It is recommended that the use of technical language be minimized as much as possible, and that, wherever possible, such terminology be accompanied by explanations or definitions.

Psychological reports have also often been criticized for containing ambiguous or vague statements (Sattler, 1982; Tallent, 1976). We have found this to be a problem in reports from other disciplines as well. Whenever statements in a clinical report allow or foster a number of different interpretations, the functionality of the report is impaired. Without a review process, there is no way of identifying vague statements, since report writers are their own worst editors— the report may be crystal clear to them. There are a number of reasons for ambiguity or vagueness in reports. First the writer may not feel that he or she has a sound basis or sufficient data to provide the reader with definitive statements about the evaluation process or recommendations. If so, it is better to be honest and state that fact, than to include statements that say little or nothing or that could lead to misinterpretation. Second, the report writer may be unsure of how to deal with conflicting or contradictory findings and, therefore, may try to avoid discussing indirectly these problems by vague statements. Again, an honest delineation of such findings is preferable. Third, some clinical report writers are reluctant to commit to a position, even when there is clear-cut support for a position. Sattler refers to this as "hedging." Whenever there is sufficient information on which to base an opinion, or the clinician has the expertise to take a position, it is more useful to report recipients if the writer expresses a professional opinion. It is implicitly assumed by parents and agency personnel that professionals accepting referrals for child and adolescent clients are those best qualified to provide direction for resolution of referral problems. Fourth, vague or ambiguous statements may only reflect poor communication skills on the part of the clinical report writer.

Conversely, clinic reports often contain statements that, although clearly stated, are professionally questionable and may even verge on being unethical. For example, definitive statements may be made about the intellectual level of a child when inappropriate instrumentation has been used or test standardization has been violated. Or assumptions of a generalized behavior problem may be based on only one observation of a child's behavior in a one-to-one testing situation, or on clinician subjective inference. In addition, the assumption of cause and effect relationships may be drawn when there is little supporting evidence or documented data available. Tallent (1976) has described related problems in this area as "exhibitionism," the tendency for a report writer to flaunt expertise, and as "too authoritative," the tendency to communicate in a dogmatic or highly opinionated manner.

Some other problems that we and other authors have encountered in clinical reports are: a) poor organization of the information included, b) inclusion of irrelevant statements or information or details, c) lack of transition statements when topics are changed, and d) poor continuity and readability. Needless to say, clinical report writers may also lack written language skills (e.g., grammar and punctuation). This may not be a serious problem if a secretary transcribing the reports has the appropriate skills to correct errrors.

Timely Delivery of Reports

A common complaint of report recipients is that of extensive delays in receiving written clinical reports, particularly following client assessment/evaluations. This appears to be a problem in many clinics, and efforts should be made to minimize the time between services provided and written report delivery. Each clinic should develop procedures to expedite the delivery of clinical reports, and should consider this to be a significant endeavor. Timelines should be specified for clinical staff for preparation of written clinical reports and for delivering them to appropriate parties. Clinic procedures should also stipulate schedules for submission of treatment progress reports in order that current information is available on the status of client and client-related interactions. Such reports are essential to supervisors and/or clinic administrators. In addition, a staffing held at the end of the intake and evaluation can provide parents and children with a verbal preliminary summary of findings and recommendations (as discussed in Chapter 6). Such information can be used by the client's family as needed while waiting for the official report.

REVIEW AND CRITIQUE PROCEDURES FOR CLINICAL REPORTS

Many experienced clinicians prepare and review their own reports on a regular basis without review by others. Unless some feedback is obtained from report recipients, this practice can result in clinical reports that are not only nonfunctional for others but may also perpetuate any communication problems in the repertoire of the report writer. It is recommended that autonomous clinical report writers submit their clinical reports on occasion to professionals in other disciplines or to colleagues or supervisors for review, and/or ask report recipients to evaluate reports for their effectiveness (ethical guidelines must be adhered to in this process). Some professionals may consider this step "beneath" them, but it is, indeed, an indication of true professionalism to seek peer review.

In some clinics, it is standard practice for all clinical reports to be critiqued and reviewed by supervisors. Although this is a time-consuming and costly process, some type of quality control is needed. In clinics where trainees or novice clinicians provide services and write reports, it should be automatic clinic practice that such reports be reviewed by a supervisor or someone else assigned the reviewing responsibility before dissemination of final reports outside of the clinic. The staff member who reviews trainee or novice clinical reports should be trained and have experience in clinical report writing, should have good command of the language, should have some knowledge of the relevant assessment/evaluation/treatment procedures, and should be skilled in reading clinical reports objectively. The reviewer should be able to read the report from the vantage point of a report recipient and assess its functionality. Whenever possible, it would be helpful if the reviewer is familiar with the client referral and assessment/evaluation conducted as well.

Assessment/Evaluation Report Critique Guidelines

Although it is generally considered easier to critique a production than to create it, the skills needed to critique adequately functional clinical assessment/evaluation reports require that the reviewer has had some diversified experiences or training. Guidelines for use in reviewing assessment/evaluation clinical reports are presented in Table 9.1.

Treatment Summary Report Critique Guidelines

For reviewing treatment summary reports, the questions in Table 9.2 should serve as guidelines.

Table 9.1. Assessment/evaluation report critique guidelines

1. Does the report conform to the format stipulated in clinic procedures?
2. Are the client, client-related, and other personal data complete and accurate (e.g., first and last names of clients and parents/guardians included, correct spelling of client names, accurate client birth date and age)?
3. Are assessment/evaluation instruments identified accurately (e.g., complete titles given)?
4. Is the language usage correct and appropriate (e.g., grammar, paragraph separations, punctuation, and spelling)?
5. Have irrelevant details or information been excluded?
6. Is the report organized in a coherent and readable form?
7. Is the report an appropriate length, not too long or too brief?
8. Is the report clear and free of ambiguous words or phrases?
9. Have any technical terms, phrases, or abbreviations, (e.g., C.A. for chronological age) been rephrased or defined for clearer communication?
10. Is all information included in the report in congruence (e.g., noncontradictory test results)? If not, have contradictions or discrepancies been explained or addressed?
11. Has any variable client performance been explained or addressed?
12. Were test result scores checked for accuracy on all report drafts, and have they been clearly described (e.g., Have percentile scores been explained)?
13. Have client behaviors observed during the evaluation been described objectively?
14. Has the referral question been answered?
15. Is all of the information contained in the report integrated into a summary that reflects and incorporates the entire evaluation process (e.g., background, clinic behavior observations, informal and formal testing)?
16. Are the recommendations provided in the report specific, feasible, and realistic?
17. Are all recommendations relevant to the referral question and related areas?
18. Are all statements supported by data or clearly labeled as opinions?

Use of Computers for Preparing Clinical Reports

Preparation of clinical reports can be facilitated through use of a computer system with word processing capability and a printer component (the role of computers and computer systems in clinics was discussed in Chapter 2). In this section of the chapter, several examples of ways a computer system may be used

Table 9.2. Treatment summary report critique guidelines

1. Is the client and client-related identifying information accurate?
2. Have the reasons for referral been addressed and referral sources identified?
3. Has specific information been included related to treatment sessions and the time period of treatment (e.g., number of sessions provided, dates of sessions or onset and termination of treatment, number of appointments not kept)?
4. Were specific treatment goals and activities identified?
5. Has data been incorporated to describe or substantiate treatment outcome?
6. How effectively has treatment been described so that another clinician could understand what was done (e.g., assertiveness training), and what were the overall results of treatment?
7. How was treatment terminated (e.g., by client request or by therapist), and why was it terminated?

in clinical report preparation are presented. First, you may opt to type your own reports directly into a computer system. By doing so, you not only eliminate the time spent in dictation or in handwriting your reports but you can also edit or significantly alter the reports during their preparation, thus saving time spent in reviewing and editing rough drafts. Your final report copies can be printed out for review by others (e.g., supervisors) or disseminated directly to appropriate individuals. Obviously, this approach has distinct advantages: a) reduction of secretarial time, b) convenience for you, and c) a decrease in report delivery time. Further, in a one-person or small clinic, the issuance of clinical reports of a professional quality to clients can be assured (Keller, 1982). The approach requires, however, that you have adequate typing skills and are at least as adept in this approach as you would be at other approaches. It also requires that you have access to a computer system.

An alternative approach that may be more practical in your clinic is to have a secretary type your dictated or handwritten report draft directly into a computer system, where it will be stored while you review and edit a printed rough draft copy. Report changes can then be made easily by a secretary, thus eliminating the need for retyping the entire report. The involvement of secretarial services may be more cost effective and efficient in clinics where there are many reports to be prepared and a number of clinicians are involved.

Computer systems may also be used to expedite clinical report preparation by means of: a) standard report formats, b) test/assessment descriptors, and c) interpretive statements or programs. You may develop your own report formats, test/assessment descriptors, and interpretive statements appropriate for use in your clinic, or you may adopt those in other systems (Vincent, 1983), or purchase software programs available. Vincent discusses a codified system of "automated interpretive statements" describing patient appearance and test behavior that can be incorporated into an automated report through computer call numbers. According to Vincent, the use of an automated report preparation system by clinicians can result in a reduction of report preparation time by one-half.

Computer usage for clinical report preparation has another advantage, in that reports can be relatively error-free when delivered to report recipients (Keller, 1982) because of computer correction features and spelling and language correction software programs. In addition, form letters developed to be forwarded with clinical reports can be printed and personalized via computer with minimal time and effort.

VALUE OF WRITTEN CLINICAL REPORTS AS A PUBLIC RELATIONS TOOL

Functional clinical reports provided to referral and other sources can be valuable in the development and maintenance of positive public relations in the community, both through private and agency contacts. As a written document of the assessment/evaluation or treatment provided by the clinic staff, the report reflects the quality of services that are available at the clinic. This is particularly so for agencies that may be situated far away from the clinic or that refer children or adolescents to a clinic for services, yet have no direct or limited involvement with clinic staff except via the functional clinical report. In these instances, the report is the major means of communication between the clinical staff and relevant individuals or referral sources. Thus, services provided by the clinic will be judged mainly by the clinical report, and additional clinic referrals from these sources may depend almost exclusively on their reaction to the report. Clinical staff are sometimes unaware of how they and their professional services may be perceived by those who have no or limited direct contact with them.

Parents/legal guardians will have had direct contact with clinic staff while services were provided. The functional clinical report will serve as a permanent record and reminder of those interactions and the services that were provided, and, if truly functional, will be used for reference after direct contact with clinicians has ended.

CLINICAL REPORT EVALUATION FEEDBACK

As suggested earlier, some type of report recipient evaluation needs to be obtained in order to ascertain how well clinic reports serve their purpose. This can be accomplished as follows:

1. A prepared feedback questionnaire can be enclosed with the report or sent separately. Self-addressed return envelopes should be included.
2. Parents or legal guardians and agency representatives, where applicable, could be contacted directly by telephone for feedback information, preferably by a clinical staff member who has not been involved in the report preparation.

We have employed a mailed questionnaire system, enclosing feedback forms along with the clinical reports, and have received a high percentage of returns. Feedback questionnaires may incorporate questions related to other aspects of clinic services provided in addition to report feedback, or may include only questions about the written report. Sample forms of feedback questionnaires for parents or legal guardians and for agencies are shown in Forms 9.3 and 9.4.

Although a telephone approach might result in obtaining feedback from more clients than mailed questionnaires, there are some possible disadvantages: a) such contacts may be perceived by clients as intrusive; b) clients may be reluctant to express honest opinions in direct encounters; c) unless appointment arrangements are made in advance, telephone contacts may be made at inconvenient times. Whatever feedback method is employed, it is important that the information obtained be communicated to clinical staff who have been involved in writing clinical reports, in order to assist them in improving the quality of their future reports. To do so, however, sources providing feedback need to be identified. Feedback sources may be less likely to provide critical comments or nega-

FORM 9.3

Client Satisfaction Questionnaire

Client name:_____
Client file #:_____

_____Clinic

1. How would you rate your impressions of the interactions (telephone or face to face) you had with the _____ Clinic staff (i.e., staff courtesy, returning calls, listening behavior, etc.)?

1	2	3	4
Excellent	Good	Fair	Poor

2. Was the specific information provided to you prior to coming to the _____ clinic clear and accurate (fees, how to locate the clinic, parking, where to go in the building, etc.)? If not, please describe in what way at the bottom of the second page.

1	2	3	4
Definitely yes	Somewhat	Only partially	Definitely no

3. Were your concerns about your child's problems adequately discussed by the staff members assigned during your first clinic visit or at other evaluation sessions?

1	2	3	4
Yes, definitely	Yes, but in a general way	Not as much as I had hoped	No, definitely not

4. To what extent did the staff members who worked with you at the clinic help you to feel at ease and comfortable?

1	2	3	4
Very much so	Adequately	Only slightly	Not at all

5. How adequately did staff members inform you about evaluation and/or assessment procedures to be conducted with your child?

1	2	3	4
Quite adequately	Fairly adequately	Somewhat adequately	Not at all adequately

7. Was the written report that you received clear, easy to read, and accurate in describing the evaluation and recommendations?

1	2	3	4
Yes, definitely	Yes, in general	No, could have been more so	No, not at all

(continued)

FORM 9.3 (*continued*)

8. To what extent did you find your referral question(s) answered by the evaluation services provided?

1	2	3	4
Almost entirely	To a limited degree	To almost no extent	Not at all

9. If follow-up services were provided, have these services resulted in a resolution of the reason for referral?

1	2	3	4
Yes, they helped a great deal	They helped somewhat	Were not much help	No, they were of no help

10. Would you recommend our services program to a friend or associate?

1	2	3	4
Yes, definitely	Probably	Probably not	No, definitely not

Please list specific dissatisfactions and/or areas where improvement is needed:

tive responses when they know they will be identified by name. Despite this potential problem, however, unless feedback sources are identified, feedback information may be too general to be useful. Also, in a clinic with more than one or two clinicians, it would be impossible to identify the appropriate clinician to receive the feedback information.

SUMMARY

Clinical assessment/evaluation and treatment reports are an essential part of services provided by clinicians, comprising a written verification of services. Further, clinical reports are permanent reference materials for client families and/or agency personnel on the functioning of the referred client. Recommendations included in clinical reports also serve as guides or cues for actions to be taken by referral sources and/or others on behalf of child or adolescent clients.

This chapter has discussed the component sections of clinical reports typically written for child/adolescent clients. We have described various ways clinical reports may be prepared and processed, including the use of computers in report preparation and processing. We have also provided guidelines for critique of written clinic reports. Finally, we stressed the value of clinical reports in developing and maintaining positive public opinion of your clinic.

READER ACTIVITIES

Using the critique guidelines in Table 9.1, see if a recent assessment/evaluation report you have written meets those guidelines. If not, identify what you might have added, deleted, or changed. When you have completed this activity, try

FORM 9.4

Agency Satisfaction Questionnaire

_____Clinic

Agency: _____ Client: _____
Person completing form:_____

1. How would you rate the quality of your interactions (e.g., staff courtesy, response to telephone calls, explanation of services available, and fee forms provided) with our staff prior to receiving evaluation services?

1	2	3	4
Excellent	Good	Fair	Poor

2. Is the written report clear and explicit in describing assessments conducted and recommendations?

1	2	3	4
Quite clear and understandable	Partially understandable	More unclear than clear	Not at all

3. Are the recommendations included in the written report useful and practical?

1	2	3	4
Yes, all of them	Most of them	Only to a limited degree	Not at all

4. To what extent did the evaluation conducted address your referral questions(s)?

1	2	3	4
Almost entirely	Only to a limited degree	Less than adequately	Not at all

5. Did anyone from your staff have personal interaction with any members of the evaluation team?

Yes   No

6. Was the staff contact conducted in a professional manner, with courtesy and respect for school district policies and staff time?

1	2	3
Yes definitely	Somewhat	Not at all

7. How would you rate the time interval between the initial evaluation appointment date and the written report delivery?

1	2	3
Quite reasonable and satisfactory	Moderately reasonable	Not at all reasonable or satisfactory

8. Overall, to what degree were you satisfied with the services provided?

1	2	3	4
Quite satisfied	Moderately satisfied	Mildly dissatisfied	Very dissatisfied

(continued)

Form 9.4 *(continued)*

9. Would you refer another child or youth to us for services?

1	2	3
Yes	Only if other services were not available	No

Specific comments:

writing one or two test descriptions for an assessment tool with which you are familiar and that you use in assessing children. Then, compare your description of the instrument with the description provided in the manual (if available). Which is better?

If you are not satisfied with your current method of preparing clinical reports, or you are adventurous and would like to increase your skills, try a different method of report preparation by writing a background section for an evaluation report from information collected during a recent parent interview. As an alternative activity, if you are satisfied with your way of preparing evaluation reports, write a case summary report for a client following the guidelines provided in Table 9.2.

REFERENCES

Goldman, J., L'Engle Stein, C. L., & Guerry, S. (1983). *Psychological methods of child assessment.* New York: Brunner/Mazel.

Keller, P. A. (1982). Word processing for the clinical office. In P. A. Keller & L. G. Ritt (Eds.), *Innovations in clinical practice: A source book* (Vol. 1, pp. 194–198). Sarasota, FL: Professional Resources Exchange.

Sattler, J. M. (1982). *Assessment of children's intelligence and special abilities* (2nd ed.). Boston: Allyn & Bacon.

Tallent, N. (1976). *Psychological report writing.* Englewood Cliffs, NJ: Prentice-Hall.

Vincent, K. R. (1983). Psychological test analysis and report writing via a word processor. In P. A. Keller and L. G. Ritt (Eds.), *Innovations in clinical practice: A source book* (Vol. 2, pp. 223–232). Sarasota, FL: Professional Resources Exchange.

10

Consultation

After reading this chapter, you should be familiar with
1. The benefits versus the cost of providing consultation
2. The various types of consultation that can be provided
3. How to determine fees for consultation
4. The role of the technical assistance consultant
5. Procedures and forms to use
6. Standards to be implemented
7. How to implement and evaluate the impact of the consultation provided

DEFINITION

Consultation covers a range of child and adolescent services in which a mental health or psychological consultant works in school systems, police departments, courts, detention centers, foster homes, religious institutions, and a host of other community agencies and settings (Haas, 1982). Consultation occurs when an agency requests and uses the services of an outsider (who is not a regular employee of that agency) to improve the functioning of the agency (Haas, 1982). The functions of a consultant are similar to those of a supervisor. The difference is that the supervisor works within the organization and is responsible for the work of those supervised. The consultant is from outside and is not responsible for the work of those in the organization; thus he or she may concentrate exclusively on helping the consultee/client (these two terms are used interchangeably in this chapter) understand the target agency problem (Adult Education Association, 1956). Both give direction, coordinate, educate and provide services.

For purposes of this chapter, *consultation* consists of services provided to individuals in an organization to help them provide better psychological services to children, adolescents, and their families (Haas, 1982). Caplan (1963) divided consultation into four useful categories:

1. Client-centered—focuses on aiding the client
2. Consultee-centered—focuses on enhancing the skills of the consultee
3. Program-centered—focuses on resolving organizational or program difficulties
4. Administrative centered—focuses on diagnosing and resolving the administration problems encountered by the consultee

The process of consultation is often ambiguous and the expectations of the consultant by consultees (those receiving the consultation) are often unrealistic or

223

vague. Because of the ambiguity and complexity of consultation, the consultant must adhere closely to a well-defined set of ethical principles (e.g., the "Ethical Principles of Psychologists," American Psychological Association [APA], 1981, see Appendix A), which can be applied in a wide variety of contexts. The actions of a consultant affect the individual consultant, his or her profession (Haas, 1982), and the agency for which he or she ordinarily works. In addition, by accepting the role of a consultant, one implicitly, if not explicitly, promises to help the consultee and society. The consultation process typically begins with the identification of specific problems the organization is having in performing its work (services) or of its need for expertise or training in specific areas, then moves toward the deeper human relations problems (e.g., trust) as confidence in the consultant grows (Nylen, Mitchell, & Stout, 1980).

WHETHER TO CONSULT: BENEFIT VERSUS COST

Consultation Benefits

It is vital that clinic administrators include in the clinic's plan of operation the function(s) that technical assistance and consultation will serve, and the type of problems that could be addressed within the areas of expertise of clinic staff. It is clearly unethical to offer consultation or any other type of service in areas in which one is not qualified by training or experience. Consultation policies and purposes must be a part of the clinic's mission and goal structure, or such service should not be offered (Miller, 1982). The purposes can range from the generation of additional revenues, to the development of good public relations with a variety of different agencies, to promoting referrals, to preventing referrals. A consultant must be aware of both his or her own expectations and those of their clinic management (Miller, 1982).

For many years universities have known the benefits of providing consultation and technical assistance, and have encouraged faculty to do so. When a staff member provides consultation, several benefits are accrued to the home agency. First, the staff member is exposed to new and different ideas. Second, the staff member is faced with new problem situations that may result in refinement of his or her skills. Third, most consultation involves some form of extra preparation. Through such preparation—including the reading of materials he or she might not ordinarily be exposed to, organizing those materials read systematically, and presenting these materials in the form of consultation/technical assistance—the consultant acquires skills that can be applied to the home clinic in the form of inservice training and/or direct practice with clients. Another benefit is that consultation provides a change of pace, enriching the consultant's job satisfaction and increasing the consultant's feelings of self-esteem and self-confidence. Benefit might also accrue to the "home" clinic since, through such consultation or technical assistance, the consultant may engage in positive public relatins activities resulting in requests for additional services from the clinic, and a feeling of goodwill toward the clinic and its staff. The potential referrals to the clinic could generate additional income that would help recoup any costs to the clinic incurred by having staff members provide consultation offsite.

The benefits of consultation for the consultee include:

1. The availability of an impartial party in accurately diagnosing problems (e.g., in why staff does not work as a team)
2. The availability of an outside facilitator and/or catalyst (e.g., in planning long-range goals)
3. The availability of someone who can be nonjudgmental and who can assess the consultee's resources and capacity for change
4. The availability of someone who understands the dynamics and realities of planned change
5. The availability of someone who can suggest new alternatives in problem solving (Burke & Schmidt, 1978)

In summary, the benefit is improved functioning of the agency contracting for consultation.

Consultation Costs

Clinics that allow or encourage staff to provide consultation and technical assistance may incur costs to their own program. The first cost is that staff will be absent from the clinic and unavailable to provide psychological or related services to the clinic's patrons, requiring other clinicians to cover some clients and clinician responsibilities. A second cost is that, for most professionals, work does not cease when they are absent; thus, upon their return they find an accumulation of clients to see, mail, telephone calls, and other activities that need to be addressed. There is also the possibility that there will be a loss of revenue to the clinic if those providing consultation do so on a private basis where the clinic does not recover the consultation fees. In this case, staff members have the benefit of obtaining some extra income. It may or may not be clinic policy to allow staff to consult privately during hours they are responsible to the clinic.

In some situations, a request to provide consultation may be received by the clinic, resulting in additional income for its programs. It is our belief that in those situations there should also be some benefit to the staff members who ultimately provide the consultation, either in terms of the location where the consultation is being provided (e.g., going to an exciting city), or by the sharing of the fees generated by the consultation (assuming that providing consultation is not in the individual's job description). It is very easy for staff to feel that they are being "ripped off" when they are repeatedly asked to provide consultation without receiving any special remuneration for such activities. This is particularly true if the consultation requires travel on weekends or early or late in the day, or overnight stays in other locations. The problem can be minimized if consultation is a part of an individual's job description and the person knows this when he or she accepts the job; or if the trips are easily handled within the normal working hours, such as providing consultation to a local school district or other service agency.

In cases where the consultation is provided as part of the clinic's normal operation, it is important that staff members providing the consultation be given time to prepare for those activities. For example, it typically takes two to three times longer to prepare a formal presentation than it takes to actually make the presentation.

Some consultation should be a routine activity for most psychology clinics. Consultation is a viable method of generating positive public relations, referrals, and additional revenues for both the clinic and the consultants.

TYPES OF CONSULTATION TO PROVIDE

Consultation entails an endless realm of possibilities. Yet, it is important to remember that a major reason for consultations is the generation of revenue. Funds generated by consultation serve to motivate staff and administrators to continue such activities, while simultaneously bringing pressure to bear on consultants to provide quality services. Few consultation activities continue over any extended period if no income results from them, especially if the consultant could be engaged in other income-producing activities during that time. In addition, regular consultation will require adjustments in job descriptions so that consultation does not become an overload to staff and thus undesirable.

Consultation to School Districts

One area of consultation that can generate revenues involves consultation to school districts. This consultation can involve several components, including the provision of full school psychology services such as:

1. Psychoeducational assessment of children and adolescents
2. Writing reports
3. Participation in child staffings or individualized education program (IEP) meetings (in the case of children classified for special education purposes)

School consultation requires that the consultant be familiar with school-related procedures (particularly those that are unique to the specific school) and that the recommendations made be very practical so they can easily be implemented in the specific school setting.

A second area of consultation in the schools involves the provision of services to either individual students or groups of students in the form of therapy. Many schools do not have adequate resources for identifying or providing services to students at risk. Assistance may be needed to minimize the long-term consequences of being at risk (such as acting out), as well as for dealing with other negative effects on the students' lives.

A third area of consultation that can be provided to the schools includes inservice training and workshops for the school staff. Likely topics would include, but not be limited to, normal and abnormal development, identifying at-risk children, behavior management in the classroom, improving students' self-concept/self-esteem, training special education staff and other specialists on new tests or assessment materials (as appropriate ethically), and conducting functional IEP meetings. The length of training and consultation would vary, depending on need and resources. In some instances, university graduate credit can be earned.

Consultation to Other Agencies

A second major category of consultation involves providing technical assistance to other agencies that serve children and adolescents, including daycare centers, mental health centers, social service agencies, foster home parents, group home parents, dentists, and police (Fitzhugh, 1982; Ingersall & Geboy, 1983; Miller, 1982). Such consultation includes services such as: assessment, writing of a report, writing recommendations for treatment, writing treatment plans to be implemented, monitoring those treatment plans, and/or providing inservice training workshops to the staff in those facilities.

FINANCIAL FEE DETERMINATION

Probably one of the most difficult tasks for a clinic is to determine appropriate fees to be charged for consultation services. Fees are typically based on: a) the reputation of the consultant/clinic, b) the ability of the client to pay, c) the urgency of the consultation requests, and d) the purpose of the consultation. Some would argue that one should charge whatever the traffic will bear. While this is nice in theory, in reality it is difficult to determine what this fee is until after requests for consultation have dwindled or ceased altogether. Also basic to fee determination are support costs related to salaries, staff benefits, travel, communications (postage and telephone), printing/copying, and so forth. When compiling such costs it is advisable to add 5%–10% to assure that overruns are covered. Any profit margin would be added to these costs.

Clearly, if consultation is a public relations activity, one may need to provide some of the services free, or at very minimal cost, in order to realize the discussed results. As a relationship is established, and a clientele generated, then an appropriate fee structure needs to be established. In setting consultation fees, clinic administrators should consider: a) cost for the professional's time and staff benefits; b) overhead expenses such as materials, travel, and secretarial time that may be involved in preparation for or follow-up of the consultation activity; c) profit; d) competition; e) economic condition; f) bad debts; g) fairness to clinic and clients; h) the role of consultation in the clinic's structure; and i) ethics and standards (Kelley, 1982).

The portion of the consultation fee charged for staff salaries and benefits may be comparable with the normal fee structure of the clinic, or it may be very different. If consultation is provided to the federal government, or to some project funded by the federal government, the maximum fee that can be charged for a senior-level consultant is $269/day. Less is allowed for more junior-level consultants, and prior approval from the government (which is seldom given) is required to pay more. In schools the fee varies considerably, generally ranging from $50 to $150 for each child assessed by a psychologist, and from $100 to $300 per day for other activities (some consultants receive as much as $1,500 per day). For other types of consultation, the daily fee generally ranges from $150/day to $500/day, with an average fee being in the $250–$300 per day range for senior consultants. In some cases, the fee includes only the consultant's professional fee, and all other expenses are added to this to arrive at the total cost for consultation.

Many ethical issues can arise in the area of fee payments. For example, consider the case where an agency needs a particular kind of consultation, but the available consultant's daily fee is higher than the rate allowed by the agency. Consequently, the agency's request for funds to pay the higher daily fee is denied. The agency administrator needing the consultation then decides he or she can indicate on paper that more days of consultation were received than is in fact true. Is it ethical for the consultant to agree to this? Is the consultant under any obligation to lower his or her fee because of the constraints of the agency? There are no simple answers to such issues, yet one must behave ethically. As Bennc (1959) has so aptly stated, solutions to ethical problems can be discovered or created only by the consultant, usually in consultation with his client. Adherance to a set of ethics discussed in part later in this chapter and in detail in Chapter 11 also helps resolve these issues. The following sections discuss in detail other factors to consider in relation to fee determination.

Other Consultation Fee Issues

When structuring a consultation fee schedule, considerations should be given to the factors listed in Table 10.1.

Benefits

The portion of a consultation fee charged for staff benefits will generally be what a clinic pays employees in fringe benefits including insurance, vacation, sick leave, and retirement. Benefits generally range from 25% to 60% of salary (Kelley, 1982).

Overhead

Overhead expenses for consultation include: a) typing, b) telephone and postage costs, c) travel costs (air and ground transportation, parking, accommodations, meals and tips), d) materials and copying/printing, and e) costs involved in initially securing the consultation contract.

Profit

The profit margin included in consultation activities depends on the type of clinic being operated. It will generally be small for public and private nonprofit clinics

Table 10.1.   Considerations in structuring fee schedules

1.   What skills are necessary to provide the needed consultation?
2.   What competition exists? High demand with little competition means charging higher fees (Kelley, 1982).
3.   Who among the existing staff has the necessary skills, and what is his or her hourly and daily cost to the clinic? If no one has the necessary skills, it is unethical to agree to provide consultation.
4.   Among those staff members who have the necessary skills, who can be freed for consultation with the least disruption to existing services? If individual clients will suffer because of the absence of a specific staff member, it is unethical to proceed.
5.   Is there a financial gain for the client/client family if the clinic's services for consultation are used? Or a loss if not (Kelley, 1982)?
6.   What is the "going rate" for such consultation?
7.   Is it possible to structure a sliding fee schedule just as is done for regular clinic services?
8.   What is the public relations value of the consultation?

(10%–20%), and higher for privately owned clinics where the risks are greater (10%–50%). Profit is generally figured as a percentage of the combined salary, benefits, and overhead (Kelley, 1982). Since the profit margin is affected by competition, if competition is high, the profit margin will have to be lower.

Competition

The impact of competition in setting consulting fees is difficult to compute. However, the answer to several questions will help determine the degree of competition. These questions include:

1.   How much competition is in the immediate geographic area?
2.   What is the reputation of the clinic and its staff? The better the reputation, the higher the fee that can be charged.
3.   What are successful competitors charging for similar services?
4.   What will those in need of consultation pay?
5.   What is the minimum dollar amount at which the clinic is willing, or able, to provide consultation?

The answers to these questions can be found by talking to consultants (local and elsewhere), directors of agencies who have used similar consultants, the clinic's own business manager, and potential client organizations. Answers can also be based on previous experiences in providing consultation.

Economic Conditions

The consultation fee that can be charged is directly related to economic conditions. During recessions, rates must be lower, but not so low that clients assume your clinic has nothing to offer. During prosperity, there are more consultation opportunities and rates can be higher. For example, in a recession, a clinic is likely to have more referrals for services related to child and adolescent problems because of pressures put on a family, thus reducing time available for consultation. Before entering into any new consultation agreement, the administrator will want to answer two questions: Have economic conditions changed since previous consultations, and what impact do such changes have on proposed consultation activities?

Collection Rates

Economic conditions also affect the degree to which payments for consultation or other services are received. In the event that payment for consultation is not rendered, legal help should be obtained—assuming that the amount justifies such action. Doing so will reduce the negative impact of resources being expended without reimbursement. Collecting at the time services are provided is the best means of avoiding bad debts; however, strict adherence to such a procedure can eliminate a percentage of potential consultation requests, as some agencies are required to process and reimburse consulting fees only after services have been delivered. Some clinics provide a 10% reduction in the fee charged if payment is made at the time services are provided to consultees. An administrator must monitor collection rates and take appropriate action to stay in business.

Fairness

Determining a fair rate structure is difficult. If a clinic is having financial difficulty making ends meet, administrators may be inclined to provide consultation services too cheaply for fear of not getting a contract. If there is no competition, there may be a tendency to charge too much. If either party feels cheated, the consultation contract will result in problems, which can affect the probability of future contracts. It is important that a fee structure be established that is fair to all parties concerned.

Answers to the following questions will help determine fairness:

1. What fee will be required in order for the consultant/clinic to be willing to provide the level of performance required to do a quality job?
2. Will the suggested fee cover the costs?
3. What fee is the consultee willing to pay for the level and quality of service required?
4. Is the fee the consultee is willing to pay acceptable to the consultant/clinic?

By comparing the answers to questions 1–3, you obtain the information necessary to answer question 4. If the answer to question 4 is *yes*, a fair contract probably exists. If the answer is *no*, more negotiating is needed to arrive at a fair contract.

Role

In some cases a clinic may charge less to provide consultation than the costs incurred in providing services. This is likely to occur when the consultation is seen as: a) essential ethically, b) a means of generating future referrals and funds, c) a community public relations activity, d) a means of gaining reciprocity, or e) being mandated in the requirements of a publicly funded clinic. The fees charged will generally be lower in public clinics, where consultation is an integral part of their mission, and higher for private clinics, where profit is critical.

The Rule of Three

The simplest method for computing consultation fees is to use the Rule of Three (Kelley, 1982). In this case one computes the consultant's salary and multiplies by three (e.g., $150/day × 3 = $450/day). The end product plus travel costs is the consultation fee charged (e.g., $450/day plus travel costs of $400 equals a total consultation fee of $1,300 for 2 days of consultation).

Other Agreements

A wide variety of other fee structures for consultation exist. These include hourly charges, fixed fees by service, contingent fees, and retainer fees (see Kelley, 1982, for more details).

The most common method for determining a fee consists of charging an hourly fee for very short activities, or a lower overall daily fee for activities that require a considerable amount of time such as ongoing consultation to a school. For example, in some cases the fee charged for consultation to schools related to assessment and placement decisions is determined on a flat fee basis per child assessed; for example, $140 per child to include a psychoeducational assessment and written report, and a very brief attendance at a staffing meeting. Great care must be taken to monitor all costs associated in the provision of technical assistance and consultation. For example, the possibility of loss of revenues in terms of other activities staff could be engaged in; hidden secretarial time or hidden material costs for preparation for these activities, both before and after the consultation has been completed; and the need for additional staff as a result of consultation by existing staff should all be taken into account. There are times when providing consultation costs more money than is generated by the work. However, such shortfalls might be recouped through future services, in which recent losses are accounted for as "seed monies." Consulting is a business, just as a grocery store is a business, and "cost centers" are sometimes necessary to attract consumers.

ROLE OF THE TECHNICAL ASSISTANT/CONSULTANT

Clarifying the Purpose

It is useful for a clinic to develop a simple contract that specifies the obligations of both parties. The quality of a consultant's service is in part dependent upon how clearly the needed services are specified in advance. It is imperative that a clinic have a clear indication of the exact service an agency wants before negotiating a contract with it, so that all parties agree in advance on what the expectations are. The consultant should take into account the following stressors and considerations when discussing expectations with the client (Miller, 1982):

1. Have the staff in the consultee agency had a chance to get acquainted with the consultant? When a consultant is invited to work with a client agency, there is an implication that client agency staff lack knowledge, skills, objectivity, confidence, or resources in the consultation area (Caplan, 1963). Client staff may feel threatened because of the implied criticism of their competence.

2. How can the consultant encourage consultee participation in the consultation? Client staff will be uneasy about what the "outsider" (consultant) will do, how to treat him or her, whether or not to trust him or her, and a whole host of other issues that keep them from expressing their feelings.

3. Have the goals of the consultation been clarified? The client may hire the consultant under the guise of solving a problem, when in fact, what is wanted is support for a specific predetermined solution. Decide if the major consulting need is for advice, "hands on" work, or facilitation of change.

4. Is the consultant familiar with factors that affect consultation? The client may try to put the consultant in the role of the "expert" who will "solve the problem," rather than someone who will assist the client staff to "help themselves." Accepting such a role can quickly result in a loss of credibility, since client staff can sabotage change efforts and blame the consultant. Yet, the consultant must be an "expert" in content or process, or he or she would not have been hired.

5. Have the views of different staff in the consultee organization been clarified? Different people will have different perspectives on what the problem is and on whether it really is a problem. Thus, appropriate diagnosis of the problem requires the collection of such information.

Credibility

The ultimate concern of the consultant is that his or her work be appropriate, acceptable, of high quality, and utilized. A consultant will offer recommendations to be implemented, but the contracting agency is free to accept or reject those recommendations and suggestions (Miller, 1982). In some agencies, as any consultant will verify, opposition to any new idea is extremely intense. If consultation is to have an impact, the consultant must first establish credibility. Though this can be accomplished in many ways, a particularly powerful strategy is to demonstrate that the techniques being proposed do, in fact, work.

Establishing a Working Relationship

An additional activity that is often very helpful in enhancing credibility is to state in advance your sensitivity to staff needs (e.g., "I understand what it is like to have someone come in from the outside"). In essence, the consultant will want to establish a working relationship and identify the feelings of the staff in terms of: a) their anxiety about someone coming in and "showing them up," and b) their concern that impractical recommendations will be made that they will be forced to implement after the consultant leaves. By engaging in direct dialogue with the staff early on, a good working relationship is facilitated. Some suggested activities for accomplishing this include:

1. Having appropriate individuals within the receiving organization list reasons why the consultant was brought in and on what the consultant should focus. The consultant should then discuss this information and clarify any misconceptions.
2. Conducting an activity that helps people relax (i.e., to get acquainted on a more human level and assure them that solutions to their problems will depend on how well the consultant and staff work together as a team).
3. Letting the staff verbalize their concerns, discuss the feelings expressed, and summarize problems as seen by the staff. Such information should be used to facilitate a positive impact of consultation. If certain issues are not to be addressed by the consultant, he or she should tell the staff.

Different Roles and Activities

The role of the consultant will vary depending on the agreement negotiated. In some cases, for example, such as in the provision of school psychology services, the consultant may act as a regular school staff member and engage in all of the varied activities in which staff members normally engage. In other cases the consultant must provide a specific service, make specific recommendations, and train staff to carry out these procedures, with follow-up activities planned to assess how well those recommendations are being implemented. Related consultant activities are provided in Table 10.2.

Table 10.2. Samples of related consultant activities

1. Becoming familiar with the context in which consultation is to be provided. For example, did organization staff have a voice in selecting the consultant, deciding if consultation was needed, or deciding what type of consultation was needed?
2. Determining the objectives of the sponsor and identifying the audience for the work to be done.
3. Obtaining informed consent from each individual in the consultee group where feasible, because it improves communication, decreases resistance, and helps protect the rights of individual clients.
4. Clarifying the roles of both consultant and client.
5. Clearly specifying the problem to all concerned (Haas, 1982).
6. Collecting relevant information.
7. Becoming familiar with control issues and how to resolve them (Haas, 1982).
8. Defining the problems to be addressed in functional terms so that impact can be measured.
9. Scheduling periodic reviews on the impact of consultation to date to assure that communication channels remain open and that consultation activities can be based on relevant information.
10. Engaging in interpersonal interactions that include: a) giving clear messages so words and actions are congruent, b) checking on the meanings of things that are said or done by client staff, c) suggesting optional methods for problem solving, d) being supportive, e) giving and accepting feedback, f) formulating issues, and g) supporting a spirit of inquiry (French & Bell, 1978).

Table 10.3.   Types of problems needing solutions by consultants

1. Most training programs and consultations teach general principles rather than dealing with specific situations. The consultant must assure that learning on the part of consultees can be applied to the specific situations that exist.
2. A mechanism needs to exist or be established to assure that staff changes are reinforced. This requires follow-up and evaluation of change efforts and a recognition by supervisors/administrators of staff who are implementing the changes.
3. Expertise must be developed within the organization if the efforts are to continue after the consultant's services are terminated.
4. Change must receive actual support from management, not just "lip service."
5. Training efforts must be directed to the appropriate level of staff. Training a supervisor who does not have time to train his or her staff, even though they are the ones who must carry out the work, is at best inefficient.
6. Continuity should be a focal point so that the activities of one consultation are related to those of the next.
7. Staff may see many consultants "come and go" with no durable changes. Thus, care should be taken to assure that the specific consultation is not just another "passing fad."

Other Problem Areas

The consultant must incorporate into consulting activities solutions to the type of problems listed in Table 10.3, as appropriate.

The Consultation Process

The consultation change process involves several steps relating to problem resolution (Lippitt, Watson, & Westley, 1958; Miller, 1982), as listed in Table 10.4

Some principles that can facilitate this change process are suggested by French and Bell (1978), including:

1. Change in any system also requires change in relevant aspects of the environment.
2. Change in behavior at one level in a system requires complementary and reinforcing changes in higher and lower organizational levels.

Table 10.4.   Steps in the change process

1. The development of a need for change in an organization.
2. The establishment of a change relationship with a consultant to institute the change process.
3. The accurate diagnosis of the organization's problem(s). Accurate diagnosis requires listening, restatement, clarification, and summarization.
4. The exploration of alternative solutions; and establishment of goals and intended actions. This process requires that four questions be answered:
   a. What is the problem from the viewpoint of the consultee?
   b. What is the cause of the problem?
   c. Where is the problem located?
   d. What resources does the consultee have for addressing the problem?
5. The initiation of the change activities.
6. The generalization and maintenance of change efforts.
7. The termination of the consultation relationship.

3. Change in client system should begin where the stress and strain exist, because motivation for change will be highest there.
4. Changes that affect the entire organization should start with the policymaking group.
5. Change in an organization must address both the formal and informal structure of the client organization.
6. Change is more effective if all organizational levels are involved in the fact finding, in diagnosis of needed changes, and in the reality testing of solutions.

PROCEDURES AND FORMS TO USE

Record Keeping

Maintaining fiscal and service records on all work done is important when providing technical assistance for a fee. One of the simplest methods for doing this is for the consultant to keep a log in which he or she records:

1. Each activity engaged in, the amount of time it took, where it was carried out, and who was present
2. Each telephone call placed, the number called, the number of minutes spent on the call, the person spoken to, and the purpose of the call
3. Each secretarial and other staff assignment, their purposes, and the time involved
4. Each cost of materials, travel, supplies, staff time, and so on
5. Each outcome achieved and how measured

Such information will help the consultant prepare a thorough and accurate accounting of all work done and the costs of doing it.

Evaluation of Impact

Evaluating the impact of consultation is critical and should be a part of each consulting experience. If the consultation activity consisted of a workshop or inservice training activity, the consultant should make every effort to evaluate the immediate response to the activities by asking participants questions such as those shown in Form 10.1, and if possible should do a follow-up contact sometime later (e.g., 30 days) to assess effect. Such an evaluation provides the consultant with feedback so that he or she can improve his or her own skills, and also provides feedback to the administrator served, on the value of the consultant's services as judged by that agency's own staff.

Evaluation of impact can also be accomplished through a subjective assessment of activities by the staff of the client agency, or through an objective measure of outcomes (e.g., in terms of change in the behavior of those served), or by formal testing to determine if the information presented was actually learned and applied by agency staff.

On-site Consultation Evaluation Form

1. I rate the value received from the consultation as:

low | | | | | high

2. I rate the clarity of the goals of consultation as:

low | | | | | high

3. The degree to which the goals of consultation were met was:

low | | | | | high

4. I rate the quality of the consultant's attitude and knowledge as:

low | | | | | high

5. The two things of most value to me as a function of the consultation are:
    a.
    b.

6. The two most important things that could be done to improve future consultations are:
    a.
    b.

7. Other comments:

A Consultation Plan

Consultation planning is critical to the success of any activity. A useful format for such a plan is shown in Form 10.2. The consultant completes portions of this form with the client (e.g., goal and objectives), and some portions with his or her own staff. The completion of the consultation form provides the consultant (and, if desired, the client) with a plan for the consultation activity, including what is to be accomplished, how, by whom, what communications are to be made, what resources are needed, fees, and when and how it will be determined that the objectives were achieved (Miller, 1982). Again, it is recommended that the goals and objectives be outcome oriented and measurable. The consultant might even include the estimated cost for each activity and by this determine whether the project is being accomplished within the budget allocated.

Consultation Format

1. Goals A. Objectives	Activities for achieving goals and objectives	Person responsible for each activity	Other resources needed	Method for evaluation	Projected start date	Projected completion date

237

Consultation Contact Form

Agency _____

Consultant _____

Date	Total hours	Problem areas addressed	Recommendations made	Success achieved	Agency/staff responsible

Table 10.5. Contract considerations for consultants

1. Name of the consultant and consultee agencies and individuals
2. Qualifications of the consultee
3. Duration of the contract
4. Clarification of the consultation method
5. Type of consultation (e.g., client-centered)
6. Description of target eligible for consultation (e.g., age, problem, etc.)
7. Financial eligibility and reimbursement mechanism
8. Accountability procedures (e.g., evaluation of work done)
9. Standards and expectations (e.g., where and when will work be done)
10. Termination, renewal, and noncompliance procedures and penalties
11. Liability, federal requirements (e.g., nondiscrimination), grievance procedures, and confidentiality issues

Other Forms

Other forms that are useful include a simple contact form such as that shown in Form 10.3. The form clearly specifies what areas are to be addressed, what recommendations should be made, and whether the recommendations were acted on successfully. Through follow-up, impact data can be gathered. One could also develop a contract that incorporates all of the factors listed in Table 10.5 (Miller, 1982).

Other forms may include: a) a standardized clinical report for assessment (see Chapter 9), b) a standardized form for treatment contact in which the consultant provides direct individual or group therapy services (see Chapter 7), and c) and a termination form. These forms are either identical or similar in nature to those that would be used if the consultant were providing therapy within the psychological clinic itself; in essence, such documents are part of good service and record keeping.

STANDARDS AND ETHICS

Every consultant should adhere to stringent, generally accepted ethical principles and standards for provision of services (see Chapter 11). Ethics are dependent on the context; thus, the consultant must be thoroughly familiar with ethical principles and standards of practice and must be able to apply them to changing environments. Haas (1982) defines unethical behavior as that which: a) causes harm, or b) violates an ethical principle without producing some other good or adhering to some other ethical principle. Service standards that are the most relevant to consultation situations include: a) clarifying for all parties concerned the level of confidentiality of information obtained, b) clarifying the role of the consultant and the client, c) providing consultation only in one's areas of competence as based on training and experience, d) always being prepared for the consultation activity in terms of having collected appropriate information and resources so that the consultation is state-of-the-art, e) keeping adequate records of activities, f) providing appropriate supervision for assistants by an appropriately qualified psychologist, and g) adhering to the "Ethical Principles of Psychologists" (APA, 1981) and *Standards for Providers of Psychological Services* (APA, 1984).

Some areas in which ethical conflicts often arise include:

1. When the consultant and consultee's expectations about their proper and necessary relationship differ. This issue is usually related to what the consultant should or should not do.
2. When the values of the client organization differ from the ethics adhered to by the consultant because of his or her professional association. This issue usually arises in the form of a client demand on the consultant (e.g., the billing issue discussed earlier).

CONSULTANT TRAITS

A consultant must have within his or her repertoire extremely good social skills and what could be called, in group process terms, group maintenance skills (see Chapter 3). In essence, the consultant should: a) be genuinely friendly; b) take the initiative to introduce himself or herself as appropriate; c) be sincerely concerned about other people; d) be willing to adhere to social overtures, or protocol, such as having lunch with the organization staff; and e) be adept at engaging in activities that will help staff at the contracting agency feel comfortable and confident. The more sensitive the consultant is to the needs, fears, and anxieties of the individuals at the contracting agency, the better will be the rapport built with the consultees and the more likely that an open and honest working relationship (Miller, 1982) will develop. The following is a listing of skills the consultant must have (some have already been mentioned here):

1. Sensitivity to the feelings and needs of consultee staff
2. Knowledge of content
3. Ability in facilitating good relations
4. Familiarity with relevant laws and ethical principles
5. Ability to develop a clear and specific contract
6. Ability to summarize information accurately, to listen well, and be candid
7. Ability to develop a consultation plan and to evaluate its impact
8. Ability to seek assistance where appropriate
9. Ability to understand and work with "power" issues (internal politics of organizations)
10. Ability to deal flexibly with the "unusual" events that occur, such as changes in timelines or personnel

SUMMARY

Consultation is a useful mechanism for generating additional funds both for the home clinic and the consultant. It can also enhance the skill development of the consultant. A clinic must decide and plan for the role that consultation will play in the clinic's function and provide support and training to staff designated to provide consultation. Fee determination, establishment of client expectations, and ethical issues will be the major obstacles to overcome.

READER ACTIVITIES

List your areas of expertise and compare them with those of other clinic staff. Develop a list of agencies or individuals who might profit from having you as a consultant. Decide what fee you would need to charge to make consultation a worthwhile activity. Have other clinic staff do the same. Develop a brochure that would market your group's services to interested parties. What skills are you aware of that greatly impact the success of consultants (e.g. sensitivity)? Do you have enough of these skills or do you need additional training before proceeding?

REFERENCES

Adult Education Association. (1956). *Supervision and consultation.* Wasington, DC: Author.

American Psychological Association. (1981). Ethical principles of psychologists. *American Psychologist,* 36(6) 633–638.

American Psychological Association. (1984). *Standards for providers of psychological services.* Washington, DC: Author.

Benne, K. D. (1959). Some ethical problems in group and organizational consultation. *Journal of Social Issues, 20*(1), 60–67.

Burke, W. W., & Schmidt, W. H. (1978). Management and organizational development: What is the target of change? In W. L. French, C. H. Bell, Jr., & R. A. Zawacki (Eds.) *Organizational development: Theory, practice, and research,* (pp. 40–50). Dallas, TX: Business Publications.

Caplan, G. (1963). Types of mental health consultation. *American Journal of Orthopsychiatry, 33*(4), 470–481.

Fitzhugh, W. P. (1982). New roles in consultation with police. In P. A. Keller & L. G. Ritt (Eds.), *Innovations in clinical practice: A source book* (Vol. 2, pp. 371–387). Sarasota, FL: Professional Resources Exchange.

French, W. L., & Bell, C. H., Jr. (1978). *Organizational development.* Englewood Cliffs, NJ: Prentice-Hall.

Haas, L. J. (1982). Ethical issues in consultation. In P. A. Keller & L. G. Ritt (Eds.), *Innovations in clinical practice: A source book* (Vol. 2, pp. 319–330). Sarasota, FL: Professional Resources Exchange.

Ingersall, B. D., & Geboy, M. J. (1983). Consultation with dentists: Innovative roles for the clinician. In P. A. Keller & L. G. Ritt (Eds.), *Innovations in clinical practice: A source book* (Vol. 2, pp. 331–347). Sarasota, FL: Professional Resources Exchange.

Keller, P. A., & Ritt, L. G. (1982). Confidentiality. In P. A. Keller & L. G. Ritt (Eds.), *Innovations in clinical practice: A source book* (Vol. 1, pp. 379–380). Sarasota, FL: Professional Resources Exchange.

Kelley, R. E. (1982). How to establish and collect consulting fees. In P. A. Keller & L. G. Ritt (Eds.), *Innovations in clinical practice: A source book* (Vol. 2, pp. 250–262). Sarasota, FL: Professional Resources Exchange.

Lippitt, R., Watson, J., & Westley, B. (1958). *The dynamics of planned change.* New York: Harcourt, Brace & World.

Miller, F. T. (1982). Consultation: A practical approach. In P. A. Keller & L. G. Ritt (Eds.), *Innovations in clinical practice: A source book* (Vol. 1, pp. 320–333). Sarasota, FL: Professional Resources Exchange.

Nylen, D., Mitchell, J. R., & Stout, A. (1980). *Handbook of staff development and human relations training: Materials developed for use in Africa.* Washington, DC: Stephenson Lithograph.

Legal and Ethical Aspects

Upon completion of this chapter, you will be able to:
1. Establish a set of client rights procedures
2. Explain the limits of confidentiality
3. Protect yourself against most job-related litigation
4. Understand the importance of adhering to stringent standards for services, ethical guidelines, and laws
5. Establish a human rights and internal and external peer review committee
6. Understand the importance of written, standard operating procedures

CLIENT RIGHTS

In the past, rights of individuals seeking help for psychological problems were often abridged and ignored. Many persons were hospitalized on wards where they received little or no treatment and were often abused and neglected. Adults with psychological problems who were confined to prisons were more likely to have their rights protected than those in state mental institutions because of the availability of criminal lawyers. More recently, the rights of clients seeking psychological assistance have become an important focus of legal and professional action. Protection for adults has improved and is beginning to improve for children and youths (Enrenreich & Melton, 1983). Adults' rights are increasingly recognized and protected by law. However, many states still lack mental health laws that specify the rights of children and youth. For example, in some states a parent can have his or her minor child involuntarily committed to a state mental institution without due process of law. Recent studies suggest that at least 40% of the mental hospital placement of children and youth are unnecessary (National Council of Community Mental Health Centers, 1985). States are hesitant to interfere with parents' rights to rear children as they choose, outside of abuse or neglect. The state tries to protect those who cannot protect themselves via what is called the *parens patriae* power. It is increasingly recognized that parents do not always act in the best interest of their children (Enrenreich & Melton, 1983). Some parents readily put the onus on the child as the person needing help when the problems are due to family strife. They may overestimate the child's need for psychiatric treatment, hospitalizing him or her because of differences in lifestyle, and take care of their own interests at the expense of their child (Enrenreich

& Melton, 1983). Little direct guidance is available to clinicians on whether their primary allegiance is to parents or to the child, on how they should make such a decision, or on their ethical or legal responsibility. According to the American Psychological Association's ([APA], 1981a) "Ethical Principles" (see Appendix A), a psychologist must "take special care to protect [the minors'] best interests" (Principle 5d). At the same time, psychologists must protect the welfare of all clients, thus leaving the psychologist in a quandary in some situations. There is no one answer to these issues, but the information that follows should help clarify options.

Obtaining Services

It is a fact that children rarely come to a clinician on a purely voluntary basis (Carroll, Schneider, & Wesley, 1985). In part this is because children and youth often do not know that they need professional help, or if they do know, they are unaware of what services are available or how to gain access to them. In addition, a child or youth, by law, cannot typically seek psychological services without parental consent, even if the child's problem is related to his or her interpersonal relationship with the parent. Many clinics do treat children without parental knowledge (Enrenreich & Melton, 1983), even when not sanctioned by law. Although providing such services can be risky, it may be necessary in order to protect the welfare of children and youth.

A clinic must establish and adhere to a policy with respect to this age-of-service issue. For very young children (3–10 years of age) it makes sense to have parents involved in consenting to treatment, selecting treatment goals, and in some cases implementing aspects of the treatment program in the home. For older adolescents (16 years and above), the clinic must decide if the minor is mature enough to seek treatment on his or her own, to provide informed consent, and to select goals so that treatment is beneficial to the minor himself or herself. Also, the clinic must determine who will pay for services or if a reduced or waived fee is involved before agreeing to see the minor without parental knowledge (Carroll et al., 1985). For the young adolescent age group (11–15 years of age), it is more difficult to decide what to do when they seek services without parental knowledge. Some individuals in this age range are mature enough to make reasonable treatment-related decisions, whereas others may not be competent to do so. These cases will have to be decided either according to a general policy (e.g., in all such cases, parents will be involved), or on a case-by-case basis. The former position may preclude some youth from receiving the services they need. The latter position will take more time to implement and will be more anxiety producing for clinicians. At a minimum, individuals in this adolescent group should be involved in selecting goals. The probabilities of a psychologist being held liable for the nonnegligent treatment of an adolescent over age 15 is extremely low. The probability for younger children is more uncertain.

Needed Legislation

Efforts to establish and protect, by law, the rights of children and youth, are long overdue. Legislation is needed that a) specifies children's rights, b) clarifies age of consent and relates it to competence for making treatment-related issues, c) addresses limits of confidentiality, and d) provides for due process before involving hospitalization. Some states already have some such legislation, while others, like Utah, are struggling with these issues. Child abuse laws have been in place for many years in all states, and yet children are still not totally protected from abusers. It is hoped that laws related to psychological services can be enacted and enforced in less time than it took abuse laws, so that more harm to children and youth is avoided.

Implications

It is critical that all providers of psychological services realize that failure to protect the rights of clients, and/or to willfully abridge those rights, can readily result in litigation against the practitioner (Schwitzgebel & Schwitzgebel, 1980) or action by professional ethics groups. Negligence suits against practitioners are increasing. In fact, the more lawyers there are in a community, the more likely is litigation (Schwitzgebel & Schwitzgebel, 1980). In addition, the ethical code for psychologists (APA, 1981a) requires psychologists to protect the welfare and dignity of those they serve. A practitioner can no longer afford to be uninformed or uninvolved when it comes to clients' rights. Most violations of the laws and codes of ethics that exist in reference to clients' rights are due to a lack of information rather than deliberate violations. A clinician must be sensitive to the impact of his or her actions on the child as well as the rights, responsibilities, and relationships that tie the child to his or her parents (Enrenreich & Melton, 1983).

Clinic Policy

The best procedure for dealing with clients' rights is for each agency or clinic to establish a program for preventing rights violations. The first step is to establish a set of client rights and appropriate procedures for protecting them. Rights and procedures should be put into written form so that all staff members have access to them. Staff should also be trained in what these rights are and how to protect them. It is also very important that clients be provided a copy of these rights (as described in Chapter 6) upon initial entry into a service system (APA, 1981a); that these rights be explained to the client; that the client (and parent or guardian in the case of minors) sign one copy indicating that the client fully understands his or her rights; that this signature process be witnessed; and that, in informing the client of his or her rights, care be taken to ensure that it is truly a case of informed consent. Handling this task requires someone with good interpersonal as well as professional skills. In most clinics the task can be assigned to the person conducting the intake interview.

Client Rights

All individuals receiving services are considered to be clients. This includes parents and legal guardians, as well as children and adolescents.

Clients have a right to:

1. Receive the best professional services within their personal belief and value system, including the right to an individualized treatment plan.
2. Ask any questions about services or about the training of the staff member(s) assigned to their case.
3. Participate in the development and approval of treatment plans and programs provided.
4. Know about and request alternative programming.
5. Request referral to a different therapist.
6. Accept that any information, verbal or written, provided will be kept confidential. No information will be communicated to other individuals or agencies unless authorized by the signature of a parent or legal guardian of a minor or by the adult client on a written letter or release of records form, with the following exceptions:
   a. Court subpoena of client records and/or testimony by the therapist. This includes court actions against the therapist.
   b. Client is referred to the clinic by the court (court ordered); all information will be available to the court.
   c. A clear emergency exists where there may be danger to the client or others.
   d. It is necessary to comply with state statutes (e.g., when child abuse is suspected or reported).
   e. Where client obligation, name, and address may be referred to outside collection agencies including small claims court if no payment is made on an account for over 60 days, unless special arrangements have been made with the therapist.
   f. Where client requests payment from third-party payer (insurance company).
7. Be informed when confidential information has been requested (e.g., health insurance, etc.), and of options available to clients.
8. Parents, legal guardians, or adult clients have the right to review their own client record or client record of their minor child or youth with the therapist within a reasonable time after making a written or verbal request.
9. In unusual circumstances, clients have the right to request a reduction in fees by submitting a written request.
10. Request that a client advocate be assigned to them to help deal with client issues such as grievance procedures.

I have read and understand my rights and those of my child.

Signature (mother/legal guardian)

Signature (father/legal guardian)

Signature (child)

Date

Informing adults of their rights is, in most cases, straightforward. When dealing with children or adolescents, things become a bit more complex. In most states parents are stipulated as the ones who can legally seek or refuse services for their children. The age at which an adolescent can seek independent services varies from state to state; thus, providers of psychological services must be familiar with state law. Should one inform the parent of the child's rights, or should one also try to inform the child of his or her rights? Whenever possible, it is best to inform the child or adolescent of his or her rights in understandable terms. With very young children or children with handicaps, this may be difficult. Nonetheless, the practitioner is obligated to try. Form 11.1 lists client rights. Although not as comprehensive as that proposed by others (Christian & Hannah, 1983; Sheldon-Wildgen & Risley, 1982), the list provides a good basis for assuring that the major rights of clients are not abridged.

Safeguards

It is not enough to have a bill of client rights available, to inform a client of them, and to have him or her sign off. In addition, it is essential that staff adhere to these client rights. The first step in protecting these rights is to have available a set of client safeguard procedures; the second step is to assure that staff are trained in how to implement the safeguards; and the third is to assure that the procedures are in fact implemented. Safeguard procedures include (Christian & Hannah, 1983) having written procedures for each of the items listed in Table 11.1.

In some cases, protecting client rights can be fairly easy; in other cases it can be extremely difficult. Is it possible, for example, that in protecting a client's rights one may be faced with a choice between adhering to a set of ethical principles such as those proposed by the American Psychological Association or following the legal requirements of the state in which one operates? For example, it is required by law that suspected cases of child abuse or neglect be reported to the appropriate authorities (police or social service system); failure to do so is a misdemeanor. Yet, it is very possible for a practitioner to be faced with a situation in which to report the abuse could be severely detrimental to the child. In accordance with the APA's ethical principles (1981a), one is bound to do whatever is best for the welfare of the client. In a situation in which reporting would result in legal authorities visiting the home and initiating an investigation of, for example, the father's sexual abuse of a young daughter, in which neither the child nor the father is removed from the home, the child is put in jeopardy. Once the situation is reported, the child could readily receive an immense amount of abuse because she "talked about private matters with someone outside of the family." A clinician faced with such a dilemma should immediately talk to the supervisor or clinic director to determine jointly the proper course of action. The written safeguard procedures should serve as a guideline for what to do and how to do it; if they do not, the procedures are inadequate and need to be revised. The best test of procedures is their utility for addressing situations that can potentially result in a violation of client rights. A clinic should have an ongoing client rights committee that reviews the client rights statement (Form 11.1) and the safeguard procedures (Table 11.1), both during and after each special situa-

Table 11.1. Written safeguard procedures

1. Providing clients/families with a written list of their rights and assuring that they understand them.
2. Protecting privacy and confidentiality.
3. Obtaining written consent before seeking or releasing client information.
4. Including the client in the development of individualized treatment plans.
5. Allowing the client to voice grievances and concerns about clinic procedures.
6. Assuring that treatment goals and objectives are measurable and that evaluation of their attainment occurs.
7. Assuring that all appropriate assessments (psychological, medical, neurological, etc.) have been conducted so alternative treatment approaches are not overlooked.
8. Assuring that a client has access to his or her treatment plan in conjunction with an appropriate staff member who can answer questions about its intent and content.
9. Assuring that treatment plans are reviewed on a regular basis.
10. Assuring that the treatment plan does not subject the client to unfair circumstances.
11. Assuring that staff are current on relevant laws, intervention strategies, and evaluation procedures.
12. Assuring that the program has a functional human rights committee that provides an external, unbiased peer review of services.
13. Assuring that procedures exist for regulating the use of aversive, coercive, and restrictive treatment procedures such as timeout and restraint and that suspected cases of abuse are investigated and dealt with appropriately. These procedures must clearly differentiate between client rights and client privileges (Schwitzgebel & Schwitzgebel, 1980).
14. Assuring that due process procedures are in place so each client is served using the least restrictive alternative.
15. Assuring that confidential written records are maintained.
16. Assuring that clinic staff are aware of client rights issues so that they protect those rights while providing services and striving to improve those services.
17. Assuring that practical alternatives to litigation for dealing with disagreements are in place, including grievance procedures, negotiation procedures, arbitration procedures, peer review committee procedures, and human rights committee procedures.

tion that arises concerning client rights and, at a minimum, once per year. These procedures and rights are not static; thus change is inherent in assuring ongoing appropriate services.

Safeguarding client rights may require consultation with a lawyer; with a local, state, or national ethics group; or with other agency personnel. It is very helpful if the standard operating policy manual for a psychological clinic includes clearly defined steps staff members should take when faced with specific or unusual client rights situations.

POLICIES OF CONFIDENTIALITY

Definitions

One area of client rights that deserves special consideration is confidentiality. The terms *confidentiality* and *privileged communication* carry different meanings; yet, the two overlap. *Privileged communication* is a term referring to a legal right that protects the client from having his or her confidences revealed publicly without permission during legal proceedings (Schwitzgebel & Schwitzgebel, 1980). The right belongs to the client and not the clinician. In all states, communication between a lawyer and his or her client is privileged. This means that the courts cannot require the lawyer to testify about anything he or she has been told by the client (Schwitzgebel & Schwitzgebel, 1980). That same privilege of communication is not accorded psychologists or other providers of psychological services in some states. It is important that a clinic determine whether that privilege exists within the state in which the clinic operates and how it differs for the different disciplines of the staff. It is also important to know if privileged communication extends to children.

Confidentiality is not a legal right; rather, it is an ethical practice (Schwitzgebel & Schwitzgebel, 1980). Principle 5 of the APA's "Ethical Principles" (1981a, see Appendix A in this book) clearly specifies that psychologists should, in advance, inform clients of the limits of confidentiality. This includes informing children and adolescents of the limits of confidentiality they can expect as negotiated with parents. Confidentiality is a broad concept that ethically binds professionals to "respect the confidentiality of information obtained from persons in the course of their work" (APA, 1981a, pp. 635–636). Information obtained is revealed only with the consent of the client or in unusual circumstances, such as where a danger exists to the client or others.

Limits of Confidentiality

One of the limits of confidentiality that should be told the client in a state in which privileged communication is not accorded to a provider of psychological services or to his or her clients is that in certain situations (e.g., if client is prosecuted for homicide) the courts can subpoena all records of the interactions that occur between the provider and the client. This and other common types of situations clinic staff should consider in informing clients of the limits of confidentiality are listed in Table 11.2. The limits in the table are expressed in general terms because it is the parents who generally hold the right to confidentiality. Clearly, there may be other instances where confidentiality may be abridged because of the specifics of an individual situation or by policy of an individual clinic. These items should all be included within the client statement of rights.

Informed Consent

Clients should be informed of the limits of confidentiality and client rights at the onset of service contact and should be required to sign a statement that they understand these rights; that is, informed consent should be obtained. In the case of children and adolescents, the parents are generally the ones who are informed, since they have the legal right within the limits of law to decide what is best for their child. If a child is seen without parental knowledge, he or she should be informed. The child should also be informed if seen with parental knowledge. Informed consent requires the following components:

Table 11.2. Sample set of limits of confidentiality

1. In virtually all states, suspected cases of abuse and neglect must be reported (Keller & Ritt, 1982).

2. If the primary client being served is a child or adolescent, the parent or legal guardian is usually the holder of the right to confidentiality, and, as such, any information disclosed by the minor may have to be shared with that parent or legal guardian on request (Rae, 1983). It is feasible to arrive at a different arrangement by agreement of all parties concerned about what information will not be shared with the parents. If this is to be done, it should be initiated at the onset of contact and should be clearly specified in written form. This does not mean that a parent cannot later change his or her mind; but it could protect the child in terms of any information that has been disclosed to the service provider up to that point.

3. In any case in which an individual is in danger of harming himself or others, it may be necessary to break the bonds of confidentiality, either to report the potential harm to authorities to initiate involuntary hospitalization proceedings (Keller & Ritt, 1982), or to inform the intended victim. Or in the case of a minor, to also inform the parent if an agreement was reached with the parent that information shared with the clinician by the child would be confidential.

4. In any case in which a client uses his or her "mental" condition as a defense in any legal proceedings, confidentiality will probably be abridged (Keller & Ritt, 1982).

5. In any legal action initiated by the client against the clinic or its staff, confidentiality may be abridged.

6. Some agencies have a policy whereby individuals who do not pay for the services they receive will have their name and certain identifying information turned over to collection agencies or to small claims court. Similar information including diagnosis is often released if the client requests third-party payment. It is best to get a signed consent form before releasing the information.

7. If the client is referred to the clinic by the court (court ordered), all information may be available to the court. The amount of information available to the court depends upon the agreement negotiated with the judge.

1. The client must act voluntarily.
2. The client must be mentally competent.
3. The client must understand the purpose of treatment.
4. The client must understand the nature and duration of treatment.
5. The client must understand the risks involved and prospects of success or benefit.
6. The client must understand the disadvantages if treatment is not undertaken.
7. The client must understand the alternative methods of treatment.
8. The client must be allowed to ask questions.
9. The client must understand whether financial compensation will be provided, should physical harm occur in situations where risk exists (Schwitzgebel & Schwitzgebel, 1980).

Existing research shows that children as young as 9 years of age can act voluntarily and can understand a simplified explanation of items 3–9 (Enrenreich & Melton, 1983). Individuals are also often mentally competent to make some decisions at even a younger age. Professionals and governmental agencies alike have suggested establishing an *age of discretion* for children (e.g., at 9 years) and requiring consent from a child older than that age before prescribing an intervention (Rekers, 1983).

ETHICS AND THE CHOICE OF THE CODE OF ETHICS

Importance of Adherence

Determining what set of principles of ethics clinic staff must abide by can be difficult and/or confusing. Members of the APA are all required to adhere to the "Ethical Principles of Psychologists" (APA, 1981a, see Appendix A). However, psychologists who are not members of the APA are not bound by these ethical principles. Although it may be foolhardy for a psychologist not to adhere to these principles, it does, in fact, happen. Keep in mind, though, that in cases in which a client accuses a psychologist of an activity that results in litigation, and that also involves ethical principles, the psychologist will be judged by most courts in accordance with the ethical principles to which he or she subscribes. In most cases, the courts will expect the psychologist to adhere to those of the APA; however, a court could also choose—since the person does not adhere to those principles—to compare the person against any other set of guidelines that the court chooses (Woody, 1983). Thus it is for the protection of the psychologist, himself or herself, and the client as well, to adhere to these principles.

Choosing

A clinic providing psychological and related services, however, may include staff from a variety of disciplines. The various principles of ethics to which these different disciplines subscribe may not all be as specific, or as comprehensive, as those of the APA. It is *essential* for a psychological service clinic to specify and include in its standard operating procedures copies of the designated ethical principles for staff. It is recommended that all staff members (including all clerical staff) be required to abide by: a) the ethical principles for their specific professional discipline, and b) a set of specific ethical principles established by the clinic (which may, in fact, be those of one of the professional associations such as the APA). For the benefit of all concerned, the clinic should utilize the most clearly defined, most stringent, and most comprehensive set of ethical principles currently available for the disciplines represented. If available principles are not stringent enough, the clinic should develop some that are and have them reviewed by external peers from the same professional disciplines. As a condition of employment, all staff, including clinical, business, professional, and paraprofessional, should be expected to adhere to the ethical principles adopted. Furthermore, failure to adhere to the principles should result in immediate termination of employment.

Updating

Ethical principles of national professional organizations are updated periodically. The clinic must also review its ethical principles and assure that they are updated annually or more frequently. If situations occur that are not clearly addressed by existing ethical principles, the clinic would be well advised, from both a moral and legal standpoint, to establish ethical principles to cover such situations, to assure that the clinic, its staff, and clientele are best protected.

Enforcement

As just stated, all staff, as a condition of employment, should be informed of the importance of ethics and policies and that violation of ethical principles *can* and *will* result in termination of their employment. An excellent compilation of professional ethics by various professional associations was published by the American Association for the Advancement of Science (Chalk, Frankel, & Chafer, 1980). Other sources of information are professional associations such as the American Psychological Association and books by Christian and Hannah (1983); Sales (1983); Schwitzgebel and Schwitzgebel (1980); and Striefel and Cole (1984).

INTERNAL AND EXTERNAL PEER REVIEW AND HUMAN RIGHTS COMMITTEES

The best policy for monitoring staff compliance with standards is a process of ongoing review of staff activities by both internal peer and external peer review committees as well as the human rights committee. Each of these three types of review is discussed in the paragraphs following.

Internal Peer Review

There are three types of internal peer review: a) evaluation of treatment plans, b) evaluation of case record documentation, and c) evaluation of staff performance (Christian & Hannah, 1983).

Evaluation of Treatment Plans

The most common evaluation of treatment plans is completed by a supervisor. The supervisor should be totally familiar with the services to be provided and can meet with treatment teams on a weekly basis to review cases for client progress and changes needed in the treatment plan (Christian & Hannah, 1983; Striefel & Cole, 1984). In these team meetings, feedback can be provided on how well the team is adhering to the clinic's ethical principles and standards. Each team member should be an active participant.

In implementing this process, a clinic should use naturally occurring treatment teams consisting of those individuals serving a particular client/family; should form interdisciplinary teams for cases in which only one staff member is involved; or have the total staff review, on an ongoing basis, each case seen by the clinic. In a large clinic, teams of three or four people can weekly review a certain number of the cases seen by the specific treatment team or by individual therapists on that team. Items team members could review include: a) the presenting problem, b) the assessment/evaluation that was conducted, c) the proposed treatment program, d) alternative treatment approaches that might be applicable as established in the literature, e) advantages and disadvantages of the particular treatment approach, f) how well the treatment approach is working, g) progress made, and h) problems that have arisen.

In addition, for each case reviewed, it is important that team members sign and date a review form indicating that the individual client treatment plan was reviewed. Recommendations should be listed on this form, and can be as simple as "continue as is"; or they may be specific and call for drastic changes. This review form becomes a part of the client's file. Christian and Hannah (1983) provide a good summary of how to conduct treatment peer reviews.

Documentation Review

The documentation review consists of reviewing client records, and provides valuable data for program and staff evaluation. Included is information such as the appropriateness and effectiveness of services received by individual clients and the degree to which staff understand the needs and rights of clients. Six procedures are included in case record review:

1. Developing standards for client records
2. Selecting or developing procedures and forms for record review
3. Selecting committees for record review
4. Conducting the client record review
5. Developing procedures and providing feedback to clinicians
6. Following up the record review to assure that suggested changes are implemented

Each of these procedures is discussed extensively by Christian and Hannah (1983).

Staff Performance Evaluation

In addition to evaluation of performance by a supervisor, each staff member can be evaluated in several others ways, including: a) having another team staff member evaluate each staff member's performance (using an evaluation check-list such as that discussed in Chapter 3), b) having clients and their families provide feedback on staff performance (a form of external evaluation as discussed in Chapter 3), c) having staff of other agencies with whom the staff member interacts conduct an evaluation of staff performance (another form of external evaluation as discussed in Chapter 3), and d) combinations of the previously mentioned procedures (Striefel & Cadez, 1983). Staff evaluation was discussed in more detail in Chapter 3.

External Peer Review

External peer reviews are most often initiated by third-party payers such as CHAMPUS, Blue Cross, and other insurance companies; but they can also be initiated by a clinic itself. In the case of third-party reviews, an insurance company will hire certain professionals, will set up guidelines on when reviews will be conducted, on what kind of information is needed for review, and on when it is to be carried out. External reviews initiated by a clinic have the advantage that feedback is typically candid and unbiased if evaluators are selected who have no vested interest in the clinic. Such review also provides a check on the reliability of internal reviews (Christian & Hannah, 1983). In addition, it provides a check on how well the clinic is adhering to community standards. External reviews can be of three types according to whether they are conducted by consumers, by professional experts, or by community personnel. Each type of review can provide the clinic with useful information. Some information may be consistent across different type of reviews and some will be decidedly different. A new clinic may find the professional expert review most useful, whereas a well-established and administratively sound clinic may be more interested in consumer or community feedback.

In all reviews a clear set of expectations, forms, purposes, applicable ethics, standards of confidentiality, type of report, and timelines should be developed in advance. A contract should be developed from these requirements, and should be signed by all reviewers prior to the start of the review.

Human Rights Committee

The third category of review is the human rights committee. The purpose of this committee is to assure that the rights of clients are protected, to protect the client against inappropriate treatment, and to assure that appropriate services are provided (Christian & Hannah, 1983). This committee should consist of a representative sample of people from the community. A few members may be clinic employees, but for the most part the committee would consist of citizens from the community. It is helpful if the membership of this committee is diverse but includes: a) other providers of psychological services, b) a legal representative, c) a local newspaper representative, and d) representatives from a variety of occupations in the community, including homemakers. It is important for this committee to: a) establish its purposes, b) determine the kind of training the group needs, and c) assure that the committee or committee members cannot be fired because they take a position opposed to clinic activities. It should not be possible for the clinic to eliminate a person from membership in the human rights committee other than as specified in the paragraph following.

The best way to organize membership in this group is to establish staggered terms of service so that a specific number of committee members are replaced each year, at the end of their term. Thus, a certain number of experienced members would always exist on the committee to assist incoming members. A good working model is to have one-third to one-fourth of the group replaced each year, with complete membership turnover every third or fourth year. The procedures for reviewing cases can be established by the clinic. It is probably best not to try to review all cases seen by a clinic; indeed, this may not even be possible. Rather, there should be a random selection of cases for review. A role for committee members could also involve helping clinic managers establish and maintain procedures for: a) educating clients and their families concerning client rights; b) ensuring that client rights, informed consent, and confidentiality are protected; c) obtaining peer reviews concerning human rights issues; and d) training staff to monitor their own performance to assure that client rights are protected (Christian & Hannah, 1983). Sheldon-Wildgen and Risley (1982) provide an excellent outline of questions for use by human rights committees during their review.

A clinic should consider instituting all three types of review committees, because their purpose is to help a clinic establish, maintain, and update its standard operating procedures so that clients are receiving the best litigation; and so that the public can be assured of quality services.

WRITTEN FORMS

It is important that each clinic have available some very simple, jargon-free forms that explicitly cover information on client rights. It may also be useful to have forms reviewed by a lawyer to assure that they are legally adequate. Some of the forms that a clinic may find useful include: a) a client rights form including a space for signature (Form 11.1), b) a billing agreement that clearly specifies billing arrangements with the individual client (Form 11.2), c) a form that clearly specifies when confidentiality will be violated (this could be included in the

---

FORM 11.2

Billing Agreement Form

Your personal fee for services will be $_____ per visit. You are expected to pay your bill at the time of each visit. If you cannot pay your complete bill at the time of the visit, arrangements for monthly payments must be made in advance with your therapist. Billing statements are made monthly. If you cannot make a scheduled appointment, you must cancel or reschedule it at least 24 hours before the scheduled time. Failure to do so will result in your being billed for the session.

Client Agreement

I have read and understand the information regarding fees. In addition, the information has been explained to me. I understand that accounts may be referred to an outside collection agency or pursued in small claims court or other courts if they are delinquent over 60 days. In this case delinquent means not making payment in accordance with the aforementioned guidelines. All court costs, attorney fees, and collection costs shall be my responsibility. It is also understood that interest at the rate of 1½% per month of the unpaid balance will be added to my account if delinquent over 30 days. By signing below, I certify that I have read and understand this agreement, have knowledge of its meaning and effect, and will adhere to it.

_____
Witness

_____
Signature of person responsible for payment

_____
Date

client rights statement, d) a consent form for testing and observation (see Chapter 6), and e) a sample release of records and request for information form (see Form 11.3).

Sample Release of Records and Request for Information

To: _____

_____
(Address)

Regarding: _____Date of birth:_____
(Client's Name)

_____
(Address)

I hereby authorize any individuals who have provided services for the client identified above, or representatives of the agency identified above, to furnish to the:

Clinical Services Program
Developmental Center for Handicapped Persons
Utah State University
Logan, UT 84322-6800

any information available whether written or verbal with respect to any psychological testing and reports, academic information, medical history, physical examinations or evaluations, consultation reports, and any treatment or programs prescribed. I also certify that I am the above-named client's legal guardian.

_____   _____
(Witness)   (PRINT Parent/Legal Guardian Name)

_____   _____
(Date)   (Parent/Legal Guardian Signature)

I hereby give my permission to the Clinical Services Program of the Developmental Center for Handicapped Persons to verbally discuss or release written evaluation/assessment and treatment reports for the above-named client to the individual or agency or agency representatives identified above. I also certify that I am the above-named client's legal guardian.

_____   _____
(Witness)   (PRINT Parent/Legal Guardian Name)

_____   _____
(Date)   (Parent/Legal Guardian Signature)

Authorization by written signature for Release of Records and Request for Information will be effective for 1 year from the date signed unless rescinded in writing before that time.

LIABILITY ISSUES

Liability Coverage

A practitioner can no longer assume that good practice and good luck will keep one out of court. As Schwitzgebel and Schwitzgebel (1980) emphasize, the farther away you can stay from the legal system the better. The point being made is that the more lawyers there are in a particular geographic area, the more likely it is that an individual or agency will be sued for one reason or another. Certainly it is advantageous to engage in quality service procedures, including peer reviews and adherence to well-defined ethical principles, standards, and the law. However, preparation alone does not preclude a lawsuit being brought against the individual clinician and/or clinic. The best defense is still a good offense. Each clinic should consider the availability of appropriate liability insurance for clinic staff members. Information can be collected from several insurance agencies on what the typical court awards are for various problems, and also on what other measures the insurance companies would recommend for protecting yourself and the clinic (see Chapter 2 for more information). At a minimum, liability insurance needs to be in the vicinity of $1–3 million per individual case.

Prevention

The maintenance of high ethical standards; clearly specified standard clinic operating procedures that include informing clients of their rights and limits of confidentiality; staff procedures dealing with clients; informing clients of alternative treatment choices, including those provided by other practitioners, and of the advantages and disadvantages of each treatment alternative; staff awareness of the treatment of choice for particular problems; and peer reviews and consultation to preclude ethical or treatment questions from arising, can go far toward protecting an agency and establishing a community reputation as a place that provides quality service. A well-established client grievance procedure is also useful. Even though staff are totally adhering to the procedures just described, an individual client could still decide to bring suit, resulting in major problems for the clinic and staff members named as defendants. It takes extensive emotional energy and time to prepare for litigation, even if one is innocent. In addition, even when an individual professional has been found innocent by the courts, community members may question whether the professional was really innocent or just had a good lawyer. In essence, any lawsuit will probably tarnish the reputation of the agency and the professional involved. For this reason, many civil suits are settled out of court.

Several alternatives designed to preclude litigation should be part of the standard operating procedures. These include: a) planned, advertised, and implemented client grievance procedures that include access to an advocate from the human rights committee; b) planned and implemented procedures for negotiating differences; c) established liaison with a lawyer whose purpose it is to preclude lawsuits; and d) established arbitration procedures.

Should a lawsuit arise, it is important that clinic administrators clarify with their insurance company that the clinic will not settle the suit out of court just for the convenience of the insurance company. Doing so may encourage additional lawsuits by individuals who know that a suit was brought, but that it was settled out of court. It also has a negative impact (i.e., the implication that the practitioner was guilty). Clearly, however, if the service provider is guilty and the odds are that courts will also find him or her guilty, it is to the clinic's advantage to settle the issue out of court with as little publicity as possible. A lawyer's advice is quite useful in such matters.

Common Areas of Litigation

There are several areas in which litigation is becoming more common. One of the most frequent and most likely sources of litigation is related to collection of fees (Wright, 1981). The scenario goes something like this. An individual is receiving treatment services for his or her child. The bill gets large and the client's family is not making regular payments. At some point, after the bill has gotten fairly large, the clinic or individual service provider begins to put pressure on the client's family to pay the bill. They, in turn, find some aspect of their child's assessment or treatment that they can question, and they bring suit. One common area is related to client evaluation, such as misdiagnosis, erroneous information incorporated into a report, or a lack of documentation (Wright, 1981).

Other common areas of litigation include: a) sexual intercourse with clients (especially minors), b) unauthorized physical contact of the client, c) negligence, and d) being a member of a governance board (e.g., being a member of an ethics committee). The best defense against litigation is to assure that there are no grounds for litigation by adhering to high standards of professional conduct as previously specified.

LEGAL IMPLICATIONS OF
WRITTEN STANDARD OPERATING PROCEDURES

Chapter 3 emphasized the importance of a clinic's having available written, standard operating procedures. Equally important is periodic review and updating of these procedures to assure that they are current legally and ethically. The procedures provide for quality control if all staff engage in the specified activities in the prescribed manner. This does not preclude latitude for individual applications with specific clients. Rather, it assures that procedures for addressing issues such as billing, client rights, and confidentiality are enforced. A supervisor can compare the performance of individual staff members with the standard operating procedures and can provide inservice training for violators. In cases of noncompliance because of disagreement with policy, a policy review can be conducted by the appropriate policy committee of the clinic. The committee can determine whether to revise the policy, reprimand the employee, or terminate the professional's employment with the clinic. Availability of written standard operating procedures and monitoring staff compliance go together. Failure to adhere to written clinic operating procedures, resulting in client injury, would in a civil court suit probably result in a judgment of negligence against staff members involved.

Clinic operating procedures should specify how a staff member would go about seeking consultation, either legal or professional, when a specific ethical or treatment dilemma arises. It is safer to pay a lawyer's consultation fee than it is to make an uninformed guess and be faced with litigation. Standard operating procedures should also address clinic procedures dealing with ethical violations by clinic staff. The procedures should adhere to both the ethical principles of the individual's profession and to those of the particular clinic. In addition, procedures must fit due process, in terms of protecting the rights of the individual accused. One cannot eliminate the possibility of staff biases. Personality conflicts between staff can result in misinterpretations of particular events. Ongoing education on ethics, professional standards, "state of the art" practice, and legal self-protection are critical to clinics and their staff.

CLIENT INVOLVEMENT AND SIGNATURES

Signatures

Information was previously provided on different forms needing the client's signature. It is critical that the person who signs the forms is in fact the legal guardian of the child or adolescent client. It is quite feasible in a reconstituted family for a child to be brought in by a stepparent who had not adopted the child client, and thus, is not a legal guardian. His or her signature on a consent form would not be sufficient protection in any kind of future court action. For example, it is common in custody disputes for the parent who does not have custody to bring a child in for evaluation. If the evaluation is carried out without court order, it can result in legal and ethical problems for a clinic and its staff.

Informed Consent

Before having the client or guardian sign any form for testing, client rights, billing agreements, or release of records, it is critical that the client understand the content. The information should be presented to the client or guardian, and they should be asked to repeat in their own words the meaning. Such a process provides the professional with one indicator of whether the client understood what was on the form before signing. Ideally, this process should be witnessed by a person other than the therapist, and all three parties should sign the form.

Some agencies videotape or audiotape the process during which a client receives an explanation of the content of a particular form. Taping may be a bit extreme for the operation of most clinics providing psychological and related services to children and adolescents. However, availability of a videotape for explaining items such as client rights at a level appropriate for use with children or adolescents and parents would be useful. The tape would assure that the specific content was provided to each client, and could also save professional time, since a secretary could play the appropriate tapes for all clients. After each tape has been observed or listened to, the therapist could provide the client with an opportunity to ask questions about the content in the presence of the secretary, and then all three parties could sign the appropriate form. In some clinics an intake worker explains the content of all forms to clients before the client sees a therapist.

Deciding whether an intake worker, the secretary, or the therapist will explain specific procedures that require signature is useful. For example, it is appropriate to keep billing forms and procedures separate from those related to therapy, because hassling with clients over billing could compromise a therapist's effectiveness. If the decision is made to separate billing activities from therapy, a secretarial staff member or the business administrator could explain the billing procedures and obtain signatures on those forms (see Chapter 4 for more information). The therapist could deal with issues such as client rights, consent for testing, and so on.

COURT TESTIMONY

Professionals working with children and adolescents may find that they are periodically required to testify in court. There are at least six areas in which court testimony is likely for those providing psychological services to children and adolescents. These areas are described in Table 11.3.

Custody procedures should be clearly specified in the clinic's standard operating procedures. Evaluation for a custody decision could include the following: a) interviewing each parent (e.g., psychiatric diagnostic interview) and each child individually; b) assessing the mental stability of each parent using an instrument such as the Minnesota Multiphasic Personality Inventory (MMPI); c) assessing the parenting skills of each parent, using something like the Knowledge of Behavioral Principles as Applied to Children Test; d) assessing each parent's ability to provide a home that offers quality parent time, emotional support, the satisfaction of basic daily needs, and a true interest in having the child; e) determining the preference of the child or adolescent in terms of individual parents; f) covering each aspect in the state law; and g) the child's availability for visitation by the parent who does not receive custody. Similar if not identical areas need to be addressed in operating procedures and assessments in case of abuse.

Techniques for Surviving Court Testimony

Testifying in court is, at best, an emotionally draining experience for most professionals. It is also an area in which they have received little or no training.

Table 11.3. Areas in which court testimony is likely

1. Testifying about aspects related to one's own area of expertise. Often this testimony will be about a matter *not* related to a specific client but, rather, to a specific content area such as the appropriate treatment for a particular type of problem. One could also be brought into court as an expert witness in the defense of a client.

2. Testifying at a commitment hearing in which a child or adolescent is considered "dangerous to self or others," requiring long-term hospitalization against the will of the child and/or his parents. States' mental health laws often do not clearly specify such procedures. The general commitment guidelines are that a person be mentally ill, be dangerous to self or others, and be unable to care for his or her basic needs. Sales (1983) provides a summary of the requirements for commitment in each state. None are cited specifically for children because they generally do not exist.

3. Testifying at a sanity evaluation in which an individual is accused of a crime and a determination is needed by the court on: a) whether this person is competent to stand trial, and b) whether this person can be judged responsible for his or her actions at the time of the crime. These two factors are quite different. Responsibility is concerned with the defendant's state of mind at the time the alleged offense occurred, whereas competence refers to the defendant's state of mind at the time of the trial (Schwitzgebel & Schwitzgebel, 1980). The younger the defendant, the more difficult the process.

4. Testifying in civil litigation where a minor has, for example, damaged someone's property and is being sued. A professional may be asked to testify on behalf of his or her minor client.

5. Testifying in child custody disputes is the major and most common area of court testimony for those working with children and adolescents. A clinic needs clearly established procedures for dealing with custody decisions. The procedures must adhere to the state law. Before agreeing to allow staff to testify in a child custody hearing, a clinic should require an agreement by all parties concerned that the clinician will: a) do an evaluation of each parent and each child involved; b) write one report and submit it to the lawyers for both parties; and c) be an advocate for the child first and the family second (Committee on the Family of the Group for Advancement of Psychiatry, 1980). The report should be written in terms of what serves the best interests of the child(ren). This procedural agreement should be written, in advance, in accordance with informed consent procedures.

6. Testifying in cases of child abuse or neglect in which, as a clinician, you have either been treating the child victim or one or both parents. Deciding who and how to serve as an advocate in such cases is difficult.

Thus, it is truly a case of throwing a "sheep into the lion's den." Yet, professionals providing psychological services to children and adolescents can survive and contribute via court testimony if appropriately prepared. Some guidelines that will help the professional survive this situation include:

1. Have supported information available. In essence, do not rely on projective tests alone, but, rather, include observations and other objective information that can be substantiated.

2. Stick to the facts. Make as few inferences as possible, even though expert witnesses are allowed to make inferences within their area of expertise.

3. Take time in answering questions. If a question cannot be answered with a *yes* or *no*, indicate this to the court.

4. Present both the advantages and disadvantages of any recommendations made, the probabilities of occurrence of each of those events, and the basis for making that probability judgment (Schwitzgebel & Schwitzgebel, 1980).

5. Be honest, be prepared, admit weaknesses, use meaningful words, and listen to the wording of the questions carefully (Schwitzgebel & Schwitzgebel, 1980).

The purpose of testimony is to provide useful and relevant information to aid the court in making legal decisions (Schwitzgebel & Schwitzgebel, 1980). Expert witnesses are asked to testify on matters such as: predicting dangerousness to self and others; competence to stand trial; responsibility for one's actions; and child custody. In each case, expert testimony can be useful and may be unopposed. It may also be opposed by an expert witness working for the other side. The adage "know what you are doing or refuse to be an expert witness" (unless so ordered by the court) is advised.

ETHICAL ISSUES SPECIFICALLY RELEVANT TO CHILDREN

A variety of ethical issues pertain to psychological practice so far as minors are concerned, including:

1. *Minors' consent to treatment.* The law is clear in terms of the need for informed consent when treating adults. Without consent, a clinician can be charged with battery and negligence. Also, an adult must be mentally competent in order for consent to be meaningful. Minors, however, are considered incompetent to give informed consent unless otherwise specified in state law (Enrenreich & Melton, 1983); it is assumed, by virtue of their age alone, that they lack the ability to consent to treatment. Parents or guardians generally possess the authority to give consent. Yet, parents do not always act in the best interest of their children. If a clinician treats a child whose parents consent to treatment, but the child has not consented, the clinician can still be liable. It is best to obtain the informed consent of both the parent(s) and the child. Getting such consent can be difficult, since few children voluntarily seek treatment (Enrenreich & Melton, 1983). In some cases children are able to give or withhold consent regardless of their parents' position. This includes legally emancipated minors or mature minors. Some states have mature minor statutes or minor consent statutes. At a minimum, a provider of psychological services should determine if a minor has the capacity to consent to treatment. Since children have no organized advocacy group to get laws changed, they continue to be treated or not treated depending on the adults in their lives. The state seldom overrides the wishes of a parent when it comes to mental health services.

2. *Fee payment.* If a parent refuses treatment for a child and the clinic provides treatment anyway, the parents probably will not be held liable for the bills incurred. Since minors often lack sufficient funds to pay for services, a problem exists. The services must either be provided free or at a low cost in order for the minor to receive treatment. If a minor is emancipated or is competent to enter into a legal contract, he or she may sometimes be liable

for service costs. Often, however, the minor is not considered liable. Serving minors is an area where psychologists can be altruistic and donate some services, as specified in the APA's "Ethical Principles" (1981a). Thus, minors could obtain treatment services that are not considered by law to be "necessities" (Enrenreich & Melton, 1983).

3. *Adequate treatment.* The courts have ruled that involuntarily institutionalized minors have a "right to adequate treatment" (Enrenreich & Melton, 1983, p. 1290). The components of adequate treatment are a human psychological and physical environment, an individualized treatment plan, and sufficient professional staff to implement the individualized plan.

4. *Confidentiality.* Parents can generally have legal access to their child's mental health records; however, disclosure of that information to others may rest in the authority of the agency, attorneys, insurance companies, or others. Most states do not grant children the right to see their own records (Enrenreich & Melton, 1983). Nor do they deal with the issue of confidentiality when a minor consents to treatment. A clinic should establish a policy regarding disclosure of information to parents, the policy should be discussed at the beginning of treatment, and any exceptions should be documented (Enrenreich & Melton, 1983).

Most adolescents over age 14 or 15 can make treatment decisions as well as adults can. They also benefit from the experience. At minimum, children should be encouraged to participate in decision making concerning their treatment, and a clinic should have clearly specified procedures concerning this process. Such policies must be established with full knowledge of relevant laws.

OTHER INFORMATION

Staff in every clinic providing psychological and related services to children should have direct access to the types of information listed in Table 11.4. These standards, laws, and principles will help staff function effectively on a day-to-day basis. Woody (1983) outlined a worthwhile set of recommendations for avoiding malpractice suits. These are provided in Table 11.5.

SUMMARY

It should be clear to the reader by now that legal and ethical issues are intertwined, and yet must often be sorted out in making the best professional judgment. Advance planning in terms of which ethical principles to adhere to; what the legal implications are for the particular clinic's practice; and what training staff need, can go far in preventing problems. By having available legal, ethical, and treatment consultants, and a human rights and peer review committee, a clinic can preclude the majority of difficulties that may arise in these areas. The availability of written, well-conceived standard operating procedures concerning these matters helps ensure quality services and the protection of staff.

Table 11.4. Necessary standards, laws, and principles

1. State licensing laws and regulations for each discipline represented by staff in the clinic (available from the State Office of Licensing).
2. State mental health policies, laws, standards, and regulations (available from the State Division of Mental Health).
3. State involuntary commitment and child abuse and neglect laws (available from the State Division of Mental Health).
4. State professional association ethical principles and standards (available from individual professional associations).
5. State child custody laws (available from the State Division of Family Services or Department of Social Services).
6. "Ethical Principles of Psychologists" (APA, 1981a).
7. *Specialty Guidelines for the Delivery of Services* (APA, 1981b). These are the standards for delivery of services by clinical, counseling, school, and organizational psychologists.
8. *Standards for Educational and Psychological Testing* (APA, 1985).
9. *Standards for Providers of Psychological Services* (APA, 1977). A revision of these standards should be available in late 1986.
10. Public Law 94-142 (the Education for all Handicapped Children Act, 1976).

READER ACTIVITY

Do you have a stringent set of ethical principles to which all staff in your clinic are expected to adhere? If not, develop a set now. List the limits of confidentiality that clients at your clinic are to be informed of. If you do not have any, develop a set now. Describe your internal peer review system. Does it really serve as a quality assurance procedure? If not, how could you change the procedure so it does? Describe the ideal membership of a human rights committee.

REFERENCES

American Psychological Association. (1977). *Standards for providers of psychological services* (Rev. ed.). Washington, DC: Author.
American Psychological Association. (1981a). Ethical principles of psychologists. *American Psychologist, 36*(6) 633–638.

Table 11.5. Recommendations for avoiding malpractice suits

1. When a complaint occurs, take a defensive posture
2. Adhere to a high standard of care and communicate it to clients
3. Have a peer available to regularly review your cases
4. Have the client/family be responsible for communication with outside agencies
5. Establish a diagnosis for each client, using professionally accepted procedures
6. Base all interventions on an established theory
7. Maintain only a professional relationship with clients
8. Do not allow clients to get behind in fee payments
9. Use an attorney when needed
10. Carry malpractice insurance
11. Clarify the clinic's legal liability for your professional activities

American Psychological Association. (1981b). *Specialty guidelines for the delivery of services.* Washington, DC: Author.

American Psychological Association. (1985). *Standards for educational and psychological testing.* Washington, DC: Author.

Carroll, M. A., Schneider, H. G., & Wesley, G. R. (1985). *Ethics in the practice of psychology.* Englewood Cliffs, NJ: Prentice-Hall.

Chalk, R., Frankel, M. S., & Chafer, S. B. (1980). *AAAS professional ethics project.* Washington, DC: American Association for the Advancement of Science.

Christian, W. P., & Hannah, G. T. (1983). *Effective management in human services.* Englewood Cliffs, NJ: Prentice-Hall.

Committee on the Family of the Group for Advancement of Psychiatry. (1980). *New trends in child custody determination.* San Diego: Harcourt Brace Jovanovich.

Education for All Handicapped Children Act of 1975. (1976). Reston, VA: Council for Exceptional Children.

Enrenreich, N. S., & Melton, G. B. (1983). Ethical and legal issues in the treatment of children. In A. E. Walker & M. C. Roberts (Eds.), *Handbook of clinical child psychology* (pp. 1285–1305). New York: John Wiley & Sons.

Keller, P. A., & Ritt, L. G. (1982). Confidentiality. In P. A. Keller & L. G. Ritt (Eds.), *Innovations in clinical practice: A source book* (Vol. 1), (pp. 379–380). Sarasota, FL: Professional Resources Exchange.

National Council of Community Mental Health Centers. (1985). Hearing targets teen services. *National Council of Community Mental Health Center Newsletter, 1.*

Rae, W. A. (1983). Teen-parent problems. In C. E. Walker & M. C. Roberts (Eds.), *Handbook of clinical child psychology* (pp. 725–740). New York: John Wiley & Sons.

Rekers, G. A. (1983). Ethical issues in child behavior assessment. In T. H. Ollendick & M. Hersen (Eds.), *Handbook of child psychopathology* (pp. 244–262). New York: Plenum.

Sales, D. B. (1983). *The professional psychologist's handbook.* New York: Plenum.

Schwitzgebel, R. L., & Schwitzgebel, R. K. (1980). *Law and psychological practice.* New York: John Wiley & Sons.

Sheldon-Wildgen, J., & Risley, T. R. (1982). Balancing client rights. In A. S. Bellack, M. Hersen, & A. E. Kazdin (Eds.), *International handbook of behavior modification and therapy* (pp. 263–289). New York: Plenum.

Striefel, S., & Cadez, M. J. (1983). *Serving children and adolescents with developmental disabilities in the special education classroom: Proven methods.* Baltimore: Paul H. Brookes Publishing Co.

Striefel, S., & Cole, P. (1984). *Clinical services handbook.* Logan, UT: Developmental Center for Handicapped Persons.

Woody, R. H. (1983). Avoiding malpractice in psychotherapy. In P. A. Keller and L. G. Ritt (Eds.), *Innovations in clinical practice: A source book.* (Vol. 2, pp. 205–216). Sarasota, FL: Professional Resources Exchange.

Wright, R. H. (1981). Psychologists and professional liability (malpractice) insurance: A retrospective review. *American Psychologist, 36*(12), 1485–1493.

12

Current Status and Future Directions

After reading this chapter,[1] you should understand:
1. The current status of psychological services available to children and adolescents
2. The role of preventive services
3. Suggested future directions

This chapter provides a brief summary of the current status of treatment and preventive services for children and adolescents. It also provides suggestions for future directions on serving these populations.

CURRENT STATUS

It has often been said, and rightly so, that children are the future hope of society. As such, the adult society should assure that the mental health and well-being of all children is nurtured. This means that society must be aware of and accept its responsibility for this valuable asset. Unfortunately, this has not generally occurred in the area of mental health prevention or in treatment services for children and adolescents. Knitzer (1984) reports that two of every three seriously disturbed children and adolescents do not receive appropriate mental health services; 40% of those children who are institutionalized are placed there because there are no community alternatives; of those children who receive community services, many receive only multiple evaluations but no treatment; and the few who receive treatment often do so only for short periods of time because, as their needs change, alternative treatments do not exist. Nationwide, the problem of inadequate mental health services for troubled children and adolescents is severe, and preventive mental health services are almost nonexistent.

How can such a situation exist if children are valuable assets? What accounts for this neglect in the development of preventive mental health treatment for children? Several factors appear to be relevant. First, attempting to deal with

---

[1]Parts of the section of this chapter on the need to prevent mental health problems in children and adolescents are adapted from: Striefel, S. (1986, November). A changing era: Preventive mental health and the quality of life for children. *In Touch, 1*(2), 1–3. Reprinted with permission from the Mental Health Association in Utah.

preventive mental health for children and adolescents, without dealing with the issue of direct treatment service, is not productive. The fact is that both are considered vitally important, with the need for prevention exceeded only by the need for child treatment (Lamb & Zusman, 1979). Yet the attention accorded both areas of concern is inadequate in this country owing to:

1. Lack of adequate funding and other resources (i.e., insufficient numbers of trained personnel) (Goldston, 1986).
2. Disagreements on how available funds should be used. For example, prevention is considered by many in the field to be a utopian idea that is neither feasible nor cost effective (Peterson & Ridley-Johnson, 1983). In addition, many service advocates argue that given limited funding, the funds available should be allocated to treatment rather than prevention. Others argue that without a preventive focus, the need for treatment services increases. Both views can be supported or refuted.
3. No public policy or statutory regulation exists at the national or state level mandating either preventive or direct mental health treatment services for children. It has been proposed that the local community and state agencies should take the lead in formulating and implementing plans for both treatment service and prevention (Knitzer, 1984; Peterson & Ridley-Johnson, 1983). It has also been proposed that the National Institute of Mental Health (NIMH) should take the leadership role (Goldston, 1986).
4. Children and adolescents are not able to advocate for their own mental health needs and, with few exceptions, no strongly organized advocacy group currently exists for doing so (McGowan, 1978).
5. Most individuals in the general community do not readily recognize the needs of children for treatment and preventive mental health services.
6. State agencies responsible for mental health often do not have staff members assigned specifically to develop treatment programs for the needs of children and adolescents, and if they do, those assigned are often inadequately trained (Knitzer, 1984).

A Changing Era

Precedent

The status of treatment services and preventive mental health for children is entering a changing era. The situation is very similar to that for persons with handicaps about 10 years ago. Whereas the needs of persons with handicaps have not all been met in the last decade, great progress has occurred as a function of many factors, including:

1. Litigation mandating specific services for persons with handicaps. For example, Partlow State Hospital was required by the court to provide specific intervention services.
2. Public Law 94-142 which mandated a free and appropriate education for every child with a handicap.

3. Section 503 of the Rehabilitation Act, which mandated nondiscriminatory practices in hiring to provide an equal opportunity for persons with handicaps.
4. The 1976 White House Conference on Handicapped Individuals, which created a great awareness of and movement for improving the quality of life for persons with handicaps.
5. The formation of due process proceedings and the establishment of legal advocacy for persons with handicaps in each state, which provided a mechanism for protecting the rights of persons with handicaps.
6. The formation of strong parent advocacy groups for protecting the rights of persons with handicaps and meeting their needs.

The precedent set for answering the needs of handicapped persons can and should be used as a guide for actions to take to prevent and treat child and adolescent mental health problems. A vast array of child-related experience, procedures, and materials is already available that could be utilized in approaching issues in mental health prevention and treatment services for children and adolescents. For example, one lesson from work with handicapped youngsters is that research in early childhood intervention shows that many developmental problems can be overcome or the effects minimized by early identification and intervention. Early intervention in the form of prevention would seem appropriate in the area of mental health. To prevent or minimize the impact of mental disorders, it would seem that the ideal population would be very young children who have not yet experienced severe damage (Knitzer, 1984).

CLIENT AND ADOLESCENT RIGHTS

In dealing with children, it must be recognized that they have rights. Client rights are an issue currently stressed by professionals, advocates, and the public. Children also have rights, and the public is beginning to recognize the impact of not protecting these rights or not meeting children's needs. Child abuse is a prime example of a problem that often results in severe mental health problems for children. It is possible that a nationwide preventive and treatment service program could alleviate or minimize the impact of abuse, as well as other mental health problems.

Levels of Prevention

A preventive mental health program may well serve children and adolescents by addressing the three preventive levels outlined by Caplan (1964). The first such level is primary prevention, which stresses the importance of preventing problems before they occur. The second is secondary prevention, which stresses minimizing the impact of mental health problems by early detection and treatment. The third is tertiary prevention, which stresses preventing long-term disabilities resulting from a disorder. Tertiary prevention is difficult to separate from direct treatment services, other than on a semantic level (Knitzer, 1984).

Most of the information in this book focuses on the procedures and practices related to provision of direct psychological and related services to children and adolescents.

Advocacy

Historically, we know that change does not usually occur unless there is a "force" applying pressure on many levels of society to produce change (Goldston, 1986). The most powerful force for producing a comprehensive continuum of mental health preventive and treatment services for children and adolescents could result from the parents of these individuals uniting into advocacy groups so their voices are heard as the "demand of the people." Advocacy groups already exist in some areas of mental health (e.g., the National Alliance for the Mentally Ill), and these groups could take up the challenge of protecting our most precious assets by advocating for the needs of children and adolescents. Existing advocacy groups could also serve as educators and support groups for newly formed child mental health prevention and treatment service advocacy groups.

FUTURE DIRECTIONS

The challenge and need is clear. A parental advocacy force can be created. What remains is a clear need for direction. Some of the initial major steps might include:

1. Creation and passage of legislation on both the national and state levels requiring establishment and implementation of a nationwide comprehensive continuum of treatment services and preventive mental health programs for children. Section 455(d) of the Public Health Services Act mandates the establishment of an administrative unit for prevention within the National Institute of Mental Health (Goldston, 1986). Its goals are to: a) establish national priorities for prevention of mental illness, b) assist state and local agencies to achieve such priorities, and c) coordinate prevention policies to assure an increased focus on prevention of mental illness and promotion of mental health. Leadership is needed to assure that the needs and rights of children and adolescents are placed high on the list of priorities.
2. The identification of the groups of children that are most likely to be unserved or inappropriately served. The information obtained in the NIMH Epidemiological Catchment Area studies could be used to help in this activity (Goldston, 1986).
3. The training of more specialized professionals to meet the specific needs of children and adolescents, including training of administrative leaders at the state and local levels.
4. The creation of an active, nationwide organized child advocacy network consisting of professional and citizen advocates. A national prevention

CURRENT STATUS AND FUTURE DIRECTIONS / 271

advocacy group for prevention for all ages has been developed and consists of researchers, service providers, and members from most major mental health organizations (Goldston, 1986). Since this group is for prevention per se, an effort must be made to assure that this group or a group similar to it focuses on preventive efforts and treatment needs of children and adolescents.

5. The allocation of dollars, taxes, and private donations, to research and implement successful, feasible, and cost efficient preventive and treatment services. The $1.5 million currently available from the National Institute of Mental Health to states to plan children's services needs to be drastically increased.

6. The integration of preventive programs into existing community structures such as classroom programs in the public schools.

7. The education of the public on preventive mental health activities to involve them in improving the quality of life for children.

8. The establishment of more clinics and other service agencies to provide psychological and related services to children and adolescents. These service agencies must have available qualified staff who provide appropriate quality services. At present, there is a nationwide effort by private corporations to establish free-standing psychiatric hospitals in communities across the nation to provide services to disturbed children and adolescents. Some of these corporations are establishing a continuum of services as discussed in Chapter 1, including community clinics that provide psychological services.

9. The funding and conduct of applied and basic research to gain new knowledge and to establish well-evaluated treatment and prevention service models.

10. The dissemination of written and video information on services available and on behaviors that are indicative of the need for mental health services to parents, children, and adolescents. For example, several cities now have available for adolescents crisis telephone numbers whereby an adolescent can contact someone for help while remaining anonymous, even to the crisis worker if so desired. In some cases, the crisis line is staffed by other adolescents. In addition, various groups offer brochures, books, and films on services or indicators of psychological problems (Steele, 1986).

11. The presentation via public television of 30-second ''spots'' indicating it is okay to seek help when you are having difficulty coping with life and its stresses. These should be geared for children, adolescents, and adults. Awareness is needed to overcome resistance to seek help. The National Council of Community Mental Health Centers and the American Academy of Child Psychiatry are calling attention to the critical mental health needs of teenagers (*National Council News,* 1986).

12. The evaluation of the quality of psychological and related services provided to children and adolescents.

13. The development of training programs to educate parents on parenting and other skills that will benefit their children and adolescents and training programs for children and adolescents themselves on skills such as coping, making friends, expressing feelings, and dealing with fears.

SUMMARY

The hope for the future and for our children will be enhanced by a concerted effort to take positive action to increase appropriate mental health treatment and prevention services. Understanding current and future needs can be useful to advocacy groups in drawing attention to the problems of children and adolescents. Active advocacy groups are essential, since children and adolescents do not advocate for themselves when it comes to the need for psychological and related services. The establishment of child and adolescent rights is one area that would set the stage for protecting the rights of these populations.

READER ACTIVITIES

Have you established a human rights committee to help you establish and or review a set of child and adolescent rights? If not, we suggest you do so, since this group can enhance your public image, can indirectly increase referrals and locate other sources of revenue, and can advocate at the community, state, and national levels. Do you have a functioning preventive program? What would a functional program consist of and how could you implement it? What advocacy activities could you engage in that would serve the community and also increase your revenue?

REFERENCES

Caplan, G. (1964). *Principles of preventive psychiatry*. New York: Basic Books.

Goldston, S. E. (1986). Primary prevention: Historical perspectives and a blueprint for action. *American Psychologist, 41*(4), 453–460.

Knitzer, J. (1984). Mental health services to children and adolescents: A national view of public policies. *American Psychologist, 39*(8), 905–911.

Lamb, L. R., & Zusman, J. (1979). Primary prevention in perspective. *American Journal of Psychiatry, 136*(1), 12–17.

McGowan, B. (1978). The case advocacy function in a child welfare practice. *Child Welfare, 52*(3), 275–284.

Peterson, L., & Ridley-Johnson, R. (1983). Prevention of disorders in children. In C. E. Walker & M. C. Roberts (Eds.), *Handbook of clinical child psychology* (pp. 1174–1197). New York: John Wiley & Sons.

Staff. (1986). Problems, services for teens, focus of Mental Health Month. *National Council News* (National Council of Community Mental Health Centers, Rockville, MD), pp. 1–2.

Steele, W. (1986). *Preventing teenage suicide*. Naples, FL: Ann Arbor Publishers.

Striefel, S. (1986, November). A changing era: Preventive mental health and the quality of life for children. *In Touch, 1*(2), 1–3.

Appendix A: Ethical Principles of Psychologists

PREAMBLE

Psychologists respect the dignity and worth of the individual and strive for the preservation and protection of fundamental human rights. They are committed to increasing knowledge of human behavior and of people's understanding of themselves and others and to the utilization of such knowledge for the promotion of human welfare. While pursuing these objectives, they make every effort to protect the welfare of those who seek their services and of the research participants that may be the object of study. They use their skills only for purposes consistent with these values and do not knowingly permit their misuse by others. While demanding for themselves freedom of inquiry and communication, psychologists accept the responsibility this freedom requires: competence, objectivity in the application of skills, and concern for the best interests of clients, colleagues, students, research participants, and society. In the pursuit of these ideals, psychologists subscribe to principles in the following areas: 1. Responsibility, 2. Competence, 3. Moral and Legal Standards, 4. Public Statements, 5. Confidentiality, 6. Welfare

Ethical principles of psychologists. *American Psychologist, 36*(6), 633–638. Copyright © 1981 by the American Psychological Association. Reprinted by permission.

This version of the Ethical Principles of Psychologists (formerly entitled Ethical Standards of Psychologists) was adopted by the American Psychological Association's Council of Representatives on January 24, 1981. The revised Ethical Principles contain both substantive and grammatical changes in each of the nine ethical principles constituting the Ethical Standards of Psychologists previously adopted by the Council of Representatives in 1979, plus a new tenth principle entitled Care and Use of Animals. Inquiries concerning the Ethical Principles of Psychologists should be addressed to the Administrative Officer for Ethics, American Psychological Association, 1200 Seventeenth Street, N.W., Washington, DC 20036.

These revised Ethical Principles apply to psychologists, to students of psychology, and to others who do work of a psychological nature under the supervision of a psychologist. They are also intended for the guidance of nonmembers of the Association who are engaged in psychological research or practice.

Any complaints of unethical conduct filed after January 24, 1981, shall be governed by this 1981 revision. However, conduct (a) complained about after January 24, 1981, but which occurred prior to that date, and (b) not considered unethical under prior versions of the principles but considered unethical under the 1981 revision, shall not be deemed a violation of ethical principles. Any complaints pending as of January 24, 1981, shall be governed either by the 1979 or by the 1981 version of the Ethical Principles, at the sound discretion of the Committee on Scientific and Professional Ethics and Conduct.

of the Consumer, 7. Professional Relationships, 8. Assessment Techniques, 9. Research With Human Participants, and 10. Care and Use of Animals.

Acceptance of membership in the American Psychological Association commits the member to adherence to these principles.

Psychologists cooperate with duly constituted committees of the American Psychological Association, in particular, the Committee on Scientific and Professional Ethics and Conduct, by responding to inquiries promptly and completely. Members also respond promptly and completely to inquiries from duly constituted state association ethics committees and professional standards review committees.

Principle 1
RESPONSIBILITY

In providing services, psychologists maintain the highest standards of their profession. They accept responsibility for the consequences of their acts and make every effort to ensure that their services are used appropriately.

a. As scientists, psychologists accept responsibility for the selection of their research topics and the methods used in investigation, analysis, and reporting. They plan their research in ways to minimize the possibility that their findings will be misleading. They provide thorough discussion of the limitations of their data, especially where their work touches on social policy or might be construed to the detriment of persons in specific age, sex, ethnic, socioeconomic, or other social groups. In publishing reports of their work, they never suppress disconfirming data, and they acknowledge the existence of alternative hypotheses and explanations of their findings. Psychologists take credit only for work they have actually done.

b. Psychologists clarify in advance with all appropriate persons and agencies the expectations for sharing and utilizing research data. They avoid relationships that may limit their objectivity or create a conflict of interest. Interference with the milieu in which data are collected is kept to a minimum.

c. Psychologists have the responsibility to attempt to prevent distortion, misuse, or suppression of psychological findings by the institution or agency of which they are employees.

d. As members of governmental or other organizational bodies, psychologists remain accountable as individuals to the highest standards of their profession.

e. As teachers, psychologists recognize their primary obligation to help others acquire knowledge and skill. They maintain high standards of scholarship by presenting psychological information objectively, fully, and accurately.

f. As practitioners, psychologists know that they bear a heavy social responsibility because their recommendations and professional actions may alter the lives of others. They are alert to personal, social, organizational, financial, or political situations and pressures that might lead to misuse of their influence.

Principle 2
COMPETENCE

The maintenance of high standards of competence is a responsibility shared by all psychologists in the interest of the public and the profession as a whole. Psychologists recognize the boundaries of their competence and the limitations of their techniques. They only provide services and only use techniques for which they are qualified by training and experience. In those areas in which recognized standards do not yet exist, psychologists take whatever precautions are necessary to protect the welfare of their clients. They maintain knowledge of current scientific and professional information related to the services they render.

a. Psychologists accurately represent their competence, education, training, and experience. They claim as evidence of educational qualifications only those degrees obtained from institutions acceptable under the Bylaws and Rules of Council of the American Psychological Association.

b. As teachers, psychologists perform their duties on the basis of careful preparation so that their instruction is accurate, current, and scholarly.

c. Psychologists recognize the need for continuing education and are open to new procedures and changes in expectations and values over time.

d. Psychologists recognize differences among people, such as those that may be associated with age, sex, socioeconomic, and ethnic backgrounds. When necessary they obtain training, experience, or counsel to assure competent service or research relating to such persons.

e. Psychologists responsible for decisions involving individuals or policies based on test results have an understanding of psychological or educational measurement, validation problems, and test research.

f. Psychologists recognize that personal problems and conflicts may interfere with professional effectiveness. Accordingly, they refrain from undertaking any activity in which their personal problems are likely to lead to inadequate performance or harm to a client, colleague, student, or research participant. If engaged in such activity when they become aware of their personal problems, they seek competent professional assistance to determine whether they should suspend, terminate, or limit the scope of their professional and/or scientific activities.

Principle 3
MORAL AND LEGAL STANDARDS

Psychologists' moral and ethical standards of behavior are a personal matter to the same degree as they are for any other citizen, except as these may compromise the fulfillment of their professional responsibilities or reduce the public trust in psychology and psychologists. Regarding their own behavior, psychologists are sensitive to prevailing community standards and to the possible impact that conformity to or deviation from these standards may have upon the quality of their performance as psychologists. Psychologists are also aware of the possible impact of their public behavior upon the ability of colleagues to perform their professional duties.

a. As teachers, psychologists are aware of the fact that their personal values may affect the selection and presentation of instructional materials. When dealing with topics that may give offense, they recognize and respect the diverse attitudes that students may have toward such materials.

b. As employees or employers, psychologists do not engage in or condone practices that are inhumane or that result in illegal or unjustifiable actions. Such practices include, but are not limited to, those based on considerations of race, handicap, age, gender, sexual preference, religion, or national origin in hiring, promotion, or training.

c. In their professional roles, psychologists avoid any action that will violate or diminish the legal and civil rights of clients or of others who may be affected by their actions.

d. As practitioners and researchers, psychologists act in accord with Association standards and guidelines related to practice and to the conduct of research with human beings and animals. In the ordinary course of events, psychologists adhere to relevant governmental laws and institutional regulations. When federal, state, provincial, organizational, or institutional laws, regulations, or practices are in conflict with Association standards and guidelines, psychologists make known their commitment to Association standards and guidelines and, whenever possible, work toward a resolution of the conflict. Both practitioners and researchers are concerned with the development of such legal and quasi-legal regulations as best serve the public interest, and they work toward changing existing regulations that are not beneficial to the public interest.

Principle 4
PUBLIC STATEMENTS

Public statements, announcements of services, advertising, and promotional activities of psychologists serve the purpose of helping the public make informed judgments and choices. Psychologists represent accurately and objectively their professional qualifications, affiliations, and functions, as well as those of the institutions or organizations with which they or the statements may be associated. In public statements providing psychological information or professional opinions or providing information about the availability of psychological products, publications, and services, psychologists base their statements on scientifically acceptable psychological findings and techniques with full recognition of the limits and uncertainties of such evidence.

    a.   When announcing or advertising professional services, psychologists may list the following information to describe the provider and services provided: name, highest relevant academic degree earned from a regionally accredited institution, date, type, and level of certification or licensure, diplomate status, APA membership status, address, telephone number, office hours, a brief listing of the type of psychological services offered, an appropriate presentation of fee information, foreign languages spoken, and policy with regard to third-party payments. Additional relevant or important consumer information may be included if not prohibited by other sections of these Ethical Principles.

    b.   In announcing or advertising the availability of psychological products, publications, or services, psychologists do not present their affiliation with any organization in a manner that falsely implies sponsorship or certification by that organization. In particular and for example, psychologists do not state APA membership or fellow status in a way to suggest that such status implies specialized professional competence or qualifications. Public statements include, but are not limited to, communication by means of periodical, book, list, directory, television, radio, or motion picture. They do not contain (i) a false, fraudulent, misleading, deceptive, or unfair statement; (ii) a misinterpretation of fact or a statement likely to mislead or deceive because in context it makes only a partial disclosure of relevant facts; (iii) a testimonial from a patient regarding the quality of a psychologists' services or products; (iv) a statement intended or likely to create false or unjustified expectations of favorable results; (v) a statement implying unusual, unique, or one-of-a-kind abilities; (vi) a statement intended or likely to appeal to a client's fears, anxieties, or emotions concerning the possible results of failure to obtain the offered services; (vii) a statement concerning the comparative desirability of offered services; (viii) a statement of direct solicitation of individual clients.

    c.   Psychologists do not compensate or give anything of value to a representative of the press, radio, television, or other communication medium in anticipation of or in return for professional publicity in a news item. A paid advertisement must be identified as such, unless it is apparent from the context that it is a paid advertisement. If communicated to the public by use of radio or television, an advertisement is prerecorded and approved for broadcast by the psychologist, and a recording of the actual transmission is retained by the psychologist.

    d.   Announcements or advertisements of "personal growth groups," clinics, and agencies give a clear statement of purpose and a clear description of the experiences to be provided. The education, training, and experience of the staff members are appropriately specified.

    e.   Psychologists associated with the development or promotion of psychological devices, books, or other products offered for commercial sale make reasonable efforts to ensure that announcements and advertisements are presented in a professional, scientifically acceptable, and factually informative manner.

f.   Psychologists do not participate for personal gain in commercial announcements or advertisements recommending to the public the purchase or use of proprietary or single-source products or services when that participation is based solely upon their identification as psychologists.

g.   Psychologists present the science of psychology and offer their services, products, and publications fairly and accurately, avoiding misrepresentation through sensationalism, exaggeration, or superficiality. Psychologists are guided by the primary obligation to aid the public in developing informed judgments, opinions, and choices.

h.   As teachers, psychologists ensure that statements in catalogs and course outlines are accurate and not misleading, particularly in terms of subject matter to be covered, bases for evaluating progress, and the nature of course experiences. Announcements, brochures, or advertisements describing workshops, seminars, or other educational programs accurately describe the audience for which the program is intended as well as eligibility requirements, educational objectives, and nature of the materials to be covered. These announcements also accurately represent the education, training, and experience of the psychologists presenting the programs and any fees involved.

i.   Public announcements or advertisements soliciting research participants in which clinical services or other professional services are offered as an inducement make clear the nature of the services as well as the costs and other obligations to be accepted by participants in the research.

j.   A psychologist accepts the obligation to correct others who represent the psychologist's professional qualifications, or associations with products or services, in a manner incompatible with these guidelines.

k.   Individual diagnostic and therapeutic services are provided only in the context of a professional psychological relationship. When personal advice is given by means of public lectures or demonstrations, newspaper or magazine articles, radio or television programs, mail, or similar media, the psychologist utilizes the most current relevant data and exercises the highest level of professional judgment.

l.   Products that are described or presented by means of public lectures or demonstrations, newspaper or magazine articles, radio or television programs, or similar media meet the same recognized standards as exist for products used in the context of a professional relationship.

Principle 5
CONFIDENTIALITY

Psychologists have a primary obligation to respect the confidentiality of information obtained from persons in the course of their work as psychologists. They reveal such information to others only with the consent of the person or the person's legal representative, except in those unusual circumstances in which not to do so would result in clear danger to the person or to others. Where appropriate, psychologists inform their clients of the legal limits of confidentiality.

a.   Information obtained in clinical or consulting relationships, or evaluative data concerning children, students, employees, and others, is discussed only for professional purposes and only with persons clearly concerned with the case. Written and oral reports present only data germane to the purposes of the evaluation, and every effort is made to avoid undue invasion of privacy.

b.   Psychologists who present personal information obtained during the course of professional work in writings, lectures, or other public forums either obtain adequate prior consent to do so or adequately disguise all identifying information.

c.   Psychologists make provisions for maintaining confidentiality in the storage and disposal of records.

d.   When working with minors or other persons who are unable to give voluntary, informed consent, psychologists take special care to protect these persons' best interests.

Principle 6
WELFARE OF THE CONSUMER

Psychologists respect the integrity and protect the welfare of the people and groups with whom they work. When conflicts of interest arise between clients and psychologists' employing institutions, psychologists clarify the nature and direction of their loyalties and responsibilities and keep all parties informed of their commitments. Psychologists fully inform consumers as to the purpose and nature of an evaluative, treatment, educational, or training procedure, and they freely acknowledge that clients, students, or participants in research have freedom of choice with regard to participation.

a.   Psychologists are continually cognizant of their own needs and of their potentially influential position vis-à-vis persons such as clients, students, and subordinates. They avoid exploiting the trust and dependency of such persons. Psychologists make every effort to avoid dual relationships that could impair their professional judgment or increase the risk of exploitation. Examples of such dual relationships include, but are not limited to, research with and treatment of employees, students, supervisees, close friends, or relatives. Sexual intimacies with clients are unethical.

b.   When a psychologist agrees to provide services to a client at the request of a third party, the psychologist assumes the responsibility of clarifying the nature of the relationships to all parties concerned.

c.   Where the demands of an organization require psychologists to violate these Ethical Principles, psychologists clarify the nature of the conflict between the demands and these principles. They inform all parties of psychologists' ethical responsibilities and take appropriate action.

d.   Psychologists make advance financial arrangements that safeguard the best interests of and are clearly understood by their clients. They neither give nor receive any remuneration for referring clients for professional services. They contribute a portion of their services to work for which they receive little or no financial return.

e.   Psychologists terminate a clinical or consulting relationship when it is reasonably clear that the consumer is not benefiting from it. They offer to help the consumer locate alternative sources of assistance.

Principle 7
PROFESSIONAL RELATIONSHIPS

Psychologists act with due regard for the needs, special competencies, and obligations of their colleagues in psychology and other professions. They respect the prerogatives and obligations of the institutions or organizations with which these other colleagues are associated.

a.   Psychologists understand the areas of competence of related professions. They make full use of all the professional, technical, and administrative resources that serve the best interests of consumers. The absence of formal relationships with other professional workers does not relieve psychologists of the responsibility of securing for their clients the best possible professional service, nor does it relieve them of the obligation to exercise foresight, diligence, and tact in obtaining the complementary or alternative assistance needed by clients.

b.   Psychologists know and take into account the traditions and practices of other professional groups with whom they work and cooperate fully with such groups. If a person is receiving similar services from another professional, psychologists do not offer their own services directly to such a person. If a psychologist is contacted by a person who is already receiving similar services from another professional, the psychologist carefully considers that professional relationship and proceeds with caution and sensitivity to the therapeutic issues as well as the client's welfare. The psychologist discusses these issues with the client so as to minimize the risk of confusion and conflict.

c.   Psychologists who employ or supervise other professionals or professionals in training accept the obligation to facilitate the further professional development of these individuals. They provide appropriate working conditions, timely evaluations, constructive consultation, and experience opportunities.

d.   Psychologists do not exploit their professional relationships with clients, supervisees, students, employees, or research participants sexually or otherwise. Psychologists do not condone or engage in sexual harassment. Sexual harassment is defined as deliberate or repeated comments, gestures, or physical contacts of a sexual nature that are unwanted by the recipient.

e.   In conducting research in institutions or organizations, psychologists secure appropriate authorization to conduct such research. They are aware of their obligations to future research workers and ensure that host institutions receive adequate information about the research and proper acknowledgment of their contributions.

f.   Publication credit is assigned to those who have contributed to a publication in proportion to their professional contributions. Major contributions of a professional character made by several persons to a common project are recognized by joint authorship, with the individual who made the principal contribution listed first. Minor contributions of a professional character and extensive clerical or similar nonprofessional assistance may be acknowledged in footnotes or in an introductory statement. Acknowledgment through specific citations is made for unpublished as well as published material that has directly influenced the research or writing. Psychologists who compile and edit material of others for publication publish the material in the name of the originating group, if appropriate, with their own name appearing as chairperson or editor. All contributors are to be acknowledged and named.

g.   When psychologists know of an ethical violation by another psychologist, they informally attempt to resolve the issue by bringing the behavior to the attention of the psychologist. If the misconduct is of a minor nature and/or appears to be due to lack of sensitivity, knowledge, or experience, such an informal solution is usually appropriate. Such informal corrective efforts are made with sensitivity to any rights to confidentiality involved. If the violation does not seem amenable to an informal solution, or is of a more serious nature, psychologists bring it to the attention of the appropriate local, state, and/or national committee on professional ethics and conduct.

Principle 8
ASSESSMENT TECHNIQUES

In the development, publication, and utilization of psychological assessment techniques, psychologists make every effort to promote the welfare and best interests of the client. They guard against the misuse of assessment results. They respect the client's right to know the results, the interpretations made, and the bases for their conclusions and recommendations. Psychologists make every effort to maintain the security of tests and other assessment techniques within limits of legal mandates. They strive to ensure the appropriate use of assessment techniques by others.

a.   In using assessment techniques, psychologists respect the right of clients to have full explanations of the nature and purpose of the techniques in language the clients can understand, unless an explicit exception to this right has been agreed upon in advance. When the explanations are to be provided by others, psychologists establish procedures for ensuring the adequacy of these explanations.

b.   Psychologists responsible for the development and standardization of psychological tests and other assessment techniques utilize established scientific procedures and observe the relevant APA standards.

c.   In reporting assessment results, psychologists indicate any reservations that exist regarding validity or reliability because of the circumstances of the assessment or the inappropriateness of the norms for the person tested. Psychologists strive to ensure that the results of assessments and their interpretations are not misused by others.

d. Psychologists recognize that assessment results may become obsolete. They make every effort to avoid and prevent the misuse of obsolete measures.

e. Psychologists offering scoring and interpretation services are able to produce appropriate evidence for the validity of the programs and procedures used in arriving at interpretations. The public offering of an automated interpretation service is considered a professional-to-professional consultation. Psychologists make every effort to avoid misuse of assessment reports.

f. Psychologists do not encourage or promote the use of psychological assessment techniques by inappropriately trained or otherwise unqualified persons through teaching, sponsorship, or supervision.

Principle 9
RESEARCH WITH HUMAN PARTICIPANTS

The decision to undertake research rests upon a considered judgment by the individual psychologist about how best to contribute to psychological science and human welfare. Having made the decision to conduct research, the psychologist considers alternative directions in which research energies and resources might be invested. On the basis of this consideration, the psychologist carries out the investigation with respect and concern for the dignity and welfare of the people who participate and with cognizance of federal and state regulations and professional standards governing the conduct of research with human participants.

a. In planning a study, the investigator has the responsibility to make a careful evaluation of its ethical acceptability. To the extent that the weighing of scientific and human values suggests a compromise of any principle, the investigator incurs a correspondingly serious obligation to seek ethical advice and to observe stringent safeguards to protect the rights of human participants.

b. Considering whether a participant in a planned study will be a "subject at risk" or a "subject at minimal risk," according to recognized standards, is of primary ethical concern to the investigator.

c. The investigator always retains the responsibility for ensuring ethical practice in research. The investigator is also responsible for the ethical treatment of research participants by collaborators, assistants, students, and employees, all of whom, however, incur similar obligations.

d. Except in minimal-risk research, the investigator establishes a clear and fair agreement with research participants, prior to their participation, that clarifies the obligations and responsibilities of each. The investigator has the obligation to honor all promises and commitments included in that agreement. The investigator informs the participants of all aspects of the research that might reasonably be expected to influence willingness to participate and explains all other aspects of the research about which the participants inquire. Research with children or with participants who have impairments that would limit understanding and/or communication requires special safeguarding procedures.

e. Methodological requirements of a study may make the use of concealment or deception necessary. Before conducting such a study, the investigator has a special responsibility to (i) determine whether the use of such techniques is justified by the study's prospective scientific, educational, or applied value; (ii) determine whether alternative procedures are available that do not use concealment or deception; and (iii) ensure that the participants are provided with sufficient explanation as soon as possible.

f. The investigator respects the individual's freedom to decline to participate in or to withdraw from the research at any time. The obligation to protect this freedom requires careful thought and consideration when the investigator is in a position of authority or influence over the participant. Such positions of authority include, but are not limited to, situations in which research participation is required as part of employment or in which the participant is a student, client, or employee of the investigator.

g.   The investigator protects the participant from physical and mental discomfort, harm, and danger that may arise from research procedures. If risks of such consequences exist, the investigator informs the participant of that fact. Research procedures likely to cause serious or lasting harm to a participant are not used unless the failure to use these procedures might expose the participant to risk of greater harm, or unless the research has great potential benefit and fully informed and voluntary consent is obtained from each participant. The participant should be informed of procedures for contacting the investigator within a reasonable time period following participation should stress, potential harm, or related questions or concerns arise.

h.   After the data are collected, the investigator provides the participant with information about the nature of the study and attempts to remove any misconceptions that may have arisen. Where scientific or humane values justify delaying or withholding this information, the investigator incurs a special responsibility to monitor the research and to ensure that there are no damaging consequences for the participant.

i.   Where research procedures result in undesirable consequences for the individual participant, the investigator has the responsibility to detect and remove or correct these consequences, including long-term effects.

j.   Information obtained about a research participant during the course of an investigation is confidential unless otherwise agreed upon in advance. When the possibility exists that others may obtain access to such information, this possibility, together with the plans for protecting confidentiality, is explained to the participant as part of the procedure for obtaining informed consent.

Principle 10
CARE AND USE OF ANIMALS

An investigator of animal behavior strives to advance understanding of basic behavioral principles and/or to contribute to the improvement of human health and welfare. In seeking these ends, the investigator ensures the welfare of animals and treats them humanely. Laws and regulations notwithstanding, an animal's immediate protection depends upon the scientist's own conscience.

a.   The acquisition, care, use, and disposal of all animals are in compliance with current federal, state or provincial, and local laws and regulations.

b.   A psychologist trained in research methods and experienced in the care of laboratory animals closely supervises all procedures involving animals and is responsible for ensuring appropriate consideration of their comfort, health, and humane treatment.

c.   Psychologists ensure that all individuals using animals under their supervision have received explicit instruction in experimental methods and in the care, maintenance, and handling of the species being used. Responsibilities and activities of individuals participating in a research project are consistent with their respective competencies.

d.   Psychologists make every effort to minimize discomfort, illness, and pain of animals. A procedure subjecting animals to pain, stress, or privation is used only when an alternative procedure is unavailable and the goal is justified by its prospective scientific, educational, or applied value. Surgical procedures are performed under appropriate anesthesia; techniques to avoid infection and minimize pain are followed during and after surgery.

e.   When it is appropriate that the animal's life be terminated, it is done rapidly and painlessly.

Appendix B:
Self-Evaluation
Checklists for
Administrators
and Clinicians

Use the following checklist to review your practices, plans, procedures and knowledge by placing a check mark in the appropriate column.

I. SELF-EVALUATION CHECKLIST FOR ADMINISTRATORS
Chapter 1

	YES	NO
1. Have you decided what your service philosophy is and have you written it down for staff use?		
2. Have you developed a mission statement for your clinic that encompasses the scope of services you plan to provide?		
3. Have you developed appropriate and measurable goals for clinic operation?		
4. Have you decided what type of clinic (specialty, model, or comprehensive) you plan to operate?		
5. Do you know the American Psychological Association requirements for providing psychological services?		
6. Have you decided how you will determine if quality services are being provided by your staff?		
7. Have you planned ways to prevent "burnout" in your staff?		
8. Have you decided how comprehensive the services offered will be?		
9. Have you decided what the standards of operation are to which staff will be expected to adhere?		
10. Have you decided whether or not to incorporate?		

Chapter 2

	YES	NO
1. Have specific funding sources and funds been identified to support the clinic for the first/next year of operation?		
2. Have you made contacts with potential funding sources in the past 6 months?		

3. Do you have a plan for marketing clinic services?
4. If expansion of services is planned or new services are to be offered, has a marketing approach been developed?
5. Have you visited or consulted with other clinic administrators to obtain information on how facilities are used by staff and clients?
6. Have you conducted a current needs assessment with staff to determine whether: a) facilities designated for their use are adequate? b) facilities for use with clients are adequate?
7. Have you determined that the facilities designated for client use are adequate?
8. Have you determined needs and allocated funds for the purchase of specialized items of furniture, equipment, and materials?
9. Are equipment inventories and equipment service records being maintained?
10. Have procedures been developed for storing and maintaining nonconsumable materials?
11. Is an inventory of consumable materials being maintained so that replacement materials are ordered and available when needed?
12. Do you have a computer system in operation and is it adequate for current and future needs?

Chapter 3

	YES	NO

1. Has a survey been conducted to determine what psychological services for children and adolescents are needed in your geographical area?
2. Have staff resources (number, skill levels, etc.) been identified to ensure that services offered can be adequately delivered?
3. Have position descriptions been prepared for all staff?
4. Are or will position descriptions for staff be updated on an annual basis?
5. Has a plan been developed for how and when staff evaluations are to be conducted?
6. Is the staff evaluation plan workable, or should it be modified?
7. Have written standard operating procedures been developed and/or reviewed for dealing with staff issues (e.g., hiring, grievance, termination)?
8. Do you have a systematic plan for maintaining and improving staff morale and motivation levels?

Chapter 4

	YES	NO

1. Have activities been identified for informing the public about available clinic services?
2. Are there current materials (e.g., brochures, pamphlets) available for dissemination that describe clinic services?
3. Have client admissions criteria been established?
4. Have you determined client fee schedules, billing practices, and fee collection procedures?
5. Have referral and other preservice forms been developed?
6. Have procedures for handling clinic referrals been developed?
7. Are all clinic staff acquainted with emergency referral practices and procedures?

8. Has a plan for client appointment scheduling been developed or updated?

9. Are all clinic staff familiar with clinic practices and procedures related to client visits?

Chapter 5

	YES	NO

1. Are you or your staff involved in the dissemination of information or guidelines to the public for referral of children/adolescents for professional services?

2. Are there established clinic policies for deciding which family members of a child/adolescent client are to be involved in the assessment/evaluation process?

3. Are there clinic policies on whether or under what circumstances family members are to be included in client treatment?

4. Is your staff well acquainted with state and community child abuse reporting laws?

5. Are there written clinic policies and procedures on reporting child abuse available for staff?

6. Are staff provided in-service training or given opportunities to learn about symptoms of physical and sexual abuse and treatment approaches?

7. Have you identified staff members' areas of expertise that could be useful in providing training to others?

8. Does your staff have access to a variety of training materials (e.g., programs, tapes, books) to facilitate their provision of parent training?

Chapter 6

	YES	NO

1. Have you obtained and made accessible to staff current information (e.g., books) on child/adolescent assessment strategies and issues?

2. Can you identify particular staff strengths and weaknesses in assessment skills?

3. Do you support staff attendance at workshops or professional meetings where their assessment skills could be expanded?

4. Do you plan for regular in-services to be conducted for staff on assessment issues and strategies?

5. Have you made contractual arrangements with professionals outside the clinic to provide assessments for clients when staff in the clinic do not have requisite assessment skills?

6. Have you budgeted for the purchase of new or replacement nonconsumable and consumable assessment materials?

7. Do you listen to and follow through on suggestions or recommendations from staff on acquisition of current assessment materials?

8. Have you developed policies and procedures on assessment/evaluation for staff to follow?

9. Have you assigned responsibilities for maintaining assessment materials in adequate condition?

10. Have you planned for efficient and safe storage of assessment materials?

11. Are assessment materials located where they are easily obtainable for staff use?

Chapter 7

	YES	NO
1. Do you support, promote, and budget for professional growth experiences for clinicians in client treatment areas through in-service training?		
2. Do you budget for provision of current resource materials (e.g., books, journals) that can be used by clinicians?		
3. Are clinicians allotted time for preparing treatment plans and client contact reports?		
4. Has a standard treatment plan format been developed for use by all clinicians?		
5. Is there a review process for checking and monitoring treatment plans and contact notes?		
6. Are clinicians expected to quantifiably or through other means demonstrate treatment effectiveness?		
7. Do you require therapists to write goals in measurable terms?		
8. Are peer reviews conducted to determine the appropriateness of the treatment provided?		
9. Do you arrange for in-service training to improve service providers skills in facilitating the generalization of therapy progress from the clinic into the client's home?		

Chapter 8

	YES	NO
1. Has a system been developed for assigning clients to therapists within their areas of expertise?		
2. Are staff encouraged to involve parental guardians in treatment decisions for child/adolescent clients?		
3. Is there a written clinic policy on charges for telephone contacts between service providers, clients, and client family members, and are staff and client families aware of the policy?		
4. Have you completed a resource chart (similar to that shown on Form 8.1) listing staff, their orientations, and their expertise on common child/adolescent referral problems?		
5. Are there written clinic policies and procedures on handling appointment changes and cancellations?		
6. Has a reference list of clinic materials been prepared and disseminated to professional service providers?		
7. Does the clinic maintain a file of copies of successful treatment plans (without specific client identification) for reference for common child/adolescent referral problems?		
8. Do you encourage appropriately trained clinicians to provide family and/or group therapy?		
9. Do you have a clinic policy for problem solving when a client is not making progress?		
10. Are you informed on the current treatment of choice for commonly referred problems?		

Chapter 9

	YES	NO
1. Have you developed specific formats for assessment/evaluation case summary reports?		
2. Have staff received training in report writing style and content adopted within the clinic?		

3. Have staff been trained on using equipment that would expedite written report preparation and editing (e.g., computers, dictating equipment)?

4. Have you budgeted for the purchase of new or replacement equipment for report preparation such as dictation instruments or computers?

5. Is there a process whereby written reports are reviewed and edited before dissemination?

6. Have you explored or adopted cost-effective procedures to enhance report preparation and delivery?

7. Is there a standard (e.g., feedback questionnaire) for obtaining feedback on client satisfaction relating to written reports received?

8. Are staff regularly consulted about more efficient methods for processing written reports?

Chapter 10

	YES	NO
1. Have you identified the types of technical assistance and consultation that will be provided by the clinic and established policies on staff involvement?		
2. Do you have a system of determining fees to be charged for provision of technical assistance and consultation?		
3. Have policies been developed to allow clinic staff consultation time independent from the clinic?		
4. Do you seek contractual arrangements for consultation or technical assistance services by clinic staff?		
5. Have you identified staff members with particular skills who could be used for consultation/technical assistance?		
6. Have you determined how much consultation or technical assistance can be incorporated into services delivery without disrupting the quality of clinic functioning?		
7. Have procedures been developed for billing and payment collection for consultation services?		
8. Are staff prepared to deal with the "stressors" related to being in a consultant role?		
9. Is there a way of ensuring that staff assigned to consultant roles are adequately prepared to represent the clinic (i.e., do they have requisite social skills)?		

Chapter 11

	YES	NO
1. Do you have a written list of client rights?		
2. Do you have/know the limits of confidentiality used at your clinic?		
3. Do you have available copies of relevant federal and state laws, standards, principles, and regulations that are pertinent to serving children and adolescents?		
4. Are all of your staff familiar with your client safeguard procedures?		
5. Do you have written procedures concerning informed consent?		
6. Do you have a set of clinic ethical procedures for use by all staff?		
7. Have you provided staff with training on the appreciation of ethical principles and standards within the last year?		
8. Do you have an internal and external peer review system?		
9. Do you have a functional billing agreement procedure and form?		

10. Do you maintain appropriate levels of liability insurance coverage for all staff?

Chapter 12

	YES	NO
1. Are there unmet child and adolescent needs for psychological and related services that could be addressed by your staff?		
2. Have you contacted your state senators and members of the U.S. Congress to advocate for child and adolescent mental health needs?		
3. Have you made presentations in the community to increase citizens' awareness of child and adolescent mental health needs?		
4. Are you familiar with precedents set in serving those who have handicaps, which could serve as models for meeting the psychological needs of children and adolescents?		
5. Do you have available for staff use a set of functional child and adolescent rights statements?		
6. Do you have a human rights committee affiliated with your clinic?		
7. Do you allow community groups who advocate for child and adolescent mental health needs to use your facilities?		
8. Do your clinic publications increase public awareness of child and adolescent needs?		

Use the following checklist to review your practices, plans, procedures and knowledge by placing a check mark in the appropriate column.

II. SELF-EVALUATION CHECKLIST FOR CLINICIANS
Chapter 1

	YES	NO
1. Are you familiar with the service philosophy to which you are to adhere?		
2. Are you familiar with the mission and goals of the clinic?		
3. Are you adequately trained to do the job for which you were hired?		
4. Are you familiar with the American Psychological Association's *Standards for Providers of Psychological Services?*		
5. Are you appropriately licensed?		
6. Do you know how the quality of the services you provide will be evaluated?		

Chapter 2

	YES	NO
1. Do you know the marketing plan of the clinic in which you work?		
2. Are you actively involved or associated with community groups or organizations that serve a public relations function?		
3. Are staff facilities within the clinic adequate?		
4. Do you inform administrators of problems with the facilities designated for clients' use?		
5. Have you taken time to review current catalogs from test and book publishers to learn about new or revised professional materials?		
6. Do you make recommendations to administrators for purchase of new or replacement equipment and materials?		

7. Do you consistently check test kits or equipment after use and report problems to ensure test readiness for storage and subsequent use?

8. Have you received or requested training on use of the clinic computer system for clinical purposes?

9. Are you sensitive to how your appearance, dress, and behavior can positively or negatively affect potential clients and referral sources?

Chapter 3

	YES	NO

1. Are you involved in administrative decisions on staff replacements, changes in staff assignments, or decisions on need for additional staff?

2. Do you have a current position description that adequately describes your responsibilities?

3. Are you satisfied with the way staff evaluations are currently conducted?

4. Do you provide administrators with suggestions on how staff evaluations could be improved or changed?

5. Do you have opportunities to provide evaluations on the performance of supervisors and administrators?

6. Are you acquainted with policies and procedures related to staff issues (e.g., hiring, grievance, harassment, termination)?

7. Do you have access to written policies and procedures pertaining to standard operations within the clinic?

8. Have you been informed of your rights as a staff member?

9. Can you identify ways that communication could be enhanced within the clinic?

10. Do you take responsibility to provide feedback to supervisors?

11. Are you aware of what liability insurance coverage is provided through the clinic for you?

12. Are you involved in planning or preparation activities for changes in clinic practices and procedures on at least an annual basis?

Chapter 4

	YES	NO

1. Are you involved in any activities to enhance public awareness of clinic services?

2. Do you know what brochures, pamphlets, or written materials are available that describe clinic services?

3. Are you acquainted with established client admissions criteria?

4. Do you understand client fee schedules, billing practices, and fee collection procedures?

5. Do you have input on what preservice forms are provided to clients?

6. Are you acquainted with clinic emergency referral practices and procedures?

7. Is the client appointment scheduling process workable for you?

8. Are your preappointment responsibilities well defined?

9. Do you attend to client and client family courtesies as an established practice?

Chapter 5

	YES	NO

1. Are you involved in the dissemination of information guidelines to the public for when parents/legal guardians should seek professional services for their child/adolescent?
2. Do you have a process for determining which family members of a client are to be involved in assessment/evaluation procedures?
3. Do you have a professional viewpoint on whether or under what circumstances family members are to be included in direct treatment?
4. Are you well acquainted with child abuse reporting laws in your state and community?
5. Do you have access to written clinic policies and practices on reporting child abuse?
6. Do you have information on child/adolescent behavioral symptoms that are suggestive of physical and sexual abuse?
7. Do you know current research findings on effective treatment techniques for child/adolescent sexual abuse victims?
8. Have you identified areas of expertise where you could provide training to family members of clients?
9. Do you seek opportunities to expand your repertoire of skills so that you could be involved in individual or group training experiences?
10. Are you open to dealing with a wide diversity of family constellations?
11. Do you understand family social and communication systems?

Chapter 6

	YES	NO

1. Do you have access to current reference materials (e.g., books within the clinic) for information on assessment/evaluation issues and strategies?
2. Can you identify your particular strengths in assessing child/adolescent clients?
3. Can you identify assessment/evaluation strategies where you feel you need greater expertise?
4. Are you familiar with clinic policies and practices on accepted assessment/evaluation strategies?
5. Are you willing to consult or request services from other service providers within the clinic on assessments in areas outside your expertise?
6. Does your clinic have arrangements with professionals outside of the clinic for meeting assessment needs that cannot be obtained within the clinic?
7. Do you make recommendations to administrators about new or replacement assessment instruments that are needed in the clinic?
8. Do you request inservice training or attend workshops to increase your assessment skills?
9. Do you seek peer review of your assessment/evaluation findings with colleagues or supervisors?
10. Do you participate in discussions of assessment/evaluation issues and strategies with other professionals?
11. Are you cognizant of and sensitive to issues on reporting

assessment/evaluation findings to parents and child/adolescent clients?

12. Are assessment materials in the clinic maintained in an appropriate manner?

13. Do you have easy access to assessment materials when needed?

Chapter 7

	YES	NO

1. Are you able to identify your particular strengths in child/adolescent treatment approaches or strategies?

2. Can you identify treatment areas or approaches where you could benefit from training?

3. Do clinic administrators support or promote professional growth experiences related to client treatment?

4. Do you have access to current resource materials (e.g., books, journals, papers) within the clinic for reference on child/adolescent treatment related to specific disorders or problems?

5. Do you maintain a personal library of current resource materials (e.g., books, journals) for reference on child/adolescent treatment?

6. Do you allot regular time to advance your knowledge of child/adolescent treatment through reading and attendance at professional meetings?

7. Do you consult with colleagues or professionals outside of the clinic on client treatment when needed?

8. Do you refer clients to colleagues or professionals external to the clinic for treatment areas outside of your expertise?

9. Has your clinic developed a standard treatment plan format?

10. Do you develop treatment plans for every client?

11. Are there clinic policies and procedures for review of client treatment plans (e.g., peer reviews)?

12. Are contact notes dictated or written following each client or client-related contact?

13. Do you write treatment goals in measurable terms so that treatment effectiveness for each client can be evaluated?

Chapter 8

	YES	NO

1. Are you well acquainted with normal child and adolescent development?

2. Do you challenge your assumptions about normal child development by reviewing current information in this area?

3. Could you identify ways of improving the client assignment process used in your clinic?

4. Do you involve parents/legal guardians in decisions on treatment approaches for child/adolescent clients?

5. Do you have a systematic way to determine whether to recommend group versus individual treatment for a client?

6. Do you feel that you adhere to the seven principles identified by Reisman (1973), discussed in this chapter?

7. Have you used telephone follow-up, and if so, is it effective?

8. Have you had training in behavioral therapy principles and intervention?

9. Are you aware of your expectations of the client and family of the client?

10. Are you acquainted with some of the most common child/adolescent referral problems and current "treatments of choice" for these problems?

Chapter 9

	YES	NO

1. Do you use standard formats for assessment/evaluation and case summary reports?
2. Are you familiar with the report writing style and content adopted within the clinic?
3. Do you know how to use dictation equipment or word processors for preparation of and/or editing of written reports?
4. Do you have access to equipment for report preparation?
5. Do you recommend ways to clinic administrators in which written reports could be improved or prepared more efficiently?
6. Have procedures been established for written report review and editing?
7. Do you check your written reports to see if you have avoided using the "potential communication inhibitors" described in Chapter 9?
8. Do you know whether report recipients are satisfied with your written reports?

Chapter 10

	YES	NO

1. If you are expected to provide consultation/technical assistance in your areas of expertise outside the clinic, are you allotted sufficient time and support?
2. Do you have or want administrator approval for you to engage in independent consultation?
3. Do you have skills that could be marketed for consultation purposes?
4. Do you think staff should provide consultation as a part of their regular job responsibilities?
5. Do you understand the different roles of a consultant?
6. Are you skilled in those processes required of a consultant?
7. Are you familiar with procedures for setting realistic consultation fees?
8. Are you familiar with procedures and forms for record keeping during consultation?
9. Are you prepared to confront a consultee's hostile staff?

Chapter 11

	YES	NO

1. Do you know your clinic's set of client rights statements?
2. Do you inform all children, adolescents, and their parents of the limits of confidentiality?
3. Do you have a working knowledge of federal and state laws, standards, principles, and regulations that pertain to serving children and adolescents?
4. Do you know your clinic's client safeguard procedures?
5. Do you know how to obtain informed consent from clients?
6. Do you know and adhere to your clinic's and your profession's ethical principles?

7. Are you satisfied that your clinic's internal and external peer review procedures will help protect you should litigation arise?

8. Do you need additional training on the application of ethical principles and standards?

9. Do you carry your own professional liability insurance, and do you know what coverage your clinic carries on your activities?

Chapter 12

	YES	NO

1. Are you aware of unmet child and adolescent needs for psychological and related services that you personally could help meet?

2. Have you advocated at the local, state, and national levels for regulations to facilitate meeting child and adolescent mental health needs?

3. Does your clinic's operation manual include appropriate statements of child and adolescent rights?

4. Does your clinic have a human rights committee, and if so, is it functional?

5. Do you affiliate with community groups who advocate for meeting child and adolescent mental health needs?

6. Do you help educate your administrators on the benefits of advocating for child and adolescent mental health needs?

7. Have you participated in activities that will help prevent psychological problems in children and adolescents?

Index

Administrators, self-evaluation for, 283–288
Admission
    criteria for, 66–67
    procedures for, 85, 87–88
Advertising, 24–25
Advocacy, 270–271
Agency referral form, 76–77
Agency satisfaction questionnaire form, 221–222
Appointment scheduling, 81–82
Assessment, 105–145, 180–195
    administration of, 139–141
    client cooperation in, 139–140
    communicating results of, 142–144
    and ethical principles, 279–280
    interpretation of, 141–142
    materials for, 39–41
    referrals for, 106
    rooms for, 28–30
    specific strategies for, 108–134
    standards for, 134, 141
    strategy selection for, 134–139
Attentional problems assessment, 137

Background information form, 80
Behavioral observation, 130–134
Billing, 69–75
    billing agreement form, 255

Case assignment, 84–85
Case staffing report form, 174
Checklists in assessment, 117–121
Child abuse, 96
Child/adolescent
    role of, 98–99
    see also Clients
Child development, 179–180

Client contact note form, 172
    see also Progress notes form
Client rights form, 246
Client satisfaction questionnaire forms, 175, 219–220
Clients
    assignment of, 181–182
    courtesies for, 88–90
    expectations of, 188–189
    identification of, 149–150, 183
    preparation of, 83–84, 87–88
    rights of, 243–250, 269
    see also Child/adolescent
Clinicians
    self-evaluation for, 288–293
Clinics, 1–2
    alternative, 3
    comprehensive, 4–5
    establishment of, 19–21
    goals of, 6–8
    mission of, 5–8
    naming of, 20–21
    philosophy of, 5–6, 107
    specialty, 3–5
Communication with clients, 89–90
Computers, 33–36, 216–217
Conduct problem assessment, 137
Confidentiality, 248–250, 277
Consent for clinical evaluation-treatment
    services/release information form, 87
Consent for services, 85, 87
Consultation, 223–241
    benefit versus cost of, 224–226
    for client family, 101–102
    contact form, 238
    evaluation of, 235–236
    fee for, 227–231
    format form, 237
    planning of, 236–239

Consultation (cont.)
  records in, 235
  role of consultant in, 231–235
  skills needed for, 240
  standards for, 239–240
Continuum of services, 14–15
Contract form, 168
Contracting, 167–170
Court testimony, 260–262
Crisis coverage, 13–14

Document review, 11

Education, see Training
Emergency services, 80–81
Employment, termination of, 53
Equipment, 32–37
Ethical principles, 251–255, 262–264,
    273–281
"Ethical Principles of Psychologists,"
    273–281
Evaluation, see Assessment

Facilities, 26–30
Family of client, 91
  in assessment, 93–94
  consultation for, 101–102
  effect of child/adolescent on, 97–98
  issues affecting child/adolescent,
    95–97
  in referral, 93
  training for, 99–102
  in treatment, 94–95
  see also Parents; Primary caregiver
Fees, 67–75, 227–231
Fees for services agreement form, 71
Forms, 70–71, 75–80, 85–87,
    236–239, 255–257, 259–260
  agency referral form, 76–77
  agency satisfaction questionnaire,
    221–222
  background information, 80
  billing agreement, 255
  case staffing report, 174
  client contact note, 172–173
  client rights, 246
  client satisfaction questionnaire, 175,
    219–220
  consent/release, 87

consultation contact, 238
consultation format, 237
contract, 168
fees for services agreement, 71
goal evaluation checklist, 160
guidelines for intake interview,
    112–116
initial contact, 78
intake schedule, 86
on-site consultation evaluation, 236
payment agreement, 75
progress notes, 173
release of records and request for
    information, 256
resource chart, 188
self-evaluation checklist for admin-
    istrators, 283–288
self-evaluation checklist for clini-
    cians, 288–293
service and billing information, 70
summary report, 210
treatment plan format, 157
Funding, 20, 57
Furniture, 30–32

Goal evaluation checklist form, 160

Handbook of operating procedures,
    61–62
Hiring, 52–53
Human rights committee, 252, 254–255
Hyperactivity assessment, 137

Initial contact, 77–78
  form for, 78
Insurance, 41
  professional liability, 59–60
  see also Liability
Intake
  interview form, 112–116
  schedule for, 85–86
Intake interview form, guidelines for,
    112–116
Intake schedule form, 86
Interviews, 79–80
  assessment, 108–117
  intake, 112–116
Inventories for assessment, 117–121

Job descriptions, 46–52

Learning problems assessment,
135–136
Legal issues, 255–264
Liability, 257–258
see also Insurance
Lounge, 26

Malpractice suits, avoiding, 264
Marketing, 21–25, 65–66
Materials, for clinics, 37–41
consumable, 39–41
nonconsumable, 37–39, 40–41
Multipurpose rooms, 27

Neuropsychological assessment, 138

Observation rooms, 29–30
Office space, 26
On-site consultation evaluation form,
236
Outcome-oriented services, 11–12

Pacing, 151
Parents
preparation of, 82–83, 85, 87
see also Family of client; Primary
caregiver
Pay increases, 52
Payment agreement form, 75
Peer review, 10–11, 215–216,
252–254
Performance evaluation, 47–52
Personnel
need for, 44–45
policies for, 61
see also Staff
Physiological assessment, 129–130
Position descriptions, *see* Job
Descriptions
Preventive mental health services,
267–272
Primary caregiver
role of, 98–99
see also Parents; Family of client

Progress notes form, 173
see also Client contact note form
Projective assessment, 127–129
Promotion, 24–25
Psychological and related services, 1–2,
9–17
current status of, 267–270
future directions of, 270–272
need for, 92–94
Psychological problems (specific),
191–195
Psychological service unit, 1–2
Psychological treatment, 152–153
Psychologist, job description of, 46–47
Public relations, 25–26
and clinical reports, 217–218

Questionnaires in assessment, 117–121

Rating scales in assessment, 117–121
Records, 79, 235
Referral services, 14
Referrals, 74–77
for assessment, 106
Release of records and request for in-
formation form, 256
Reports, clinical, 201–222
evaluation of, 218–222
peer review procedures for, 215–216
preparation of, 203–217
computer, 216–217
in public relations, 217–218
Resource chart form, 188
Resources, determination of, 187–188
Restrooms, 26

Scheduling of clinic rooms, 85
Self-evaluation checklist for admin-
istrators form, 283–288
Self-evaluation checklist for clinicians
form, 288–293
Self-management steps, 153
Self reports in assessment, 120–121
Service and billing information form,
70
Social emotional problem assessment,
137–138
Special needs assessment, 139, 141

Staff
  communication of, 56
  improvement of, 50–51
  inservice training of, 59
  management of, 57–58
  morale of, 54–56
  motivation of, 54–56
  orientation of, 53–54
  rights and responsibilities of, 54
  supervision of, 58–59
  see also Personnel
Staffing, 12–13
  procedures for, 52–59
Standard operating procedures, 60–63,
    258–259
Standards, 15–17, 239–240
State-of-the-art services, 10
Summary report form, 210

Tests, 37–40
  in assessment, 121–127, 134, 141
Therapeutic relationship, establishment
    of, 150–152
Therapist expectations, 189
Toys, 38–41
Training
  for client family, 99–102
  for staff, 10, 59
Treatment, 152–175, 180–195
  adjustments of, 190–191

case staffing reports in, 171–172,
    174
of choices, 181–183
and client age, 184
client contact notes in, 171–173
of common psychological problems,
    191–195
evaluation of, 173–175, 189–190,
    218–222
follow-up of, 186–187
goals of, 153–155
in hospital, home, or clinic, 185–186
and implementation methods,
    165–169
individual versus group, 183–185
ineffective, 189–190
materials, 39–41
monitoring progress of, 169–173
and plan format, 155–158
  form for, 157
plans of, 154–165
rooms, 28–30
termination of, 173–175
and therapist principles, 184–185
Triadic model, 165–166

Utah mental health services, 15–16

Waiting areas, 27–28